Palgrave Studies in Islamic Banking, Finance, and Economics

Series Editors
Mehmet Asutay, Business School, Durham University, Durham, UK
Zamir Iqbal, Islamic Development Bank, Jeddah, Saudi Arabia
Jahangir Sultan, Bentley University, Boston, MA, USA

The aim of this series is to explore the various disciplines and sub-disciplines of Islamic banking, finance and economics through the lens of theoretical, practical, and empirical research. Monographs and edited collections in this series will focus on key developments in the Islamic financial industry as well as relevant contributions made to moral economy, innovations in instruments, regulatory and supervisory issues, risk management, insurance, and asset management. The scope of these books will set this series apart from the competition by offering in-depth critical analyses of conceptual, institutional, operational, and instrumental aspects of this emerging field. This series is expected to attract focused theoretical studies, in-depth surveys of current practices, trends, and standards, and cutting-edge empirical research.

Nabil El Maghrebi · Abbas Mirakhor ·
Tarık Akın · Zamir Iqbal

Revisiting Islamic Economics

The Organizing Principles of a New Paradigm

Nabil El Maghrebi
Wakayama University
Wakayama, Japan

Tarık Akın
İstanbul, Türkiye

Abbas Mirakhor
La Junta, CO, USA

Zamir Iqbal
Islamic Development Bank
Jeddah, Saudi Arabia

ISSN 2662-5121   ISSN 2662-513X (electronic)
Palgrave Studies in Islamic Banking, Finance, and Economics
ISBN 978-3-031-41133-5   ISBN 978-3-031-41134-2 (eBook)
https://doi.org/10.1007/978-3-031-41134-2

© The Editor(s) (if applicable) and The Author(s), under exclusive license to Springer Nature Switzerland AG 2023

This work is subject to copyright. All rights are solely and exclusively licensed by the Publisher, whether the whole or part of the material is concerned, specifically the rights of translation, reprinting, reuse of illustrations, recitation, broadcasting, reproduction on microfilms or in any other physical way, and transmission or information storage and retrieval, electronic adaptation, computer software, or by similar or dissimilar methodology now known or hereafter developed.
The use of general descriptive names, registered names, trademarks, service marks, etc. in this publication does not imply, even in the absence of a specific statement, that such names are exempt from the relevant protective laws and regulations and therefore free for general use.
The publisher, the authors, and the editors are safe to assume that the advice and information in this book are believed to be true and accurate at the date of publication. Neither the publisher nor the authors or the editors give a warranty, expressed or implied, with respect to the material contained herein or for any errors or omissions that may have been made. The publisher remains neutral with regard to jurisdictional claims in published maps and institutional affiliations.

This Palgrave Macmillan imprint is published by the registered company Springer Nature Switzerland AG
The registered company address is: Gewerbestrasse 11, 6330 Cham, Switzerland

Foreword

There are few subjects of central concern to the Islamic world that need to be thoroughly re-examined and reconsidered in light of the Islamic revelation as what has come to be known as Islamic economics. Much has been written on this subject by Muslim scholars themselves but rarely with full consideration of the worldview on which modern economics is based and which is often adopted without questioning by most of those who write on Islamic economics and who accept the whole philosophical basis of Western economics save for the subject of interest or *ribā*. As a result, putting the matter of interest aside, most of what is called Islamic economics these days shares with Western economics belief in a purely material basis of this dimension of human life for which the claim of centrality is made.

Most modern Muslim economists, even when speaking of Islamic economics, forget that Islamic civilization flourished on every level including the economic for centuries without even having a term for economics in the modern sense. The Greek word *oikonomia* was translated into Arabic quite rightly as *tadbīr al-manzil*, literally taking care of the household, and the word *iqtiṣād*, that is used for economics today in the Islamic world, meant balance or moderation as in the title of the famous book of al-Ghazzālī, *al-Iqtiṣād fi'l-i'tiqād* usually translated as *Moderation in Belief*. Modern Muslim scholars adopted the term in its modern Western sense like sleepwalkers even if some did try to modify it when it came to the question of *ribā*. Few, however, dealt with the central truth that in traditional Islamic society what is now called *iqtiṣād* was never separated from the *Sharīʿah*, Islamic ethics, religious obligations toward God's creation and yes, also beauty combined with utility and the needs of the soul combined with those of the body. The case of the traditional guilds demonstrates fully this integrated perspective on economic production.

Fortunately during the last few years a small number of knowledgeable Muslim scholars, deeply rooted in their own tradition and at the same time well acquainted with modern economics and finance, have been turning their attention to the crucial question of what "Islamic" means when we speak of Islamic economics. The four authors of the present book belong to this small group. Some of them have already written valuable books on the subject and in this work all the authors bring their considerable knowledge and experience together to provide an in-depth criticism of the prevailing ideas in the field and at the same time present a new paradigm for the study and practice of economics that is authentically Islamic and not the product of colonized minds.

What is lacking in modern economics from the Islamic point of view? Why should what is called Islamic economics today be criticized? What is the role of Islamic ethics in economics? What is the relation of an authentic Islamic economics to other aspects of Islamic civilization and the Islamic sciences and forms of knowledge? These and many other basic questions are treated here in a masterful manner and with clarity by the authors in this important work. Anyone concerned with the future of the Islamic world and its civilization will benefit greatly from the message of this book.

This work is not meant to be only read and then put in one's library. It is a book that delineates a plan of action based on authentic knowledge. I hope, therefore, that it will not be read only by scholars of Islamic thought, but also by those men and women of action who are engaged in economic activity that has a bearing upon the future of our society including especially those in positions of political and social authority whose decisions often have dire consequences for society. I also hope that this book becomes taught throughout the Islamic world where economics is taught in courses in colleges and universities.

The problems with which this book deals are not confined to only one or two Islamic countries but are widespread. It is, therefore, fortunate that the authors hail from different Muslim nations and each has deep knowledge of the state of affairs in his own country. In the pages that follow, these different rivers of knowledge meet in an integrated manner so that the result is of pertinence for the Islamic world as a whole. I hope and pray that this book is disseminated widely and will reach those who are in need of its message wherever they might be.

Wa'Llāhu a'lamu bi'l-ṣawāb

Dhu'l-ḥijjah, 1444 AH
June 2023 AD

Seyyed Hossein Nasr
University Professor of Islamic
Studies
The George Washington
University
Washington, DC, USA

Introduction

There are important questions about the meaning and essence of our earthly existence. From the origin of man and cosmic phenomena to the meaning of life and means of livelihood, answers may depend on the strength of belief and degree of knowledge and expertise. For Muslim thinkers, faith and convictions are founded on the Qur'an, the fountainhead of all Islamic paradigms, ideas, and conceptions of reality. That reality is not one of a purely earthly creature in the Promethean mode of existence, but of a theomorphic man integrating knowledge of the Sacred with the pursuance of spiritual and material life. The reality is that economic prosperity ensued for centuries of Islamic civilization not because of advances in theoretical and applied economics in the modern sense, but in the absence of an original term for economics altogether. The reality is that as a religion based on Unity, Islam does not separate the spiritual from the temporal and religious from profane in any domain, including economic life. It does not seek to achieve spiritual uplifting by repudiating worldly life. It was well understood then, but it is not clear to be the case now, that the economic and social edifice cannot hold on solely to science, and reason, and that it is the soul, in the words of Malik Bennabi, that allows humanity to soar.

The decay and fall of civilization do not happen by chance, but as a matter of necessity as the scale of values is reversed, and the sense of justice is lost. There was a gradual long-term process of social degradation, economic deterioration, and transition to intellectual wilderness and confusion, where economic wisdom from men of integrity, piety, as well as spiritual and material discernment was gradually replaced by ersatz ideas that are alien to the Islamic worldview. It is natural that after long decades of approaching the study of economic phenomena from strictly a materialistic point of view, a new universe of discourse called Islamic economics emerged from pressing needs to reflect again on the problem of economic development and renaissance from an Islamic perspective. The paradigm of "Islamic Economics" adopted a narrow view of the concept of "Islamization of Knowledge," developed in the 1980s, proposed to "Islamize" the dominant paradigm of Economics by supplementing it with "Islamic values and ethics." In the sight of many Muslim critics, however, Islamic economics has failed to gain acceptability, bring change, and promote itself on the public agenda. It seems to suffer from the same internal contradictions of the very discipline it was meant to replace.

It is virtually impossible to traverse or navigate this universe of discourse without raising difficult questions about the authenticity of Islamic economics and the inability to build an identity for itself. To what extent does Islamic economics deviate from its primary function of desecularizing and resacralizing economic knowledge? Is its agenda for economic change inherently weak and deeply flawed to the point that it remains unheeded? Has it grown accustomed to the same assumptions of modern economics, while invoking the Qur'an more as a jargon than truly authentic reason and justification? Does the uncritical adoption of the same philosophy of materialism and methodology of empiricism render Islamic economics incapable of answering the very questions it raises? The ultimate question is not so much whether a discipline uprooted from its Islamic worldview has a policy agenda of its own, but whether it has still a purpose at all.

These difficult questions have no universally acceptable answers because the prefix "Islamic" attached to many so-called Islamic paradigms has come to mean different things to different people, who may not like the truth, or part of the truth that does not suit their own argument. It may be easier to commit to established beliefs, and reject specific criticism than to embrace change. Facts, however, always trump sentiments, and impartiality is essential for scholarly research. The irrefutable fact is that no authentically Islamic discipline can ever be separated from the Islamic worldview and authentic knowledge. A conjunction of secular philosophies with Islamic knowledge to serve as means to the end of establishing an Islamic paradigm is not a necessity but a false idealism. A sort of compromise between Islamic and secular worldviews exposes Islamic economics to sharper and wider criticism. It may be regarded as potential threat to religious faith by dint of its inconsistency with secular concepts, and potential danger to scientific inquiry by dint of the latter's incapacity to accommodate ethics or prove revelation to be false.

To provide some answers to these important questions in a balanced methodological manner, the opening chapter of this book considers the polar visions of the economy, and contends that in its present form, Islamic economics is bound to converge toward the dominant secular paradigm of neoliberal economics that supports the predatory economic system of capitalism. It argues that the methodology of achieving a synthetic discipline by imbuing conventional economics with Islamic values requires a compromise of the latter, and inevitable loss of authenticity. It is reminiscent of Christianity's compromise of the essential values of benevolence, grace, and selflessness, inter alia, to accommodate the ideology of neoliberalism, which redesigned capitalism into its present form. A union of neoliberal economic and Islamic economics based on two diametrically opposite visions of the economy, a synthesis of two incomparable, incompatible, and hence incommensurable paradigms with different worldviews is a logical impossibility.

To reinforce the above logical arguments, Chapter 2 provides a brief critical history of political economy and overview of the science and dogma of neoclassical economics, whereas Chapter 3 provides a brief critical examination of the contents and discontents of Islamic economics, the contentious relation between religion and economics, and the secularization of Islamic Law. It is argued that there are fundamental flaws in the assumptions underlying economic theory. The notion of consumer sovereignty is not consistent with the argument of resources scarcity, as the acceptance of the latter should logically preclude the former. The rationality postulate holds also a sacrosanct status in neoclassical economics as an empirically irrefutable metaphysical proposition by virtue of ubiquitous self-interest behaviour. Self-interest itself is taken as self-evident by virtue of the very assumptions of economic rationality and resources scarcity. Also, critical arguments about the usefulness of mathematical economics stem from fundamental flaws in connecting the abstract world of mathematics with the reality of economic life. This methodological monism does not admit value judgements or references to alternative worldviews, religious beliefs, and moral convictions.

Under the current conditions, Islamic economics can neither emerge on its own nor exist within the realm of conventional economics. The dualism of worldviews cannot be resolved into a harmonious unity because a secular paradigm that discards the metaphysical foundations of Islamic economics is conducive to a mere vision of "ethical capitalism" that is bound to be shattered by strenuous relations between the open-ended processes of secularization and Islamization. It is important for Muslim legal scholars and economists to grasp the reality that there are no merits in intellectual attempts to fit secular ideals and ideologies into Islam. Secularization, as a philosophical program based on secular life and secular destiny, can only sever the connection of Muslim's consciousness with the Islamic worldview. It contributes to intellectual confusion and error in knowledge. In a secular scheme of things, there are no profound legal maxims or economic principles that can be truly Islamized either. Islamic jurisprudence plays an important role in shaping Islamic economic thought, but without the three authentic pillars of Islamic Law, including intellectual creed, spiritual worship, and justice system, it is impossible for Islamic economics to set a policy agenda of its own for the organization of an ideal Islamic economy.

Chapter 4 examines the role of ethics in the polar case to economics, iqtiṣād that derives its ontology directly from the Qur'an to organize an ideal Islamic economy. Based on the moral philosophy of Islam aimed at promoting economic and social justice, the internalization of rules and virtues of Islam determines all facets of an economy ranging from the rules of market conduct, production, consumption, distribution, and redistribution. The organizing principle of risk-sharing in financial transactions and other forms of exchange has a rich ethical dimension which fills the gaps observed in prevailing economic systems. It minimizes the exploitation inherent to interest-based or risk-transfer systems, leads to efficient allocation of resources, reduces typical information asymmetry and agency problems in economic dealings, enhances cooperation and solidarity in the societies, and promotes financial and social inclusion.

The central message of this book, with its ontological, epistemological, philosophical, and ethical arguments, is not new. Chapter 5 reiterates the fact that it is a response to the earlier call by a number of distinguished Muslim philosophers, religious scholars, and social critics that genuine and lasting solutions to the malaise of Muslim societies, including economic problems, are contained in the Qur'an and Hadith. The analytic perspectives about the cycle of civilization and problem of knowledge are provided by eminent philosophers and social critics in the past century and half, including Muhammad Iqbal's treatise about economic science, Malek Bennabi's seminal work on the conditions of renaissance, Sa'eed Nursi's *magnum opus Letters of Light*, and al-Shaheed Muhammad Baqir as-Sadr's comprehensive insights about Islamic economy. Further insights are provided by Sayyid Hossein Nasr and Sayyid Naquib al-Attas on the problem of knowledge and the notion that the Qur'an is the fountainhead of ideas for every generation to conceive and implement its vision for future societies. The disorder and chaos faced by the Muslim world can only be the result of confusion in knowledge about Islam and its worldview. As it is impossible to accommodate Islam to the ideals of secular minds, or to graft the Islamic worldview onto secular ideas, it is imperative to reaffirm the nature of authentic knowledge and its true sources, in order to project justice in all spheres of responsibility and rebuild the socio-intellectual foundations of Islamic civilization and ideal economy.

Together with Chapters 1 and 5, Chapter 6 constitutes the core message of this book. It builds on the examination of polar visions of the economy, and earlier call by distinguished Muslim philosophers to reaffirm the nature of authentic knowledge, to present the Impossibility Theorem about the Islamization of Economics. An examination of the historical and philosophical underpinnings of economics reveals major issues that make impossible emergence of an Islamic Economics, a conception that proposes to graft dimensions of Islamic belief onto economics, that would make logical sense and can guide policy toward solving economic problems. The impossibility is indicated by the fact that economics is so strongly immunized against anything metaphysical, transcendent, moral, and ethical that even such ideas coming from the inside of economics are rejected. The chapter concludes that iqtiṣād, the Qur'an's vision of the economy is a theonomy that is so radically different from Economics that there is no basis to allow grafting of Islam onto economics or economics onto Islam. The Impossibility Theorem implies a conception of iqtiṣād, a paradigm based on the immutable, consistent, and sacred system of rules prescribed by The Creator, while a system with fallible, unstable, and everchanging concepts based on human judgement is doomed to failure.

The institutional structure and behavioural norms of the iqtiṣād-driven economy are, thus, described in Chapter 7. The institutional framework is based on a unique set of principles governing property rights, and contracts, which derive directly from the Islamic worldview. The institution of markets is also built on the three pillars of property rights, contracts, and trust. The organic relationships between these institutions depend on compliance to behaviour norms at each level, and on incentives systems that promote trust, information transparency, and risk-sharing. The behavioural norms and institutional rules, which are designed to resonate in the entire fabric of society and economic life, are asserted in the Qur'an and demonstrated by the Noble Prophet with a level of clarity and consistency that renders recourse to alternative paradigms necessarily associated with a loss of authenticity. The rules for the creation, exchange, and transfer of property rights are immutable, but the institutional structure is flexible to accommodate the shifting economic dynamics over time and space.

It is imperative to rethink the essence of macroeconomic policies in light of the institutional structure and behavioural norms. Chapter 8 argues that viable redistribution mechanisms based on the organization principle of risk-sharing are needed to regulate the dynamics of an ideal Islamic economy. In contrast to interest-based financial systems which are inherently unstable, it is possible to design and implement asset-based redistribution and risk-sharing universal basic assets, which provide opportunities for investment in the real economy and generation of stable income from development projects. The argument is made that both fiscal and monetary policies used to regulate economic activity based on the very interest-based mechanism that promotes economic rents cannot arguably be part of the solution to the problem of economic inequalities.

Finally, the stabilizing role of risk-sharing in an iqtiṣād-driven economy is also examined in Chapter 9, in relation to the nature of economic uncertainty. It is argued that there is an irreducible amount of randomness in economic systems, where failure to predict the future cannot be explained solely by flaws and deficiencies inherent to human knowledge. The notion that uncertainty and imperfect knowledge are part of economic life precludes the argument that it is also possible for certain economic agents to insulate themselves from losses through debt agreements based on risk transfer. There is also evidence that interest-bearing debt is the source of financial instability and that central bankers are losing traction of the interest-rate transmission mechanism, and thereby, control of monetary policy. Financial regulation does not seem to be so much concerned about preventing the next banking crises as about increasing the capacity of the banking system to withstand one. In contrast, risk-sharing in an iqtiṣād-driven economy promotes financial stability, which is the *conditio sine qua non* for economic development and full employment. This organizing principle provides remedies to the central contradiction of capitalism as it prevents capital from reproducing itself faster than output increases, and the past from devouring the future.

Thus, this book is a humble attempt to rethink Islamic economics, the primary causes of a long divergence from authenticity, and the need for paradigm shift toward iqtiṣād, the Qur'an's vision of how individuals and collectivities must manage the resources gifted to them by their Creator. The principal contention behind The Impossibility Theorem, explained in the central chapters of this book, is that the current paradigm of Islamic economics is not viable. It is not viable because it offers a secular philosophy for the organization of the economy that is, *a posse ad esse*, discernible from conventional economics only in hopium. There is no rationale for persistence because the *status quo* can only retard the organization of an ideal Islamic economy that serves the whole of humanity is that the foundational pillars of iqtiṣād are so radically different from the foundational structure of modern economics as to render each alien to the other. It is impossible for the Islamic worldview, which cannot be the subject of human inference or philosophical speculation, and for the certainty of religious knowledge to be fused with heteroclite secular ideas without a loss of authenticity. This authenticity is the basis of legitimacy of whatever concepts, ideas, or thoughts that bear "Islam" as prefix.

It is impossible to change economic reality with the secular mind of corrupt leadership and scholarship that advocates confusion and error in knowledge. It is the hope of the authors that this humble work will induce open-minded readers to reflect on the deep psychosis of inferiority complex and insecurity among so many Muslims that impairs correct thought and action, and leads to civilizational bankruptcy. It is a call to reflect on why Islam is deemed erroneously as a source of obscurantism while credence is uncritically given to secular ideologies that now pose an existential threat to humanity. With a distinctive worldview, Islam offers humanity a radically different choice of direction in all aspects of life, and it is incumbent on Muslim thinkers and leaders to elucidate, on the basis of authentic knowledge, the properties of an ideal Islamic economy, draw policies, and implement plans of action accordingly. The truth is that once humanity is presented with a concrete solution to economic problems, that a person with spiritual, intellectual, and material discernment is at liberty to make the right choice.

Contents

1	**Polar Visions of the Economy**	1
	Authenticity and Islamic Economics	2
	The Western Conception of Authenticity	3
	Inauthenticity and Islamic Economics	5
	The Term "Islamic Economics" and the Evolution of Its Content	6
	Hopes, Aspirations, and Inspirations of This Book	8
	Rethinking "Islamic Economics"	9
	Economics: The Operating System of Predatory Capitalism	10
	Neoliberal Economics Assumes the Mantle of "Conventional Economics"	13
	Neoliberal Capitalism Dominates World Economies	13
	The Empire of Neoliberal Economics	14
	The Dire Costs of Neoliberal Economics	17
	A Blending of "Economic Science" and the As-Sharī'ah	17
	Is Scarcity the Problem or Distribution?	19
	Secularism and the Blending of Conventional Economic and the Sharī'ah	22
	Secularism as Foundational Philosophy of "Conventional Economics"	23
	The Rationality Axiom and Islamic Economics	27
	Economic Rationality Is a Part, Albeit a Small Part, of the General Concept of Rationality	27

xvii

Al-Qur'ān *and Rationality*	30
Al-Qur'ān *and "Self-Interest"*	32
The Logical Impossibility of the Proposed Union	35
Attasian Conception of Islamization of Knowledge	36
Sadrian Discourse on Al-Iqtiṣād	40
As-Sadr's Discourse on Contemporary Socio-Economic System	42
As-Sadr's Conception of Ideal Socio-Economic System	44
As-Sadr and Al-Iqtiṣād *Paradigm*	48
Notes	60
References	68

2 Critiques of Conventional Economics 77
A Critical History of Political Economy 78
General Equilibrium Paradigm 83
The Science and Dogma of Neoclassical Economics 89
Economics Between the Rigour of Mathematics and Relevance of Morality 95
Rationality as the Hard Core of Economic Theory 100
Notes 106
References 108

3 Critiques of Islamic Economics 113
A Brief History of Islamic Political Economy 116
The Contents and Discontents of Islamic Economics 118
Theoretical Doctrine Between Analytical Rigour and Practical Relevance 123
The Contentious Relationship Between Religion and Economics 125
Islamic Law and Islamic Jurisprudence 133
The Secularization of Islamic Law 136
Islamic Law of Transaction and Economic Development 137
Notes 144
References 147

4 Ethics of *Iqtiṣād* 151
Growing Critic of Conventional Economics' "Moral Muteness" 152
Meta-Ethics of Iqtiṣād 155
   Unity of Creation 155
   Model of Man 156
   Justice and Equilibrium 157
   Preservation of Rights 157

Internalization of Virtues	158
Respecting and Protecting Environment	159
Virtue-Based Ethics of Islam	159
Truthfulness and Integrity	162
Trustworthiness	162
Honesty	162
Goodness and Excellence (Ihsān)	163
Compassion and Generosity	163
Cooperation and Solidarity	163
Mindfulness of Vices or Unethical Practices	164
Prudence and Humility	164
Ethical Dimensions of **Iqtiṣād**	165
Ethics of Risk-Sharing	165
Business Ethics	172
Conclusion	174
Notes	175
References	178
5 The Crisis of Civilization and the Problem of Knowledge	**183**
A Brief Biography of Muslim Philosophers and Social Critics Over the Past Century	185
The Determinants of Shift in Economic Power	187
The Problem of Knowledge and Intellectual Challenges	191
Consistent Perspectives on Economic Development and Economic Justice	197
Call for Paradigm Shift in Islamic Economic Thought	203
References	206
6 Islamization of Economics? An Impossibility Theorem	**209**
A Brief Note on Key Philosophical Terms	212
Economics: Its Etymology and the Evolution of Its Definition	215
Economics: Its Definition and Method	219
Etymology, Definition, and Philosophy of Iqtiṣād: An Introduction	224
Transcendental Nature of the Ontology and Epistemology of Iqtiṣād System	228
Summary: An Impossibility Theorem	231
Notes	234

7	**Behavioural Norms and Institutional Structure of *Iqtiṣād***	241
	Etymology and Quranic Foundations of Iqtiṣād	244
	Behavioural Rules and the Promotion of Economic Justice and Social Welfare	248
	Institutional Framework of an Organic Iqtiṣād-*Driven System*	258
	Property and Property Rights	259
	Contracts and Contractual Obligations	264
	Markets and Information	270
	Risk-Sharing and Shared Prosperity	272
	Notes	277
	References	283
8	**Rethinking the Essence of Macroeconomic Policies in the *Iqtiṣād* Paradigm**	285
	The Nature of Economic Inequalities and Redistribution Proposals	287
	The Linkage Between Wealth Residual and Interest-Based Debt	289
	The Quantity Channel	291
	Collateral	291
	State-Independent Payoffs	293
	The Price Channel	295
	Leverage	295
	Asset Prices	297
	Risk-Sharing and the Notion of Wealth Residual	299
	Risk-Sharing Asset Redistribution	303
	Risk-Sharing Universal Basic Assets (RUBA)	308
	Blueprint for the RUBA: Public Basic Asset Fund (PBAF)	313
	Establishment of the Public Basic Asset Fund	315
	Investment in Risk-Sharing Instruments	316
	Trading PBAF Shares in Secondary Markets	317
	Notes	319
	References	321
9	**The Risk-Sharing Organizing Principle of *Iqtiṣād***	327
	Economic Uncertainty and the Notion of Risk	329
	The Pervasiveness of Risk-Transfer Relations	333
	Debt and Financial Instability	335
	Interest Rates and the Transmission of Monetary Policy	337
	Monetary Policy as a Source of Economic Uncertainty	339

Debt and the Making of Financial Crises	341
Prudential Regulation and the Procyclicality of the Financial System	343
Risk-Sharing and Economic Stability	345
Interest Rates and Expected Rates of Return	347
Iqtiṣād and the Islamic Financial System	348
Iqtiṣād, Equity Financing and State-Contingent Claims	352
Risk-Sharing and Economic Prosperity	356
Conclusion	360
References	361
Index	367

CHAPTER 1

Polar Visions of the Economy

This book is about visions of how societies organize the management of their resources to serve the needs of their people. Specifically, it is about two polar visions of the economy and the dominant foundational paradigms that provide them theoretical support. These are: (i) capitalism and the currently dominant paradigm of neoliberal economics, and (ii) the system envisioned by the supportive paradigm "Islamic economics" presently dominating the universe of discourse about the Islamic economy. The reason that necessitates this investigation is that the latter paradigm—based on a narrow conception of the methodology of "Islamization of Knowledge (IOK)" and equally narrow conception of the "Objectives of *as-Sharī'ah*"—converges to the dominant paradigm, neoliberal economics, that supports the economic system, capitalism, which now dominates contemporary economies and has done so for at least the last four decades. The economy that such paradigm would support has yet to be designed, much less implemented. Nevertheless, it is possible to extrapolate the paradigm to envision the resulting economic system based on its axioms. Doing so yields the outline of a system not much different from the form of capitalism now being practised.

The essence of the methodology of this paradigm suggests that introducing Islamic concepts and terms (including Islam's conception of morality and ethics) into the present economic paradigm Islamizes "conventional economics." The main contention here is that this methodology requires a compromise of Islamic values in order to achieve such a synthesis. The resulting system will not be much different from that which emanated from the synthesis of Protestant Christianity and capitalist ideologies undertaken in the nineteenth and twentieth centuries.[1] That compromise unleashed a predatory economic system that has produced severe economic and financial crises, an obscenely skewed income and wealth distribution, and an environmentally existential threat to humanity. Lessons from the history of Protestant Christianity's compromise with capitalism and its consequences[2] are constructive references as researchers, writers, and scholars attempt to develop the discipline that is to explain the design and operations of the economy that the most authentic source of Islam, *Al-Qur'ān*, envisions. These attempts should be guided by authenticity, which is fundamental to Islamic economics and the system it sets out to describe.

AUTHENTICITY AND ISLAMIC ECONOMICS

For the purpose of discussions here, authenticity refers to the immutability of a source with which congruent systems of thought, phenomena, and behaviour identify and define themselves. For adherents of Islam that source is *Al-Qur'ān*; the Verbatim Word of Allah *subhānahu wa taala* (swt) transmitted to the Noble Messenger, *salla Allah 'alaihi wa aalih (saa)*. *Al-Qur'ān* itself defines as authentic any thought, action, and identity that reflects belief in and adherence to that which has been transmitted by Allah swt to humanity through the Noble Messenger.[3] For example, the primordial human nature (*al-fitrah*) is identified in *Al-Qur'ān* as authentic because Allah swt has Created it as immutable (*Al-Qur'ān*, Verse 30: Chapter 30). Its authenticity can be temporarily covered and suppressed by cultural, ideological, or other external forces, but it will not be fully submerged or lost; it is invincible, pervasive, and never loses its inbuilt compass that directs it toward its Creator.

In the context of the subject matter of this book, it will be argued that an authentic paradigm of the discipline meant to articulate and explain *Al-Qur'ān's* vision of the economy has to be one which is fully congruent with *Al-Qur'ān* and presents an indisputable representation of its vision of the economy. It will be argued also that there is a comprehensive, coherent, and comprehensive vision of the economy discernible from *Al-Qur'ān*. The axiomatic belief, which constitutes also the premise of this book, is that an authentic discipline should be able to discover that vision and the rules that govern it. It will be explained how such a paradigm will have to be an authentic, coherent, and logically consistent body of knowledge whose core axioms and principles stand in sharp contrast to those of the presently dominant paradigm, referred to in this book as "Economics." This mutual exclusivity negates compromise of Islamic values in order to obtain an "Islamized" Economics.[4]

There is no clear evidence regarding who coined the term "Islamic economics" or when, but it appears that not much thought had been given to the paradox that the term presents by placing a transcendental and sacred system of thought side-by-side with a secular, desacralized and grossly profane, highly materialistic discipline. Similarly, there is no clear explanation or etymological justification for the term and the legitimacy of combining the two terms composing it. As will be discussed, Economics has roots that are historically, philosophically, and culturally specific. The question arises as to the degree of compatibility of the specificity of Western experience that led to the birth of Economics with the Islamic experience to legitimize combining the two terms. The puzzle of the choice of the term becomes even more striking when realizing that Islam has its own authentic term "*Al-Iqtiṣād*," with roots in *Al-Qur'ān*, to describe the system and the discipline dealing with behaviour and processes involved in the operations of an economy. Within the Islamic framework, the question of authenticity is quite crucial and relates to the degree that the contents ideas, behaviour, or phenomena have direct connection with *Al-Qur'ān*. It is this connection of Al-Iqtiṣād with Al-Qur'ān that consitutes its authenticity, and thus legitimacy.

THE WESTERN CONCEPTION OF AUTHENTICITY

In contrast to Islam, conception of authenticity is a contested subject in Western thought. The concept first appeared in the writings of Jean-Jacques Rousseau (1712–1778) who, in criticism of emerging modernity, argued emerging modernity argued that authenticity is derived from the natural self and appealed for the return to the inner self. He defined inauthenticity as behaviour resulting from influences of the external forces bearing upon the natural self.[5] With the expansion and strengthening of secularism, materialism, and modernity, the late nineteenth and twentieth centuries witnessed growing criticism of the interiority search for the authentic self by philosophers such as Theodor Adorno (1903–1969)[6] and Michel Foucault (1926–1984).[7] Adorno criticized existentialism (especially Martin Heidedgger (1889–1976)) for (specially Heidegger) for developing an ontology and a language (jargon) attempting to reproduce a Christian character without the Christian belief.[8]

A clear example of inauthenticity is the way the nineteenth-century Protestantism accommodated economics (Davenport, 2008). At first glance, it appears as a puzzle how the Christian values of selflessness, humility, compassion, sacrifice, and benevolence can accommodate the capitalist ideology of possessive individualism, self-interest, self-promotion, greed, competition, and emphasis on exclusive personal success, by aggressively seeking the best of material world for oneself. The way this was accomplished is articulated in Maximilian Weber (1864–1920)'s book, The Protestant Ethic and the Spirit of Capitalism.[9] Weber argued for the Protestant "ethic" contained in the doctrine of "calling"—a divinely inspired inner impulse toward a particular course of action—summarized in the practice of worldly asceticism, particularly hard work, extreme frugality, postponed gratification combined with the "Spirit" of capitalism—rationality, self-interest, competition—to legitimize the expansion/of capitalism. The combination promised worldly rewards by the "spirit of capitalism" and otherworldly rewards promised by Protestantism through the practices of the ethic of worldly asceticism. By the mid-nineteenth century, capitalism had become a pervasive way of life so much so that Weber described the capitalist economy as an "immense cosmos into which the individual is born, and which presents itself to him, at least as an individual, as an unalterable order of things in which he must live. It forces the individual, in so far as he is involved in the system of market relationships, to conform to capitalistic rules of action."[10] Thus, the "philosophy" of Economics provided theoretical support, analyses, policies, and the means of indoctrination of the young through the educational system for over a century with consequences that are now posing an existential threat to humanity. The natural question arises as to whether Islam's compromise with conventional economics would produce better results?

INAUTHENTICITY AND ISLAMIC ECONOMICS

A tentative look at the inauthenticity of one such compromise may be instructive in response to the question posed above. The last few decades have witnessed the emergence and growth of "Islamic banking" which is, in all but the name, a replicate of interest-based, risk-transfer banking. It usurps terms developed in Islamic Jurisprudence (*Fiqh Al-Mu'āmalāt* related to Islamic Law of Transactions) as "Islamic" jargon, to camouflage basically a non-Islamic character as it integrates interest rate or, at best, quasi-interest rate, charges into financial dealings. Sometimes it even invents jargons that, to the un-initiate, sound Islamic. For example, its practitioners invented "*sukūk*"—plural of *sakk*, an Arabized Persian instrument called "check" (French *chèque*)—as a name for interest-based "Islamic bonds." This development has brought it into convergence with conventional banking to the degree that it has made the former an "asset class" in the latter. It appears that the paradigm that presently dominates discussions of "Islamic economics" is moving in similar direction.

There is still time to initiate a course correction and return to the authentic path of discovering the vision of *Al-Qur'ān* for the economy and establish the discipline to support it. Arguably, that discipline is a work in progress and will remain so for some time. Presently, it is passing through the agonizing stage of its infancy and the struggle for self-identification. While half a century may justifiably seem a long period of time to the young researchers, it is worth remembering that, by the reckoning of some historians of economic thought, the roots of the discipline of "conventional economics" have been in the making for over a millennium or longer.[11] In that sense, even the late start of Muslim articulation in English of thinking on the subject matter, dating to the 1960s, seems to have been hasty in labelling the discipline as "Islamic economics" without considering the etymological, epistemological, and doctrinal misconceptions and misunderstandings that combining the two terms would create.

The Term "Islamic Economics" and the Evolution of Its Content

In the second half of the nineteenth and early twentieth centuries when economics was introduced to Muslim societies, the term was translated as "*Al-Iqtiṣād*" apparently without the awareness of the fact that "*Al-Iqtiṣād*" as an authentic concept, with roots in *Al-Qur'ān* (from the root *qaṣada*, see, for example, Verse 19: Chapter 31 of *Al-Qur'ān*), was etymologically quite different from the Western conception of "economics." From there, it was a short step to combining Islam and "economics" in the 1970s and 1980s while all the while the intention may well have been to investigate the vision of Islam for the economy. In the event, major writings on the subject in the 1980s focused on an apparent view that Islam was summarized in "*as-Sharī'ah*," and the latter was represented by Islamic Jurisprudence (*Fiqh*) and, in the context of "conventional economics," that meant the Jurisprudential rules governing transactional relationships, i.e. *Fiqh Al-Mu'āmalāt*. Hence, efforts were devoted to defining the discipline of Islamic economics along the lines of Islamic Jurisprudence.[12] Other writers, judging this approach inadequate, began exploring, in the second half of the 1980s, the writings of the classical Muslim scholars and discovered the concept of *Maqāṣid as-Sharī'ah* that summarized the objectives of Islam in five principles: protection of religion, life, property, intellect, and lineage, articulated in the tenth through the fourteenth centuries.

This line of inquiry proposed developing "Islamic economics" based on this conception of the objectives of Islam. What it overlooked was the historical circumstances, ideological and political orientations, and purposes of the advocates of this narrow conception of the objectives of Islam. Concurrently, a number of Muslim philosophers and educators postulated that educational systems in Muslim countries were responsible for the malaise of these societies. Hence, they proposed a program of "Islamizing" the educational system in Muslim societies. Initially financed by rich Muslim countries, Islamic universities were organized in a few Muslim countries, such as Malaysia and Pakistan, to serve as model for the rest of Muslim countries. Their task was to develop "Islamized" curricula. By the end of the old millennium and the first decade of the new, an Islamic economic paradigm emerged that integrated the idea of "Islamization" with the narrow conception of the objectives.

The point worth emphasizing is that focusing on five principles as containing the objectives of *as-Sharī'ah* (usually equated to the objectives of Islam) and then to suggest that a discipline of economics should be built on this basis disserves Islam's vision of the economy. Continued focus on five principles is somewhat puzzling since over time writers on the subject have continuously expanded the list based on their understanding of *Al-Qur'ān* and *As-Sunnah*.[13] The contention of the philosophers and educators who proposed Islamization of Knowledge, however, was that a search for authentically Islamic model of education, as well as social science disciplines, should rely directly on *Al-Qur'ān* and *Sunnah* of the Noble Messenger (*saa*).

Accordingly, it is hoped that the discussions in this book will be helpful—in this yet early and nascent stage—in the formation, development, and emergence of a paradigm that explains the authentic vision of the economy as is contained in *Al-Qur'ān*, and explicated and operationalized by the *Sunnah* of the Noble Messenger (*saa*). The implementation of such an authentic Islamic economy will have the power to radiate out and sanctify the actions of its participants resulting in stable and prosperous society. However, this requires a firm belief in the metaphysical conceptions of *Al-Qur'ān* that could not and would not be possibly entertained by the Western secular foundations of "conventional economics." For example, one of the most important metaphysical and transcendental axioms of Islam which plays a significant role in the operations of the vision of the economy in *Al-Qur'ān* is the belief in al-Ghayb, meaning a conviction that there is a metaphysical universe with its rules and operative relations that cannot be explained in terms and language of philosophies and discourses that deny metaphysics and transcendence. Nor can the language of *Al-Qur'ān* referring to the universe of al-Ghayb and its connections with humans and their behaviour be understood or acknowledged by underlying systems of thought that gave rise to the contemporary Western conception of economics: secularism, materialism, and empiricism. To illustrate, one such a rule with significant implications for material prosperity in the life of individuals and societies is that of "*Barakah*" which, as a metaphysical concept, cannot find acceptability in the system of thought that produces the Western conception of economics (although, as will be remarked later in this chapter, there are economic concepts that approximate "Barakah" in effect but not in conception). The operations of this rule in *Al-Qur'ān* vision of the economy is described in Verse 96 of Chapter 7 of *Al-Qur'ān* which enunciates the necessary and sufficient conditions for the prosperity of human societies.

Hopes, Aspirations, and Inspirations of This Book

This book is a response to the call by a number of distinguished Muslim philosophers, religious scholars, and social critics—such as Said Nursi (1877–1960), Muhammad Iqbal (1877–1938), Malek Bennabi (1905–1973), and Muhammad Baqir As-Sadr (1935–1980), as well as Seyyed, Seyyed Hossein Nasr, and Syed Muhammad Naquib al-Attas—that genuine and lasting solutions to the malaise of Muslim societies are contained nowhere other than in *Al-Qur'ān*. It is important to note, in this context, that the fundamental task of an authentic Islamic economic paradigm is not to produce a theory of how an existing economic system operates but to specify the institutional scaffolding of the system that *Al-Qur'ān* envisions for human societies. The task of theorizing begins after such a system has been defined and its institutional structure—that is the rules governing its operations—are identified. Therefore, theorizing in this context would mean to postulate how such a system can be implemented and, from there, hypothesize empirical propositions to be tested. In other words, unlike the Western conception of economics in which theories aim at discovering rules that govern economic behaviour, then predict and control such behaviour, authentic Islamic economics takes as axiomatic the rules governing behaviour as prescribed in *Al-Qur'ān* and searches for ways and means of implementation in a given society within the context of cultural, demographic, and natural conditions.

The most important task of a Muslim economist—that is one who has internalized the knowledge of the authentic economy as envisioned in *Al-Qur'ān*—is to design and propose policies that would transform a non-Islamic economy to the vision of *Al-Qur'ān* to the relevant authorities for implementation. Therein lies one of many fundamental differences between the Western conception of economics and the authentic Islamic economics as envisioned in *Al-Qur'ān*. To illustrate, it is generally understood that economics as defined by the ideology of neoliberalism redesigned capitalism into a new form.[14] This means that a discipline defines a system which is then implemented by policymakers who are convinced by the arguments of its advocates. It is generally acknowledged that the current system was created when the President of the

US and the Prime Minister of UK at the time (in the 1980s) implemented policies designed by those who professed neoliberal economics. In contrast, the fundamental principles of authentic Islamic economics are immutable because they are derived from *Al-Qur'ān*. This and other salient differences, to be considered later in this chapter, raise the question of epistemological legitimacy of "Islamizing" Economics. The possibility that such efforts may well lead to an epistemological schizophrenia should give pause.

Rethinking "Islamic Economics"

An opportunity to rethink may be helpful to a deeper understanding of philosophical, logical, and methodological issues involved in present efforts to "Islamize" Economics through a union of economics and a narrow conception of *Maqāṣid as-Sharī'ah* as well as a constrained understanding of the philosophy of the concept of "Islamization of Knowledge," a term first used by 'Allamah Muhammad Iqbal of Lahore[15] with its logical and philosophical bases elaborated by Syed Muhammad Naquib al-Attas.[16] Indeed, the deeper understanding makes clear that this union represents such a narrow understanding of Islamization of Knowledge, which is not even compatible with the underlying philosophy and the proposed methodology of Ismail Al-Faruqi (1921–1986),[17] Abdul-Hamid Abu-Sulayman (1936–2021),[18] Taha Jabir Al-Alwani (1935–2016), and their colleagues[19] at the International Institute of Islamic Thought (IIIT), much less with philosophical and metaphysical arguments of al-Attas. Efforts at Islamizing conventional economics via application of the narrow conception of *Maqāṣid as-Sharī'ah* (as the five objectives popularized by the writings of classics in the tenth through fifteenth centuries, CE) converges necessarily to the secular, neoliberal economics out of which grew the current form of predatory capitalism that now dominates economies across the globe. As important as the Objectives of Islamic Law (*as-Sharī'ah*) are, for humans the priority belongs to compliance with the rules (institutions) that govern the individual and collective behaviour prescribed in *Al-Qur'ān* and which define the vision of Allah *swt* for the economy that serves human societies. Emphasis on a *Fiqhi* approach, through the narrow view of the Objectives,[20] has led to the neglect of *Al-Qur'ān* in this important task. There has been a woeful lack of scholarship in extracting, articulating, and drawing policy implications from the analysis. Exception are efforts by Darraz (1950 [1973]) and that of Al-Hakimi et al. (1992).[21]

In order to demonstrate the inauthenticity of the Islamic economic paradigm that currently dominates discussions and which proposes to "Islamize" mainstream economics through the union of the two, it is necessary to investigate the historical, cultural, and philosophical foundations of the "economics" which is to be "Islamized." This "economics" forms what, in the language of computers, Norgaard calls "the operating system" of today's capitalism.[22] Accordingly, attention focuses on the historical, methodological, philosophical, and ideological development of the reigning paradigm of economics which provides the theoretical support and justification for global capitalism.[23] Throughout the post-Scholastic period, especially during the seventeenth and eighteenth centuries, political economy's centuries, the main task of political economy was to explain and justify the existing economic systems, but not to create one. However, the present form of capitalism owes its existence to neoliberal economics formulated in the 1930s and 1940s in Europe, came to fore in the 1960s and 1970s, and implemented as national policy first in the US and UK in the 1980s. Thereafter, it spread to the rest of the world attesting to the power of major capitalist economies to influence world economies.

Over a period of four decades of operation of this system, significant damage was done to societies around the world. It will be argued here that the adoption of a paradigm of Islamized Economics, as is presently formulated, to design an economic system will produce no better results. An alternative path—offered to researchers in the second half of the 1960s but not taken—to discoverning an authentic *Qur'ānic* paradigm of economics complete with its philosophical, logical, and methodological underpinnings will be presented at the end of the chapter.

Economics: The Operating System of Predatory Capitalism

The presently dominant paradigm of neoliberal economics evolved from "orthodox" or "conventional" economics. The latter, in turn, evolved from the discipline of political economy. Western thought about the economy dates to the seventeenth century, even though concerns about activities that are termed "economic" has always been an inseparable part of human life. From its inception, political economy viewed the economy as embedded within the social system and not separate from it. Political economy was the discipline that studied the management of the resources of the society in provisioning material resources for its members within the historical, cultural, and the belief frameworks existing at the time that formed the structure of Western societies. Among these were the class and hierarchical structure of these societies. Hence, the management of the economy involved path-dependent, cultural values, historical processes, institutions, and organizations which defined Western experience in the seventeenth century. A chief characteristic of this experience was, and continues to be, unequal distribution of power, resources, income, and wealth. The economy was the domain in which this unequal power exercised its privileges.

It is worth noting that the discipline of political economy did not include scarcity as an axiom, as did its offspring "economics." As Thomas De Gregori (1987) and Tae-Hee Jo (2011) note, resources were not considered scarce because it was recognized that they were made available when the need for them arose in the production processes. The above two scholars argue that (1987) and Jo (2011) argue that causal ordering runs from production to natural resources and not the reverse. If so, then scarcity of resources cannot serve as an index of prices. Without a scarcity index, price mechanism cannot legitimately be considered as the coordinator of market activity. Indeed, it has been argued that most prices for goods and services are determined outside of the market. They are administered prices determined by profit margins.[24]

To Adam Smith (1723–1790), the issue of purpose of political economy was finding ways and means of empowering the people to provide their own means of material life as well as providing revenue for the state. Clearly, the issue of scarcity was not a primary concern of Smith.[25] Even after him, political economy's concern was discovering laws governing production and distribution of wealth. While economists like David Ricardo (1772–1823) and John Stuart Mill (1806–1873) focused on these issues, Karl Marx (1818–1883)'s concern was with the question of accumulation of capital through exploitation of the process of distribution and usurpation by capitalists of surplus wealth created by labour. Again, there was no strong emphasis or an overriding concern with scarcity.

In the last three decades of the nineteenth century with the growth of acceptance of marginalism and utilitarianism calculus of pleasure and pain advocated by Stanly Jevons (1871) and Carl Menger (1871), political economy shifted focus from studying the dynamics of production, distribution, and accumulation of wealth to individual behaviour positing humans as calculating beings in search of maximum pleasure with minimum pain.[26] Maximization of utility defined rational behaviour, and optimization became the sole concern of economic agents allowing the discipline that studied it to become deductive and mathematical, abstracting from historical, cultural, and social contexts.[27] In the process, the issue of scarcity of means to satisfy unlimited wants became an axiom that provides the basis for the rationalization of fierce competition for resources and profits.[28]

The end of the nineteenth century saw economics evolving away from the original paradigm of political economy to another in which the notion of scarcity, defined as paucity of resources as means to satisfaction of unlimited wants, is essential. Scarcity as manifestation of desire and fear and as "the starting point of the economy" in Western thought has been traced to Thomas Hobbes (1588–1679). But the economic crises.[29] The economic crises of the 1930s helped buttress the idea of scarcity as a major problem of capitalist societies instead of problems of production and distribution as envisioned by classical, Marxian and, to a large extent, Keynesian economists. Thus, by mid-twentieth century, problems of capitalist system defined in terms of production and distribution were no longer a major concern of economics. Thus, scarcity economics. Instead, scarcity became the focal issue of economics—in the perspectives of economists like Lionel Robbins (1898–1984), George Stigler (1911–1991), Paul Samuelson (1915–2009), and Milton Friedman (1912–2006), Stigler, Samuelson, and Friedman—defined as a study of how scarce resources with alternative uses are allocated to satisfy unlimited wants. This perspective, which altogether skirted the problems of production and distribution in capitalism, was not the result of scientific deliberation and careful research but, as Angus Burgin asserts, there was an ideological purpose aimed at creating a "science" that rationalized and justified neoliberal market fundamentalism at the centre of *laisser-faire* capitalism that challenged communism, Keynesianism, and institutionalism.[30] By the 1970s, neoliberal economics that had argued this ideological position most aggressively since the late 1930s had gained acceptability among conservative politicians and had managed to place itself on the public agenda.

Neoliberal Economics Assumes the Mantle of "Conventional Economics"

At the heart of neoliberal economics is a political ideology that holds that the primary bond between humans is not religious, cultural, societal, familial, moral, ethical, or metaphysical but purely economical. All human relations, associations, and interactions are driven purely by self-interest and motivated by what can be gained from these relationships. Self-interest is the driver of human progress.[31] In this ideology,[32] the idea of use of state power to enforce or even advocate civil rights was a "corruption" of the ideal of liberalism. The term "liberal" in neoliberalism is inspired by the classical liberalism of the eighteenth and nineteenth centuries. Its main focus was on economic liberty, meaning that all individuals have the freedom to dispose of their resources as they see fit. Given that this ideology contends that human progress is driven primarily by self-interest, it follows that any constraint on the economic liberty of individuals to exercise their freedom would constitute a barrier to human progress and must be removed.

Neoliberalism is, in effect, a relatively new philosophical thought that makes certain claims on human conditions and uses these claims to gain support for a new form of capitalism. Liberalism emphasizes individual freedom exercised within the framework of the rule of law and limits the power of state to constitutional provisions. Neoliberalism advocates total freedom of individual behaviour within an institutional scaffolding that includes: strong private property rights, free markets, and free trade, state power exercised only to preserve and strengthen markets where they exist and establish new ones where there is none. It holds individuals fully responsible for all consequences of the choices and decisions they make. Given these conditions, social injustices, poverty, hunger, massive inequalities, and environmental degradation are acceptable since they are the result of behaviour of free individuals in the free market. The state must not interfere, through its redistribution policies, to correct the results, whatever they may be, of operation of free markets and free individuals.

Neoliberal Capitalism Dominates World Economies

Neoliberal economics has been the fundamental articulation of the specifics of the reigning capitalist system.[33] It gave capitalism a new life. Before WWII, following the economic crises of the 1920s and 1930s, capitalism was under considerable stress. Communism and socialism were making inroads in Western Europe and in the US where capitalism and policies to support it were being blamed for the Great Depression and other crises. Historians have even argued that failures of capitalism were responsible for the rise of fascism in Europe. After WWII, leading Western intellectuals were motivated by the need to find ways and means of sustaining peace and strengthening capitalism by stabilizing relationships between economic classes in society as well as between nations. John Maynard Keynes had already proposed the outline of a new economic system that represented a compromise between capitalism and socialism a decade before the end of WWII. Basically, this new vision would continue to allow capitalists to maintain control over the means of production "guided by market forces."

This vision, however, recognized that, left to itself, capitalism creates "disequilibrium" that leads to bouts with inflation, recession, depression, and mass unemployment as well as to frequent financial crises. To counteract the excesses of capitalism, Keynesian solutions called for government intervention by designing fiscal and monetary policies to adjust the economy whenever there was fear of emergence of disequilibrium in form of inflation or recession. As well, laws and regulations were proposed to "leash" capitalism in order to limit its excesses. Moreover, progressive taxation would provide the needed resources to fund social welfare and safety nets as ways and means of provisioning for the economically disadvantaged.

The Empire of Neoliberal Economics

Between the end of the WWII and 1970s, Keynesian paradigm dominated economies. There was economic growth with relative stability. Social welfare programs that provided health, education, and retirement funding allowed a reasonably tolerable income and wealth distribution. However, a number of economic and geopolitical shocks, including the Vietnam War (a fiscally un-provisioned war) and price shocks emanating from monopolization of oil and other extractive industries led to slow growth with rising prices. As a result, a new economic phenomenon emerged in the form of "stagflation": high unemployment combined with inflation. Upper economic classes had tolerated high taxes and had reluctantly consented to have their economic power be "leashed" through regulation during the post-WWII so long as their share of the economic pie remained essentially unaltered.[34] However, the economic elite found intolerable that their economic take was eroding because of the low growth of the 1970s. In the event, they and their political allies began searching for ways and means by which the crises of the period could be used to wrest back control over the economy lost during the post-WWII period.

In the immediate post-WWII period, a group of European economists, members of Mont Pelerine Society,[35] had already developed a body of philosophical and analytic research highly critical of Keynesian economics. The Society's most prominent member, Fredrick Von Hayek (1899–1992) and Milton Friedman, made a philosophical case that reframed all government interventions as restricting human freedom and, therefore, they constituted an attack on the central values of Western civilization. This way, the need for governments to regulate to protect the economy, the society, and the environment against abuse and harm that individuals and corporations can cause was reasserted as arbitrary attempts to constrain human freedom.

Neoliberalism first came to public notice in the decade between the second half of the 1960s and the first half of the 1970s. During this period, there was discontent and agitation, particularly among the European and American youth. While the mass protests were spearheaded by opposition to the war in Vietnam, it represented a deeper underlying resentment against what the protestors considered government policies restricting individual liberties. By the late 1960s and early years of the 1970s, these movements crystalized their position with a focus on the "intrusive" role of the state and demanded reforms. This provided the neoliberal intellectuals a platform which they used skillfully throughout the 1970s to place their views on public agenda.[36] As pure economic ideology, neoliberalism had a simple message, establishing free markets and minimizing the role of the state in regulating the market, cloaked in the rhetoric of individual liberty, political equality, and human rights.[37]

With support from allies among political and economic elites, neoliberalism capitalized on the popular discontent to guide it toward reinventing a much stronger form of capitalism. In this effort, neoliberalism achieved its major success in intensifying the formulation of government policies aimed at serving the interests of capitalism with the election of Margaret Thatcher as the Prime Minister of UK in 1979 and Ronald Regan as the President of the US in 1981, both strong converts to neoliberalism. From then on, neoliberal economics would become the doctrine according to which domestic economic policies in Western countries and across the globe would be formulated. Internationally, implementation of the neoliberal economic policies, summarized as "the Washington Consensus"[38] were promoted through international financial institutions as "Adjustment Programs." Neoliberal economic policies brought deep changes in the structure of economies across the globe. Multinational corporations could move, with ease, financial and technical resources and production, across borders, to where labour was the cheapest while increasing the income and wealth gap between rich and poor. By mid-1990s, the power of economic decision-making had begun to shift from states to economic elites and their political allies through implementation of neoliberal policies.

By the end of the 1990s, the neoliberal capitalism had begun weakening its host governments to the degree that John McMurthy (1999) diagnosed the period as "the cancer stage of capitalism." The "disease" was sapping the strength of "the resources of social immunity and the civil commons that bear them"; resources that were "life bases of successful response" to the disease.[39] McMurtry (1999, p. 257, italics in orginal) warned that human life is in pathological competition with neoliberal capitalism. He explained that competition becomes *pathological competition* "when life is not *raised* to higher or more enabled levels of vital life compasses of thought, feeling, and action, but is *reduced* to lower levels and, at worst, permanently disabled or destroyed."

Even at the time of his writing, late 1990s, McMurtry (1999, pp. viii, 257–8, italics in original) further argued that the market paradigm has mutated "into its recent carcinogenic eruption and metastasis" and now it "has at this stage of social evolution become humanity's primary pathological competition. For it does not enable more comprehensive, vital life for humanity or the planet, but disables the world's species and environmental habitats, increasing hundreds of millions of malnourished, unemployed, homeless, insecure and money-subjugated people, and societies in general which have been variously stripped of their civil commons across the world—all in a period of greater technical powers and rising riches ... This competition is pathogenic not only because its calculus of value rules out life's requirements, but because its programme prescribes the defunding of precisely what protects and fulfils these requirements. Yet all of this is said to be necessary 'to be more competitive'—which it can only be from the standpoint of the disease invasion itself."[40] These warnings went unheeded.

The Dire Costs of Neoliberal Economics

Two decades later and after nearly forty years of domination of world economy by neoliberal capitalism—under which corporations have operated without government interference and without accountability—neoliberal reforms have stacked the deck in societies in favour of economic elite, disempowered states, and empowered multinationals. The resulting massive inequality and much higher concentration of wealth in the hands of the economically powerful have allowed the economic elite to dictate their objectives to policy and law makers. There is, regrettably, no countervailing power either in form of labour unions or states not captured by the economic elite. The rapidity with which societal institutions collapsed in face of the 2008/2009 financial crisis and again during the 2019/2020 Covid-19 pandemic is evidence of the powerlessness of states and the failure of the "free market" ideas of neoliberal economics as the death toll from Covid pandemic across the globe approached 7 million by May 2023 according to the World Heath Organization, though The Economist estimated it in excess of 10 million by May 2021.

Above all else, the inability to deal effectively with the pandemic reflects the most glaring example of market failure. As noted by Parker (2021, pp. 28–29), nothing in the pandemic has escaped reference to economics, as "measured by a combination of unprecedented trillions that powerful governments and their central banks have poured into their economies; by the exorbitant costs for crash development, production, and successful distribution of vaccines; by the massive financial losses imposed by the shutdowns or curtailment of businesses; by the physical shortages caused by disruptions to what is anodynely called 'the global supply chain;' and by the abrupt disappearance or curtailment of jobs worldwide—and with those jobs, the personal income that purchased food, paid for homes and cars and clothing, indeed supplied all the variegated necessities and luxuries we have grown accustomed to assuming were always simply there."[41]

A Blending of "Economic Science" and the As-Sharī'ah

The typical idea that "Islamic economics is a distinctive blend of *Sharī'ah* principles and conventional economics" and that "as long as concepts and principles do not contradict Islamic principles, they can be adopted in Islamic economics,"[42] recognizes the secular nature of "conventional economics," nevertheless, it accepts, with apparently minor modifications, the axioms of this "science." For example, it replaces "scarcity" with "relative scarcity"[43] and argues that "any disagreement" with relative scarcity "as the prime cause of the economic problem will not only deprive us from developing the new discipline scientifically but will also deviate us from meanings mentioned in the Holy Book of Allah the Almighty." This position betrays an uncritical devotion to "conventional economics" at a time when this discipline is facing the most serious crisis of legitimacy within the profession itself. Aside from the fact that the claim has neither a theoretical nor an empirical content in the sense that could claim "scientific objectivity," relativity here is used, in the sense of means-ends, to relate resources to "peoples' needs" unlike the "conventional" economics which relates "scarcity" to "wants"; a broader concept than "needs."

Invoking *Al-Qur'ān*—more as a jargon than truly authentic justification as is done in this context—raises a difficult question. Precisely within the context of the selected verses used and the peculiar meaning attached to them, begs the question about the justice of creating a species without providing them with sufficient resources to meet its needs. Indeed, *Al-Qur'ān* insists that ontologically there is no scarcity and that Allah swt has created everything in sufficient amounts, both in terms of stocks and flows, to sustain all in the created order (see, for example, Verse 30: Chapter 17; 21:15; and 8:30). However, *Al-Qur'ān*, as well as *As-Sunnah*, also assert that serious problems such as poverty, deprivation, and massive inequalities of income and wealth are caused by non-compliance with rules of distribution and redistribution as prescribed rather than by the paucity of resources. The logic of means-ends relationship provides the reason and justification for the existence of "conventional economics" which, in turn, necessitates the invention of the concept of scarcity as related to "wants." Human wants could be assumed as "unlimited," in terms of insatiable desires and wishes, unlike "needs" which have a limit, at least within the constraints of what life needs to sustain itself comfortably.

Acceptance of scarcity as an axiom as well as the adoption into "Islamic economics" of the rest of the discipline of conventional economics, "as long as they do not contradict Islamic principles" not only secularizes the knowledge of how *Al-Qur'ān* orders the economy and thus desacralizes it, with far-reaching implications, it has also an impact on understanding Divine Justice as it begs the question of the justice of creating a being without making sufficient provisions available to carry out the responsibilities assigned to it. Since the ninth–fourteenth centuries AD, there has always been a strand of thinking among Muslims that excludes "Justice" as an attribute of the Creator because, it argues, it would impose a constraining condition on the Divine's Omnipotence and on His Absolute Power to do as He pleases. Injustice however does not befit the nature of Allah, the Just and the Judge.[44]

Is Scarcity the Problem or Distribution?

Focusing on scarcity rules out distribution (and redistribution) as the main problem of economies as envisioned in *Al-Qur'ān*. The model of the union of *as-Sharī'ah* and "conventional economics" focuses on "relative scarcity" as "the prime cause of the economic problem." This is similar to what happened to economics in the later decades of the nineteenth century when the Marginalist school shifted attention away from the primary concern of classical and Marxian economists with production and distribution to one of studying a much more limited means-ends issue, with "scarcity" as a focal axiom. Never mind that the theoretical and empirical validity of scarcity as an axiom has not been demonstrated, this brand of Islamic economics argues for the concept of scarcity as if it were an irrefutably established fact.

To reject scarcity as a fundamental axiom of Islamic economics, in consonance with clear verses of *Al-Qur'ān*, is not to deny that individuals, societies, and states operate under budget constraints, sometimes very hard budget constraints. Rules governing spending and consumption behaviour prescribed in *Al-Qur'ān* impose constraints, yet *Al-Qur'ān* denies the existence of ontological scarcity. It attributes the existence of problems such as poverty, hunger, and destitution to reasons stemming from maldistribution and/or non-compliance with rules governing redistribution as directed by the Creator. If anything, a major function of Islamic economics must be de-secularization and resacralization of economic knowledge as was the original intention of the Islamization of Knowledge project as advanced by Al-Attas who made a compelling argument, philosophically, metaphysically, and logically, for desecularizing and resacralizing knowledge. Economic knowledge, relying on the teachings of *Al-Qur'ān* would reject the axioms of conventional economics, including that of scarcity.

The absurdity of the idea of scarcity as the main reason for the "economic problem" is becoming more and more obvious empirically. How can the proposition of scarcity "as a prime cause of the economic problem" have any validity when Oxfam reported that in 2020, thirty billion US dollars—only a fraction of the US $130 billion owned by the wealthiest individual in the world—could have eradicated world hunger. What is a more serious "economic problem" than hunger? Similar fraction of the wealth of the second wealthiest individual in the world could provide education, health, and welfare for most people in the world. Is scarcity then the "prime cause," or obscene distribution of wealth, when a fraction of the wealth of only two individuals could eradicate hunger, poverty, and disease? Is scarcity "the prime cause," or the absurd levels of waste, extravagance, and opulence that have depleted natural wealth of humanity to such a high degree that ecological crisis is now an existential threat to its survival? Scarcity is not a "scientific" fact—it is an artifact invented to create a specific mindset, an attitude, capitalizing on basic emotions of fear, desire, and greed in order to distort the objective reality that humans live in a world abundance. This view about reality was essentially held over the history of economic thought with the exception of approximately the last hundred and fifty years. Compliance with the rules that limit undue consumption, on the one hand, and distribute income and wealth more fairly would not see scarcity as a binding constraint.

Robin Kimmerer, The anthropologist, Robin Wall Kimmerer (2013, p. 376) finds it paradoxical that: "Modern capitalist societies, however richly endowed, dedicate themselves to the proposition of scarcity. Inadequacy of economic means is the first principle of world's wealthiest peoples."[45] As Charles Eisenstein (2011) explains: "It is an attitude of scarcity, not of abundance, that has led to the depletion of our natural commons. Competition and the accumulation of more than one needs are the natural response to a perceived scarcity of resources. The obscene overconsumption of our society arise from our poverty: the deficit of being that afflicts the discrete and separate self, the scarcity of money in an interest-based system, the poverty of relationship that comes from the severance of our ties to community and to nature, the relentless pressure to do anything, anything at all, to make a living. In contrast, the natural response to an atmosphere of abundance is generosity and sharing. This includes sharing within the human realm and beyond it as well."[46] Eisenstein then asks: "Whence our frenetic race to convert nature into commodities that don't even meet real needs, if not from insecurity? Think about it. Is it from an attitude of scarcity or abundance that someone buys fifty pairs of shoes? Is it the secure person or the insecure person who buys a third sports car and a 10,000-square-foot house? Whence this urge to own, to dominate, to control? It comes from a lonely, destitute self in a hostile ungiving world."

Al-Qur'ān addresses precisely these kinds of problems of the alienated self and provides ways and means of resolving them. By arguing that the Creator has and continues to provide everything in exact measure for everyone and every generation, that humans should never worry about their sustenance, and that they should work hard and share their income and wealth with others, *Al-Qur'ān* removes fear as a motivation for predatory behaviour. It negates the idea of scarcity as stimulant for fear, greed, and savage competition upon which capitalism thrives. Instead, *Al-Qur'ān* focuses on distributive justice, warns of severe consequences for the society from violation of the rules of distribution and redistribution prescribed by Allah swt. By focusing on scarcity as "a prime cause of the economic problem," the dominant Islamic economics paradigm either excludes consideration of distribution, redistribution, and social justice or assigns it lower priority than could be justified. In the process of diverting attention away from the alternative axiom of fundamental abundance, such a convenient position absolves human responsibility in establishing social justice contrary to the clear verses of *Al-Qur'ān* (see, for example, Verses 18 and 21: Chapter 3; 135: 4; 8: 5; 60 and 103: 9; 29: 7; 90: 16; and 25: 57). Social Justice is thus the prime directive.

Excluding distribution and redistribution and, ultimately, social justice, as the central concerns of Islamic economics and, instead, focusing on and reiterating scarcity as a fundamental cause of "the economic problem" cannot access the spiritual capital that an authentically structured economy governed by the rules prescribed in *Al-Qur'ān*, with an organic connection to al-Ghayb, would provide. Conventional economics with its underlying philosophy of materialism and its methodology of empiricism would reject any concept or idea whose source is metaphysical. For example, it could never take seriously the concept of *Barakah*, a very important and operational dimension and a source of expansion in an economy whose institutional scaffolding is constituted by the rules prescribed in *Al-Qur'ān* and where participants in the economy are in full compliance with these rules (see, Verse 96 of Chapter 7 of *Al-Qur'ān*). Islamic economics as a combination of sacred and profane would rob such a discipline of value as a subject matter in what Talal Asad calls an "authorizing discourse," even if it partakes of jargons of authenticity.

Such a paradigm becomes vacuous in terms of its ability to propose authentically Islamic policy measures addressed to problems such as poverty, hunger, health, education, and environmental challenges. Like its conventional counterpart, its policy discourse has to take scarcity seriously as the central cause of these problems. Focusing on scarcity obviates the need for designing policies, based on *Al-Qur'ān* and *As-Sunnah*, addressed to correcting maldistribution and weak, or nonexistent, redistribution policies. This position necessarily converges toward that of neoliberal economics that excludes questions of distribution, redistribution, and social justice and instead offers capitalism as the solution to the false "economic problem" ostensibly caused by scarcity. As well, it converges to the position of those who exclude justice as belonging to the Five Principles of *Maqāṣid as-Sharī'ah*.[47] In contrast, Fazlur Rahman holds that justice is the main principle of *Al-Qur'ān* and that communicating the divine concept of justice is the main function of *Al-Qur'ān*.[48]

SECULARISM AND THE BLENDING OF CONVENTIONAL ECONOMIC AND THE *SHARĪ'AH*

The view of Islamic economics stated above holds that the science of economics possesses a "wealth of economic knowledge, theories and policies" which could benefit Islamic economics.[49] Indeed, conventional economics has developed concepts, terms, and ideas that can be useful in formulating explanations for prescribed rules governing the economy and the behaviour of its participants. However, there are very few (some will be mentioned later) of these that do not, in a fundamental way contradict *Al-Qur'ān*. As a whole, however, "conventional economics,"[50] relying heavily as it does on secularism, materialism, and possessive individualism as its underlying philosophy has very little in terms of "principles" that would not contradict Islamic values and principles. Consider, for example, its conception of human as "economic man."[51] While the practitioners of conventional economics claim that this is only an abstraction intended to simplify a more complex conception of human beings, their policy recommendations for individuals and governments behaviour in the real world bear the mark of "economic man" as a crucial pillar of their "science."

Within the narrow context of conceptualization of Islamization of Knowledge (IOK), it may be argued, as is done, that once one accepts the fundamental axioms of the conventional economics, i.e. self-interest, scarcity, and rationality, much of the rest of the "science" can be incorporated into Islamic economics. This position however contradicts the philosophy and methodology of the broader conception of IOK as conceived by its originator, Syed Muhammad Naquid Al-Attas who held de-secularization of Western knowledge, especially the social sciences, as the first condition of Islamization.[52] However, secularism has been a foundation of economics, and political economy before it, ever since the Enlightenment.[53] The focus of secularism consists of desacralizing thought and action, and replacing metaphysical and sacred explanations with "knowledge" based on empirical evidence discernible by senses, rationality, and formal logic. Secularism became essential, and remains so, to the "science" of economics which has assumed a sovereignty of its own, sourced separately from the Divine origin. It is rather astonishing that at a time when the legitimacy of conventional economics—as well as its axioms and methods, and as the theoretical mother of present predatory capitalism—is being challenged[54] more aggressively than ever before within the Western culture that gave birth to it and in the profession that has been practising it, Muslim writers uncritically find in it redeeming qualities that can help Islamic economics build an identity for itself.[55]

Secularism as Foundational Philosophy of "Conventional Economics"

Economics evolved out of political economy which began as an Enlightenment project of moral philosophy. A salient feature of the Enlightenment desacralizing the world is the process of "rationalization," which makes information and technical reasoning the essence of knowledge. The intention was replacing the concept of Supreme Creator as a source of all knowledge. Whereas political economy dealt with the subjects of conscience, virtue, and personal liberty, economics was concerned with secular, worldly mundane issues like production, exchange, trade, and taxation without any connection, ontological or otherwise, with the sacred. The only idea of "spirit" it was willing to countenance was that of the "animal spirit" in humans that motivated investment.[56] Economic historians have argued that the emergence and expansion of political economy was due to the decline of religion. Harold J. Laski (1936), an economic historian, argued that the birth of political economy established an intellectual tradition which based its "foundation of social inquiry" on human–human relations "instead of the relations of man with God."[57] Davenport (2008, pp. 23–24) suggests: "This shift in intellectual life from the vertical to the horizontal had begun centuries earlier, but Adam Smith was first to take this perspective into the realm of economics, an Enlightenment venture that was as promising as it was dangerous both for nations and for the religiously committed."[58]

Enlightenment thinkers valued highly the idea of personal freedom—meaning not subject to rules prescribed by the Creator, in the first place, and the state. Finding the right kind of organization of an efficient social order consistent with strict individual freedom had been a dilemma. A solution was offered by Adam Smith who synthesized two ideas of Enlightenment, that of personal freedom and that of the Newtonian physics and mechanics. According to the latter, the planetary system resembled "a clockwork: a closed, autonomous system, ruled by endogenous, mutually independent factors of a highly selective nature, self-regulating and moving toward a determinate, predictable point of equilibrium. The Newtonian paradigm, in line with eighteenth-century thinking, represents economic events as a reality independent of the observer."[59] Observer was assumed rational, meaning in possession of the faculty of reason. While separate from the object, the observing subject could understand the object through reasoning. The objective reality, according to this system of thought, was subject to natural law.[60] The latter consists of the precepts, norms of the "Eternal Law" that govern the behaviour of humans, as rational (able to use the power of reason) beings possessing free will.

The vision of the economy Adam Smith presented in his book The Wealth of Nations—in exclusion of his book on The Theory of Moral Sentiment written a decade and half before The Wealth of Nations—was what he called a "commercial society" in which the "invisible hand" directs rational individuals possessing free will to achieve the good of the whole by pursuing their own individual self-interests. Thus, his vision which harmonized the two ideals of Enlightenment: freedom of individual with the ideal of "a rational and efficient social order," resolved a conflict between the two that had confounded Enlightenment social thinkers. Smith was interpreted as replacing "God" with the invisible hand of the market which directed individuals to achieve an efficient and rational social order while pursuing their self-interests. Thus, implying that the ideal of the freely acting, autonomous individuals pursuing their own self-interests required a removal of the religious, moral, and ethical ideas that constrained human behaviour.

This interpretation required that economic action had to be decoupled not only from Divinely ordained rules of behaviour but even from secular moral concerns. This, in turn, required an abstract vision of human being as an "economic creature" or an "economic agent" who pursues only "the end of maintaining, expanding, and enjoying his own life as a singular individual" and who as a "practical agent" conceives of no world other than the world of empirical facts. All values are extrinsic. Things do not interest the "agent" because of the intrinsic values they hold but because they serve as means to the end of singular pursuit of self-interests. Here, the most important extrinsic value criterion the "agent" has is that of efficiency, of getting the most out of all means that serve agent's self-interests. The agent may cooperate in a social project but only if it serves as means to the end: "*self-interest.*"[61]

The economics that emerged between the time of Adam Smith and the present gradually but surely became a conjunction of philosophies and ideologies of empiricism, logical positivism, individualism, and materialism[62] all of which require secularism as a foundational ideology. Secularism is a foundation stone of conventional economics—the myth system that provides theoretical and logical support for capitalism. Generally, it is understood that "secularism" is antithetical to religious values. What is not often acknowledged is that both concepts "religion" and "secularism" were developed in a historical context, specifically that of Western Christianity. The term "religion" originated in the Roman law while "secularism," meaning rejection of religion, developed at a time when Europeans were searching for a collective identity. While the roots of secularism are in the Renaissance period, it came to its full fruition during the Enlightenment and a period of de-Christianization attempts in Europe. Hence, concepts of religion and secularism are not universal, objective, and value-free as they are often portrayed.[63] As Jakobsen and Pellegrini (2008) argue, "secularism was linked at its origin to a particular religion and a particular location, and it was maintained through a particular set of practices."[64] Yet, its advocates treat it as a universal concept that encompasses modernism, freedom, and progress while holding religion as a regressive force. All these claims are subjective and non-verifiable, and, as Talal Asad has argued (2003), secularism serves a larger project to establish modernity as a hegemonic political goal.[65]

Secularism provided a fertile ground for the birth of the idea of the "market" as is understood by contemporary economics as secular, free of religion, and devoid of moral values. While secularism may not oppose privatization of religion, religious values have no place in the "market." As Weber suggested, secularism's separation from religion meant freedom for the market. However, secularization also meant that economic actors and systems became autonomous in dealing with the natural environment as its sovereign master with licence to exploit nature as they saw fit, no longer accountable to the Creator for actions of their own that harm nature. Conventional economics is directly responsible for the free-market-based, consumption-led theories that appeal to greed derived from its axiom of self-interested "rational" economic man. The resulting economic system, capitalism, created, in turn, artificial wants and found means to motivate the desire on the part of the consumers to fulfil them. This way, human beings became means, as insatiate consumers, necessary to sustain economic growth. The severe deterioration of the ecological capital that belongs to the humanity as a whole and the consequent environmental disasters are the direct results of the exploitive mindset created by the secular conventional economics.

In contrast, Islam considers nature and all its components as created by Allah *swt* and represent, individually and collectively, His Signs thus deserving respect and reverence. Humans, as trustee-agents of the Divine Reality are charged with the preservation of nature. Any exploitation or abuse of nature by humans means shirking in performance of their responsibility and failure as agents of Allah *swt* for which they are held accountable. To exploit nature and its endowments and in the process cause harm results in a degradation of Human-Creator relation or at least negligence or disrespect of that relation. As Seyyed Hossein Nasr argues, since the natural world and its components are created as signs of Allah *swt* for humans (Verse 190: Chapter 3), any act of economic exploitation that destroys any "object or phenomena of nature" is an act of defiance against their Creator.[66] The contrast between the attitudes of secular conventional economics and Islam toward nature is so deep and intensive to beg the question, once again, of how can one possibly entertain a marriage proposal between the two as proposed by the dominant Islamic economics paradigm?

The Rationality Axiom and Islamic Economics

Another crucial axiom of conventional economics—along with self-interest and scarcity—is that of "rationality" which poses a challenge of justification for those who propose to incorporate it into Islamic economics. Just like the concept of sucularism, that of rationality, in its general meaning and as an ideological instrument, was developed during the Enlightenment period. That context was meant for "reason" to replace inherited religious reasoning for the individual whom the Enlightenment glorified, as did the Renaissance, which openly declared "the individual's supreme worth"[67] along with strong belief in human reason. Rationality has different meanings depending on the context. Alasdair MacIntyre (1988) suggested "rationality itself, whether theoretical or practical, is a concept with a history: indeed, since there is a diversity of traditions of enquiry, with histories, there are ... rationalities rather than rationality."[68] Irani (1986) argued for "modes of rationality"[69] and considered that, generally, rationality is "the search for order and thereby for understanding."[70]

The notion that the concept of rationality has a history and that there are varieties of rationalities is confirmed by R. G. Collingwood (1946). He traced it to the Greco-Roman humanism that considered man "as essentially a rational animal, by which I mean the doctrine that every individual human being is an animal capable of reason. So far as any given man develops that capacity and becomes actually, and not potentially, reasonable, he makes a success of his life: according to the Hellenic idea, he becomes a force in political life; according to Hellenistic-Roman idea, he becomes capable of living wisely, sheltered behind his own rationality, in a wild and wicked world."[71]

Economic Rationality Is a Part, Albeit a Small Part, of the General Concept of Rationality

In economics rationality, as a postulate, has specific meaning focused on the means-end logic. In this role, rationality is used instrumentally—in the sense that economics focuses on how means are used to specific ends. It is not able to judge the rationality in the choice of those ends or their quality. Even within the profession itself, views on the role of rationality differ. Some consider that the rationality postulate has a descriptive function meaning that it describes the behaviour of economic agents. Another view holds that the crucial function of the postulate is to emphasize the necessity of consistency in the behaviour of economic agents. Specifically, consistency means transitivity of preference ordering. This condition, simply stated, requires that if, for example, a consumption basket A is preferred to consumption basket B and B is preferred to a third basket C, then A is preferred to C. A third view holds that the postulate is helpful in developing theories that can make decision-making more effective even if the behaviour of economic agents is not always and everywhere consistent. Tony Cramp (1991) suggested that economics, in its attempt to "cut loose from its earlier mooring in moral philosophy," developed the twin axioms of "private rationality" and "private greed." The first means that people behave consistently, and the latter means that people prefer more to less; "neither can be proved."[72] Hence, in economics, rationality and greed are correlates.

In an attempt to "find the mathematically complete principles which define 'rational behavior' for the participants in a social economy, and derive from them the general characteristics of that behavior," John von Neumann and Oskar Morgenstern (1944) proposed five axioms of utility that would make economic behaviour consistent and predictable, therefore rational. An individual who can express preferences based on their notion of utility would be rational by definition according to these axioms: (i) comparability, meaning that an individual can not only express preferences but can also compare them; (ii) measurability, this axiom means that preferences are measurable; (iii) independence axiom requires that the original preference orderings be independent of new preference alternatives; (iv) ranking axiom requires ordinal ranking of preferences; and (v) consistency axiom requires that the comparisons the individual makes among preferences remain consistent over an array of alternatives. The essential axiom of economics that individuals always prefer more to less, the greed axioms, lurks in the background as the individual rank-orders preferences.

Even at the analytic level of von Neumann-Morgenstern's instrumental rationality, human behaviour's reasoning ability is reduced to revealing no inconsistencies in his choice behaviour, in exclusion of all else. It is for this reason that Amartya Sen (1977) called the economic man "a bit of rational fool." He argued that an individual may be rational "in the limited sense of revealing no inconsistencies in his choice behavior," but if the individual's "one preference ordering" does not reflect—and Sen intimates that it does not—the person's self-interest nor "represent his welfare, summarize his idea of what should be done, and describe his actual choices and behavior," then "he must be a bit of a fool." Sen then proceeds to argue that economic theory "has been preoccupied with this rational fool bedecked in the glory of his one all-purpose preference ordering."[73] In response, Frank Hahn and Martin Hollis (1979) allowed "economics probably made a mistake when it adopted the nomenclature of 'rational' when all it meant is correct calculations and an orderly personality."[74] This takes economics back to defining rationality as consistency and requiring that a rational economic agent prefers more to less.[75] This conception of means-ends rationality cannot be reconciled with ideal human behaviour as envisaged in *Al-Qur'ān*.

Frank Hahn's plea for a change in the meaning of economic rationality did not get much traction in the profession, perhaps because it involves value judgements, even though it is closer to the idea of "reasonableness," as understood outside the field. Its rejection by the profession may have been due to the fact that it did not yield itself easily and precisely to marginal utility analysis despite the fact that the definition of utility, its measurement, and aggregation have been ambiguous throughout the history of the concept. Tony Cramp (1991, p. 56) quotes Kenneth Boulding as saying that economists "do not know what utility is, but cannot do without it." It is, however, argued that both the concept of utility as "satisfaction" derived from consumption and the idea that satisfaction declined with marginal consumption are verifiable by "introspection."

At one point in the history of the evolution of the concept (early decades of the twentieth century), a useful policy proposal to justify redistribution of income in order to reduce income inequality was argued by Arthur Cecil Pigou (1912) and Hugh Dalton (1920a, 1920b). Pigou proposed that since the marginal utility of an additional income is much higher for the poor than for the rich, a redistribution of income from the rich to the poor will increase total utility hence the total welfare of the society, as an aggregate of total utility, measured cardinally. Dalton formalized the idea which became known as Pigou-Dalton Principle. It states that, ceteris paribus, a social welfare function should prefer allocations that are more equitable. This means that in the face of income inequality, the value of social welfare increases. Stated differently, a mean-preserving transfer of income from richer to poorer people increases the sum of societal satisfaction.[76] The profession rejected the idea, however, arguing ostensibly that interpersonal comparisons of utility are not permissible. In contrast, redistribution is a major principle as well as a mechanism for reducing income inequality in Islam and is governed by rules prescribed in *Al-Qur'ān*.

AL-QUR'ĀN AND RATIONALITY

Rationality as the use of reason in guiding decision and action is quite radically different in Islam in contrast to the rationality axiom of economics. Whereas in the latter it is a process of reasoning ruled by acquisitive self-interest in exclusion of all else, in the former, the process of reasoning is one of reflective and meditative response in decision-action situations in compliance with the rules prescribed by Allah swt. In *Al-Qur'ān*, two pillars form the foundations upon which rationality is based and which direct the reasoning process of a believer: *Al-Fitrah and Al-'Aql* and *al-'Aql*. The first is the primordial nature of mankind kneaded into being by the Creator with the distinction that it bears the imprint of the cognition of His Oneness and Uniqueness (Verse 30: Chapter 30). Humans who are fully aware of their "self" and of their Creator are constantly oriented and focused toward Him and Him Alone (79: 6). In such individuals, *al-fitrah* commands the depth of their consciousness and ensures consistency of the focus in the reasoning process due to the active, intimate, and permanent awareness of the ever-presence of the Creator. There is no impulsive response to stimuli calling for decisions for immediate gratification. Individual humans may temporarily lose touch with their primordial nature, perhaps due to forgetfulness or temporary disharmony between the requirements of the belief and actions—what Aristotle called "akrasia." Nevertheless, the call to humans to return to the primordial nature always harkens deep in their "self." Islam articulates such call to the entire humanity to return to their primordial nature through compliance with the rules governing behaviour prescribed in *Al-Qur'ān*. In this sense, it can be argued that rationality, as discernible from *Al-Qur'ān*, is the process of rule-based reasoning[77] fortified by its second pillar, *al-'Aql*.

Al-'Aql, as used in *Al-Qur'ān* and in the sayings of the Noble Messenger (saa), has no exact equivalent in English. The root verb of *al-'aql is 'a-qa-la, which* means "to bind together," "to restrain," or "to withhold" perhaps signifying that utilization of *al-'aql* in the reasoning process keeps human focused on the primordial its primordial nature active, fully aware, and free to bind the individual to the Creator. Hence, *al-'aql* can be regarded as the faculty with which the Creator has endowed humans to employ in the process of reasoning in their decision-action circumstances in compliance with the rules He has prescribed in *Al-Qur'ān*. In practice, this concept of rationality operates through the process involving three stages of *Ta'qqul* (process of intellection), *Tafakkur* (thinking process), and *Tadabbur* (meditation and contemplation on the consequences of each alternative course of action) that constitute rational decision-making. The first employs *al-'aql* to meditate on and assess the decision-action situation, the second, the faculty to reflect on the alternative courses of action, and the third is employed to contemplate and consider the consequences of each alternative course of action it terms of compliance with the prescribed rules. To summarize, rationality, according to *Al-Qur'ān* is a rule-based process of meditative, contemplative, and reflective reasoning.

As Yarmine Mermer (1996)[78] argued, rationality within the context of *Al-Qur'ān* means not only sound "reasoning and logic but more importantly that which is in accordance with fitrah (human nature)." This is in sharp contrast to the independent reasoning which is the ultimate arbiter of reasoning itself and self-sufficient onto itself and a "commitment to reason in the name of reason."[79] *Al-Qur'ān* refers to independent rationality—that which is not anchored on *al-fitrah* and *al-'aql* and unheedful of guidance of the Creator—as "*hawā*," meaning whim and caprice (see, for example, Verses 43–44: Chapter 25; and 50: Chapter 28). In the Allah-centred rationality, every and all things have meanings pointing to the Ultimate Source of their existence. These meanings guide the believer facing a decision-action circumstance. Hence, by necessity, rationality according to *Al-Qur'ān* has a strong metaphysical dimension. When faced with decision-action choices, the believer's internal compass turns toward the rules prescribed by the Creator. He/she is, in turn, guided by these rules in the course of intellective-deliberative-meditative-reflective process of rationality. Hence, it is apparent that independent economic rationality cannot accommodate the rationality discernible from *Al-Qur'ān*. The two are in no way compatible.

Al-Qur'ān and "Self-Interest"

Turning to self-interest as one of the trio of fundamental axioms of conventional economics, with scarcity and rationality, it is noted that of the three axioms, self-interest has the longest history in Western thought. There is however a major difference between the concept as it is now an integral part of the foundations of neoliberal economics and as it has been considered throughout the history of the concept prior to the emergence of neoliberal economics. While Western philosophy has always argued that acting in the interest of oneself stems from an essential human characteristic: self-love, which motivates self-preservation, it has also expressed the concern that self-love has manifest potential of doing harm. Plato, for example, considered selfishness the greatest of evils: "Of all evils the greatest is one which in the souls of most men is innate, and which a man is always excusing in himself and never correcting; I mean, what is expressed in the saying that 'everyman by nature is and ought to be his own friend.' Whereas the excessive love of self is in reality the source to each man of all offences" and considered; "for the lover is blinded about the beloved, so that he judges wrongly of the just, the good, and the honorable, and thinks that he ought always to prefer himself to the truth."[80]

It has been a challenge for Western thought to find the right balance between admitting what it considered the inevitability of pursuing self-interest in service of self-love and mitigating its harmful manifestations. Adam Smith believed that self-interest would be tempered by sympathy inherent in the human nature. Economics as developed in the twentieth century however subscribed to the "psychological egoism" theory that argued all human behaviour is motivated exclusively by self-interest. All behaviour that seems motivated otherwise, such as charity, is disguised self-seeking. Albert O. Hirschman (2013, p. 196) understood that the concept of self-interest in economics is in line with this conception. After saying that "the construct of the self-interested, isolated individual who chooses between alternative courses of action after computing their prospective costs and benefits to him-or herself that is, while ignoring costs and benefits to other people and to society at large" is central in Economics, he proceeded to give examples of the "inefficient and harmful" effects of "the unfettered pursuit of private interest." These include "the decision problem known as the Prisoner's Dilemma, the obstacles to collective action because of free riding, and the problem of ensuring an adequate supply of public goods in general."[81]

As discussed so far, two of the three fundamental postulates or axioms of Economics are incompatible with Islamic teachings. The self-interest axiom can also be shown to be incompatible with the teachings of *Al-Qur'ān*. For this purpose, it will be helpful to understand the meaning of the two components of the concept: "self" and "interest" within the context of *Al-Qur'ān*. It is striking that there has been very little or no attempt (to our knowledge) in the economics literature to unpack "self-interest." While interest can be understood as economic interest, as is apparent from Hirschman's arguments quoted above, the "self" is not defined in contemporary economics. It is however possible to comprehend a sense of the concept of the "self" as understood in Economics from the writings of the intellectual ancestors of the discipline. Of these thinkers, John Locke (1632–1704) had perhaps the greatest influence on the formation of the philosophical foundation of economics and specially on neoliberal economics. For example, Locke's fundamental conception of existence of deep antagonism between man and nature, self and universe which underlie his philosophy helped the formation of the view predominant in economics that humans had mastery over nature allowing its exploitation and that of its resources as means of economic advancement.

Locke defined the "self" as "that conscious thinking thing (whatever substance made up of, whether spiritual or material, simple or compound, it matters not) which is sensible, or conscious of pleasure and pain, capable of happiness or misery, and so is concerned for itself, as far as that consciousness extends."[82] For Locke, sense experience, in terms of pleasure or pain, constitutes the dominant character of humans. Nature, he said, "has put in man a desire for happiness, and an aversion to misery: these indeed are innate practical principles, which (as practical principles ought) do continue constantly to operate and influence all our actions without ceasing."[83] The innate principles constitute the moral notions of "good" and "evil" to Locke: "Things are good or evil, only in reference to pleasure or pain. That we call good, which is apt to cause or increase pleasure, or diminish pain in us; or else to procure or preserve us the possession of any other good, or absence of any evil. And, on the contrary, we name that evil, which is apt to produce or increase any pain, or diminish any pleasure in us; or else to procure us any evil, or deprive us of any good."[84]

Lock's idea that sense experience of pleasure or pain provides the axis around which human thought rotates leads directly to his philosophy of individualism which was also adopted enthusiastically by economics. The reason is, Locke argued, that while everyone can agree that happiness is the aim in life, general agreement on a uniform definition of happiness is not possible. Therefore, since thoughts come from individual sense perceptions, then actions too must come from individual experiences. Individual sense experience provides the knowledge that drives and controls individual actions. And, the more rational the more clearly will the individuals perceive of where true happiness lies. From here, it was a short distance to the formation of economic liberal individualism which argued that the individual should be free to use his own resources as he chooses. Frank Knight (1885–1972) explained that "the primary immediate objective of liberalism was freedom for the individual in relationships of exchange, of goods and services, i. e., relations of *quid pro quo*."[85] Accordingly, markets must be free of state interference. The state had only one legitimate use of the power of coercion: to prevent encroachment on the freedom of individuals by others.

It appears that economics adopted without change Locke's definition of "self" as well as the "love" for it and incorporated it into its own concept of self-interest without Adam Smith's concept of "sympathy" meant to mitigate the excesses of "psychological egoism." Locke's definition of "self" purely as the "thing" whose world revolves around physical sense perceptions of pleasure and pain, happiness and misery stands in sharp contrast with the conception of self as "*nafs*" encountered in *Al-Qur'ān* where it is identified as a being created, standing between the body (*badan*) and spirit (*rūh*). This self is inspirationally (in the sense of *ilhām*) and ontologically cognizant of "good and evil" (Verse 7: Chapter 91). It has been empowered to order its possessor—who has been granted freedom of will—to do evil (*nafs ammarah bis-sū'*; 53: 12) as it can blame and accuse its possessor when he/she wills to do evil (*nafs lawwūmah*; 2:75), or achieve certitude and tranquility in its relationship with its Creator (*nafs mutma'innah*; 27:89). At any moment in time the possessor of the "self as *nafs*," the human being, has a clear insight of the stage in which his "self" is positioned even if he gives ostensible excuses for his/her behaviour commanded by the "*nafs*" (Verse 15: Chapter 75) that knows its own "self-interest" defined by its position with respect to the three stages of *ta'aqqul, tafakkur, and tadabbur*. Those interests change as the "self" progresses through these stages. Progression is determined by the degree of compliance with the rules governing behaviour prescribed in *Al-Qur'ān* and explicated by the Noble Messenger (*saa*).

The interactions between this self and its possessor determine the degree of compliance. The more the possessor of the *nafs* is in control, the more compliant the behaviour, depending on the strength of the former to dominate the latter in the process of cleansing the "self" from its whims and caprice. If the *nafs* becomes dominant to the point where it can order its possessor to rebel against its Creator by rule violation, then it converges qualitatively to the greedy, worldly, individualistic "self" defined by John Locke and the neoliberal economics since it no longer recognizes the Sovereignty of Allah swt. At the beginning stages where the self is dominant, it takes on an adversarial role with respect to its possessor and their "interests" are in conflict. As the dominance of the self over the person declines—through the Grace and Mercy of its Creator Who provides the human being with the needed guidance—its role becomes one of cooperation. Hence, the interests of the "self" and those of its possessor begin to converge as the person's control over the whims and caprice of the "self" increases through rule compliance.

The Logical Impossibility of the Proposed Union

Noting that the whole reason for the existence of a discipline that deals with issues arising from the operations of an economic system is to discover and explain the rules governing its operation that guarantees the results envisioned by the underlying worldview or ideology, neoliberal economics serves well this function by explaining the rules that guide the predatory capitalism now dominating world economies. Considering all that has been discussed above, it is clear that a union of neoliberal economics and Islamic economics—that is the discipline that could discover and explain the rules governing the vision of economic system discernible from *Al-Qur'ān*—is a logical impossibility. These are two incomparable, incompatible, hence incommensurable paradigms with different worldviews.[86] Clearly, the proposed union will differ from the paradigm discernible from *Al-Qur'ān*. Different worldviews provide different perspectives and different ideologies allowing different solutions to issues faced in the economy. The result is confusion and disagreements. The solution to the conflict is a shift in perspective, a "paradigm shift" from the paradigm suggested by the proposed union to the one discernible from *Al-Qur'ān: Al-Iqtiṣād*.

Many consider that the conventional economics is in an existential crisis of legitimacy, thus in need of new paradigm. A number of proposals are being discussed.[87] Some also consider the present configuration defining Islamic economics too is in crisis[88] and in need of a paradigm shift. The former has created significant problems which itself is now incapable of solving. The latter, employing a narrow understanding of the project of Islamization of Knowledge project as well as a narrow understanding of the Objectives of *as-Sharī'ah*, proposes a naive model of Islamization of economics[89] that will replicate both the creation of problems—most importantly, obscene levels income inequality and environmental disasters which it now finds intractable—and the inability to solve them. Consequently, this paradigm is not viable, either theoretically or from a practical policy perspective. But what about the authentic version of the Islamization of Knowledge? Can it provide a basis for the development of an authentic Islamic economic paradigm?

Attasian Conception of Islamization of Knowledge

The idea of Islamization of Knowledge developed along two paths.[90] The first—a broader, more comprehensive view—has a holistic vision of knowledge that needs to be Islamized. It has a clear, unambiguous philosophical foundation and a methodology developed by Syed Muhammad Naquib Al-Attas of Malaysia. The second approach was proposed by Ismail al-Faruqi and his colleagues at the International Institute of Islamic Thought (IIIT) in Herndon, Virginia, U.S.A. The latter provided a methodology for Islamization of knowledge which became ostensibly the predominant methodology of the present paradigm of Islamization of Knowledge present Islamization of economic paradigm.[91] Within the Faruqian methodology, *Al-Qur'ān* is the first source for Islamization of knowledge—most emphatically articulated by Taha Jabir Al-'Alwani. However, in actual practice of articulating an Islamized economics paradigm, priority was given to *fiqh* and the ideas of writers of tenth–thirteenth centuries, for example, Al-Juwayni, Al-Ghazali, Al-Shatibi, Ibn Khaldun, and others.

The first path proposed by Al-Attas was based firmly on an ontological and epistemological Islamization of Knowledge aimed at the de-secularization and resacralization of knowledge.[92] This objective is shared by many Western scholars who believe that secularization and desacralization of knowledge has gone too far resulting in considerable damage to humanity and to nature, much of it through the discipline of economics and the predatory capitalism which it supports.[93]

De-secularization requires combing through the teachings of a field of knowledge and purging it of all secularized notions and ideas. The methodology of resacralization, according to Al-Attas, requires the reintroduction into Muslim societies and their educational systems the system of *"Ta'deeb,"* meaning a process of acquiring *"Ādāb,* plural of *adab,*[94] meaning proper conduct in compliance with the rules of behaviour governing relationships with the Creator, other humans and nature, and the "self"—as prescribed in *Al-Qur'ān* and exemplified by the Noble Messenger (saws). *Ta'deeb* then is a process of educating the *nafs* (self) to give recognition to and acknowledgement of its proper place in relation to its Creator, itself, its community, and society. This schooling, and character-building of the *"nafs* or self" manifests in one's behaviour and disposition (*akhlāq*). *Ādāb* is a crucial element of Attasian discourse of Islamization of knowledge (de-secularization and resacralization). The loss of *ādāb* is identified as the principle cause of turmoil in Muslim societies. Al-Attas points to this loss as the cause internal to Muslim societies and secularism as the external cause which in an organic combination set a dynamic path of degradation of Muslim character, thought, and behaviour.[95] In general, the Attasian proposal is that Muslim societies should undertake a process of counter-secularism which simultaneously means resacralizing human societal relationships. This combined process means that Islam reasserts its societal influence, returns to public sphere, cultural subsystems, education, and social sciences. In doing so, all actions, including those economic, become sacred.

Muslim philosophers and writers such as Said Nursi, 'Muhammad Iqbal, Seyyed Hossein Nasr, and Syed Muhammad Naquib Al-Attas have for long emphasized that the image of humans sacralized by the Breath of the Creator is the only one that can protect them from the terror of existence. It is the image that truly liberates humans, provides them with the highest conceivable freedom to experience that knowing which is above knowledge and which provides humans access to the "dynamic passage of the universe to unending unity."[96] Their activities become correlated with their belief as they engage in the economic creative processes, along with the abundant resources that their Creator has provided, as an act of communion with Him rather than one of exploitation of nature to satisfy personal greed for self-gratification and senseless accumulation. Their existence becomes timeless, their work and their world sacred such that every act in compliance with rules of behaviour guarantees multiple returns leading to the flourishing of their society and its economy (see, for example, Verse 96: Chapter 7).

Such a movement would challenge the long-standing belief of the West that its own historical, cultural, and civilizational experience had universal validity. Extended to Muslim societies this meant the assertion that this civilization needed its own "Enlightenment," "Reformation," and "Liberal Consciousness"[97] to gain the benefits of "modernity." Therefore, Muslims needed their own Luther and-or Erasmus.[98] Generations of Muslims have responded to this call by formulating their own worldview, including their understanding of Islam and Islamic civilization, through the Western prism. Generations "of Muslim students and intellectuals accepted passively and uncritically" the assessment made of Islam and its civilization by Western scholarship. This meant "a deconstruction of the corpus of thought that constitutes the worldview of Muslims." Through this process of deconstruction taking place in the twentieth century, Allawi (2010) argued, the "world of Islam, indeed the comprehension of the world, was being disenchanted and de-sacralized right in front of the eyes of Muslims, without their full recognition of what was taking place."[99] Allawi considers the idea of Islamization of Knowledge proposed by Al-Attas in the context of the current system of education in Muslim countries representing "an uncompromising environment" in which "Islam's legacy of profound respect for learning had been long abandoned." These systems were characterized by a bifurcation composed of anachronistic traditional schools (*madāris*, plural of *madrasah*) and Islamic colleges, on the one hand, and the new secular schools, colleges, and universities uninterested "in propagating the worldview of Islam when their models and standards were firmly anchored in the West."[100]

In this context, Al-Attas proposed his conception of Islamization of Knowledge. He conceived knowledge as being composed of primary, or first order, and secondary, or subsidiary, knowledge. The first order knowledge is that of Allah *swt* which has the position of centrality in Islam and which leads to truth and certainty. The second order knowledge, while based on first order knowledge, "comes from observation and experience intermediated through Man's rational faculties." De-secularization and re-saclarization of any field of knowledge would be accomplished through the first order knowledge and *ta'deeb*.[101]

Within the Attasian universe of discourse, Islamization of economics—certainly more authentic given Al-Attas' deep engagement with the ontology and epistemology of Islam than the narrow vision of Islamized paradigm of economics with its jargons of authenticity—would mean a thorough purging of the discipline from secular and secularized ideas, concepts, and theories. Once this is accomplished, Al-Attas' methodology would require resacralization of economics through *ta'deeb*. This would mean accessing the primary knowledge in *Al-Qur'ān*—understanding, internalizing, and applying the rules governing economic behaviour as prescribed in *Al-Qur'ān*, and explicated and operationalized by the Noble Messenger (saa). For example, participating in the market with *Ādab* would mean that producers, traders, consumers must all know and internalize the prescribed rules governing the market and market behaviour before actually engaging in transactions. Given the present conditions of Muslim economies and their thorough immersion in neoliberal economics where their policies are continuing to be formulated within a slightly reformed "Washington Consensus," desecularization of institutions of the economy appears imperative in conjunction with resacralization of economic policies. This process of Islamization of the economy and economics produces an Islamic economic paradigm that converges to *Al-Iqtiṣād*. Of course, it is possible to start with a clean slate and go directly to *Al-Iqtiṣād* as the authentic Islamic economics paradigm. This would avoid having to desecularize the present neoliberal economics which would at any rate seem altogether impossible since secularism is such an essential element of the philosophy and methodology of this discipline.

To illustrate, let us take a leaf from the philosophers' playbook by engaging in a thought experiment. Suppose there is a large newly formed community of Muslims wishing to organize their society and its economy. Assume further that they have *Al-Qur'ān* and the *Sunnah* of the Honored Messenger (saa) but no knowledge of the evolution of *fiqh* and no access to the ideas of Muslim writers, old and new. Moreover, they have no knowledge of the history, culture, economy, and evolution of sciences in the West. They most certainly know nothing about economics and the evolution of thought in this field. The question is then, how will this group organize its society and its economy? The only option available to them would be to start by understanding the vision of the economy in *Al-Qur'ān*, extracting from the fountainhead of all Islamic paradimgs the rules that govern the society and the economy as envisioned there as well as the way in which the Noble Messenger operationalized the foundations and the rules of the envisioned society and its economy. This is how any authentic Islamic economic paradigm must begin. There is no need for drawing the organizing principles of the society and its economy from elsewhere. Once the society and its economy are formed, *fiqh*, history, the writings of the earlier generations as well as terminologies and technical concepts developed elsewhere would have to be considered but only if they help in explicating the contents of the vision of the society and its economy in *Al-Qur'ān*.. One such paradigm was developed by as-Sayyid as-Shaheed Muhammad Baqir as-Sadr in the 1960s but which was mostly ignored by Muslim economists.

Sadrian Discourse on *Al-Iqtiṣād*

M. B. As-Sadr was an extraordinary and unique genius whose personal and intellectual accomplishments as a believing and practising Muslim were those of an archetypal human that serves as example for others striving for perfection intended for humans by their Creator. Those who knew him well have written and spoken about his personal integrity, disposition, *akhlāq*, compassion, commitment, modesty, courage, and charisma.[102] *As-Sadr* will continue to inspire generations as an example of a human personality fully immersed in and completely devoted to the high values and ideals of Islam. The way he lived his life, the sacrifices he made, and the immensely valuable intellectual legacy he left behind will continue to serve as a beacon of virtuous conduct, effort, and sacrifice on behalf of human freedom and dignity, social justice, truth, and tolerance.

Aside from being a model and standard of what it means to live a life in full compliance with the high values and ideals of Islam, he was a towering intellect who set for himself a grand and difficult task of analytically rejuvenating Islamic thought in accordance with the rigour of logic and analysis demanded by his time. He did so systematically with meticulous logic presented in a way accessible to his contemporaries—especially the young Muslims alienated from Islam and seduced by "modern" ideologies. In the process, he challenged the philosophical, social, political, and economic foundations of dominant ideologies of his time.

He understood well that the current compartmentalized and specialized approach to knowledge was inadequate in representing Islam's alternative solutions to the socio-political and economic problems of mankind. Accordingly, his approach to scientific revitalization and representation of the teachings of Islam—based rigorously on *Al-Qur'ān* and *As-Sunnah*—was, and still is, far deeper, broader, and more coherent than other contemporary efforts. He envisioned Islam's teachings as a unified system—a network of interrelated and eminently empirical set of rules compliance which guaranteed spiritual felicity and material prosperity for human societies.

The depth and the breadth of the full spectrum of *As-Sadr's* intellectual legacy fills one with a sense of awe, humility, and admiration, even four decades after his martyrdom. This impression becomes even more forceful when one realizes the early age in which As-Sayyid As-Shaheed As-Sadr began his study of Western schools of thought, along with the traditional curriculum of seminaries. According to a biographer, one of his teachers in grade school with Marxist tendencies reported that at the age of twelve, As-Sadr asked to borrow from him books on Marxism. Upon returning the books, as-Sadr astonished him by providing answers to a number of questions about Marxism that had engaged his teacher's mind for some time.

Two of his major works, *Falsafatuna* (*Our Philosophy*) and *Iqtisāduna* (*Our Economy*), were published before the age of thirty. These books display a surprising masterly grasp of the main Western ideas of his time. Given the limited scholarly sources available in Arabic translation at the time, one can only wonder whether his scholarly contributions would have been much more enriched had a wider bibliography of topics of his interest published at the time in other languages were available to him. One would be justified in answering the query in the affirmative given *As-Sadr's* unique genius. In terms of foundational philosophical and logical approach to the analytical explanation of problems faced by Muslim societies and solutions provided by *Al-Qur'ān*, As-Sadr's system of thought converges to that of 'Allamah Muhammad Iqbal and Shaykh Said Nursi[103]. It is arguably more focused on the analytics of socio-economic system envisioned in *Al-Qur'ān*. In early decades of the twentieth century, 'Allamah Iqbal, having mastered major philosophical groundworks of the Western socio-economic system, issued a clarion call to Muslims to return *Al-Qur'ān* for solutions to their problems.

Like Nursi and As-Sadr, 'Allamah Iqbal had a grand comprehensive vision of ideal human society each dimension of which would be structured in consonance with the prescription of Islam. He too envisioned a coherent system composed of a network of rules. He argued that *Al-Qur'ān* fostered rational and concrete (analytic) habit of thought. It was the Muslim scholars' preoccupation with Greek thought that constrained their ability to cognate the empirical orientation of *Al-Qur'ān* which urges humans to observe natural phenomena, meditate on their observation, validate, internalize, and appreciate the greatness of their Creator. *Al-Qur'ān*, said Iqbal, emphasizes action not abstract ideation only, analytic and critical thinking rather than pure speculation, and reliance on facts rather than abstraction. *Al-Qur'ān* constantly appeals to reason and experience laying great emphasis on the observation of nature and study of history as source of human knowledge. In his classic book, The Reconstruction of Religious Thought in Islam, Iqbal asserts unequivocally: "The birth of Islam ... is the birth of inductive intellect." This view was rigorously and analytically articulated by As-Sadr some four decades later in his book, The Foundations of Inductive logic.[104]

AS-SADR'S DISCOURSE ON CONTEMPORARY SOCIO-ECONOMIC SYSTEM

The focus of As-Sadr's thought was on the presentation of his vision of an economy embedded in a social system structured on the teachings of *Al-Qur'ān* and *As-Sunnah* within the contemporary context. Before he could do so, he had to dispense with the intellectual hegemony of the two systems that were dominant at the time: Capitalism and Communism. He met the two systems on their own terms logically, philosophically, and critically. He demonstrated the philosophical and logical weaknesses of their arguments without resorting to or invoking his own religious dogma. In his analysis, he focused on the logical and philosophical underpinnings of materialism which gave rise to both systems as well as the logical implications of this philosophy for humanity.

His analysis focused on the flawed vision of human beings and their collectivities as defined in the philosophy of materialism. He pointed out that in this philosophy, humans were envisioned as beings whose gaze was constantly centred on life on earth, its wealth and pleasures while ignoring the heavens. He showed the devastating effects of the spirit of materialism on human morality and ethics. He saw that the axiomatic structure of such systems of thought leads to emergence of "one-dimensional" human beings, materially greedy, non-empathic, acquisitive, and focused on the immediate gratification of base drives. He stated a theorem that in a society composed of such humans, efforts to coordinate and harmonize private and social interests—the grand objective of the Enlightenment project—will fail with disastrous consequences. After managing to seriously and successfully challenge the two ideologies on their own turf and using their own "rules of the game," he presented his vision of how Islam provided more efficient, logical, coherent, and effective solutions to the "economic problems" faced by societies. A review of research materials available will show that before As-Sadr, no Muslim scholar of his calibre, background, and standing in the religious scholarly community had managed to analyse, critique, and explain the philosophical flaws of the materialistic foundations of communism and capitalism with as much clarity, eloquence, fairness, and precise logic as had As-Sadr. In the process of developing his comprehensive analysis of the two systems, he offered a number of original insights into socio-economic-psychological problems of modern societies operating under the dominance of a materialist philosophy.

To explain, consider a major problem facing humanity, one that has grown with amazing speed over the last few decades to the point of threatening life on earth: the environmental degradation. Major cause of this problem as well as the difficulty in solving it are referred to by a variety of terms and titles: "collective action problem"; "coordination problem"; "tragedy of the commons"; "free-rider problem." These terms refer to the phenomenon of damage to public goods and natural resources when individuals have freedom to use them but carry no responsibility toward preserving them. The problem occurs both in materialist "command systems" where individual freedom is severely restricted and in "market capitalism" with ostensible devotion to "individual freedom."

A careful reading of As-Sadr's writings will reveal that he analysed this phenomenon and asserted the impossibility of coordination of private and public interests in socio-economic systems founded on materialism. This subject became the centre of attention of Western scholarship years after As-Sadr provided philosophical, logical, and economic arguments in support of his theorem that it is impossible to achieve effective harmony between public and private interests in capitalism. He further provided arguments, first in *Falsafatuna* and then in *Iqtisāduna*, that the two materialist systems, dominant at the time, either sacrifice private interests in favour of social interests, as does communism, or sacrifice social interests in favour of private interests, as does market capitalism. The latter, As-Sadr argued, focuses on materialization of private interests in its definition of a "free society." Hence, it emphasizes unconstrained freedom of property ownership, freedom of exploitation and sovereignty of consumption.

While a capitalist society functions through individuals, the frame of reference of epistemological orientation of individual's economic behaviour is devoid of moral, ethical, and spiritual values. If it ever includes these values, their origin will have to be external to the epistemological framework of the individual as defined by materialism. The same argument was made in both of his major works regarding communism in which, at least in case of the Soviet system, even the behaviour of ruling classes in the bureaucracy's epistemological framework did not include these values.

A major implication of his discussion of the philosophical and logical flaws of the two systems meant that they were unstable and non-viable in the long run. This penetrating insight of As-Sadr proved prescient as the communist system failed about two decades after his works were published. Capitalism too in the form he knew at the time of his writing came to an end. That system was transformed into a new form of predatory neoliberal capitalism through the dominance of neoliberal economics and the promotion of ideas advanced by this paradigm by the major political authorities in the West. Even in its new form, there are doubts whether contemporary capitalism can survive the crisis-prone system it has created. Many among contemporary scholars of capitalism argue that operations of capitalism, in its various forms, have led to the destruction of the environment, enormous inequalities of income and wealth, polarization of societies, alienation of a major part of humanity, and diminished human solidarity.

As-Sadr's Conception of Ideal Socio-Economic System

While the writings of As-Shaheed As-Sadr were quite timely and important in his own time, understanding them at the present is crucial as the search for alternative socio-economic paradigms that can more effectively respond to the problems of humanity has intensified. Importantly, it is quite clear that over the last forty years no other comprehensive, consistent, and internally logical presentation of Islam's vision of a society optimally formed and its ideal economy has emerged. Moreover, not enough has been done to make his writings available to non-Muslim audiences. Additionally, the articles or books written over the last forty years by Muslim researchers on the topics that As-Sadr addressed show that while they have borrowed ideas from his writings, these are selective and partial not reflecting the entire vision of As-Sadr, thus creating confusion and misdirection.[105]

As-Sadr's writings constitute an integrated and interrelated whole. Singling out a specific topic in exclusion of analysis of how it is related to his philosophy—especially ontology and epistemology which unify in his discourses—does not do justice to him, to his writings, or to his readers. Understanding his views on economy, for example, requires cognition of all other parts of his writings which form a unique Sadrian universe of discourse. This understanding transforms the "one-dimensional" worldview of transactional human-material relationships to the three-dimensional worldview of Creator-man-nature which, once it finds expression in the formation of society, attains justice in all its operations. Compelling arguments have been made that paradigms representing the one-dimensional worldviews that leave human–human relations as well as human-nature relationships to be governed by human caprice have created enormous tragedies to the point that at the present, they do threaten the survival of humans on earth. As François-Marie Arout, better known with his nom de plume de Voltaire (1694–1778) once said: "It would be very singular that all nature, all the planets, should obey eternal laws, and that there should be a little animal (man), five feet high, who, in contempt of these laws, could act as he pleased, solely according to his caprice."[106]

The three-dimensional paradigm, so clearly and effectively articulated by As-Sadr's, expresses the resulting justice and harmony in human socio-economic relations analogous to that prevailing in the universe when human behaviour complies with "eternal rules" prescribed by the Creator. Unfortunately, there is an inertia in the "modern" secular mind that resists expending effort in the cognition of the intricacies of this paradigm. And rather fortunately, an important feature of the contribution of the Sadrian universe of discourse is its simplicity and clarity of expression as well as coherence and logical structure of its arguments which should make understanding less cumbersome.

It will perhaps not be a mischaracterization to suggest that before all else As-Sadr was a first-rate logician whose discourses accorded logic and objective truth central and active roles, firmly believing that humans have desire to know truth and can do so through the exertion of effort. His discourses teach how to think logically, structure thoughts coherently, express them clearly, and organize narratives consistently, dispassionately, and analytically. Such effort, however, need not diminish the creative force of passion for what constitutes our beliefs.

In all of his discourses, As-Sadr does not lose an opportunity to display the passion of his belief that Islam provides solutions to problems societies face. For example, in *Falsafatuna* he argues that it is the framework of the *deen*—the way of life that is Islam—within which a harmony can be forged between individual and social interests.[107] Humans need incentives to forsake some or all of their interests in favour of others' interests. The *deen* has the spiritual power capable of providing the incentives, in form of material and non-material rewards, to motivate individuals to make sacrifices. That said, this section of the chapter is a modest attempt to provide a brief commentary on a number of As-Sadr's insights in presenting the theory and practice of *Al-Iqtiṣād* (Islam's vision of ideal economy). The point bears emphasis that this chapter is not a commentary on the entirety of the views of Al-Sadr on *Al-Iqtiṣād*; to do some degree of justice to his views requires volumes. The chapter instead focuses on some of his insights—those that economic analysis itself discovered years after him, with the purpose of indicating that the *Iqtiṣādi* contributions of As-Sadr and his genius deserve far deeper and more intensive scholarly treatment than they have received so far. While the entire Sadrian universe of discourse is derived from the authentic sources of Islam, the choice of words, expressions, and terms as well as the underlying philosophical and logical framework he employed to expound his understanding of *Al-Iqtiṣād* (Islamic paradigm of organizing an economy) as envisioned by *Al-Qur'ān*, *As-Sunnah*, and *fiqh*, are unique. This is not to suggest that these views are the last word on *Al-Iqtiṣād* but to emphasize that greater effort must be devoted to the specific elements as well as the totality of his vision of *Al-Iqtiṣād* and its implications for theoretical, empirical, and policy issues.

It is noteworthy that As-Sadr himself displayed no inertia in modifying his views and their explanations when the need arose. A major example is his views on governance of Islamic society. Initially, he conceptualized governance within the framework of "Shūra"—consultative paradigm of governance as ordained by *Al-Qur'ān*. He modified this view after the Islamic Revolution of Iran. Or consider explanatory articles he published throughout his life that expounded on major issues treated in *Falsafatuna* and *Iqtiṣāduna* with somewhat different expressions and orientations. This is, for example, quite palpable when one considers his position on banking and finance in his paper on Al-Bank Alla Ribāwī and his explanations of Islamic methods of banking and finance after his first paper became widely known. The latter clarified both the theory and application of the concept of *Mudharabah* where there is emphasis on the necessity of the sharing of risks between the participants in investment projects. *Iqtiṣāduna* asserts, supported by verses of *Al-Qur'ān* and *Al-Hadeeth*, that the fundamental Islamic principle of fraternity requires risk-sharing.

To begin the discussions of As-Sadr's insights on the organizing principles of socio-economic system, a digression on the concept of *Al-Iqtiṣād* would seem useful. This term is often translated as "economics." As-Sadr, however, provides a taxonomy that uses the term *Al-Iqtiṣād* in the general sense of its meaning as "the economy" while using it as a prefix, *Iqtiṣād Islāmi* or *Al-Iqtiṣād Al-Islāmi*, to denote the discipline that deals with the workings of that economy. As-Sadr goes to a great length to argue that ontologically and epistemologically there are significant differences between the nature and logic of economics and *Al-Iqtiṣād*. In translation, however, the term *Iqtiṣād* became "economics" and "Islamic economics." Currently, the difference between "economics" and "Islamic economics" is quite blurred. Some believe that the incorporation of *as-Sharī'ah* into "conventional economics" will render it Islamic. As discussed in detail earlier, and further explained also in the rest of the book, a union of the two is logically *impossible*.[109] The term "*Iqtiṣād*" is unique to Islam, making its appearance both in *Al-Qur'ān* and *As-Sunnah*, which makes a one-to-one mapping of the term to European languages questionable.[110]

Arguably, the term "Islamic economics" as translation of *Al-Iqtiṣād* lacks accuracy and precision doing injustice to the careful and logical arguments and the analytic method by which As-Sadr drew philosophical and logical distinction between *Al-Iqtiṣād* and capitalist "economics."[111] While the term "Islamic economics" is used often by writers, it always requires preliminary explanations regarding its major differences with conventional "economics." Moreover, the term *Iqtiṣād* serves two distinct purposes. First, it represents Islam's vision of an economy (including its finance paradigm) in a society formed on the basis of prescriptions of *Al-Qur'ān* and *As-Sunnah*. While arguably mapping *Iqtiṣād* into "Islamic economy" can be justified, translating *Al-Iqtiṣād* to "Islamic economics" in its second meaning—as the discipline which discovers the structure and operation of Islamic economy, as well as study the transactional relationships within that economy—cannot.

Arguably even the oft-used term "*Al-Iqtiṣād Al-Islāmi*" involves redundancy, since, as mentioned earlier, *Al-Iqtiṣād* is a uniquely Islamic concept which was in existence and use extensively many centuries before the appearance of the word "economics." In his successful effort to lay out a holistic, unified, coherent, and consistent vision of *Al-Iqtiṣād*, As-Sadr employs, to the extent needed, ideas from philosophy, history, logic, psychology, sociology, physics and mechanics, morality, and ethics, as well as explanation, *tafseer*, of *Al-Qurān*. The rest of the chapter is based on the available corpus of his vision of *Al-Iqtiṣād*.

As-Sadr and *Al-Iqtiṣād* Paradigm

Even a cursory reading of the writings of As-Sadr reveals its systematic, pragmatic, and practical vision of *Al-Iqtiṣād*. This vision begins with the definition of the subject matter. Accordingly, in its first meaning, *Al-Iqtiṣād* is defined as the economy envisioned in *Al-Qur'ān* and *As-Sunnah*. In its second meaning, *Al-Iqtiṣād* is defined as the discipline which deals with the theory and empirics of the workings of such an economy. The initial stage involves discovering rules prescribed by *Al-Qur'ān* and *As-Sunnah* that are to govern the transactional relationships between humans themselves and between them and nature. The empirics of *Al-Iqtiṣād* refers to the scientific study of the operations of these rules in practice.

Al-Iqtiṣād in its second meaning is the study of life as experienced in a society organized according to the blueprint *Al-Qur'ān* has provided within which *Al-Iqtiṣād* is embedded. The latter would be, therefore, the study of lived experience in the economy envisioned in *Al-Qur'ān* and *As-Sunnah*. It becomes relevant only after *Al-Iqtiṣād* in its meaning as economy comes into being. The former, As-Sadr calls the *Madh'hab* of *Iqtiṣād* and the latter as the '*Ilm* of *Iqtiṣād*. The role of *Madh'hab* is broader than defining the economy. It provides the organizing principle of the society in which the economy is embedded and whose fundamental reason for existence is Justice. The central focus of *Al-Iqtiṣād* of such society too is justice. As-Sadr identifies justice as the axis around which the *madh'hab* of *Iqtiṣād* rotates. For him the Objectives of *Al-Qur'ān* (*Maqāṣid Al-Qur'ān*) are summarized in Social Justice (*Al-'Adālah Al-Ijtimā'iyyah*), General Mutual Support (*At-Takāful Al-'Ām*); and Social Balance and Harmony (*At-Tawāzun Al-Ijtimā'ī*) for the society.

As-Sadr's definition of *Al-Iqtiṣād* has provoked debate and discussion among scholars and writers on its logic and content.[112] As-Sadr carefully and analytically differentiated between the *madh'hab* and science of *Al-Iqtiṣād*. The existence and functioning of the latter are conditional on the operationalization of the former. *Madh'hab Al-Iqtiṣād* exists in a society organized and targeted to achieving justice based on prescriptions annunciated in *Al-Qur'ān* and *As-Sunnah*. An example could perhaps explain the distinction between the *Madh'hab* and the "science" of *Al-Iqtiṣād*. In the vision of As-Sadr, justice is the spirit and functional essence of Islam crystalized in the society. It has an axial role in the entire socio-economic system envisioned for humanity in *Al-Qur'ān*.[113]

Justice in Islam is a concept whose identification is possible through its effects. Unlike other conceptions which see justice as a principle or a virtue among others to be cultivated in individuals and the society, in Islam justice is intricately and integrally bound with the degree of individual and social compliance with the prescribed rules of behaviour. When it exists in a human society, it represents a mapping of the balance and harmony that prevails in the heavens. Whereas its existence in the heavens reflects the full submission of all cosmic elements to their Supreme Creator, in earthly human societies its existence and operation depend on the volition of individuals as manifestation of the gift of freedom of will granted by their Creator. Hence, whether justice prevails in a society and among its members is an empirical question; therefore, subject to examination by the "science" of *Al-Iqtiṣād*. As-Sadr had studied the works of the major Western philosophers of the time, for example, those of British empiricists. While the works of such philosophers as Karl Popper (1902–1994) as well as Emre Lakatos were not available to him, he understood the sentiment of the time on the reliance of anything scientific on empirical verification. He chose to make the dichotomy between the axiomatic Iqtiṣād drawn from *Al-Qur'ān* not subject to verification and theoretical-empirical part that dealt with hypotheses regarding how the first part of *Al-Iqtiṣād* could be implemented in order to create the socio-economic system envisioned in *Al-Qur'ān* and operationalized by *As-Sunnah*. As-Sadr emphasized that existence of poverty and deprivation (effects) in a society is *prima facie* evidence of lack or impairment of justice (cause). It is the role of the "science" part of *Al-Iqtiṣād* to empirically study the degree of rule compliance and, therefrom, the degree to which justice prevails in the society through the empirical examination of observed levels of poverty and deprivation. The next step for the "science" part of *Al-Iqtiṣād* would be to formulate solutions based on the *madh'hab* part and formulate testable hypotheses.

It is the *madh'hab's* role to discover the principles and rules prescribed in *Al-Qur'ān* that are to govern individual and collective behaviour which the Creator has deemed necessary for a harmonious, balanced, and fair social life for all humans. It is this discovery that allows society to organize its social and economic life according to Islam's conception of justice. Supported by *Al-Qur'ān* and *As-Sunnah*, As-Sadr asserted unequivocally that individual and societal problems are created by injustice and ingratitude, both manifested ultimately by non-compliance or violation of prescribed rules.[114] While the discovery, analysis, and explanation of rules are the function of the *madh'hab* part, it is the role of the "science" part of *Al-Iqtiṣād* to determine the ground reality of the degree to which individuals and their collectivities are rule-compliant. Furthermore, he argued that it is the role of "science" of *Al-Iqtiṣād*, as a discipline which studies lived experience, to suggest to legitimate authority (*ulu al-amr*) a menu of policy prescriptions that bring individual and collective behaviour into compliance with prescribed rules based on its analysis of the ground reality of actual behaviour. This is evident from As-Sadr's argument that the distinction between *madh'hab* and "science" of *Al-Iqtiṣād* is not to be found in their subject matter but in their methodology and objectives.[115]

The distinction that As-Sadr drew between *Madh'hab al-Iqtiṣād* and "science" of *Al-Iqtiṣād* (*'Ilm al-Iqtiṣād*) has precedence in the history of economic thought. Some decade and half before writing The Wealth of Nations (WN), Adam Smith wrote The Theory of Moral Sentiments (TMS) that until a few decades ago was all but ignored by economists. Arguably, this book lays down the Philosophy and logic of the system that became known as capitalism. For all intents and purposes, TMS explains the *Madh'hab* of the economic system envisioned by Adam Smith. His second book, The Wealth of Nation can be considered as the "science" (*'ilm*) of that system.

The dichotomy of *Madh'hab* and "science" (*'Ilm*) provides a solution to the so-called "Adam Smith's problem." From about the middle of last century until recently, scholars contended that there is such a contradiction between the two books of Adam Smith to appear as if two different authors wrote them. If granted consideration that TMS explains the *Madh'hab* and WN its "science" (*'Ilm*), then it would resolve "the Adam Smith" problem. The vision that Smith held for the economy was far from what developed later. As discussed earlier in this chapter, what

Smith envisioned was a system anchored on a collection of moral/ethical values that, he believed, should govern human behaviour in transactional relationships within the society in which they were embedded. Smith envisioned justice as the most important among these values. The source of these values was a deist belief that asserted a doctrine of a harmonious order (what As-Sadr would call "tawāzun") in nature guided by its Creator whom Smith called "The Author of Nature," among others.[116] Smith then applied this doctrine with precise logical consistency to the economic order. His later book The Wealth of Nations devotes itself to analytics and empirics of the working of this economic order.

Major difference in the conceptions of justice between Adam Smith and As-Sadr is that the former conceived of justice as the most important among the virtues, along the Aristotelian thought. He believed that a virtue such as self-interest, not regulated by justice degenerates into vice. As-Sadr, on the other hand, gives justice the axial role in the entire edifice of the philosophical underpinning of *Al-Iqtiṣād* order, in consonance with the teachings of *Al-Qur'ān*. Since the last decades of 1990s much research work has been published in an attempt to bring Smith's TMS into mainstream economic thinking.[117] Smith's last book, published after his death and based on his students' notes, is Lectures on Jurisprudence whose objective was focused on the ways and means of developing the legal structure (*fiqh*) that would institutionalize rules he had developed in his doctrinal Theory of Moral Sentiments.

The purpose of drawing attention to the writings of Adam Smith is not to establish an equivalence between his ideas and those of As-Sadr. Instead the purpose is to suggest that the idea of As-Sadr—that the essence of *Al-Iqtiṣād Al-Islāmi* is its *madh'hab* and its *'ilm*, which is the scientific study of lived experiences in an economy designed according to the Madhhab—has an approximate analogous precedent in the works of Adam Smith. It is important to note that the position of As-Sadr on *'Ilm Al-Iqtiṣād* does not mean that no scientific empirical studies using the methodology of *Al-Iqtiṣād* can be done unless there is an Islamic economy already established. His position is that no *discipline* of *'Ilm Al-Iqtiṣād* can exist in the absence of an Islamic economy. To suggest that according to his position a researcher cannot empirically test a hypothesis drawn from *Madh'hab Al-Iqtiṣād* in Islam would have to meet the challenge of substantiating the claim based on As-Sadr's writings.

To explain, consider his discussion of his theory of knowledge (epistemology) masterfully presented in *Falsafatuna* where he points out to two ideas of conception and judgement. The role of logic in the formation of judgement as it progresses from conception is crucial. The logic of the argument asserts that judgements are what allow capturing the essence of reality. It is this epistemology that allows him to make judgement that materialism is flawed and so are economic systems that are based upon this philosophy. While all of his arguments in this context stand on strong logical ground and are objectively and powerfully reasoned, it would not be realistic to assume that he did not draw on the intellectual wealth of *Madh'hab Al-Iqtiṣād* in formulating hypotheses with which he began studying the philosophical foundation of materialism. Consider also the fact that he proposed an Islamic method of finance for non-Islamic systems. While he drew the outline of his proposal from the *Madh'hab*, it was the *'Ilm* that had to devise ways and means of implementing it.

There are many propositions and hypotheses that can be formulated based on the content of the *Madh'hab Al-Iqtiṣād* and tested empirically. Two examples may help illustrate this point. One can hypothesize that, in a society not fully organized according to the teachings of Islam, a believer's behaviour in transactional relationships would be different from a non-believer under the conditions defined by the transaction because they would operate under different rules. Experimental methods—which As-Sadr referred to in his writings years before the discipline of experimental economics actually developed—could then provide the ways and means of testing such hypotheses. In a recently published book, Dr. Hazik Mohamed reports on such an experiment using game theory. He tested a hypothesis regarding the question of whether compliance with rules prescribed by *Al-Qur'ān* and *As-Sunnah* would elicit a different response from a believing Muslim than from a non-believer under the same set of circumstances.[118]

In a second example, Dr. Tarik Akin, interpreting Islamic finance method as one of sharing risks and rewards of investment projects,[119] designs and empirically tests a related and elaborated simulation model positing that the major problem of inequality of income and wealth distribution stems from an interest-based finance system, and that risk-sharing Islamic finance provides an effective solution to the inequality of income and wealth that plagues contemporary societies.[120]

A third example requires a brief introduction. In his explanation of how, in an Islamic society, concepts (*Mafāheem*) derived from the Belief (*Al-'Aqīdah*) generate inclinations (*'Awātif*) and sentiments (*Aḥāsees*) that lead to rule-compliant actions, As-Sadr refers to the concept of

"*Taqwā*," a crucially important concept because of its organic affinity with justice as well as its attribute that it becomes operational when a person is always and everywhere conscious of Allah *swt* and acts always with the intention of achieving the pleasure and approval of Allah *swt*. This is the ground of "righteous action" (*Al-'Amal As-Sālih*).[121] In this context, As-Sadr argues that the concept of *taqwā* is an indicator of honour (*karāmah*) and deference (*tafādhul*) among human beings which, gives rise to the Islamic sentiments or inclinations, related to *taqwā*, of high esteem (*ijlāl*) and respect (*ihtirām*).

This understanding of As-Sadr can be interpreted as meaning that a *Muttaqi* (the person who possesses *taqwā*) earns a reputational capital implying that the person is considered as trustworthy. In a recent book, Dr. Omid Torabi modelled how the reputation earned through behaviour that stems from *taqwā* can make equity-crowdfunding successful. More importantly he demonstrated analytically the operation of the concept of "*barakah*," a concept of nonlinear scalar leading to multiple returns, that results from reputational behaviour governed by *taqwā*.[122]

Conventional economics is not unfamiliar with multiplicity of returns to appropriate behaviour. The concept operative at the micro-economics level is referred to as X-efficiency. The theory reflects the observation that two firms operating under the same set of circumstances, with the same quality and quantity of resources perform differently with one doing better than the other in terms of productivity and profits. This effect was attributed to efficiency in resource use whose source was not known, hence, X-efficiency. Since its early appearance, analytic studies have identified sources such as inter alia, labour-management relationships, participation by labour in decision-making process, degree of job satisfaction of labour, and programs of profit sharing with labour.

The analogous concept at the macroeconomics level is referred to as "total factor productivity." This idea relates to two different growth rates in two countries with similar resource profiles, comparable resource availability, cultural similarity, and comparable geography. One country has higher level of growth and development. Initially, it was thought that the reason may be due to different levels of technical progress. Empirical studies showed that even when this difference is accounted for, still one country performed better than the other.[123]

As-Sadr's view on groundwork upon which ideal Islamic society and its economy are grounded.

As noted earlier, Islamic economy is embedded in an Islamic society. Hence, As-Sadr argued that it is not possible to study Islamic economy without first understanding the society which Islam envisions. The latter organizes the social life and its economy organizes the *Iqtiṣādi* behaviour of the members of the society. The latter is possible only after the society has become fully familiar with Islam's view of life, and its members have internalized belief in Allah *swt* to the point of cognition of the fact that such a belief (*Iman bi-Allah*) means complying with the rules of behaviour that Allah *swt* has prescribed. It is only then that appropriate ground conducive to emergence of Islamic society is prepared. That, in turn, requires methods of nurturing, educating, and training of individuals to follow Islamic teachings to yield a society with the full Islamic colouring (*As-Sibghah Al-Islamiyyah*). It is in such a society where *Al-Iqtiṣād* not only orders *Iqtiṣādi* relationships harmoniously but provides also the ways and means of achieving prosperity (*Ar-Rakhā'*) and felicity (*As-Sa'ādah*).

As-Sadr then proceeds to focus on the ingredients required for preparing the ground out of which Islamic society would emerge—what Malek Bennabi called *At-Turbah*). He derives three elements necessary for the emergence of Islamic society: the central principle (*Al-Qā'idah Al-Markaziyyah*) of Belief (*Al-'Aqīdah*); Concepts (*Al-Mafāhīm*) derived from Belief reflecting the view of Islam in understanding phenomena; and inclinations (*'Awātif*) and sentiments (*Ahāsees*) that are invoked by concepts derived from Belief. As mentioned, he used the example of the concept of *at-taqwā* derived from Belief which invokes the sentiments of deference, respect, and esteem among people for the person practising it.

The axial element of Belief around which the worldview of Islam rotate is *at-tawheed*; the axiom of Unity. It means that all that was, is, and will be has One Creator, Sustainer, and Provider Who is Omniscient, Omnipresent, and Omnipotent. A corollary of this axiom states the unity of all creation including human beings. This is the underlying reason for the universality of Message of Islam that humans, in their creation, are but one irrespective of apparent multiplicity of humanity and seeming differences among them.

The belief in the Unity of the Creator and of humanity gives rise to the concept of fraternity (*Al-Ukhuwwah*) which in turn manifests itself in form of the sentiment of love of other humans with significant implications for social relationships, including sharing in economic and financial transactions. Another concept derived from the belief in *at-tawheed* is that Allah *swt* is the ultimate Owner of all things and Has the First claim on them. As-Sadr asserted that while everything belongs to Allah *swt*, He Has permitted individual humans to claim the right of conditional possession of things they produce combining their labour with resources Allah swt has Created for all humans. Therefore, he built a strong logical case for his assertion that work is the fundamental basis for the creation of conditional property-rights claims in Islam.

In this context, As-Sadr introduces a concept, derived from the Belief, that explains the idea that all value added to a product—as it goes through complex production and exchange network to get to its final destination—belongs to the original producer. He called it "immutability of property ownership" (*Thabat Al-Milkiyyah*). This is an important concept that provides a logical foundation for the sentiment of sharing. For long before As-Sadr, sharing in the form of *Sadaqāt* (plural of *sadaqah*, including *sadaqah jariyah, zakah, khumus, qardh hasan, infaq fi sabil Allah*, among others) were considered "charity" and "poor tax." However, the concept of the immutability of property claim provides a crucial insight that strengthens the justification for legislation sharing as mandated by Allah swt.

The logic of the justification for sharing is as follows: (1) Everything belongs to Allah *swt*; (2) This Owner Has declared that all the resources He Has Created belong to all humans, meaning that all have the right to access these resources; (3) Some members of the humanity are unable, due to a number of factors, to exercise the right of access to these resources, hence; (4) Some, who have the opportunity, will use more of these resources than those who are unable to do so, meaning that the former use the right of accessing these resources that belonged to the latter; (5) Regardless of how many hands these resources change or how many complex processes they go through to create income and wealth for the able group, the right of the Original Owner remains; (6) It is that Owner Who has legislated that the second group (those who are able to access resources) must compensate the first because it has used the right of access that belonged to those who were unable to exercise their right of access to resources to produce income; (6) Income and wealth of the second group contains a share that rightly belongs to the first group; (7) The Original Owner of the resources not only Has ordained that the latter group be compensated by the second group, He Has legislated also the ways and means of doing so. Hence, not only *Sadaqāt* are not "charity" in any sense of the word, they are indeed the redemption of the rights of the "poor" (those who are unable to use their rights of access to resources provided for them by their Creator) in the income and wealth of the rich.

There are important insights in As-Sadr's explanation of the elements of the groundwork. The three elements provide humans with the ability to focus their internal and external dispositions intensely on Allah swt (the Belief) and abandon servitude to any other entity. Thus, becoming liberated from servitude to internal and external idols. Based on his discussions of causality and motion in *Falsafatuna*, As-Sadr argued that the process involved in this liberation movement is one of gradual transformation of potentiality into actuality. Potentiality, existing in the essence of the duality of materiality and spirituality within the constitution of human beings, is actualized experientially as humans use their spiritual capital provided by their Creator in their very essence as expressed in His Message to humanity.[124]

The concept of spiritual capital (As-Sadr uses two terms for spiritual capital, *Ar-Raṣīd Ar-Rūhi* and *At-Tamwīn Ar-Rūhi*) is As-Sadr's important insight which he derived from the Belief (*Al-'Aqīdah*). It is the erosion and loss of spiritual capital and its replacement by the dominant ideology that As-Sadr considered as the major cause of problems of Muslims and their society. Loss of spiritual capital leads to loss of social capital because the former is the source of the latter.[125] Social capital, according to As-Sadr, emerges when a critical mass of believing individuals engage in social transactions with self-confidence borne from the internalization of commitment to the three elements of the groundwork.

When such a critical mass of individuals comes into existence and behaves in compliance with the rules prescribed by their Creator, the society will have available a stock of spiritual and social capital that promotes solidarity, stability, prosperity, and social welfare. The reason is that social capital includes elements of mutual trust, cooperation, and coordination that bring individual self-interests and social interests into harmony. Once spiritual capital is eroded, and eventually lost, social capital becomes impaired or destroyed leading to loss of social solidarity and cohesion. Pursuing objectives solely borne out of self-love and self-interest becomes the ruling paradigm which, in turn, leads to intense competition for accumulating wealth, and society becomes a "winner-take-all" society.

The ideas of spiritual and social capital, essential insights of As-Sadr, had to wait for their articulation by scholars of conventional economics until the last decades of the twentieth century. Even then, social capital was first to make its appearance. In the last decade few researchers have been attempting to bring spiritual capital into mainstream economic thinking. However, this effort has yet to gain much traction. These attempts, while acknowledging that the main source of spiritual capital is religion, in an attempt to broaden the appeal of this concept have tried to downplay the role of the latter.[126] This is analogous to attempts by philosophers and ethicists to develop "godless morality."[127]

The three elements, the belief, concepts, and sentiments, constitute the organizing principles of Islamic society. They are also the foundational principles of *Al-Iqtiṣād* in that without them, the two most important pillars of Islamic social justice discussed in the Sadrian discourse: "general mutual support" (*At-Takāful Al-'Ām*) and "social harmony and balance" (*At-Tawāzun Al-Ijtimā'ī*) would be undermined. Collectively, the three principles and their specific characteristics are unique to Islam. They distinguish Islamic society and its economy from all other systems. Notwithstanding disagreements and debates regarding specific issues in philosophy, logic, or other subjects treated in the Sadrian universe of discourse, there can be no denying that the latter provides a pragmatic and practical blueprint for organizing an Islamic society with its own unique economy. The challenge, however, is the absolute necessity of a critical mass of individuals who have already internalized the three elemental organizing principles before the ideal society comes into existence. This is the reason why As-Sadr placed such strong emphasis in his discourses on nurturing, education, and training of individuals.

Given his penchant for pragmatism and practicality, As-Sadr argues for a type of education and training that reflects the universality of the Message of Islam and its ability to be articulated in terms, expressions, and frameworks that are capable of addressing the ground reality upon which the contemporary generation experiences life. This is the reason he focused on the necessity of change in the outlook and methodology of *Al-Ijtihād*—that is achieving expertise in religious studies. He specified the condition for the type of *Ijtihād* that can articulate an up-to-date Islamic vision to address the contemporary problems of humanity. This was to be an *Ijtihād* that is not chained by a commitment to preserving the *status quo*, is not influenced by any personal biases of the *mujtahid*—the person exercising *Ijtihād*—, does not abuse the absence of rules related to specific circumstances in the authentic sources in order to render a *fiqhi* decisions that justify his/her prejudices.

In short, As-Sadr argued for an *Ijtihād* that was not only logically rigorous but was also objectively devoid of prejudices, biases, and ignorance but well-informed about current socio-political-scientific developments. It is this kind of *Ijtihād* that could educate and train human beings worthy of the office of *Khalīfah* (trustee, agent) of Allah on earth. As-Sadr had no doubt that Islam has optimal solutions to the current problems of mankind. He emphasized that what gives rise to these problems are injustice (*dhulm*) and ingratitude (*Kufrān An-Ni'mah*). The two together create internal conflicts within individuals which if not resolved lead to external conflicts with others and conflicts with nature, leading to destruction of social harmony, cohesion, and solidarity as well as damage to nature. In order for viable solutions to society's problems to emerge, however, humans have to remake themselves into Islamic humans by internalizing the three principles. In short, they have to become fully compliant with the rules their Creator Has prescribed.

Long before the world became intensely concerned about environmental disasters, As-Sadr, employing unique thematic interpretations of *Al-Qur'ān* (*At-Tafsīr Al-Mawdhū'ī*), explained that the verses of *Al-Qur'ān*[128] assert that the more human relationships among themselves and with nature are based on equity and justice, the greater social solidarity. As a result of the internalizations of Islamic values such as fraternity, love, and care for others, even at the cost of self-sacrifice, the society accumulates social capital (trust and cooperation) that allows more efficient use of resources, higher productivity, and hence greater prosperity.

This brief account has touched only a part of the collection of insights of the creative genius of as-Sayyid as-Shaheed as-Sadr. In every field that As-Sadr found essential to his grand vision, he achieved new insights. Whether in philosophy, logic, history (in which the rigour of his analysis is at par or superior to that of Hegel, among others), psychology, sociology, and economics, he either found a new way of explaining concepts better or created new ones that enriched his discourses.

After a comprehensive discussion of the organizing principles of a just society based on *Al-Qur'ān* and *As-Sunnah*, As-Sadr proceeds to specify the paradigm of *Al-Iqtiṣād* both as a system and discipline. He retains social justice as the primary and principle Objective of Islam for society and its economy. Deriving arguments from *Al-Qur'ān*, As-Sadr provides justification for arguing that the system of *Al-Iqtiṣād* is defined and served by the practical ways and means of achieving and serving the Objective of Islam: social justice. This is done by discovering the rules that govern the system of *Al-Iqtiṣād* as prescribed in *Al-Qur'ān* and operationalized by the *Sunnah* of the Honored Messenger (SAA). This constitutes the function of *Madh'hab Al-Iqtiṣād*. These rules govern: governance of the economy; property relations and acquisition of conditional rights of property ownership; use of natural resources and their allocation before production; employment of human resources; production; formation of markets and market behaviour; post-production distribution; consumption; redistribution and its mechanisms; accumulation of wealth; and financial transactions, *inter alia*.[129]

As-Sadr was quite mindful that all *Iqtiṣādi* relationships are derived firmly from the three organizing principles of Islamic society: '*Aqīdah*, *Mafāhīm*, and '*Awātif* which build the concept of sharing within the fabric of socio-economic relations. As illustration, he focuses on *Mudhārabah* as the ideal framework of *Iqtiṣādi* financial system. Having dealt with probability theory in his work on logic (Foundations of Inductive Logic), As-Sadr was fully aware that in focusing on *Mudhārabah* as the archetype of financial contracts in Islamic financial system, he was arguing—well justified by *Al-Qur'ān*—for a financial system whose main engine would be risk and reward-sharing. Risk-sharing is clear from the contract of *Mudhārabah* requirement that the sharing ratio be established between the financier and the entrepreneur before the start of a given project. Since the outcome of the venture is unknown before the start, it makes the decision on the sharing ratio subject to uncertainty and, therefore, risky. Thus, *Mudhārabah*, before becoming a profit-loss sharing contract at the completion of the project, is a risk-sharing contract at its beginning. From this initial proposition, the whole system of Islamic finance can be spanned.

Once *Madh'hab Al-Iqtiṣād* provides the overall framework of *Al-Iqtiṣād* system, the "science" of *Al-Iqtiṣād* (*'Ilm Al-Iqtiṣād*) can develop testable propositions regarding the implementation of the requirements of operationalization of the system. It designs and articulates policies to bring the actual economy in convergence with the ideal.[130] For example, developing policies to implement a fiscal system (government tax and spending) that serves the Islamic economy in achieving social justice is a function of the "science" of *Al-Iqtiṣād*; justice having been established as the Objective of the system based on *Madh'hab Al-Iqtiṣād*. Similarly, designing policies that implement an Islamic risk-sharing financial system is the responsibility of the practitioners of the "science" part of *Al-Iqtiṣād* as the discipline that studies the practical aspects of implementing the requirements of *Madh'hab Al-Iqtiṣād*. In summary, *Al-Iqtiṣād* paradigm as envisioned by As-Sadr, is composed of two distinct parts: (i) *Madh'hab Al-Iqtiṣād* whose main task is the discovery of the rules governing Islamic economic system; and (ii) *'Ilm Al-Iqtiṣād* which studies the ground reality of the operations of the actual economy and propose ways and means of bringing it to convergence with the ideal.

Notes

1. See Weber (1958). For Protestant Christianity's compromise with capitalism in nineteenth-century America, see Davenport (2008). Catholicism has been much more reluctant to make compromises with capitalism. See, for example, Von Nell-Breuning (1936), Dulles, (1999), and Donders (2005). See also, Sandelands (2010). Before America's full commitment to neoliberal capitalism, there were American economists who had a different vision of the economy. See, for example, Ryan (1916).
2. For a remarkable book that analyses this compromise, and the resulting problems, see Goudzwaard (1979a).
3. See, for example, Verse 41: Chapter 2; 53:3; 136:4; 44–49:5; 3:7; 21:31; 2:47; and 4:97.
4. See Hamid and Mirakhor (2020).
5. Rousseau's idea echoes a saying attributed to the Noble Messenger: "Whoever comes to know his inner self (*nafs*), knows His Creator, Sustainer, and Nurturer (*Rabb*)." This search of interiority has been a task of the body of time-honoured teachings (*'Irfān*) that has provided guidance for those who wish to know their inner self.
6. See, especially, Adorno (1973).
7. See Foucault (1983, 1994).
8. In recent times the debate about authenticity has been revived, see, for example, Bauer (2017) and Rings (2017).
9. Translated by Parsons (1958).
10. Ibid., p. 91.
11. See, for example, Spengler and Allen (1960), Lowery and Gordon (1998), and Samuels et al. (2007).
12. In this context, see Khan (2002).
13. See, for example, Ibn Ashur (2007). See also, Kazemi-Moussavi (2011).
14. See, for example, articles in the July 2021 issue, number 96, of the journal Real-World Economic Review.
15. See Saiyidain (1942). See also, Khurshid (1962).
16. Al-Attas (1978, 1980).
17. Al-Faruqi (1988).

18. Abu Sulayman (1989).
19. See, for example, Al-'Alwani (1996).
20. See Nur (2020).
21. See Darraz (1950 [1973]) and Al-Hakimi et al. (1992). In this context, a book that attempts to derive, from *Al-Qur'ān* and *As-Sunnah*, rules (institutions) that govern the process of economic development and growth is that of Al-Reyshahri and Al-Hosseini (2001).
22. See Norgaard (2021).
23. For a fuller discussion of the evolution of capitalism and the economics that supports it, see Mirakhor and Askari (2017, Chapters 2 and 3).
24. See De Gregori (1987) and Jo (2011), see also, Jo (2016) and Lee (2013).
25. For a view of Adam Smith's system of thought as consisting of a moral foundation, as depicted in The Theory of Moral Sentiments, upon which the economy of a "commercial Society" was to be structured and which provided the moral framework within which that economy was to operate, see Pack (1991). See also, Schultz (2001).
26. For an excellent summary of these developments, see Katouzian (1980).
27. Henry (2009).
28. Baranzini and Scazzieri (1986), see also Roncaglia (2005).
29. Opdebeeck (2018).
30. Burgin (2012).
31. Friedman (2002).
32. While ideology is a rather ambiguous and controversial concept, based on available consensus among writers, it can be argued that the evolution of economics between the 1930s and now shows ideologically positive commitment and not neutrality. That is the theories developed during this period have been structured to serve a particular ideology. For example, classical economics was based on a liberal ideology and neoclassical was based on neoliberalism. The term "ideology" made its first appearance during the French Revolution by the philosopher Antoine Destutt de Tracy (1754–1836) to mean "a science of ideas." Since then the term has been invested with emotive contents. At times it has carried a negative and pejorative sense specially. In the Hegelian and Marxian thought, for example, ideology is referred to as "false consciousness." When a thought is not well understood or hotly debated the word is hurled at one side or the other accusing a person as being "ideological." Thomas Piketty (2020, p. 3), in his new book Capital and Ideology, defines ideology as "a set of a priori plausible ideas and discourses describing how society should be structured. An ideology has social, economic, and political dimensions." Piketty then proceeds to offer a typology of ideology (p. 9). According to Piketty's definition, neoliberalism qualifies as an ideology. See also, Katouzian (1980, pp. 149–211).

Katouzian traces the term ideology to Plato and discusses the concept in general and in the context of evolution of economics. White (1973, p. 22) in his book Metahistory: Historical Imagination in Nineteenth-Century Europe, defines ideology as "a set of prescriptions for taking a position in the world of social praxis and acting upon it (either to change the world or to maintain it in its current state); such prescriptions are attended by arguments that claim the authority of "science" or "realism."" He proposes "four basic ideological positions: Anarchism, Conservatism, Radicalism, and Liberalism." It is noted that while there is no such a concept as "ideology" in Islam defined as is in the Western scholarship, the concept to of "*Millah*" attributed to the stance of Prophet Ibrahim, the True in faith called "*Millat Ibrāhim Al-Hanīf*" called "Millah of Ibrahim Haneef" referring to the Oneness (Tawheed) of the Creator (see, for example, Verse 130: Chapter 2; 125: 4; 161: 6; 123: 16; and 78: 22) comes close in capturing the essence of Ideology.

33. Even at this early stage of this chapter, attention is directed at the claims made based on the 5-principles Maqasid model to speak of "freedom of property ownership," "freedom of expression," "freedom of religion," and so on, presumably without constraints. It should not be difficult to draw parallels between this narrow conception of *maqāṣid* and neoliberal economics.
34. See Glyn (2007) and Piketty (2014).
35. For the history of the emergence of neoliberalism, the nature and membership of the Mont Pelerin and their influential policy work, see Mirowski and Plehwe (2015).
36. See Harvey (2006).
37. See Mirowski (2015), particularly insightful is section titled "A Neoliberal Primer" (pp. 433–440) in which Mirowski presents what he calls "the tenets" of Neoliberalism.
38. The "Consensus" includes the following principles: Austerity (usually reduction in government spending for social program and safety nets); tax reduction for individuals, businesses, and corporations; deregulation; trade liberalization; flexible exchange rates; privatization; financial, capital, and labour market liberalization; protection of property rights; public investment should go only to infrastructure, public health, and education, all done through the private sector. Note that these principles exclude any accommodation with social justice. In fact, one of the most influential members of the neoliberal intellectuals, Friedrich Hayek, had strong disdain for social justice calling it meaningless and a mirage (see Hayek [1980] who saw no justification for the state to redistribute income and wealth). See also, Askari and Mirakhor (2020, pp. 145–149). Note also that the narrow conception of the Objectives of *al-Shari'ah*

with five principles does not include justice as one of the *Maqāṣid as-Sharī'ah*. It would thus appear that the narrow conception of *Maqāṣid* can be accommodated within the neoliberal framework.
39. See McMurtry (1999, p. x). For the diagnostic of the neoliberalism as "cancer" and the "social immune system," see pp. 37–189.
40. Ibid., p. viii and pp. 257–256. See also, Finn (2006).
41. See Parker (2021).
42. See, for example, Ahmed (2002, p. 11).
43. Ibid., p. 23.
44. See Fakhry (2004, p. 218), see also, Martin et al. (1997).
45. See Sahlins (1998, p. 7), also Polanyi (1947), and Dalton (1961).
46. See Eisenstein (2011, p. 247), see also Skidelsky and Skidelsky (2012).
47. For an analysis of the historical debate and controversies that arose between the doctrines advocated by the school of thought, Mu'tazilite, that held Divine Justice as one of five fundamental principles of belief in Islam and the school that opposed it, Ash'arite, see Martin et al. (1997). See also Vishonoff (2011, pp. 135–139, 248–250, 276), Reilly (2011, pp. 78–83), Hoodbhoy (1990), and Najjar (2001, pp. 12–13, and 115–121).
48. See Rahman (1980).
49. See Ahmad (editor) (2002, p. 23).
50. By the time the volume edited by Professor Habib Ahmad appeared, "conventional economics" had already become the neoliberal economics that had dominated all other economic paradigms for at least 20 years.
51. For a philosophical view on the two major conceptions of models of human beings in Western thought, see Hollis (1977) and the series of papers in Meeks (editor) (1991). See also, Bensusan-Butt (1978).
52. See Al-Attas (1993) and Allawi (2010).
53. In this context, it is important to note that Adam Smith, though a product of the Enlightenment Project, wrote The Theory of Moral Sentiments which a number of Adam Smith scholars consider to be the moral framework within which Smith believed his conception of a "Commercial Society" were to operate. There are others who disagree. See Mirakhor and Hamid (2009).
54. See, for example, various papers in the *Real-World Economics Review*, issue 96 (July 2021).
55. For an exception, see Ertuna (2009). For a critique of the axioms of "free market" and claims made on its behalf by neoliberalism, see Finn (2006).
56. The term was coined by Keynes in his General Theory, 1936. Its contemporary explanation is provided by George Akerlof and Robert Shiller (2009).
57. Laski (1936, p. 19).

58. For a radically different view of Adam Smith's contributions, see Pack (1991).
59. Weisskopf (1979).
60. For a discussion of natural law, see Askari and Mirakhor (2020, pp. 33–44).
61. See Mure (1958, pp. 21–23). This is an excellent book as a critique of empiricist-positivist philosophy and its influence on economic thinking. Seyyed Hossein Nasr labels such beings as "Promethean" humans. That is in rejecting all things religious and all things not perceptible by physical senses as superstitious, this being in essence rebelling against the Creator. Promethean is anyone who like Prometheus—a Titan god in Greek mythology who rebelled against all other gods by providing humans with fire, an act prohibited by the gods—rejects anything sacred. See Nasr (1968). Professor Nasr was one of the few Muslim philosophers who issued explicit early warnings about the onset of environmental crises that has now become an existential threat. Even at the relatively early stage of the diagnosis of adverse effects of economic growth policies that would create environmental crisis and when the warnings of the MIT project on Limits to Growth was still some four years away (Meadows et al. 1972), Professor Nasr (1968) warned that the consequences of the damaging effects of the behaviour of the Promethean economic agent against nature—while assuming a prerogative to "conquer nature" as means of serving the end of self-interest—will be dire. He argued: "Few realize that by the very fact that nature is finite its boundaries cannot be pushed back indefinitely. Man simply cannot continue to conquer and dominate nature endlessly without expecting a reaction on the part of nature to re-establish the equilibrium destroyed by man" (Nasr 1968, pp. 118–119; see also 1996). In the secular "conventional economics" paradigm, there is no room for explicit consideration of restoration of environmental equilibrium since it is based on exploitation of nature for the sake of human economic prosperity. The best it can do is to relegate the responsibility of performing this task to the price mechanism in the "free market."
62. For definition and explanation of these and their relation to economics, see Katouzian (1980).
63. On the contrary, Nasr (2004) argues that "secularism is the common enemy of all the Abrahamic traditions, and the erosion of moral authority in secular societies that we observe today poses as many problems for Jews and Christians as it does for Muslims."
64. See, Asad (1993, 2003) and Jakobsen and Pellegrini (2008, p. 3).
65. Asad (2003), ibid., p. 13.
66. See Seyyed Hossein Nasr (1968).
67. Lukes (1973 [1990], p. 47).

68. MacIntyre (1988, p. 9). See also, Audi (2001). A survey of the literature on rationality fails to produce a comprehensive, coherent, and universal theory of rationality.
69. Irani (1986, pp. xi–xx).
70. Irani, ibid., p. xx.
71. Collingwood (1946, p. 41).
72. Cramp (1991).
73. Sen (1977, 1991).
74. Hahn and Hollis (1979, p. 12).
75. Mirakhor and Hamid (2009).
76. See Pigou (1912) and Dalton (1920a, 1920b). See also, Atkinson and Brandonili (2015).
77. Gwynne (2004).
78. Mermer (1996, 1999).
79. In this context, see Trigg (1973).
80. Plato (2016).
81. Hirschman (2013).
82. Locke (1975, Book II. 27. 17, p. 341, and Book II. 27. 17).
83. Locke, ibid., I. 3. 3.
84. Locke, ibid., II. 20. 14.
85. Knight (1939, pp. 8–9).
86. Kuhn (1970).
87. See papers in issue No 96 of Real-World Economic Review, July 2021.
88. Zaman (2012).
89. Javaid and Suri (2020).
90. In this context, see Stenberg (1996).
91. See Faruqi (1982). This paradigm has been discussed, used, and critiqued far more extensively than its Attasian counterpart. See, for example, Zarqa (2003).
92. Al-Attas' views are expounded comprehensively in his book, Prolegomena to the Metaphysics of Islam: An Exposition of the Fundamental Elements of the Worldview of Islam (1995). Elements of the Worldview of Islam are subject of a shorter treatise. See, for example, Al-Attas (1976, 1978, 1985, 2015).
93. See, for example, Berger (1999), Opdebeeck (2018), Goudzwaard (1979b), Sandelands (2010), Eisenstein (2011), Finn (2006), McMurtry (1999), McCarraher (2019), and Long (2000). See also the two books of Nelson (1991, 2001) in which he makes compelling case that economics has many characteristics that make it a religion.
94. For more discussion of $\bar{A}d\bar{a}b$, see its treatment and explanation in Leaman (2001) and Daiber (2001, p. 842). It is noted that in these sources $\bar{A}d\bar{a}b$ is understood in an ethical framework in societal relations whereas in the Attasian discourse it has a broader definition and application covering all relations.

95. See Daud (2010, pp. 37–38), Jah (2010) and Musawi (2010). Also, Waghid (2010) restates, in the first part of this paper, Al-Attas' views on Islamization of education which in some crucial respects echoes insightful remarks of Richard Parker on how Western universities across the world are organized to indoctrinate newcomers in the ideology of neoliberal economics (see, Parker 2021).
96. Boas (1961, p. 14). Also, Boas (1961, p. 12) suggests that "[s]hrewed as man's calculations have become concerning his means, his choice of ends which was formerly correlated with belief, with absolute criteria of conduct, has become witless."
97. See Allawi (2010, p. 60).
98. Much admiration, respect, and rewards awaited those who were willing to play this role. For example, in 2004, the Dutch awarded three Muslim intellectuals: Sadik al-'Azm, Fatema Mernissi, and AbdulKarim Soroush, the Erasmus Prize. Erasmus was the Renaissance Dutch humanist. Significantly, according to its official announcement, the Erasmus Prize is "awarded annually to a person or institution that has made an exceptionally important contribution to European culture, society, or social science."
99. Ibid., p. 59.
100. Ibid., p. 67.
101. Ibid., pp. 70–75.
102. See, for example, Al-Sayyid al-'Allamah 'Ammar Abu Ragheef (1989).
103. For a selective summary of Said Nursi's views comprehensively covered in his Tafseer, Risale-I Nur, in English, see Michel (2013).
104. See As-Sadr (1981 [2019]). In this book, As-Sadr shows how certainty of belief can be reached through repeated and sequenced experiences. The notion that one can experientially achieve certainty of belief on a given proposition among all other alternatives increases through experience was developed by As-Sadr in his proof of the existence of the Creator showing that this proposition is like any in natural sciences.
105. As an example, note the use, or rather the abuse, of his writings on the theory and practice of "Islamic banking."
106. Quoted in Klein (1985, p. 238).
107. There is close convergence between the views of As-Sadr and Al-Attas on their understanding of religion (*deen*). See for example, Al-Attas (1992).
108. For a contemporary view of "Islamization" project, see Abou El Fadl (2014, p. 345).
109. See Al-Hasani (1989).
110. Ibid., pp. 24–26.
111. See, for example, Yousefi (1980), Mir Moezzi (2006), and Sadr (2019).
112. The view of As-Sadr on justice is another testimony to his creative genius when one considers that it was not until the 1940s that scholars, such as

Tahir ibn Ashur, included justice in the lists (there is now a number of them) of *Maqāṣid as-Sharī'ah*.
113. Important to this discussion is the pioneering work by Al-Hakimi et al. (1992). Particularly helpful is the painstaking effort of the authors in collecting relevant Ahaadeeth relating to the subject matter particularly on justice which they too consider as axial objective of *Al-Iqtiṣād*.
114. On the important issue of methodology, see Zia'uddeen (2006), inter alia.
115. For more detail, see Mirakhor and Hamid (2009). In his Theory of Moral Sentiments, Smith uses different titles other than "The Author of Nature" to refer to the Supreme Creator as "the great Director of Nature"; "the final cause"; "the great judge of hearts"; "Providence"; "the divine Being"; "an invisible hand"; "Providence"; and "God."
116. For more detail, see Askari et al. (2015, pp. 3–7; 307–312, and the bibliography of this book).
117. See Hazik et al. (2019).
118. In *Iqtiṣāduna*, As-Sadr focuses on the necessity of sharing based on *Al-Qur'ān* and *Ahādeeth*, especially in investment projects that take time to gestate. Both in his *Al-Bank Alla Ribāwi* and his shorter explanatory notes on his proposal he refers to the risks and the need for sharing them. In books on al-Bay' and al-Makasib, particularly more contemporary treaties and/or commentaries, varieties of partnerships and risks associated with them are discussed. See, for example, Moddarrisi (1993, especially pp. 272–311 with commentaries in the footnotes). It is crucial to note that conditions regarding the sharing of profits or losses have to be determined *ex ante* at the time of the contract. However, while the parameters of sharing are being agreed to, no participant in the contract knows the outcome. Therefore, each participant has to make decisions under conditions of risk and uncertainty. Hence, at the beginning of contracts, all are sharing the risks of the project being undertaken. Once the outcome is known (whether loss or profit), the sharing parameter activates. That is, activation takes place only after the end of project when profits (or losses) are shared according to the share parameter agreed upon at the beginning of the project. Consequently, to refer to Islamic finance as "profit-loss sharing" is inaccurate. Islamic finance is risk-sharing *ex ante* and profit-loss sharing *ex post*.
119. See Akin and Mirakhor (2019).
120. For an understanding of the definition of righteous conduct (*Al-'Amal As-Sālih*) in the Sadrian discourse, see Al-Sadr (1982 [2013]).
121. Based on *Al-Qur'ān* and *As-Sunnah* of the Messenger (*saa*), Barakah can be defined as a nonlinear scalar that leads to multiple returns to righteous actions. As-Sadr deals with the concept of Barakah while interpreting Verse 96 of Chapter 7. See Torabi and Mirakhor (2020).

122. The idea that any righteous action leads to multiple returns begs the question: Are the rules of behaviour prescribed by Allah *swt* so universal that compliance with them by agents, regardless of the degree of belief, will invoke and trigger Barakah?
123. Sadr al-Deen al-Shirazi (Mulla Sadra) explained comprehensively the nature and the process of this "motion-in-substance" in his book Al-Asfar Al-Arba'ah.
124. For more detail on how Islamic belief gives rise to social capital, see Ng et al. (2015).
125. See, for example, Rima (2013).
126. See, for example, Holloway (1999).
127. He focuses on: Verse 16: Chapter 72; 66:5; 96:7; 92:21; 52:23.
128. These rules are enumerated and explained in Askari, Iqbal, and Mirakhor (2015).
129. For an exposition of the ideal *Iqtiṣādi* system based on the ideas expounded in the Sadrian discourse, see Mirakhor and Askari (2017).

References

Abou El Fadl, Khaled. 2014. *Reasoning with God: Reclaiming Shari'ah in the Modern Age*. New York: Rowan & Littlefield.

Abu Ragheef, Al-Sayyid al-'Allamah 'Ammar. 1989. "Al-Sayyid Muhammad Baqir Al-Sadr: Theoretician in Iqtiṣād." In *Essays in Iqtiṣād*, edited by B. al-Hasani and A. Mirakhor, 7–19. Maryland: Nur Corporation.

Abu Sulayman, AbdulHamid A., ed. 1989. *Islamization of Knowledge: General Principles and Work Plan*. Herndon, VA: IIIT.

Adorno, Theodor W. 1973. *The Jargon of Authenticity*. Translated by Knut Tarnowski and Fredric Will. Evanston: Northwestern University Press.

Ahmed, Abdulrahman Yousri. 2002. "The Scientific Approach to Islamic Economics: Philosophy, Theoretical Construction and Applicability." In *Theoretical Foundation of Islamic Economics*, edited by Habib Ahmad. Book of Readings, No. 3. Jeddah: Islamic Development Bank.

Akerlof, George, and Robert Shiller. 2009. *Animal Spirit: How Human Psychology Drives the Economy, and Why It Matters for Global Capitalism*. Princeton: Princeton University Press.

Akin, Tarik, and Abbas Mirakhor. 2019. *Wealth Inequality, Asset Redistribution, and Risk-Sharing Islamic Finance*. Berlin: Walter de Gruyter.

Al-'Alwani, Taha Jabir. 1996. *The Islamization of Knowledge: Yesterday and Today*. Herndon, VA: IIIT.

Al-Attas, Syed Muhammad Naquib. 1976. *Islam: The Concept of Religion and the Foundation of Ethics and Morality*. Kuala Lumpur: Muslim Youth Movement of Malaysia.

Al-Attas, Syed Muhammad Naquib 1978. *Islam and Secularism*. Kuala Lumpur: Muslim Youth Movement of Malaysia.
Al-Attas, Syed Muhammad Naquib. 1980. *The Concept of Education in Islam*. Kuala Lumpur: Muslim Youth Movement of Malaysia.
Al-Attas, Syed Muhammad Naquib. 1985. *Islam, Secularism and the Philosophy of the Future*. London: Mansell.
Al-Attas, Syed Muhammad Naquib. 1993. *Islam and Secularism*. Kuala Lumpur: International Institute of Islamic Thought and Civilization.
Al-Attas, Syed Muhammad Naquib. 1995. *Prolegomena to the Metaphysics of Islam: An Exposition of the Fundamental Elements of the Worldview of Islam*. Kuala Lumpur: International Institute of Islamic Thought and Civilization.
Al-Attas, Syed Muhammad Naquib. 2015. *On Justice and Nature of Man: A Commentary on Surah Al-Nisa' (Chapter 4; Verse 58) and Surah Al-Mu'minun (Chapter 23: Verses 12–14)*. Kuala Lumpur: IBFIM.
Al-Faruqi, Ismail Raji. 1988. Islamization of Knowledge: Problems, Principles and Perspectives. In *Islam: Source and Purpose of Knowledge*. Islamization of Knowledge Series Number 5. Herndon, VA: International Institute of Islamic Thought (IIIT).
Al-Hakimi, M. R., M. Al-Hakimi, and A. Al-Hakimi. 1992. *Al-Hayat*. Makatab Nashr Al-Thaqafah Al-Islamiyyah. 5 Vols., 7th printing. Tehran.
Al-Hasani, Baqir. 1989. The Concept of Iqtiṣād. In *Essays on Iqtiṣād*, edited by Al-Hasani and Mirakhor, 21–44. Maryland: Nur Corporation.
Allawi, Ali. 2010. "Re-Islamizing the World." In *Knowledge, Language and the Civilization of Islam: Essays in Honor of Syed Muhammad Naquib al-Attas*, edited by Wan Mohd Nor Wan Daud and Muhammad Zainiy Uthman, 59–81. Johor Bahru, Malaysia: Universiti Teknologi Malaysia (UTM).
Al-Reyshahri, M., and S. R. Al-Hosseini. 2001. *Al-Tanmieh Al-Iqtisadiyyeh Fee Al-Kitab wa Al-Sunnah*. Ghom: Dar Al-Hadeeth.
As-Sadr, Muhammad Baqir. 1981 [2019], *Al-Usus Al-Mantiqiyyah Lil-Istiqra', Logical Foundations of Induction*. Translated by Talib H. Janabi. London: University Press of London.
As-Sadr, Muhammad Baqir. 1982 [2013]. *Al-'Amal as-Salih fee Al-Qur'an*. Buhuth Islamiyyah. Dar Al-Kutub Al-Islamiyyah.
Asad, Talal. 1993. *Genealogies of Religion*. Baltimore: The Johns Hopkins University Press.
Asad, Talal. 2003. *Formation of the Secular: Christianity, Islam, Modernity*. Stanford: Stanford University Press.
Askari, Hossein, Zamir Iqbal, and Abbas Mirakhor. 2015. *Introduction to Islamic Economics: Theory and Application*. Singapore: Wiley.
Askari, Hossein, and Abbas Mirakhor. 2020. *Conceptions of Justice from Islam to the Present*. New York: Palgrave Macmillan.

Atkinson, Anthony B., and Andrea Brandonili. 2015. "Unveiling the Ethics Behind Inequality Measurement: Dalton's Contribution to Economics." *Economic Journal* 125 (583): 209–234.

Audi, Robert. 2001. *The Architecture of Reason: The Structure and Substance of Rationality*. Oxford: Oxford University Press.

Baranzini, Mauro, and Roberto Scazzieri, eds. 1986. *Structure of Inquiry and Economic Theory*. Oxford: Basil Blackwell.

Bauer, K. 2017. "To Be or Not to Be Authentic: In Defense of Authenticity as an Ethical Ideal." *Ethical Theory and Moral Practice* 20 (3): 567–580.

Bensusan-Butt, D. M. 1978. *On Economic Man*, 113–173. Canberra: Australian National University Press.

Berger, Peter. 1999. "Desecularization of the World: A Global Overview." In *The Desecularization of the World: Resurgent Religion and World Politics*, edited by Peter Berger. Grand Rapids: William B. Eerdmans Publishing.

Boas, George. 1961. *The Limits of Reason*. New York: Harper and Brothers.

Burgin, Angus. 2012. *The Great Persuasion: Reinventing Free Markets since the Depression*. Cambridge: Harvard University Press.

Collingwood, R. G. 1946. *The Idea of History*. Oxford: Oxford University Press.

Cramp, Tony. 1991. "Pleasure, Prices and Principles." In *Thoughtful Economic Man*, edited by Gay Meeks, 50–73. Cambridge: Cambridge University Press.

Daiber, Hans. 2001. "Political Philosophy." In *History of Islamic Philosophy*, edited by Seyyed Hossein Nasr and Oliver Leaman. New York: Routledge.

Dalton, George. 1961. "Economic Theory and Primitive Society." *American Anthropologist* 63: 1–25.

Dalton, Hugh. 1920a. "The Measurement of the Inequality of Incomes." *Economic Journal* 30 (119): 348–361.

Dalton, Hugh. 1920b. *Some Aspects of Inequality of Incomes in Modern Communities*. London: Routledge and Kegan.

Darraz, Muhammad AbdAllah. 1973 [1950]. "Dustur Al-Akhlaq fee Al-Qur'an." Abd Al-Sabur Shaheen, Sayyid Muhammad Badawi and Sami Al-Ghariri. *Reprinted with additional explanatory footnotes in Ghom*, Islamic Republic of Iran: Dar Al-Kutub Al-Islamiyyah.

Daud, Wan Mohd Nor Wan. 2010. "Al-Attas: A Real Reformer and Thinker." In *Knowledge, Language, Thought and the Civilization of Islam*, edited by Nor Wan Daud and Muhammad Zainiy Uthman, 37–38. Johor Bahru, Malaysia: UTM.

Davenport, Stewart. 2008. *Friends of the Unrighteous Mammon: Northern Christians & Market Capitalism*. Chicago: The University of Chicago Press.

De Gregori, Thomas R. 1987. "Resources are Not; They Become: An Institutional Theory." *Journal of Economic Issues* 21 (3): 1241–1263.

Donders, J. G. 2005. *John Paul II: The Encylicals in Everyday Language*. Maryknoll, NY: Orbis Books.

Dulles, A. 1999. "Centesimus Annus and the Renewal of Culture." *Journal of Markets and Morality* 2 (1): 1–7.
Eisenstein, Charles. 2011. *Sacred Economics: Money, Gift and Society in the Age of Transition*. Berkeley, CA: Evolver Editions.
Ertuna, Ibrahim Ozer. 2009. *Wealth, Welfare and the Global Free Market*. Burlington, VT: Ashgate Publishing.
Fahim Khan, M. 2002. "Fiqh Foundations of Islamic Economics." In *Theoretical Foundations of Islamic Economics*, edited by Habib Ahmad. Jeddah: The Islamic Development Bank.
Fakhry, Majid. 2004. *A History of Islamic Philosophy*. 3rd ed. New York: Columbia University Press.
Faruqi, Ismail. 1982. *Islamization of Knowledge*. Herndon, VA: IIIT.
Finn, Daniel K. 2006. *The Moral Ecology of Markets: Assessing Claims About Markets and Justice*. Cambridge: Cambridge University Press.
Foucault, Michel. 1983. "The Subject and Power." In *Beyond Structuralism and Hermenutics*, edited by Hubert L. Drefus and Paul Rabinow. Chicago: University of Chicago Press.
Foucault, Michel. 1994. *The Order of Things: An Archeology of Human Sciences*. New York: Vintage Books.
Friedman, Milton. 2002. *Capital and Freedom*. Chicago: University of Chicago Press.
Glyn, Andrew. 2007. *Capitalism Unleashed*. Oxford: Oxford University Press.
Goudzwaard, Bob. 1979a. *Capitalism and Progress*. Translated and edited by Josina Van Nuos Zylstra. Toronto: Wedge Publishing.
Goudzwaard, Bob. 1979b. *Capitalism and Progress: A Diagnosis of Western Society*. Toronto: Eerdmans Publication.
Gwynne, Rosalinda Ward. 2004. *Logic, Rhetoric and Legal Reasoning in the Qur'an: God's Arguments*, 61–105. London: Routledge, Taylor and Francis Group.
Hahn, F. H., and M. Hollis, eds. 1979. *Philosophy and Economic Theory*. Oxford: Oxford University Press.
Hamid, Idris Samawi, and Abbas Mirakhor. 2020. "On the Logical Character and Coherence of Islamic Economics." In *Handbook of Analytical Studies in Islamic Finance and Economics*, edited by Nabil Maghrebi, Tarik Akin, Zamir Iqbal, and Abbas Mirakhor. Berlin/Boston: De Gruyter.
Harvey, David. 2006. *A Brief History of Neoliberalism*. Oxford: Oxford University Press.
Hayden White. 1973. *Historical Imagination in Nineteenth-Century Europe*. Baltimore, MD: The Johns Hopkins University Press.
Hayek, Friedrich A. 1980. *Law, Legislation and Liberty*. Volume 2: The Mirage of Social Justice. Chicago: University of Chicago Press.

Hazik, Mohamed, Abbas Mirakhor, and S. Nuri Erbas. 2019. *Belief and Rule Compliance: An Experimental Comparison of Muslim and Non-Muslim Economic Behavior*. London: Academic Press.

Henry, John F. 2009. "The Illusion of the Epoch: Neoclassical Economics as a Case Study." *Studi e Note di Eonomia* 14 (1): 27–44.

Hirschman, Albert O. 2013. "The Concept of Interest: From Euphemism to Tautology." In *The Essential Hirschman*, edited by Jeremy Adelman. Princeton: Princeton University Press.

Hollis, Martin. 1977. *Models of Man: Philosophical Thought on Social Action*. Cambridge: Cambridge University Press.

Holloway, Richard. 1999. *Godless Morality: Keeping Religion out of Ethics*. Edinburgh: Canongate books Ltd.

Hoodbhoy, Perviz Amir Ali. 1990. *Islam and Science: Religious Orthodoxy and the Battle for Rationality*. London: Zed Books.

Ibn Ashur, Muhammad Al-Tahir. 2007. *Treatise on Maqasid al-Sharia'h*. Herndon, VA: The International Institute of Islamic Thought.

Irani, K. D. 1986. "Introduction: Modes of Rationality." In *Rationality in Thought and Action*, edited by Martin Tamny and K. D. Irani. Westport, CT: Greenwood Press.

Jah, Omar. 2010. "Al-Balagh." In Daud and Uthman (eds.), pp. 83–96.

Jakobsen, Janet R., and Ann Pellegrini, eds. 2008. *Secularism*. Durham: Duke University Press.

Javaid, Omar, and Wahab Suri. 2020. "The Possibility or Impossibility of Islamization of Knowledge in a Neoliberal Market Order." *Journal of Islamic Business and Management* 10 (1): 148–169.

Jo, Tae-Hee. 2011. "Social Provisioning Process and Socio-Economic Modelling." *The American Journal of Economics and Sociology* 70 (5): 1094–1116.

Jo, Tae-Hee. 2016. "What If There Are No Conventional Price Mechanisms?" *Journal of Economic Issues* 50 (2): 327–344.

John von Neumann and Oskar Morgenstern. 1944. *Theory of Games and Economic Behavior*, Princeton: Princeton University Press.

Katouzian, Homa. 1980. *Ideology and Method in Economics*. New York: New York University Press.

Kazemi-Moussavi, Ahmad. 2011. "Rethinking Islamic Methodology with Reference to Maqasid al-Shari'ah." *Islam and Civilizational Renewal* 2 (2): 272–287.

Khurshid, Ahmad. 1962. *Principles of Islamic Education*. Lahore: Islamic Publications Ltd.

Kimmerer, Robin W. 2013. *Braiding Sweetgrass*, Milkweed Editions.

Klein, Morris. 1985. *Mathematics and the Search for Knowledge*. Oxford: Oxford University Press.

Knight, Frank H. 1939. "Ethics and Economic Reform -I- The Ethics of Liberalism." *Economica* 6 (21): 1–29.
Kuhn, Thomas. 1970. *The Structure of Scientific Revolution*. Chicago: University of Chicago Press.
Laski, H. J. 1936. *The Rise of the European Liberalism*. New York: Harper.
Leaman, Oliver. 2001. "Islamic Humanism in the Fourth/Tenth Century." In *History of Islamic Philosophy*, edited by Seyyed Hossein Nasr and Oliver Leaman, 156–157. New York: Routledge.
Lee, Frederic S. 2013. "Post-Keynesian Price Theory: From Pricing to Market Governance to the Economy as a Whole." In *The Oxford Handbook of Post-Keynesian Economics*, edited by Harcourt and Kriesler, vol. I, 467–484. Oxford: Oxford University Press.
Locke, John. 1975. *An Essay Concerning Human Understanding*. Edited by Peter H. Nidditch, Book II. Oxford: Clarendon Press.
Long, D. Stephen. 2000. *Divine Economy: Theology and the Market*. New York: Routledge.
Lowery, S. Todd, and Barry Gordon, eds. 1998. *Ancient and Medieval Economic Ideas and Concepts of Social Justice*. Leiden: Brill.
Lukes, Steven. 1973 [1990]. *Individualism*. Cambridge: Basil Blackwell Ltd.
MacIntyre, Alasdair. 1988. *Whose Justice, Which Rationality*. Notre Dame: University of Notre Dame Press.
Martin, Richard C., Mark R. Woodward, and Dwi S. Atmaja. 1997. *Defenders of Reason in Islam*. Oxford: Oneworld Publications.
McCarraher, Eugene. 2019. *The Enchantments of Mammon: How Capitalism Became the Religion of Modernity*. Cambridge: Harvard University Press.
McMurtry, John. 1999. *The Cancer Stage of Capitalism*. London: Pluto Press.
Meadows, D. H., D. L. Meadows, J. Randers, and W. W. Behrens III. 1972. *The Limits to Growth*. New York: Universe Books.
Meeks, Gay, ed. 1991. *Thoughtful Economic Man*. Cambridge: Cambridge University Press.
Mermer, Yamine. 1996. "Induction, Science and Causation." *Islamic Studies* 35 (3): 265–286.
Mermer, Yamine. 1999. "The Hermeneutical Dimension of Science: A Critical Analysis Based on Said Nursi's Risale-i Nur." *The Muslim World* 89 (3–4): 270–296.
Michel, Thomas. 2013. *Insight from the Risale-I Nur*. Clifton, NJ: Tughra Books.
Mirakhor, Abbas, and Hossein Askari. 2017. *Ideal Islamic Economy*. New York: Palgrave Macmillan.
Mirakhor, Abbas, and Idris Samawi Hamid. 2009. *Islam and Development*. New York: Global Scholarly Publications.

Mir Moezzi, Sayyid Hossein. 2006. "Criticism and Analysis of Shaheed Sadr's Views on the Nature of Iqtiṣād Islami." In *Studies on Iqtiṣādi Thoughts of AyatuAllah Shaheed Sadr* (ra), edited by Sayyid Zia'uddeen Kia' Al-Hosseini, 131–154. Qum: Mofid University Publications.

Mirowski, Philip. 2015. "Defining Neoliberalism." In Mirowski and Plehwe (eds.), pp. 417–455.

Mirowski, Philip, and Dieter Plehwe, eds. 2015. *The Road from Mont Pelerin: The Making of the Neoliberal Thought Collective.* Cambridge: Harvard University Press.

Moddarrisi, Al-Sayyid Mohammad 'Ali. 1993. *Al-Shirkah Fee Al-Islam.* Qum.

Mure, G. R. G. 1958. *Retreat from Truth.* Oxford: Basil Blackwell.

Musawi, Ahmad Kazemi. 2010. "Shifts of Language and Turns in Worldview: Naquib Al-Attas' Perspective." In Daud and Uthman (eds.), pp. 97–102.

Najjar, Ibrahim, trans. 2001. *Faith and Reason in Islam: Averroes' Exposition of Religious Arguments.* Oxford: Oneworld Publications.

Nasr, Seyyed Hossein. 1968. *The Encounter of Man and Nature: The Spiritual Crisis of Modern Man.* London: George Allen and Unwin.

Nasr, Seyyed Hossein. 1996. *Religion and the Order of Nature.* New York: Oxford University Press.

Nasr, Seyyed Hossein. 2004. *The Heart of Islam: Enduring Values for Humanity.* New York: HarperCollins.

Nelson, Robert H. 1991. *Reaching for Heaven on Earth: The Theological Meaning of Economics.* Lanham: Rowan and Littlefield.

Nelson, Robert H. 2001. *Economics as Religion: From Samuelson to Chicago and Beyond.* University Park: The Pennsylvania State University Press.

Ng, Adam, Abbas Mirakhor, and Mansor H. Ibrahim. 2015. *Social Capital and Risk Sharing.* New York: Palgrave Macmillan.

Norgaard, Richard B. 2021. "Post-Economics: Reconnecting Reality and Morality to Escape the Econocene." *Real-World Economic Review* 96: 49–66.

Nur, Hasan. 2020. "Relationship of Maqasid al-Shari'ah with Ususl al-Fiqh." *Ulul Albab: Jurnal Studi dan Penelitian Hukum Islam* 3 (2): 231–245.

Opdebeeck, Hendrik. 2018. *The Economy and Meaningfulness—A Utopia.* New York: Peter Lang.

Pack, Spencer J. 1991. *Capitalism as a Moral System: Adam Smith's Critique of the Free Market Economy.* Northampton, CT: Edward Elgar.

Parker, Richard. 2021. "Of Copernican Revolutions- and the Suddenly-Marginal Marginal Mind at the Dawn of the Anthropocene." *Real-World Economics Review* 96: 28–48.

Pigou, Arthur Cecil. 1912. *Wealth and Welfare.* London: Macmillan.

Piketty, Thomas. 2014. *Capital in the Twenty-First Century.* Cambridge: Harvard University Press.

Piketty, Thomas. 2020. *Capital and Ideology.* Harvard University Press.

Plato. 2016. *Laws.* Translated by Tom Griffith and edited by Malcom Schofield, Book 5, pp. 169–197. Cambridge: Cambridge Texts in the History of Political Thought, Cambridge University Press.
Polanyi, Karl. 1947. "Our Obsolete Market Mentality." *Commentary* 3: 109–117.
Rahman, Fazlur. 1980. *Major Themes of the Qur'an.* Minneapolis: Bibliotheca Islamica.
Reilly, Robert R. 2011. *The Closing of the Muslim Mind.* Wilmington, DE: Intercollegiate Studies Institute.
Rima, Samuel D. 2013. *Spiritual Capital: A Moral Core for Social and Economic Justice.* Farnham, Surrey, UK: Gower Publishing Limited.
Rings, M. 2017. "Authenticity, Self-Fulfillment, and Self-Acknowledgement." *The Journal of Value Inquiry* 51 (3): 475–489.
Roncaglia, Alesandro. 2005. *The Wealth of Ideas: A History of Economic Thought.* Cambridge: Cambridge University Press.
Ryan, John A. 1916. *Distributive Justice.* Revised edition, 1927. New York: The Macmillan Company.
Sadr, Seyed Kazem. 2019. "The Methodology of Islamic Economics." *Iranian Economic Review* 23 (4): 897–917.
Sahlins, Marshall. 1998. "The Original Affluent Society." In *Limited Wants, Unlimited Means,* edited by John Gowdy. Washington, DC: Island Press.
Saiyidain, K. G. 1942. *Iqbal's Educational Philosophy.* Lahore: Islamic Publications Ltd.
Samuels, Warren, Jeff E. Biddle, and John B. Davis, eds. 2007. *A Companion to the History of Thought,* 11–45. Malden, MA: Blackwell Publishing.
Sandelands, Lloyd E. 2010. *God and Mammon.* New York: University Press of America.
Schultz, Walter J. 2001. *The Moral Conditions of Economic Efficiency.* Cambridge: Cambridge University Press.
Sen, Amartya. 1977. "Rational Fools: A Critique of the Behavioral Foundations of Economic Theory." *Philosophy and Public Affairs* 6: 317–344.
Sen, Amartya. 1991. "Beneconfusion." In *Thoughtful Economic Man,* edited by Gay Meeks, 12–16. Cambridge: Cambridge University Press.
Skidelsky, Robert, and Edward Skidelsky. 2012. *How Much Is Enough? Money and the Good Life.* New York: Other Press.
Spengler, Joseph J., and William R. Allen, eds. 1960. *Essays in Economic Thought: Aristotle to Marshall.* Chicago: Rand McNally & Company.
Stenberg, Leif. 1996. *The Islamization of Knowledge: Four positions on Developing an Islamic Modernity.* Lund: Lund University Press.
Torabi, Omid, and Abbas Mirakhor. 2020. *Crowdfunding with Enhanced Reputation Mechanism.* Berlin: Walter de Gruyter.

Trigg, Roger. 1973. *Reason and Commitment*. Cambridge: Cambridge University Press.

Vishonoff, David R. 2011. *The Formation of Islamic Hermeneutics*. New Haven, CT: American Oriental Society.

Von Nell-Breuning, S. J. 1936. *Reorganization of Social Economy*. Translated by Bernard W. Dempsey. New York: The Bruce Publishing Company.

Waghid, Yusef. 2010. "Reflections on Al-Attas' Conception of the Islamic University: Implications for Academic Freedom, Institutional Autonomy and Philosophy of Education in South Africa." In Daud and Uthman (eds.), pp. 103–118.

Weber, Max. 1958. *The Protestant Ethic and the Spirit of Capitalism*. Translated by Talcott Parsons. New York: Scribner.

Weisskopf, Walter A. 1979. "The Method Is the Ideology: From a Newtonian to a Heisenbergian Paradigm in Economics." *Journal of Economic Issues* XIII (4): 869–884.

Yousefi, Ahmad 'Ali. 1980. "Introduction: The Nature and Structure of Iqtiṣād Islami from the Point of View of Shaheed Sadr." In *The Nature and Structure of Iqtiṣād Islami*, edited by Ahmad 'Ali Yousefi (with cooperation of Sa'eed Farahani and 'Ali Ridha Lashgari), 23–54. Qum: The Center for publication of Islamic Culture and Thought.

Zaman, Asad. 2012. "Crisis in Islamic Economics: Diagnosis and Prescriptions." *Journal of King AbdulAziz University: Islamic Economics* 25: 147–169.

Zarqa, Muhammad Anas. 2003. "Islamization of Economics: The Concept and Methodology." *J.KAU: Islamic Economics* 16 (1): 3–42.

Zia'uddeen, Sayyid Kia' Al-Hosseini. 2006. "Application of Induction in the Derivation of Maktab Iqtiṣādi of Islam in the vision of AyatuAllah Shaheed Sadr (r'a)." In Zi'uddeen Kia' al-Hosseini (ed.), pp. 89–121.

CHAPTER 2

Critiques of Conventional Economics

The ideology of self-interest as the driver of human progress constitutes the foundations of neoliberal economics, which in turn assumes the mantle of conventional economics. Critiques regard neoliberalism as a spurious philosophical thought and the source of policy confusion and ineptitude. Indeed, as argued in the opening chapter of this book, sustainable economic growth and prosperity have been elusive as conflating policies continue to exacerbate poverty, destroy nature, strain economic livelihoods, and undermine social life. The objective of the present chapter is to briefly review some critiques of economic doctrines, economic laws, and economic methodologies. There is mounting criticisms and intense scholarly debates about rational economic behaviour, *wertfreiheit* economics, morality, ethics, the notion of invisible hand, the theory of general equilibrium, Keynesianism, utilitarianism, monetarism, *inter alia*. There are also concerns about measurement without theory as well as pluralism in economic methodology, which refers to the various approaches pursued by scholars to justify and validate, or otherwise disprove and refute particular economic theories.

At the heart of the universe of economic discourse are issues related to the epistemological rationalism, and ontological scarcity, among others. In contrast to Islamic economics, conventional economics is axiomatically regarded as a descriptive rather than normative discipline. As explained in

© The Author(s), under exclusive license to Springer Nature
Switzerland AG 2023
N. El Maghrebi et al., *Revisiting Islamic Economics*,
Palgrave Studies in Islamic Banking, Finance, and Economics,
https://doi.org/10.1007/978-3-031-41134-2_2

the previous chapter with reference to the Sadrian discourse, it is clear from its doctrine (*madh'hab*) and science *'ilm* that *Al-Iqtiṣād*, which derives its rules or behaviour from *Al-Qur'ān* and *As-Sunnah*, does not lend itself to the positive-normative dichotomy. The organizing principles of *Al-Iqtiṣād* center on how the economic system should be structured and how economic agents should behave rather than merely how systems are actually structured and how agents actually behave. An overview of critiques of Islamic economics, universe of discourse clearly distinguishable from *Al-Iqtiṣād* paradigm and from conventional economics, will be presented in the next chapter, but for the purposes of discussion in the present one, the focus is placed on the logical consistency, or lack thereof, of mainstream economic doctrines, and their associated methodological principles.[1]

Thus, if economic thinking underlies the choices of policy-making and regulation, and if the apparent serious flaws in economic policies are reflective of inconsistencies inherent to economic doctrines, then it is crucially important to consider the epistemological foundations of economics. The focus hereafter is placed on competing definitions of economics before addressing critical arguments related to the science and dogma of classical and neoclassical economics. The critical review considers issues related to the underlying assumptions of economic rationality, resource scarcity, and consumer sovereignty, as well as the role of mathematical reasoning, morality, and ethics, and among others.

A Critical History of Political Economy

Human sustenance and subsistence have been the persistent challenge of societies throughout history. The "economic problem" regards the satisfaction of unlimited wants with limited resources as indemonstrable axioms. The scarcity of resources and insatiable wants are, however, at odds with the Islamic worldview derived from sacred knowledge, which regards economic issues as the consequence of the condition of material existence that cannot be separated from cosmic reality. The Islamic worldview, which challenges the rationalistic secular philosophies underlying the economic doctrines, is introduced in the opening chapter and further explained in other parts of the book. The critical history of political economy, presented here, focuses on scholarly efforts to formulate the economic problem. It is of singular interest to note that it is a fragmented discipline that fails to provide a coherent account of the economy or provide consistent remedies to its ailments. Instead, the economic debates seem to harden the hearts of men absorbed in the mechanistic worldview of mass and motion in the direction of nothingness, and make it impossible to reflect beyond the limited self to discover the inner being and the nature of reality.

The term "economics" has its roots in the Greek *Oikonomia*, which refers to the management of household affairs. As argued by Fred D. Miller (1998), the word *oikonomiké* in Aristotle (384–322 BC)'s vocabulary did not mean "economics" in the modern sense, but "the art of household management."[2] An extension from the wealth of households to the wealth of nations is mostly apparent in classical economic thought. Adam Smith (1723–1790) in his seminal work on *The Wealth of Nations* defined economics as an inquiry into the nature and causes of the wealth of nations. However, interpretations of the Smithian work as purely wealth-centric inquiry into human interpretations based solely on competition opened the door to criticism about the founder of modern economics as a Social Darwinist. Perhaps a lack of consistent reading of his collective work may better explain the observed variations in economic thought over time. In his equally important, albeit relatively overlooked, work *The Theory of Moral Sentiments*, Adam Smith presents arguments about moral psychology, including sympathy, fellow feelings, and the virtue of propriety, which are consistent with Aristotle's thesis on justice.[3]

Adam Smith (1776, p. 453) in *The Wealth of Nations* argued that "the great object of the political economy of every country, is to increase the riches and power of that country." More precisely, he defined political economy as a branch of the science of a statesman or legislator, with "two distinct objects: first, to provide a plentiful revenue or subsistence for the people, or more properly to enable them to provide such a revenue or subsistence for themselves; and secondly, to supply the state or commonwealth with a revenue sufficient for the public services." It is, thus, a discipline that proposes to enrich both the people and the sovereign. Notwithstanding the diverging views about the methodology of economics, many scholars have in a similar vein, developed alternative definitions that revolve around the central concept of wealth. In *The Principles of Political Economy and Taxation*, David Ricardo (1772–1823) argued that the principal problem in Political Economy is to determine the laws which regulate the distribution of the whole produce of the earth as rents for landownership, profits for capital, and wages for labour. The objective of his work was to demonstrate that "the rate of profits can never be increased but by a fall in wages, and that there can be no permanent fall of wages but in consequence of a fall of the necessaries on which wages are expended." Thus, the analysis of the "natural" rate of profit is constrained by the price dynamics of necessities, and demographics of active population.

Earlier arguments about economic constraints were made by by Thomas Robert Malthus (1766–1834) who suggested, first, that the question of productive labour cannot be addressed without an appropriate definition of wealth as *"material* objects, necessary, useful, or agreeable to man, which are voluntarily appropriated by individuals or nations." He proceeded, then, to claim that a nation "will therefore be rich or poor, according to the abundance or scarcity with which these material objects are supplied, compared with the extent of territory; and the people will be rich or poor, according to the abundance with which they are supplied, compared with the population" (Malthus 1798, pp. 28–29). *The Principle of Population* proposed by Malthus indicates that overpopulation is bound to exert pressure on available resources if it grows faster than food supplies. The argument is that a rapid growth in population, if left unchecked, is also regarded as the cause of not only economic hardship and misery but environmental damage as well. Thus, the remedy, it is argued, should lie in the adoption of control measures such as wage ceilings at bare subsistence levels in order to restrain population growth. As noted by Todd G. Buchholz (2021 [1989], p. 63), Malthus' fatalistic pessimism implies that if wages are allowed to rise beyond their upper limits, "workers would have more children, leading to food shortages and inescapable decline in the standard of living."

A departure from philosophical radicalism about population growth was marked by a shift in focus from man's reproductive functions to man's desire to accumulate wealth. John Stuart Mill (1806–1873) argues in Essays on Some Unsettled Questions of Political Economy (1884, p. 111), that "[w]hat is now commonly understood by the term 'Political Economy' is not the science of speculative politics, but a branch of that science. It does not treat of the whole of man's nature as modified by the social state, nor of the whole conduct of man in society. It is concerned with him solely as a being who desires to possess wealth, and who is capable of judging of the comparative efficacy of means for obtaining that end." It is noted that he also regarded the desire to possess wealth as a means to happiness. Indeed, the essence of the utilitarianism doctrine "is, that happiness is desirable, and the only thing desirable, as an end;

all other things being only desirable as a means to that end." However, he warranted new insights on self-interest and utilitarianism as he noted that since all selfish interests must be confined by the certainty of death, it is important to cultivate fellow relationships with the collective interests of mankind. Thus, utilitarianism should not be confounded with, nor detached from, the concept of self-interest as individuals acting on utilitarianism should behave with the required moral virtues of trustworthiness, integrity, and fairness to promote overall well-being. There are important applications of utilitarianism and morality in economic thought in order to address issues related to the ethics of global poverty, philanthropy, and altruism.[4]

Part as a reaction to Mill's definition of Political Economy and views of a society where the interests of all members should be regarded as equally important, Walter Bagehot (1826–1877) suggested, in *Economic Studies*, that John Stuart Mill "is open to the charge of having widened the old Political Economy either too much or not enough." Bagehot (1880, p. 5) argued that Political Economy "may be defined as the science of business, such as business is in large productive and trading communities... And it deals too with the men who carry on that commerce, and who make it possible. It assumes a sort of human nature such as we see everywhere around us, and again it simplifies that human nature; it looks at one part of it only. Dealing with matters of 'business,' it assumes that man is actuated only by motives of business. It assumes that every man who makes anything, makes it for money." Thus, the science of business, theory of commerce, desire for money, and accumulation of wealth remain as the central issues of Political Economy.

It is clear from the brief historical review that few centuries after Adam Smith's seminal contributions to the definition of Political Economy and important essays on its scope, methodology, and fundamental principles, there are diverging views about the genuine achievements of these intellectual debates. For instance, Gavin Kennedy (2008, pp. 1–2) argues that "by the new millennium, the original conflict of 'free trade versus protection' was back in contention; markets versus state management remained as divisive as ever, and competing solutions to problems of poverty, domestic and global, were stuck, intellectually, practically where Adam Smith had left them. The dominant feature of economics today is the divisive non-agreement on basic practical policies and, for all its hard-science pretensions, it remains in an unsettled state." The above argument that economics has not come of age in the ensuing centuries is founded on a lack of consensus on economic policies, a perpetuation of financial crises and economic depression, and exacerbating economic inequalities. Arguably, economists of many persuasions may agree on the enhanced theoretical understanding of the importance of exchange relationships in pushing the agenda for free trade, but the discipline has contributed only a modicum of economic policies addressing the plight of large segments of humanity living in desperate poverty.

Joseph Stiglitz (1991) presents an account of the achievements of economic science over the past century and argues that despite its methodological triumphs, there is no basic model to describe the economy. The development of the neoclassical Walrasian paradigm introduced by Kenneth Arrow (1921–2017) and Gérard Debreu (1921–2004) presented a theoretical framework for a formal demonstration of Adam Smith's invisible hand theory with unintended social benefits deriving from individual actions based on self-interest. This analytical approach offered also important insights into market equilibrium and the fundamental theorems of welfare economics. Another major contribution to the development of new economic thinking is associated with *The General Theory of Employment, Interest and Money* by John Maynard Keynes (1883–1946). Keynesian economics challenged the prevailing wisdom that market equilibrium is conducive to full employment and demonstrated the existence of unemployment equilibria, which can be caused by inadequate aggregate demand and the absence of short-term market adjustment to reduce the amplitude of the business cycle.

The countercyclical fiscal policies advocated by Keynesian economics should, thus, rely on government spending on labour-intensive projects during periods of economic recessions and mass unemployment. The demand-driven measures were met with counterarguments from the Austrian School of Economics led by Ludwig Von Mises (1888–1973) and Friedrich Hayek (1899–1992), *inter alia*, that economic suffering subsequent to economic excess is both necessary and inevitable. Government spending, therefore, would only inhibit the necessary process of adjustment and aggravate the economic conditions. Whereas interest in Keynesian economics grew with the Great Depression, belief faded with the onset of stagflationary conditions characterized by high inflation coupled with anaemic growth. An alternative school of thought based on monetarism contends that Keynesian economics does not provide a sound response to stagflation and that it is money supply that constitutes the main determinant of economic output and price levels. The monetarist school founded on the *Quantity Theory of Money* and led by Milton Friedman (1912–2006), suggests that high inflation rates are due to rapidly rising money supply. As fiscal policies are ineffective in regulating the business cycle with aggregate demand, recourse should be made to monetary policies to adjust the level of money supply and alter interest rates in the economy. The New Classical School argues that both Keynesian and Monetarist policies can be ineffective when market participants are able to anticipate changes in fiscal and monetary policies and offset their effects.

Thus, economic theory, which is defined by Paul Krugman (1994, p. 6) as "essentially a collection of models," has expanded along countless lines of thought. Some economic models are more cited than read. Others have successfully pushed the neoclassical model to its logical conclusions, which warrant new economic thought. On aggregate, however, the general impression is that the discipline lacks coherence and that intellectual progress has rarely been convincing enough to ignore the seminal work of earlier thinkers. Part of the reason is that the split of the broad subject of *Political Economy* into politics and economics has yielded little intellectual insights. Indeed, John Kenneth Galbraith (1987, p. 299) argues that "[t]he separation of economics, politics and political motivation is a sterile thing. It is also a cover for the reality of economic power and motivation. And it is a prime source of misjudgement and error in economic policy." He expressed also the hope that economics "will be reunited with politics to form again the larger discipline of political economy." With the proliferation of economic models and the miscellany of analytical methods, new insights may have ensued. As noted by *The Economist* (2011), "Economics is producing a torrent of research, coursing in all directions. The rivers have overflowed their banks."[5] Thus, scepticism remains about the future of a fragmented and disoriented discipline that fails to provide a basic model to describe the economy and provide remedies to its structural problems.

GENERAL EQUILIBRIUM PARADIGM

Understanding the general equilibrium theory developed by Léon Walras (1834–1910) is important because it may provide some useful insights into the role of market prices in the economy, and it establishes the equilibrium relationship between the important decisions about production and consumption. John Hicks (1939, pp. 60–61) argues that the reason for the sterility of the Walrasian equilibrium theory is that it did not address the laws of change, and states "Walras does give one a picture of the whole system; but it is a very distant picture, and hardly amounts to more than an assurance that things will work themselves out somehow, though it is not very clear how they will work themselves out." In the Walrasian equilibrium theory, prices adjust through a *tatônnement* process described by Rothschild (1994, p. 322) among others, as "(blind) groping in the dark." As noted by Ackerman (2002), the process of *tatônnement* may be mathematically tractable but it is rather unrealistic in the sense that it implies that the rate of change in the price for any commodity is proportional to excess demand, and that no trades are permitted until equilibrium prices have been achieved. Indeed, the Sonnencheim-Mantel-Debreu theorem suggests that the excess demand function can take any shape under the assumption of rational utility-maximizing agents, precluding thereby the uniqueness and stability of general equilibrium. Also, if the dynamics of price adjustment are such that the addition of a new commodity may destabilize an otherwise stable system, then there are legitimate concerns that the model results arrived at with small economies may not necessarily be valid for larger scales.[6]

Following the development of the Walrasian abstract theory of exchange, Arrow and Debreu (1954) demonstrated the existence of general equilibrium for a competitive economy under the conditions of state-contingent commodities, perfect competition, and an integrated system of production and consumption that accounts for a circular flow of income. As noted by Maurice Salles (2017), Arrow and Debreu used the mathematical fixed-point theorem proposed by Shizuo Kakutani (1911–2004) to develop analytical concepts that provide the basis for the present-day microeconomic theory.[7] The Arrow–Debreu model of competitive general equilibrium, as argued by Kenneth J. Arrow (1994, p. 451), "the only coherent account of the entire economy." However, the question arises, as noted by Frank Ackerman (2002), as to whether after a few decades of its development, the general equilibrium reached a "mathematical dead end." The reasons for the failure of the general equilibrium theory do not lie so much with esoteric model features as with internal design issues directly related to the neoclassical economic theory. In order to address the underlying problems, a modification of the economic theory is needed with new modelling of consumer choice, nonlinear analysis of social exchanges, and revision of institutional and social constraints.

It is important to note that the equilibrium model provides the basis for the development of welfare economics and social choice theory. The two fundamental theorems of welfare economics stipulate that competitive markets are conducive to Pareto efficient outcomes and that any efficient equilibrium is achievable through competitive markets with the required redistribution of income and wealth. Thus, whereas the first theorem remains silent as to whether the allocation is fair or just, the second implies that market failures provide the most important economic argument for government intervention. Market failures are the manifestation of inefficiencies stemming from many sources including information asymmetry, monopolies, transaction costs, and externalities where individual actions affect the utility of others. Market failures are intrinsically related to conditions of imperfect information. For instance, high information costs can inhibit arbitrage activities, which are needed to ensure the law of the single price. The economics of information, proposed by Joseph Stiglitz, has evolved over the past half-century into an integral branch of economics aimed at explaining the implications of information asymmetries on economic policy. In this regard, Joseph Stiglitz (2017) notes that "information failures are associated with numerous other market failures, including incomplete risk markets, imperfect capital markets, and imperfections in competition, enhancing opportunities for rent seeking and exploitation." Because of the important role of governments in addressing market failures, the economics of information has raised interest in institutional economics, as another branch of economics concerned with institutional arrangements for economic behaviour. But as noted by Eric Crampton (2007), the same informational problems that explain the occurrence of market failures in the first place may also hinder the necessary government intervention to improve economic outcomes.

Arguably, it is the failure of governments to mitigate market failures that results in inefficient economic outcomes, unrealized potential growth, and unfair income distribution. In particular, government policy failures to correct the distortive incentives for rent seeking and exploitation are inevitably conducive to economic injustice and macroeconomic instability. For instance, it is obvious that insofar as labour markets are governed by the iron law of wages, workers cannot afford consumption above the subsistence levels sufficient to cover the bare necessaries of life. The Ricardian notion of a "natural" price of labour converging toward long-term levels of minimum wages needed to preserve the physiological capacity to work and breed a sufficient number of children to sustain active population may be predicated on the Malthusian theory of population. But it is difficult to argue that the iron law no longer casts a shadow on labour markets, collective bargaining agreements, and constitutes, in turn, a primary source of poverty trap and economic inequality.[8]

The imperfect wage adjustments and the existence of a "natural" rate of unemployment constitute significant market failures, but they do not seem to warrant serious government intervention. Part of the reason may have to do with the intricacies of political and technocratic calculus. *The Economist* (2022) argues that an "overreliance on boffins lulls politicians into the idea that there is a correct answer to every problem. Rather than accepting that there are competing interests, whether based on economics or class or place, technocrats turn politics into an impossible search for nirvana. Clever-clever solutions beat simple ones. Puritans fear that someone, somewhere, may be happy; technocrats worry that a middle-class family may enjoy a free lunch." Thus, even when market failures are evident and fortitude is needed, government inertia is often justified based on economic theory as a rational choice.

There is, however, no for government intervention, as argued by John Kenneth Galbraith (1987, pp. 84–85) because even an injection of capital and technology cannot elevate the market price of labour indefinitely. He adds that it is difficult to defend Ricardo's reputation from the serious implications of his fundamental conclusions, and his commitment to the inevitable misery of those who live under capitalism. He condemned the arguments about the futility and error of government intervention, which derive from Ricardo's principle: "Like all other contracts, wages should be left to the fair and free competition of the market, and should never be controlled by the interference of the legislature." The iron law of wages is not consistent either with Adam Smith's arguments about social harmony and the notion of Pareto optimality developed later as part of welfare economics. As expressed in *The Wealth of Nations*, "[w]hat improves the circumstances of the greater part can never be regarded as an inconveniency to the whole. No society can surely be flourishing and happy, of which the far greater part of the members are poor and miserable. It is but equity, besides, that they who feed, clothe, and lodge the whole body of the people, should have such a share of the produce of their own labour as to be themselves tolerably well fed, clothed, and lodged." In this sense, fairness demands that wages should not be dictated by the "natural" rate of profit but be commensurate with the level of welfare and standards of living in the whole society. Poverty and neglect can be, indeed, the result of income inequalities caused by market failures in terms of unfair labour remunerations and inefficient government regulations. Thus, it can be argued that the government's failure to exert corrective actions to mitigate market failures is conducive to a maldistribution of income and wealth, which precludes convergence toward efficient economic equilibrium.

There remain deep concerns that the Arrow–Debreu general equilibrium model suffers also from serious conceptual limitations. The restrictive model assumptions that market participants are price-takers preclude the existence of an overriding cause-and-effect mechanism that explains departure from equilibrium and ensures convergence. In this regard, Mark Blang (1980, pp. 166–167) points to the "curious anomaly that perfect competition is possible only when a market is in equilibrium. It is impossible when a market is out of equilibrium for the simple reason that perfectly competitive producers are price-takers, not price-makers. But if no one can make the price, how do prices ever change to produce convergence on equilibrium? This problem is perhaps a minor blemish in an apparatus which has no role for money, for stock markets, for bankruptcies, or for true entrepreneurship." There are attempts, as in Peter H. Friesen (1979), to extend the model to include financial markets, but the essential features and implications of macroeconomic equilibrium models are likely to remain unperturbed.

There is arguably, an inevitable trade-off in economics between rigour and relevance. Indeed, as noted by Mark Blang (1980, p. 167), "Theories that are truly rigorous are rarely practically relevant and theories that are eminently relevant are rarely analytically rigorous. If we argue in favour of a market economy compared to a command economy because of the dynamic characteristics of a competitive regime in fostering technical dynamism and cost-cutting innovations, and perhaps even political freedom to match economic freedom, our argument is anything but rigorous; it is, however, extremely relevant. On the other hand, if we prove that multimarket equilibrium is possible no matter how large the number of markets, our demonstration is rigorous but has no relevance whatsoever." The existence of multiple solutions to the mathematical equations describing the economic equilibrium results in locally unique points of dynamic attraction, which can be finite or infinite.

Macroeconomic equilibrium may be unique when market clearance takes place with a unique set of prices, but the non-uniqueness of dynamic equilibrium occurs when the laws of motion are conducive to several asymptotic states. The conditions of multiple equilibria can be described by several factors including irrational exuberance, a phrase first used by former Chairman of the Federal Reserve Board Alan Greenspan, and subsequently defined by Robert J. Shiller (2000) as the psychological basis for speculative bubbles. Asset bubbles can be conducive to multiple equilibria because, as argued by Costas Azariadis (2008), they are indeterminate in their initial states and laws of motion, with essentially unpredictable deflation pressures depending on shifts in investor sentiment.

However, some critics hold that economics has already developed beyond the old Arrow–Debreu framework of general equilibrium. Alternative theoretical frameworks include new models of endogenous preferences, asymmetric information, chaos and complexity theory, and applications of game theory. Broadly defined as the mathematical modelling of certain conditions of human conflict and cooperation, game theory may have enjoyed several decades of contributions to both normative and descriptive research. It is the seminal contributions of John von Neumann (1903–1957) and Oskar Morgenstern (1902–1977) and their joint work on *Theory of Games and Economic Behavior* (1944) that provide the theoretical foundations of game theory.[9] As noted by Oskar Morgenstern (1964), "the theory is and was designed to give meaning to what common sense vaguely calls 'rational behaviour.' What does it mean to be rational in a situation where the outcome does not depend on you alone, nor on chance alone, but on others also who have opposite aims but likewise lack the ability to achieve them because they depend on your actions too?"

Notwithstanding the clarity of its theoretical objectives, game theory became the subject of strong criticism on the grounds of unimpressive results. Anthony Kelly (2003) suggests that part of the criticism is based on the main issues of rationality, inconsistency, and indeterminacy. Serious criticism is levied against the indeterminacy of economic outcomes which do not necessarily represent a social optimum. As argued by Frank Ackerman and Alejandro Nadal (2004, pp. 3–4), "In the prisoner's dilemma, the ubiquitous introductory example of game theory, the optimum (short sentences if neither prisoner confesses) is unstable, while the worst outcome (long sentences if both confess) is stable. More generally, the 'folk theorem' of game theory -a result that was apparently so damning that no one wanted to claim credit for it- shows that essentially anything can happen in an infinitely repeated game. In such a game, multiple equilibria are the norm, while theory in general places very few restrictions on the possible outcomes of the game." Thus, while game theory is presented as a promising development beyond the old Arrow–Debreu framework of general equilibrium, it is associated with the same concerns about the existence of multiple equilibria and unstable outcomes.

The Science and Dogma of Neoclassical Economics

Economics can be regarded as presenting either dogmatic assertions about fundamental principles accepted at face value and unchallenged as true or scientific propositions susceptible of falsification and verification. Understanding the methodology of neoclassical economics is important because testing the validity of economic theories depends on setting the appropriate standards of proof and methods of logical thinking. As argued by Thomas Edward Cliffe Leslie (1825–1882), "no branch of science, no scientific body, confines itself to the observation of phenomena without seeking to interpret them or to ascertain their laws" (Leslie 1879, p. 376). In order to understand the essence of economic phenomena, such as recurrent financial crises and economic recessions, an examination of the nature of underlying causes not just their periodicity is essential. Statistical science should be concerned with the laws of social phenomena, as well as the phenomena themselves, as further argued by Thomas Leslie (1879, pp. 376–377) "A theory of a decennial recurrency of commercial crises, for example, was based on the occurrence of crises in 1837, 1847, and 1857. Had the cause of commercial crises been examined, it would have been discovered that they are extremely various and uncertain in their occurrence; that a war, a bad harvest, a drain of the precious metals, anything, in short, which produces a panic, may cause a crisis; and as there is no decennial periodicity in the causes, there can be none in the effects." Thus, economic inquiry requires that economic phenomena should be the subject of not only measurement but also sagacious observation, measurement, and rigorous logic.

The recurrence of financial crises in more recent times is not just a matter of statistical analysis, but the subject of profound thought about the inherent instability of interest-based financial systems barely connected with investment risk and investor sentiment in the real economy. In a quest to achieve the level of respectability enjoyed by natural sciences, it is tempting to dispense with inquiry into psychology, theology, sentiment, and mental forces at work in order to establish the natural laws that govern economic phenomena. Bold attempts to recognize as natural laws the assumed associations between, for instance, wages and food and between desire for wealth and aversion to work can be used to justify the Ricardian notion of reducing the "natural" price of labour to the price of labour subsistence. Such attempts can be useful also in dismissing policies aimed at full employment, and advocating instead, a "natural" rate of unemployment and a "natural" rate of interest that neither stimulates nor depresses the real economy. The term "natural" may be the source of confusion in Political Economy as well as in the philosophy of law. In his treatise about the reign of natural law, Pierre Samuel Dupont de Nemours (1739–1817) proposed the notion of "*Physiocratie*," where he defined natural law and the role of government in the organization of human society. Natural law is thus defined as inclusive of physical and moral laws, arguing that "natural laws can be either physical laws or moral laws. We mean here by physical law the regulated course of any physical event or the natural order evidently most advantageous to humankind. We mean here by moral law the rule of all human action of the moral order that is in conformity with the physical order and most advantageous to humankind" (de Nemours 1879, p. 32; authors' translation).[10]

Thus, it may be argued that the *laisser faire* economic doctrine is derived from the system of natural liberty, in compliance with the ideal code of nature, including the "natural" rights of liberty, and "natural" rights of property. However, John Kells Ingram (1823–1907) in *A History of Political Economy* argues that the *laisser-faire* doctrine, long considered as the watchword of economic orthodoxy extending from the system of natural liberty, "is a result not so much of scientific thought as of the pressure of practical needs – a cause which has modified the successive forms of economic opinion more than theorists are willing to acknowledge. Social exigencies will force the hands of statesmen, whatever their attachment to abstract formulas; and politicians have practically turned their backs on *laisser faire*" (Ingram 1888, p. 243) (italics in original).

The issue remains, however, as to whether positive legislation that should be an extension of natural laws, is conducive to positive outcomes and a "natural" organization of society to achieve economic prosperity for all humankind. Any natural-law system, as argued by O'Brien (2004, p. 27), involves a set of fundamental propositions, including the existence of an underlying order in natural phenomena, which are discoverable by reasoning through observation and innate moral sense. The discovery of the natural order results in the formulation of natural laws, which should be reflected in positive legislation. He further argues that "a natural-law system may also involve the following further propositions: that natural laws are productive of immutable forces which man cannot deflect or impede - this will be called *determinism*; that if freedom is accorded, then society will progress harmoniously to a better state - this will be called *harmony theory*; and that therefore the operation of natural laws requires a great degree of freedom to achieve their ends - this will be called the doctrine of *natural liberty*" (italics in original). Thus, the application of natural laws to economic phenomena is predicated on compelling evidence of the existence of an underlying order in economic phenomena. It is conditional on the notion that the economic order is discoverable through reasoning. It is based on the notion that the discovery of the economic order allows for the formulation of economic laws, which in turn, pave the way for the establishment of positive legislation.

Given the above proposition of the natural law system, it is noted that at the heart of scientific discovery lies the problem of induction, which poses the question of whether, and under what conditions, inductive inferences are justified. In this respect, Lee Loevinger (1993, p. 151) argues that the validity of any conclusion is a matter of the standard of proof that depends on the validity of the process leading to that conclusion. Whereas the process in mathematics relies on compliance to rigid formal rules internally consistent within the logical system, it is rather intuitive and does not necessarily follow rigorous rules in law and most other disciplines. In contrast, "[s]cience frequently uses mathematical reasoning, but its application to data necessarily involves reasoning or assumptions that are less than mathematically rigorous. Syllogistic reasoning, Bayes' theorem, Boolean algebra and other forms of logic are particular methods of attempting to prescribe formally rigorous rules that will guarantee valid reasoning."

Whether the formal rigorous rules guarantee valid reasoning is rather a controversial issue in scientific endeavours. In the *Logic of Scientific Discovery*, Karl Popper (1902–1994) argued that an attempt to derive the principle of induction (or principle of universal causation suggested by Immanuel Kant (1724–1804)) from experience would break down because it leads to infinite regression. There is no justification either for inferring universal statements from singular ones because it does not matter how many times a singular or basic statement is found to be valid, a conclusion about its universality remains false. The widely used example is that it does not matter how many white swans we may have observed, it suffices to observe one single black swan to prove that the conclusion that all swans are white is wrong. It is also argued that statements decided by agreement are not universal but singular, and if scientific statements are required to be objective, and the basic empirical statements are required to be inter-subjectively testable, then *"there can be no ultimate statements in science"* (Popper 1935 [2002], p. 25, italics in original) Since theories are tested through the deduction of statements of a lesser level of universality, these inter-subjectively testable statements must be tested, and the deduction and testing process would be repeated *ad infinitum*.

Most importantly, Popper (1935 [2002], p. 91) argues that from a logical perspective, "the testing of a theory depends upon basic statements whose acceptance or rejection, in its turn, depends upon our decisions. Thus it is *decisions* which settle the fate of theories" (italics in original). A recourse to probability in evaluating the validity of statements based on inductive inference should be justified on a new principle of induction, which itself should be justified, and so *ad infinitum*.[11] Perhaps it is because the decisions themselves depend in part on choices guided by utility that Popper reached the conclusion that the various difficulties associated with inductive logic are "insurmountable" (Popper 1935 [2002], p. 6). With respect to the difficulties associated with inductive logic, further insights about the probabilistic nature of theoretical predictions are provided by Mark Blang (1980, p. 22), who suggests that "Whenever the predictions of a theory are probabilistic in nature (and what predictions are not -any laboratory experiment designed to confirm even so simple a relationship as Boyle's law will never find the product of pressure and volume an exact constant), the notion of assessing evidence without invoking normative methodological principles is an absurdity."

The central argument is that there is still a need for normative principles in the validation or refutation of competing theories, including sociological factors such as hierarchy, and reference groups. The ultimate decisions to refute or validate theories may be also reflective of epistemological rationalism including *a priori* methodological rules based on scepticism against new ideas. As argued by Mark Blang (1980, p. 22) "scientists typically have a greater fear of accepting a falsehood than of failing to acknowledge a truth; that is, they behave as if the cost of Type II errors were greater than that of Type I errors. We may deplore this attitude as stodgy conservatism, a typical manifestation of the unwillingness of those with vested interests in received doctrines to welcome new ideas, or we may fail it as a manifestation of healthy scepticism, the hallmark of all that is salutary in the scientific attitude. But whatever our point of view, we must perforce conclude that in this way what are considered methodological rules enter into the very question of whether a statistical fact is accepted as a fact."

This brings the discussion about economics as a science back full circle, as the initial recourse of the discipline to scientific methods to establish natural laws for economic theory is met with the reality that it is rather human decisions that ultimately settle the fate of scientific theories. Attempts to meet the rigorous rules of exact science should confront the reality that there are no canons of scientific methodology. Economics it may be argued is not a science of precise laws, but its basic statements may only be expressed as economic tendencies. Indeed, as argued by Todd G. Buchholz (2021 [1989], p. 383), "higher output usually means lower prices, except when Weblenesque goods enter the scene. A higher money supply usually means lower interest rates, except when fears of inflation push interest rates higher. Stock prices usually represent rational predictions of future cash flows, except when 'animal spirits' panic or excite investors into dramatic swings. Investors usually take risks until the marginal benefits equal the marginal costs, except for Schumpeterian Übermensch entrepreneurs, who perceive values better than the market." Thus, in every aspect of economic exchange from production to money supply, finance, and real investment, each basic statement is expressed in terms of rules and exceptions. It is arguably difficult to build a general equilibrium theory with imprecise principles. It is noted, however, that "[t]hese imprecise forces that disrupt the scientific approach are not necessarily irrational (that is, crazy). They may be non-rational and unpredictable, as in quantum physics, where electrons do not act crazily – they simply defy our current methods of modelling. As economists, we haven't figured out everything."

Thus, part of the reason for the difficulties of objective inquiry into economic phenomena following the methodology of natural phenomena, is that the principle of *determinism* is constantly violated. Indeed, economic laws are not based on immutable forces that human action can neither deflect nor impede. Human actions are rather the essence of economic phenomena, and any discoverable economic order and economic laws are reflective of human action not independent from it.

With respect to the *harmony theory*, it is noted that economic investigation should be aimed at promoting economic prosperity for the whole society. As argued by John Kells Ingram (1888, p. 241), "if we overlook this, our economics will become a play of logic or a manual for the market, rather than a contribution to social science; whilst wearing an air of completeness, they will be in truth one-sided and superficial. Economic science is something far larger than the Catallactics to which some have wished to reduce it." Thus, given the difficulties in establishing the existence of an underlying order in economic phenomena through observation and inductive reasoning, it is left for reasoning based on the innate moral sense to provide relevant evidence. Without recourse to the innate moral sense to make decisions on basic statements about the existence of economic order, it is difficult, in turn, to formulate economic laws and consistent positive legislation.

The difficulties in understanding the direction of causality and the existence of confounding variables leading to spurious associations between economic variables affect the ability of economic models to reflect the complex structure of the economy, capture its dynamic workings, and provide reliable predictions. If theories are to be judged solely on the basis of predictive power, then economic theories including the general equilibrium theory may not be taken seriously. Reuven Brenner (1994, p. 19) argues that "there cannot be such a thing as a "general theory" about any of the following questions: How does the general level of a government's expenditures, in particular, its debts and deficits, affect either the total production of goods and services or the national income earned from production? How do the debt and deficits affect employment? How do the debt and deficits affect the allocation of resources between current consumption and investment?"

The argument is that it is not possible to determine the net effects of government expenditures, debt, and deficit because they may or may not raise consumption or decrease investment. Likewise, near-zero interest rates intended to provide incentives for borrowing and spending, can be also a source of speculative bubbles and financial instability. Ambiguity about the long-term impact of changes in interest rates on the behaviour of savers and investors, adds to difficulties in isolating the factors that affect national income, employment, and economic growth. As the direction of causality between the economic variables embedded in any theory remains indeterminate, it is difficult to draw strong conclusions from weak premises. Thus, part of the reason for difficulties in articulating a consistent theory of economic equilibrium is that the theoretical arguments about convergence toward equilibrium remain inconsistent, and that corrective policies following the second theorem of welfare economics are, in turn, bound to be erratic and ineffective.

It is difficult to ignore the criticism levied against the pursuance of an elusive status of exact science for a discipline whose intellectual construct can hardly be contained in an abstract theory with precise logical statements. John Neville Keynes (1852–1949) argued in *The Scope and Method of Political Economy* (1890, p. 145) that not all science is of the demonstrative type, and that "it would be a great mistake to narrow our conception of political economy to the pure theory alone, simply in order to attain perfection of logical form." Descriptive economics, as argued by Hollis and Nell (1975) also, can dispense with optimizing models. However, "no science of any kind can be divorced from ethical considerations, as suggested by Kenneth E. Boulding (1969, p. 2). No science can be freed from the high values placed not only on exact measurement and careful experiment but also on veracity and objectivity. "The question as to exactly what values and ethical propositions are essential to the scientific subculture may be in some dispute. The fact that there are such values cannot be disputed." Thus, as the debate about the science and dogma of neoclassical economics continues, and the longing for exact science remains irresistible, the temptation to lay down economic principles as undeniably true should be equally resisted. Perhaps, if the difference between natural and economic phenomena is only of one degree, that degree is a huge one. And if the difference between economic theories and economic realities is only of one degree, that degree is an even eager one.

ECONOMICS BETWEEN THE RIGOUR OF MATHEMATICS AND RELEVANCE OF MORALITY

As explained above, economic theory has expanded with extensive efforts in theoretical and empirical modelling, but the question remains as to whether the rigours of mathematics have shifted economics away from the restraints of moral philosophy into the realm of science. Readers may be excused for thinking that economists who do not always concur on the essence of the discipline may be less likely to agree on its methodology. Disagreements about both the theoretical and methodological foundations abound. The historical fact is that for Aristotle and early philosophers including Saint Thomas Aquinas, economics was not considered as a theoretical science but a practical one.[12] Also, the economic thinking of Adam Smith and other classical economists deeply versed in moral philosophy reflects a cognition of the natural law tradition. Individuals should be free to pursue their objectives insofar that such freedom does not abridge the rights of others to do the same. The harmony theory is consistent with the doctrine of natural liberty and the corollary of harmonious social progress, but it stands in contrast to Herbert Spencer (1820–1903)'s theory of *Social Statics*, which favours a version of economic and social *laisser-faire*. It is also at odds with his arguments about the evolution of society driven by the mechanism of natural selection and survival of the fittest.

Thus, as argued by O'Brien (2004, p. 29), "The physical scientists were trying to find a harmony in nature through empiricism and the experimental method; and the natural-law philosophers tried to find the same in society. The economists who followed the philosophers were however much less convinced of the inherent harmony. But economics grew out of the natural-law systems; it was long treated as part of a comprehensive social science, moral philosophy." Nevertheless, Wesley Phoa et al. (2007) argue that economics is in a "phase of transition from a 'dismal science' whose conclusions can hardly be proved to a 'hard science' firmly rooted in empirical facts so that its conclusions and its theoretical foundations can be empirically proven as is the case with the physical sciences." As noted also by Thomas Edward Cliffe Leslie (1879, p. 404), no science can reach perfection and it should be judged on the appropriateness of its methods of investigation rather than the extent of its progress. However, given the disagreements about the essence of economics and its strained relationship with mathematics, a smooth transition from dismal to exact science may prove to be rather difficult.[13]

To illustrate this point, it is noted for instance that the principle of ergodicity proposed by Paul Samuelson (1915–2009) was regarded as a necessary mathematical axiom to advance economics from history to science. Indeed, Samuelson (1969, p. 184) argued that "economics as a science assumes the ergodic axiom." The notion that, conditional on the set of available information, the expected value of a random variable must be a fair game, is shown to be useful in the examination of market efficiency. But the ergodic axiom invited also criticism centred on the significance of its implications for economic analysis. It is essentially argued that what ergodicity means in the context of economics is not clear. Sheila Dow (2005) contends that the economic system is rather non-ergodic as there is no reason to assume that structures will remain stable. The individual behaviour of economic agents is likely to be stochastic, and thus unpredictable, because it is driven by sentiments and complex motivations. As argued by Donald W. Katzner (2003, p. 566), "[t]he unidirectional movement of time in individuals' lives means that tomorrow is not, and in many respects cannot be, the same as today or yesterday. Thus, mathematics based on assumptions of ergodicity, or the idea that the forces determining economic environments, endowments, preferences, and objectives will establish and repeat fixed patterns, can sit oddly with the actual facts of human experience."

Indeed, human beings are not inanimate objects, and their behaviour may obey complex motivation systems. This implies that in the absence of ergodicity, future patterns of behaviour may not be predictable with the precision required by mathematical systems. As a result, "when the bridges break down for these or other reasons, the fault is not with the mathematics, but with the economics to which that mathematics relates" (Katzner 2003, p. 566). Also, Miguel Carrión Alvarez and Dirk Ehnts (2016) argue that it is not possible to provide empirical evidence as mathematical systems can be ergodic or non-ergodic, but the economic reality cannot, simply because the economic system is not a mathematical system. They concur with Paul Davidson (2015, p. 7)'s argument that axioms used as the basis for the development of a given theory must be accepted as true, necessitate no proof, and they add that no proof, in fact, can be given. The natural question arises, then, as to how an "axiomatic" statement that needs no proof, and no proof can ever be established, can be in fact accepted as a universal truth.

It was William Stanley Jevons (1835–1882) who set the agenda for the adoption of mathematical methods in economic analysis. Indeed, Jevons argued in *The Theory of Political Economy* (1871, p. 3) that "Economics, if it is to be a science at all, must be a mathematical science," He argued that the simple elements, including wealth, utility, value, commodity, labour, land, and capital, upon which the science of Political Economy depends should be treated with the most care and precision. As "value depends entirely upon utility," an examination of the nature of the laws of thought, philosophy of mathematics, and logical empiricism is important in understanding the philosophy of economics. He is widely credited for the transformation of economic thought from classical to neoclassical economics. The recourse to mathematical methods in the analysis of economic equilibrium resulted in the development by Léon Walras of the marginal theory of value and the general equilibrium theory. There are competing views as to whether the Walrasian theory of exchange through *tâtonnement* has benefited or suffered from seminal contributions by several economists including Vilfredo Pareto (1848–1923) and Knut Wicksell (1851–1926), among others. The derivation of the conditions for Pareto optimal allocation is both regarded as a significant attempt to consolidate the relation between economic theory and the real economy. It is also regarded as instrumental in the demise of the Walrasian model of equilibrium, as argued by Alan Kirman (2021), among others.[14] Mathematical economics, which was expected to advance the discipline and reconcile economists about controversial issues in economic theory, became itself, paradoxically enough, the subject of controversy.

A desire to gain scientific respectability may explain in part, as suggested by Donald Katzner (2003, the increasing role of mathematics in economic analysis.[15] However, Thomas Edward Cliffe Leslie (1879, p. 241) argued that "[t]he bane of political economy has been the haste of its students to possess themselves of a complete and symmetrical system, solving all the problems before it with mathematical certainty and exactness. The very attempt shows an entire misconception of the nature of those problems, and of the means available for their solution." At the same time, the desire to view economics as a science can be also regarded as one of the reasons for resistance to change in the discipline.

Also, John Kenneth Galbraith (1987, p. 284) noted that "in the academic world, where economics is taught, the standard of intellectual precision is set by the hard sciences. To the intellectual reputation of chemists, physicists, biologists and microbiologists, economists and other social scientists, perhaps inevitably, aspire. This requires that the ultimately valid propositions of economics be essentially given, like the structure of neutrons, protons, atoms, and molecules. Once fully discovered, they are known forever." Thus, it is perhaps a sense of security that mathematics projects in an uncertain world that some economists prefer to maintain and enjoy the established orderliness in the theoretical modelling of the real economy. The sense of comfort and confidence in regulating the economic reality with mathematical equations may be also the source of resistance to change of paradigm in economic thinking.

Critical arguments about the usefulness of mathematical economics stem from the perceived fundamental flaws in connecting the abstract world of mathematics with the reality of economic life. In this respect, Subroto Roy (1989, pp. 161–162) argues that "[n]either mathematical economists nor their critics seem to have asked whether modern mathematical economics *can* be made to say all that has been claimed for it. It is true that mathematics *by itself* is silent even about the great questions of physics such as whether or not actual space is euclidean or non-euclidean or euclidean in the small and non-euclidean in the large (as Hilbert and probably Frege and Russel and Wittgenstein would have maintained) then is it *logically* possible for it to be made to answer such momentous questions in political economy as to what happens to be the optimum scope of civil government everywhere or anywhere?" (italics in original). Thus, the projection of economic phenomena on abstract mathematical domains coupled with the apparent independence of mathematics from empirical analysis raises some philosophical difficulties about the practical bearing of mathematical concepts and theorems upon economic life. In particular, it is not clear whether mathematical propositions in economics can be construed as basic statements that are *true* or universal statements *known* to be true.

An "amoral economic theory," in the words of Gunnar Myrdal (1987, p. 274), is pursued with a complete neglect of the fact that the original foundations of economics lie in moral philosophy. For instance, arguments about welfare economics are advanced in terms of individual or social utility. "But if the approach is not entirely meaningless, it has a meaning only in terms of a forlorn hedonistic psychology, and a utilitarian moral philosophy built upon that psychology." It is hardly surprising as argued again by Gunnar Myrdal (1987, p. 274), that "the psychologists and philosophers have left the economists alone and undisturbed in their futile exercise." Part of the reason for the lack of interdisciplinary interest in economic theory is that it is developed on peculiar utilitarian elements of moral philosophy that have no basis in human nature. For instance, it is difficult to discern the moral philosophy behind David Ricardo's conception of the "natural" price of labour as that which allows labourers to subsist and perpetuate their race. In this respect, Thomas Edward Cliffe Leslie (1879, pp. 384–385) argued that Ricardo "disposed altogether with psychology, and with all inquiry into the mental forces at work... Had he been an English Lasalle or Karl Marx, and his main subject to sow enmity between capital and labour, he could not have devised a doctrine better adapted to the purpose."

With respect also to the absence of morality and ethics in the welfare theory, Kenneth E. Boulding (1910–1993) noted in *Economics as a Moral Science* (1969, pp. 5–6) that Pareto-optimality is often assumed to be self-evident, when in fact it relies on implausible ethical propositions. The conditions of Pareto optimality imply that "there is no malevolence anywhere in the system. It implies, likewise, that there is no benevolence, the niceness of economists not quite extending as far as good will. It assumes selfishness, that is, the independence of individual preference functions, such that it makes no difference to me whether I perceive you as either better off or worse off. Anything less descriptive of the human condition could hardly be imagined." However, the abstraction of economic theory from values and sentiments may be explained by the reliance on exchange relations as a tacit social organizer. Exchange, however, is not the only facilitator of human and economics relationships. Trust and learning process play also an important role in the functioning of markets, division of labour and allocation of resources. Exchange relations are, indeed, more likely to be repeated among those who have a positive exchange history. Thus, exchange relations are not merely the outcome of the maximization of utility, which may or may not be driven by sentiment, but certainly governed by trust.

Rationality as the Hard Core of Economic Theory

An exodus from moral philosophy may be explained in part by the belief that mathematical economics cannot be developed on the foundations of moral sentiments. As a substitute for the aggregate system of complex human motivations and feelings, economic rationality is believed to be more amenable to analytical modelling using the mathematical methods of optimization.[16] As noted by Blaug (1992, p. 230), there is a strong perception that the rationality postulate is so pervasive in neoclassical economics that it is virtually impossible to develop any economic theory without utility maximization. Thus, the utility maximization paradigm provides the basis for the examination of the consumers' choice problem or the firm's profit maximization in a competitive economy. Katzner (2003, p. 571) argues that economic rationality has its foundations in cultural conditions, and it should not be surprising that rationality represented by constrained utility maximization is held as a methodological necessity in societies where self-interest is dominant. Consumer behaviour may not be necessarily "rational" in societies where optimization based on the logic of self-interest is not dominant. This implies that the rational behaviour of economic agents may be driven by various factors including moral values, altruism and benevolence, *inter alia*.

Invariably, however, economic theory defines rationality as the pursuit of self-interest associated with an internal consistency of choice. A textbook definition, following Gregory Mankiw (2016), suggests that given the available opportunities, rational people systematically and purposefully attempt to achieve their objectives. They are assumed to make decisions, not just often but systematically, in consideration of the relationship between marginal benefits and marginal costs. Rationality dictates that action is undertaken only under the condition that its marginal benefit is higher than its marginal cost. Walter Bagehot (1880, p. 5) who placed business and commerce at the heart of political economy, argued that man seeks to achieve the most benefits with the least costs, and added that as a matter of course, "we know that this is not so, that men are not like this; but we assume it for simplicity's sake, as an [sic] hypothesis. And this deceives many excellent people, for from deficient education they have very indistinct ideas what an abstract science is."

This definition of economic rationality fails, however, to recognize that internal consistency of choice may be also conducive to persistence in error. Gao and Schmidt (2005) suggest that there is sufficient empirical evidence that economic agents are not necessarily utility maximizers as they often make sub-optimal choices and remain nevertheless satisfied. Amartya Sen (1987, pp. 13–14) notes that "[i]f a person does exactly the opposite of what would help achieving what he or she would want to achieve, and does this with flawless internal consistency (always choosing exactly the opposite of what will enhance the occurrence of things he or she wants and values), the person can scarcely be seen as rational, even if that dogged consistency inspires some kind of an astonished admiration on the part of the observer."

Systematic patterns of irrational behaviour introduce another level of complexity in the definition of economic rationality. Indeed, Joseph Stiglitz (1991, p. 138) argues that "advances in sociology and psychology (see, for example, the work of Tversky) have shown that there may be systematic patterns to individual behaviour, even when they are irrational. Economic science is concerned with exploring predictable behaviour; the fact that behaviour is not rational, in some sense, does not mean that is not predictable." Thus, internal consistency may not suffice in the definition of rational choice. It may be argued that rational behaviour demands consistency, but rationality does not derive from self-interest alone as it can be justified also with reference to individual codes of behaviour that may appear to be, at times, in conflict with the exclusive pursuance of self-interest. This implies that rationality cannot be defined exclusively in terms of persistent pursuance of self-interest.

Given the difficulties in defining rationality on the basis of self-interest alone, the notion of bounded rationality acknowledges the reality that economic decisions depend on limited cognitive faculties that constrain problem-solving abilities, and on the nature of information that may be incomplete and unavailable on timely basis. Thus, economic rationality does not necessarily imply "rational" choices, but "reasonable" ones defined by finite intelligence and incomplete information. There are many interpretations of rationality and bounded rationality. Herbert Simon (1984 [1963]) refers to "limited rationality" and "approximate rationality." As argued by Esther-Mirjam Sent (2018), *bounded self-interest* can be defined as the propensity of human beings to sacrifice their own interest to help others.

The principle of economic rationality paves the way to the corollary of consumer sovereignty. Indeed, insofar as individual behaviour is driven by self-interest, both the consumer decisions and producer decisions are bound to be governed by utility maximization. Consumer sovereignty derives from the fact that it is consumer choices that define producer choices, not vice versa. The direction of causality implies that it is consumer satisfaction that rules over producer interests. In this respect, John Kenneth Galbraith 1971, p. 73) argued that consumer sovereignty does not allow for socially desirable upper boundaries for individual consumption. As there are no consumption thresholds, there are no binding conditions and constraints on producers either to satisfy unlimited wants. Thus, he noted that "the instruction of the neoclassical model to the economist on this is strikingly clear. The consumer wants more. Theirs not to reason why, theirs but to satisfy." It is further argued that the assumption of consumer sovereignty obscures questions about cultural factors that have an important bearing on consumer behaviour.

The question also arises as to how the assumptions of consumer sovereignty with the principle of scarce resources can be reconciled. The orthodox definition of economics rests also on the notion of scarcity, which is part of the legacy of Friedrich Hayek's arguments against Keynesian economics. Regarding scarcity as a universal law, Lionel Robbins (1889–1984) defined the entire discipline of economics in terms of scarce means, describing it as "the science which studies human behaviour as a relationship between ends and scarce means which have alternative uses" (Robbins 1932, p. 16). Thus, economic decisions that involve a devotion of time and scarce resources to achieve one end result in abandoning the satisfaction of another. The assumption of resource scarcity may also serve the broader interest of producers. In his critique of self-regulating markets, Karl Polanyi (1886–1964) suggested that in market-oriented economies, goods are assumed to be scarce in order to be valuable as commodities.

The assumption of scarcity represents also a marked shift from traditional patterns of thought. As alternative cultures and worldviews imply alternative economic assumptions and theories, it is the notion of natural abundance that dominated the debate among ancient Greek writers about *oikonomia*. From their perspective, argued Dotan Leshem (2016, p. 226), "the main task of economic rationality is to advance the good life as they understood it, which means support for philosophy, for involvement in public life, and also for not giving in to what they viewed as the unnatural urge to pursue economic goals or luxuries for their own sake." Thus, given the competing notions of scarcity and abundance, the elevation of the scarcity postulate to the status of an irrefutable universal principle required an illogical leap in thinking. It may be argued that a shortage of space, usually construed as scarcity of arable land, is responsible for food scarcity. The counter-argument is that hunger, starvation, destitution, poverty, and famine are not the inevitable result of a shortage economy, but the natural outcome, as suggested by Amartya Sen among others, of political instability, and inconsistent social and economic policies. The shortage economy should not be confounded with an economy of scarcity, which shapes the thinking of governments to avoid measures that address market failures, and absolve policymakers from the responsibility to design and implement economic policies that ensure the basic needs of the poor are fully and unconditionally met under all internal and external contingencies.

Rational choice under scarcity reinforces individual bias toward risk aversion and shapes the government policies of austerity. Alain Parguez (2013) argues that austerity is "a permanent regime devoid of any sound foundations," and that it is irrelevant to anticyclical or stabilizing policies.

Indeed, the Malthusian prophesy of impending food scarcity in the face of a burgeoning population constitutes an untestable empirical prediction about a potentially capital-scarce, labour-abundant economy that did not come to pass. Dismal prophecies are testament to the fallibility of fragmented human knowledge about important aspect of nature and human existence, including scarcity and abundance. A distinction is usually made in economic theory between absolute scarcity and relative scarcity. It is argued that the former results from the inability to increase, renew, or substitute resources, whereas the latter results from an inability to satisfy all the desires and needs of consumers. It is clear that absolute scarcity does not invariably apply to physical and non-physical resources since trust and knowledge are not scarce in absolute terms. Most importantly, the principle of scarcity does not hold in knowledge-based economies, and as noted by Geoffrey Martin Hodgson (2001), neither biology nor anthropology lend support to assumptions of universal competition under conditions of scarcity. The real scarcity in the world today, argued Joseph Stiglitz (2017), "is related to our planetary boundaries: if we 'ruin' this planet through an excessive emission of greenhouse gases, we cannot move to another."

There are fundamental flaws in the assumptions underlying economic theory. The notion of consumer sovereignty is not consistent with the argument of resources scarcity. It may be argued that acceptance of the latter should preclude the former. The assumptions of limited resources and unlimited wants seem to be rather contradictory as rationality demands that if resources are, indeed, of limited supply, then consumer wants should be constrained rather than unbounded. Given limited resources, consumer demand should be moderated rather than permitted to grow *ad infinitum*. If it can be plausibly argued that resources are limited, then it should be inevitably admitted that moderating rules and harmonizing limits to individual consumption should be formulated in the stead of promoting the sanctity of consumer sovereignty. As argued by William Redmond (2000), to the extent that consumer behaviour based on self-interest leads to overspending and low saving rates, consumer sovereignty is conducive to deviations from economic rationality. Indeed, unlimited wants lead to excessive consumption and borrowing, which are conducive, in turn, to the formation of asset bubbles, and financial crises that threaten economic stability and human development. Despite the inherent logical inconsistencies, there are no indications that neoclassical economics is ready to abandon the postulates of self-interest, wealth insatiability, resource scarcity, and consumer sovereignty.

Thus, the rationality postulate holds a sacrosanct status in neoclassical economics as an empirically irrefutable metaphysical proposition by virtue of ubiquitous self-interest. Economic theory has created perfectly suitable sacred language where self-interest is regarded as a self-evident truth. It is self-evident by virtue of the assumptions of economic rationality and resources scarcity, which are, in turn, ascertained as true by virtue of human experience. Methodological monism does not admit value judgements and references to alternative worldviews, religious beliefs, or moral convictions. However, suppressing inconvenient worldviews and ethical beliefs does not promote real progress in a subject that is of importance not just to human existence but to the cosmological order as well.

Indeed, Amartya Sen (1987, p. 15) argues that a definition of rationality in terms of self-interest implies "*inter alia* a firm rejection of the 'ethics-related' view of motivation." This argument implies that individual codes of behaviour based on self-interest are exclusive of ethical values. It is possible, however, to regard the rules-based behaviour founded on moral beliefs that transcend individual motivations as rational as well insofar that such a behaviour ensures systematic departure from self-centred decisions. It is difficult to reduce human nature to instincts and motivations based solely on self-interest. In this regard, Adam Smith (1759 [2006], p. 3) argued in *The Theory of Moral Sentiments*, that "how selfish soever man may be supposed, there are evidently some principles in his nature, which interest him in the fortune of others, and render their happiness necessary to him, though he derives nothing from it except the pleasure of seeing it." Thus, it is ironical that in its incessant quest for wholeness and respectability, conventional economics, a discipline traditionally regarded as an integral branch of ethics and moral science, shuns and brushes aside alternative worldviews about resource abundance, altruism, morality, ethics, and religious beliefs.

A crisis of confidence besets economics with the onset of every single financial crisis, which alone should suffice as empirical evidence to warrant a restructuring of the axiomatic foundations of economic theory. There is instead a state of denial about the inevitability of systemic failures and the impotence of macroprudential policies. Financial crises are swiftly dismissed as unpredictable events due to sunspot equilibria rather than by-products of predictable boom-bust credit cycles. In any case, it is difficult for a discipline that sanctifies human rationality and ontological scarcity to justify, on the basis of the economic principle of optimal allocation of resources, the devotion of intellectual capital to the rationalization of speculative asset bubbles and elusive steady-state growth.

There is studious scepticism that further theorizing in terms of refining model assumptions and mathematical modelling of imaginary shadows of the real economy can generate substantive insights that would enhance our ability to understand the implications of economic policies. If economic theory must proceed only by neglecting the real impact of uncertainty on economic behaviour, rent seeking, and the central contradictions of capitalism, among other serious flaws, then it is difficult to resist the conclusion that economic crises are events that economic theory is not designed to predict or prevent in the first place. Thus, in view of the conceptual and methodological difficulties discussed in this chapter, the real question remains as to whether the intellectual discourse about the past and future of Political Economy can be useful in deriving the fundamental principles for the organization of an ideal economy. In the absence of a proper understanding of human nature, human existence, cosmological order, and economic uncertainty, it is clear that economy theory would have nothing to offer in terms of economic principles to promote economic justice and prosperity, except for an arid *laisser-faire*, do-nothing economic policy.

Notes

1. The crisis of modern economics is perhaps best illustrated by the critical notes made by Prof. Charles P. Kindelberger in 1982 prior to the publication in 1983 of a study by Ben Bernanke about the nonmonetary impact of the financial crisis on the economic depression. The work that provided the basis for the Nobel Prize for Bernanke in 2022 was regarded as "a most ingenious solution to a non-problem… If one believes in rational expectations, a natural rate of unemployment, efficient markets, exchange rates continuously at purchasing power parities, there is not much that can be explained about business cycles or financial crises." The comments highlight the fact that there was and there still is a strong denial that real problems exist about major assumptions in modern economics. In particular, there is a clear criticism about the paper's rejection of money illusion on the ground of rationality, and about the adoption of rational assumptions, ignoring thereby the fallacy of composition, where individual participants may be rational but the market as a whole may not.

2. See for instance, Fred D. Miller (1998) for a discussion of Aristotle's economic thinking.
3. Regarding the importance of justice in both Aristotle and Adam Smith's arguments, see for instance, the comparative analyses by Laurence Berns (1994), and Alexander Broadie (2010), among others.
4. See for instance, Jeffrey Sachs (2005) and Peter Singer (2009) who argue that it is a moral obligation to end extreme poverty, which is often accompanied with conditions of powerlessness, by identifying practical ways of providing assistance to the poor to escape the poverty trap.
5. Also, *The Economist* (*The Canon of Economics*, February 24, 2011) notes that "[e]conomics has fragmented in the past 15–20 years, both in subject and technique. No aspect of human behaviour is off-limits and a miscellany of methods are in vogue, adding laboratory experiments, randomized trials and computer simulations to the traditionalist's blackboard and chalk."
6. It is noted that Walras law implies that the sum of excess demand values should be zero irrespective of the conditions of general equilibrium.
7. Kakutani (1941) provided a generalization of Brouwer's fixed point theorem, which is useful in mathematical derivations in general topology as well as in game theory. Indeed, Kakutani fixed-point theorem was also used by John F. Nash (1928–2015) to demonstrate the existence of equilibrium in randomized strategies for finite formal-form games.
8. David Ricardo (1821 [2006], p. 85) argued that "labour, like all other things which are purchased and sold, and which may be increased or diminished in quantity, has its natural and its market price. The natural price of labour is that price which is necessary to enable the labourers, one with another, to subsist and to perpetuate their race, without either increase nor diminution."
9. John von Neumann and Oskar Morgenstern (1944) developed also the foundations of expected utility theory, where rationality is modelled as the maximization of the expected value.
10. The original excerpts in de Nemours (1879, p. 32) are as follows: "*les hommes réunis en societe doivent être assujettis á des lois naturelles & á des lois positives. Les lois naturelles sont ou physiques or morales. On entend ici par loi physique le cours réglé de tout évenement physique de l'ordre naturel évidemment le plus avantageux au genre humain. On entend ici par loi morale la régle de toute action humaine de l'ordre moral conforme a l'ordre physique évidemment le plus avantageux au genre humain.*"
11. Popper (1935 [2002], p. 6) thus argues that "Nothing is gained, moreover, if the principle of induction, in its turn, is taken not as 'true' but only as 'probable'. In short, like every other form of inductive logic, the logic of probable inference, or 'probability logic', leads either to an infinite regress, or to the doctrine of *apriorism*."

12. Donald Boland (2016, p. 25) also argues that "[f]or St. Thomas and all before him back to Aristotle, Economics is not a theoretical science, but a decidedly practical one. The very language used in economic theory, such as value, signifying some good or utility, as the object of human action or behaviour, plainly indicates that the discussion is within a practical science. Yet, the discussion has been treated as if Economics were of a natural or purely theoretical kind."
13. With respect to mathematics, Kenneth E. Boulding (1983, p. 7) notes that "[i]t is customary to divide the world of scholarship into the sciences and the humanities, but this distinction is rather arbitrary. Acquiring scholarly knowledge follows essentially the same processes as acquiring folk knowledge, but in more refined forms. Thus the use of language may be more important and languages used more specialized – the most specialized of all, of course, being mathematics."
14. See for instance, Donald Walker (1987) and Roberto Marchionatti (2007) on the intense debate about the mathematical derivation of Walrasian equilibrium theory, involving Léon Walras, Francis Edgeworth, and Ladislaus von Bortkievicz, among others.
15. Donald Katzner (2003, p. 561) suggests that "mathematics may have become so important in economics for four reasons: (1) to make use of existing human capital, (ii) [sic] to attain scientific respectability, (3) to help assure security with respect to claims of truth, and (4) because economics was created primarily by Western economists to understand Western economic behavior."
16. See for instance, Katzner (2003, p. 573) who argues that "the use of mathematics in economics flows naturally from the subject matter of economics because (Western) economists consider the primary propellant of economic behavior to be culturally determined rationality. And the obvious way to represent that rationality in economic explanation is with the mathematical notion of optimization."

REFERENCES

Ackerman, Frank. 2002. "Still Dead After All These Years: Interpreting the Failure of General Equilibrium Theory." *Journal of Economic Methodology* 9: 119–139.

Ackerman, Frank, and Alejandro Nadal. 2004. *The Flawed Foundations of General Equilibrium*. London: Routledge.

Arrow, Kenneth. 1994. "Beyond General Equilibrium." In *Complexity: Metaphors, Models and Reality*, edited by George. A. Cowan, David Pines, and David Meltzer. Avalon Publishing.

Arrow, Kenneth J., and Gérard Debreu. 1954. "Existence of an Equilibrium for a Competitive Economy." *Econometrica* 22: 265–290.
Azariadis, Costas. 2008. "Multiple Equilibria in Macroeconomics." In *The New Palgrave Dictionary of Economics*, edited by S. N. Durlauf and L. E. Blume. London: Palgrave Macmillan.
Bagehot, Walter. 1880. *Economic Studies*. Edited by Richard Holt Hutton. London: Longmans, Green and Co.
Berns, Laurence. 1994. "Aristotle and Adam Smith on Justice: Cooperation Between Ancients and Moderns." *Review of Metaphysics* 48: 71–90.
Blang, Mark. 1980 [1992]. *The Methodology of Economics*. 2nd ed. Cambridge Surveys of Economic Literature. Cambridge: Cambridge University Press.
Blaug, Mark. 1992. *The Methodology of Economics: Or How Economists Explain*. 2nd ed. Cambridge Surveys of Economic Literature. Cambridge: Cambridge University Press.
Boland, Donald, 2016. "Economic Science and St. Thomas Aquinas: On Justice in the Distribution and Exchange of Wealth." *En Route Books and Media*. USA: St Louis.
Boulding, Kenneth E. 1969. "Economics as a Moral Science." *The American Economic Review* 59 (1): 1–12.
Boulding, Kenneth E. 1983. "The Optimum Utilization of Knowledge—Some Central Concepts." In *The Optimum Utilization of Knowledge*. Westview Press.
Brenner, Reuven. 1994. *Labyrinths of Prosperity: Economic Follies, Democratic Remedies*. University of Michigan Press.
Broadie, Alexander. 2010. "Aristotle, Adam Smith and the Virtue of Propriety." *Journal of Scottish Philosophy* 8: 79–89.
Buchholz, Todd G. 2021 [1989]. *New Ideas from Dead Economists*. Penguin Random House LLC.
Carrión Alvarez, Miguel, and Dirk H. Ehnts. 2016. "Samuelson and Davidson on Ergodicity: A Reformulation." *Journal of Post Keynesian Economics* 39: 1–16.
Crampton, Eric. 2007. "Market Failure." In *Encyclopedia of Law and Society*, edited by David S. Clark, 983–984. Thousand Oaks: Sage Publications..
Davidson, Paul. 1981–1982. "Rational Expectations: A Fallacious Foundation for Studying Crucial Decision-Making Processes." *Journal of Post Keynesian Economics* 5 (2): 182–197.
Davidson, Paul. 2011. *A Response to John Kay's Essay on the State of Economics*. Institute for New Economic Thinking.
Davidson, Paul. 2015. "A Rejoinder to O'Donnell's Critique of the Ergodic/Nonergodic Explanation of Keynes's Concept of Uncertainty." *Journal of Post Keynesian Economics* 38 (1): 1–18.

de Nemours, Pierre Samuel Dupont. 1879. *Physiocratie, ou Constitution Naturelle du Gouvernement le Plus Avantageux au Genre Humain*. Dupont des Sociétés Royales d'Agriculture de Soissons & d'Orléans.

Dow, S. C. 2005. "Axioms and Babylonian Thought: A Reply." *Journal of Post Keynesian Economics* 27 (3): 385–391.

Friesen, Peter H. 1979. "The Arrow-Debreu Model Extended to Financial Markets." *Econometrica* 47: 689–707.

Galbraith, John Kenneth. 1971. *Economics, Peace and Laughter*. The New American Library.

Galbraith, John Kenneth. 1987. *Economics in Perspective: A Critical History*. New York: Houghton Mifflin.

Gao, Lei, and Ulrich Schmidt. 2005. "Self Is Never Neutral: Why Economic Agents Behave Irrationally." *The Journal of Behavioral Finance* 6 (1): 27–37.

Hicks, John. 1939. *Value and Capital: An Inquiry into Some Fundamental Principles of Economic Theory*. London: Oxford University Press.

Hodgson, Geoffrey Martin. 2001. *How Economics Forgot History: The Problem of Historical Specificity in Social Science*. Routledge.

Hollis, Martin, and Edward J. Nell. 1975. *Rational Economic Man: A Philosophical Critique of Neo-Classical Economics*. Cambridge: Cambridge University Press.

Ingram, John Kells. 1888. *A History of Political Economy*. Edinburgh: Adam and Charles Black, Ltd.

Jevons, William Stanley. 1871. *The Theory of Political Economy*. London and New York: Macmillan and Co.

Kakutani, Shizuo. 1941. "A Generalization of Brouwer's Fixed Point Theorem." *Duke Mathematical Journal* 8: 457–459.

Katzner, Donald W. 2003. "Why Mathematics in Economics?" *Journal of Post Keynesian Economics* 24 (4): 561–574.

Kelly, Anthony. 2003. "A Critique of Game Theory." In *Decision Making Using Game Theory*, edited by Anthony Kelly. Cambridge: Cambridge University Press.

Kennedy, Gavin. 2008. "General Introduction: Why Adam Smith?" In *Adam Smith: Great Thinkers in Economic Series*. London: Palgrave Macmillan.

Keynes, John Neville. 1890 [1917]. *The Scope and Method of Political Economy*. 4th ed., 145. Augustus M. Kelly Publishers.

Kirman, Alan. 2021. "Walras or Pareto: Who is to Blame for the State of Modern Economic Theory?" *Review of Political Economy* 33 (2): 280–302.

Krugman, Paul. 1994. *The Fall and Rise of Development Economics*, 1–15. MIT Press Direct.

Leshem, Dotan. 2016. "Retrospectives: What Did the Ancient Greeks Mean by 'Oikonomia?'" *The Journal of Economic Perspectives* 30 (1): 225–238.

Leslie, Thomas Edward Cliffe. 1879. *Essays in Political and Moral Economy*. Dublin University Press Series.
Loevinger, Lee. 1993. "Standards of Proof in Law and Science." *Interdisciplinary Science Reviews* 18 (2): 144–152.
Malthus, Thomas Robert. 1798. "Principles of Political Economy," vol. I. Edited by John Pullen, Cambridge University Press, 1989.
Mankiw, Gregory. 2016. *Principles of Microeconomics*. 8th ed. Boston, MA: Cengage Learning.
Marchionatti, Roberto. 2007. "On the Application of Mathematics to Political Economy. The Edgeworth-Walras-Borkievicz Controversy." *Cambridge Journal of Economics* 31: 291–307.
Mill, John Stuart. 1844. *Essays on Some Unsettled Questions of Political Economy*, Cosimo, Inc. 2007, New York.
Miller, Fred D. 1998. "Was Aristotle the First Economist?" *Apeiron* 31: 387–398.
Morgenstern, Oskar. 1964. *On Some Criticisms of Game Theory*. Economic Research Program Research Paper. Princeton University.
Myrdal, Gunnar. 1987. "Utilitarianism and Modern Economics." In *Arrow and the Foundations of the Theory of Economic Policy*, edited by George R. Feiwel, 273–278. London: Palgrave Macmillan.
O'Brien, Denis Patrick. 2004. *The Classical Economists Revisited*. Princeton: Princeton University Press.
Parguez, Alain. 2013. "The Fundamental and Eternal Conflict: Hayek and Keynes on Austerity." *International Journal of Political Economy* 41: 54–68.
Phoa, Wesley, Sergio M. Focardi, and Frank J. Fabozzi. 2007. "How Do Conflicting Theories About Financial Markets Coexist?" *Journal of Post Keynesian Economics* 29 (3): 383–391.
Popper, Karl Raimund. 1935 [2002]. *The Logic of Scientific Discovery*. London and New York: Routledge.
Redmond, William H. 2000. "Consumer Rationality and Consumer Sovereignty." *Review of Social Economy* 58: 177–196.
Ricardo, David. 1821 [2006]. *Principles of Political Economy and Taxation*. New York: Cosimo Inc.
Robbins, Lionel. 1932 [1945]. *Essay on the Nature and Significance of Economic Science*. 2nd ed. London: Macmillan.
Rothschild, Emma. 1994. "Adam Smith and the Invisible Hand." *The American Economic Review* 84 (2): 319–322.
Roy, Subroto. 1989. *Philosophy of Economics—On the Scope of Reason in Economic Inquiry*. Routledge International Library of Philosophy.
Sachs, Jeffrey D. 2005. *The End of Poverty: Economic Possibilities for Our Time*. Penguin Books.

Salles, Maurice. 2017. "Kenneth J. Arrow, 1921–2017." *European Journal of the History of Economic Thought* 24 (5): 1123–1129.

Samuelson, Paul A. 1969. "Classical and Neoclassical Theory." In *Monetary Theory: Selected Readings*, edited by R.W. Clower. Harmondsworth: Penguin Modern Economics Readings.

Sen, Amartya. 1987. *On Ethics and Economics*. Blackwell Publishing.

Sent, Esther-Mirjam. 2018. "Rationality and Bounded Rationality: You Can't Have One Without the Other." *The European Journal of the History of Economic Thought* 25 (6): 1370–1386.

Shiller, Robert J. 2000. *Irrational Exuberance*. Princeton, NJ: Princeton University Press.

Simon, Herbert. 1984 [1963]. "Testability and Approximation." In *The Philosophy of Economics*, edited by D. Hausman. Cambridge: Cambridge University Press.

Singer, Peter. 2009. *The Life You Can Save: Acting Now to End World Poverty*. New York: Random House.

Smith, Adam. 1759. *The Theory of Moral Sentiments*. New York: Dover Publications.

Smith, Adam. 1776. *An Inquiry into to the Nature and Causes of the Wealth of Nations*. Printed for W. Strahan and T. Cadell, in the Strand, London.

Stiglitz, Joseph E. 1991. "Another Century of Economic Science." *The Economic Journal* 101 (404): 134–141.

Stiglitz, Joseph E. 2017. "The Revolution of Information Economics: The Past and the Future." NBER Working Papers 23780, National Bureau of Economic Research.

The Economist. 2011. "The Canon of Economics." *Finance and Economics*, February 24, 2011.

The Economist. 2022. "Why Labour's Silly Energy Policy is Smart Politics: The Limits of Technocracy," August 18, 2022.

von Neumann, John, and Oskar Morgenstern. 1944. *Theory of Games and Economic Behavior* (Sixtieth Anniversary Edition, 2004). Princeton, New Jersey: Princeton University Press.

Walker, Donald. 1987. "Edgeworth Versus Walras on the Theory of Tatonnement." *Easter Economic Journal* 13: 155–165.

CHAPTER 3

Critiques of Islamic Economics

As with conventional economics, Islamic economics invites criticism on many grounds. There are fundamental ontological and epistemological questions about a discipline devoted to the study of the organizing principles of an Islamic economy, including the important issues of whether such an economy is warranted or it can possibly exist. Part of the criticism of a normative discipline focuses not so much on what it has achieved as what it has not. The principal failure to emerge as an independent discipline is manifested in the paucity of consistent textbooks to influence patterns of critical thinking in new generations and absence of coherent policies to substantiate real change in the economy. Muslim scholars, it is argued, frequently preach value-laden innocuous policies that are rarely put into practice. The economic ideology, it is argued again, is so vague and antiquated as to be of little significance for prediction and policy-making purposes in modern economies.

Another critical view regards the development of a novel discipline unwarranted when it is possible to incorporate Islamic values and design new policies within the realm of conventional economics. The argument is based on the premise that Islamic economics shares with conventional economics the latter's hard-core principles of economic rationality and optimal allocation of scarce resources, *inter alia*. As argued in the opening chapter however, these are polar visions of the economy, which are, as

© The Author(s), under exclusive license to Springer Nature Switzerland AG 2023
N. El Maghrebi et al., *Revisiting Islamic Economics*, Palgrave Studies in Islamic Banking, Finance, and Economics, https://doi.org/10.1007/978-3-031-41134-2_3

explained in another central chapter of this book, fundamentally irreconcilable given the ontological, axiological, epistemological and teleological differences. As shown in the previous chapter as well, the very principles of conventional economics are regarded as maxims only by dint of repetition as they have no basis in the primary sources of Islamic knowledge. It is argued also that to imbue economic models with assumptions about Islamic values and test their empirical implications does not amount to the development of a genuine discipline of Islamic economics. As Islamic economics ventures into the well-trodden path of neoclassical economics, its enthusiasm for compromise may lead to entanglement with a secular paradigm where the historical tensions and potential conflicts between Islamic worldview, moral philosophy and philosophy of science can hardly be contained. A fatal compromise is inevitable as manifested by the promotion of *sukūk* products as interest-based "Islamic" bonds into a new asset class. A convergence toward conventional banking seems to be impossible without a secularization of Islamic jurisprudence to circumvent the maxim of interest prohibition.

Thus, it is tempting at this point to reflect upon the current state of Islamic economics and conclude that it can neither emerge on its own nor exist within the realm of conventional economics. In the absence of a deeper understanding of the *raison d'être* of the *homo economicus* and how economic life is anthropologically shaped, it is difficult to develop a coherent discipline of Islamic economics with an ostensibly distinctive future agenda. A secular paradigm that discards the metaphysical foundations of Islamic economics leads to a merely "ethical" but skewed version of capitalism that would be inevitably shattered, at some point, by the serious tensions and conflicts between the open-ended processes of secularization and Islamization. Indeed, a dualism of worldviews cannot be resolved into a harmonious unity. Attempts at developing Islamic economics on the foundations of mainstream economics are stalled at the same impasse.

It is tempting also to reconcile the different paths taken in the development of Islamic economics as an academic discipline entrusted with the task of elucidating the organizing principles of an ideal Islamic economy. It should be understood, however, that if all approaches are deemed to be equally valid and important, it is not clear which path can be *a priori* excluded. The principal contention of this book is that the differences in metaphysical and methodological foundations of conventional economics and *Al-Iqtiṣād*, a paradigm for an ideal economy derived from the authentic sources of Islamic knowledge, are so stark that a path of reconciliation with the grafting of one polar case onto the other is rather impossible. The reality is that a path of reconciliation is inconceivable because, as demonstrated in the previous chapter, there are inherent flaws in the dogma and science of conventional economics. The critical analysis provided in the present chapter reinforces the argument that a path of convergence can only compound the problems of divergence of the current universe of discourse called Islamic economics from the paradigm of *Al-Iqtiṣād*, which is based on the authentic sources of knowledge, *Al-Qur'ān* and *As-Sunnah*.

Thus, the focus in this chapter is placed on critiques of the philosophical foundations of the current paradigm of Islamic economics, its scope and methodology. The primary concern is about departures from what Muhammad Baqir As-Sadr called *Madh'hab Al-Iqtiṣād*, rather than its science or *'Ilm Al-Iqtiṣād*, which are explained in the opening chapter. Indeed, the existence of a science of Islamic economics is conditional upon the operationalization of its madh'hab, since no science can be more secure than the metaphysics that it tacitly presupposes, as argued by Alfred North Whitehead (1861–1947). The chapter provides, first, a brief historical account of Islamic political economy. As with conventional economics, various definitions of Islamic economics are, then, presented in order to understand the scope, contents, and discontents of the discipline. There is also concerns about the lack of theoretical doctrine in Islamic economics, and the traditional trade-off that arises between analytical rigour and practical relevance.

The chapter offers also a critical discussion of the relationship between religion and economics, and the cardinal doctrine of the unity of Being, which should form the metaphysical foundations of a discipline of Islamic economics firmly grounded on the Islamic worldview. The focus is placed also on the process of desacralization of knowledge, and replacement of the theocentric worldview with secular ones. Finally, some perspectives are provided about the role of Islamic jurisprudence in shaping Islamic economic thought, and in particular, the secularization of Islamic law as one of the principal sources of departure of Islamic economics from the authentic paradigm of *Al-Iqtiṣād*, the *Qur'anic* vision of an ideal economy.

A Brief History of Islamic Political Economy

The influence of Islamic ideas on the development of economic thought and institutions does not date back to a number of notable contributions by leading Muslim economists some decades ago. Any attempt to promote the notion that Muslim scholars made no significant contributions to economic thought over many centuries is can be rather easily refuted on the historical grounds of scholarly contributions. It is possible indeed to dismiss the idea of *The Great Gap*, which refers to Joseph Schumpeter's leap in his *History of Economic Analysis* from the Greco-Roman economics to Saint Thomas Aquinas. The unfounded proposition implies that for as many as five centuries, the role of Muslim scholars who preceded the Scholastics was to merely transmit Greek thought. It is not possible however, as argued by Abbas Mirakhor (1987, p. 248), to "extract the economic thought of Saint Thomas through a search of his work including *Opra Omni*, *Summa Theologica*, and *Summa Contra Gentiles*, among others… without seeing some references to Muslim scholars particularly in areas where these scholars are taken to task for their ideas which were contrary to the Christian dogma." Indeed, the extensive corpus of intellectual work by Abu Nasr Muhammad Al-Farabi (*Alfarabius*, 870–950), Abu Ali Al-Husayn ibn Abdallah ibn Sina (*Avicenna*, 980–1037), and Abu Hamid Muhammad ibn Muhammad Al-Tusi Al-Ghazali (*Algazelus*, 1058–1111), and Abu Al-Walid Muhammad ibn Ahmad ibn Rushd (*Averroes*, 1126–1198), *inter alia*, can hardly be overlooked given their significant contributions to the development of thought in political philosophy, natural philosophy, science, and social psychology, among others.

Major contributions to the development of the broader field of social studies were also made by other Muslim scholars, including the Forerunner of Social Sciences Abdur Rahman Ibn Khaldun (1332–1406) whose treatise on universal history, *Al Muqadimah*, was described by the world historian Arnold Toynbee (1889–1975) as "undeniably the greatest work of its kind that has ever been created by any mind in any time or place." The pioneering historical treatise is the result of a keen interest in understanding major events and their social dynamics rather than merely narrating history. New insights are provided about the nature of economic power, social changes, and political regimes, as well as human geography, economic justice, taxation, production, commerce, and industry, among others. The scholarly work provides original insights into the rise and fall of civilizations, economic prosperity, and political leadership. It offers as such an intellectual account of reflections on the subject of political economy, which precede by nearly four centuries, the inquiry into the nature and causes of the wealth of nations as expressed by Adam Smith (1723–1790), widely recognized as the father of modern economics. Abdul Azim Islahi (2014) provides further evidence about the missing link in the history of economic thought of Muslim economists on issues related to the theories of value, market pricing, production, distribution, money, finance, the role of the state, and economic development.

Also, Seyed Kazim Sadr (2016) presents, in the words of Mirakhor (2016), a comprehensive economic hermeneutic of policies implemented by the Messenger (saas) in Medinah, drawing from early insights by Muhammad Abdul Malik Ibn Hisham (n.d–833) based on the original biography of the Prophet (saas) by Abu Yusuf Yaqub Ibn Ishaq AlKindi (805–873), and later contributions by Hakim Naishaburi (933–1012), Abul Hasan Ali Ibn Muhammad Al-Mawardi (972–1058), Ibn Qudamah AlMaqdisi (1147–1223), and Ibn Hajar Al-Asqalani (1372–1449), *inter alia*. Thus, it is important to consider the intellectual heritage of Muslim scholars in the history of Islamic economic thought and its impact on the European Renaissance. Insofar as Muslim contributions are concerned, it may be argued that Schumpeter's unwarranted leap leading to misconception of *The Great Gap* was not a period of drought in economic thought, but one of valuable insights.[1]

The significant contributions of Muslim scholars to economic thought may be regarded as precursor to the formal development of Islamic economics as the study of the organizing principles of an ideal economy extracted from the Islamic sources of knowledge. It is often argued, however, that definitions of Islamic economics tend to be vague and hopelessly abstract. Ziaul Haque (1992) noted that there is no consensus on the definition of Islamic economics, with research spanning multi-disciplinary subjects related to history, law, philosophy, and religion. He argued that "Islamic economists appear to be more interested in medieval socio-religious and ethical concepts and institutions, laws and rituals than the real economic problems of their present-day societies" (Ziaul Haque 1992, p. 1069). The literature, it is argued, portrays the image of a nascent discipline anchored in medieval scholarship. In this respect, Muhammad Akram Khan (2013, p. 40) also argues that despite several attempts, "there is no standard and generally accepted definition of Islamic economics."

The Contents and Discontents of Islamic Economics

There is an abundance of definitions of Islamic economics. For instance, Muhammad Abdul Mannan (1970, p. 3) defines the discipline as "a social science which studies the economic problems of a people imbued with the values of Islam." According to Hasanuz Zaman (1984, p. 50), "Islamic economics is the knowledge and application of injunctions and rules of the *Shari'ah* that prevent injustice in the acquisition and disposal of material resources in order to provide satisfaction to human beings and enable them to perform their obligations to Allah and the society." An alternative definition that emphasizes the importance of the Islamic worldview is suggested by Mohamed A. M. Haneef (1997, p. 50), who states that Islamic economics can be broadly defined as "an approach to interpreting and solving man's economic problems based on the values, norms, laws and institutions found in, and derived from, the sources of knowledge in Islam."

With reference to the Islamization of human knowledge in the field of economics, Zubair Hasan (1998, p. 21) argues that Islamic economics may be defined as "that part of Islam's social doctrine that deals with the problems of choice in the face of uncertainty and resource scarcity so as to promote *falah* in a holistic framework." Alternatively, Umer Chapra (1990, p. 33) argues that "Islamic economics may be defined as that branch of knowledge which helps realize human well-being through an allocation and distribution of resources that is in conformity with Islamic teachings without unduly curbing individual freedom or creating continued macroeconomic and ecological imbalances." Alternatively, Ahmad Yusri (2002, p. 28) defines Islamic economics as "the science that studies the best possible use of all available economic resources, endowed by God, for the production of maximum possible output of *Halal* goods and services that are needed by the community now and in future and just distribution of the output within the framework of the *Shari'ah* and its intents."

The failure to reach consensus even on a benchmark definition of Islamic economics is reflective of diverging views about its vision, scope, and methodology. Muhammad Akram Khan (2013) argues that most of what has been proposed in the name of Islamic economics amounts to nothing more than Islamic teachings, which can be regarded as theology, not economic theory. This criticism is consistent with the argument advanced by Timur Kuran (1989, p. 170) that support for prescriptive Islamic economics rests on "selective quotations from scripture, leaving it open to the charge that an Islamic justification may be found for a wide variety of mutually inconsistent policies." It is a discipline that proposes only sterile and inconsistent policies that do not amount to a genuine blueprint for the organization of the economic system in ways that promote justice.

Part of the reason for these policy failures has to do with misguided attempts at defining Islamic economics in relation to conventional economics, which embraces a positive science concerned with the actual behaviour of economic agents. Islamic economics, in contrast, should aspire for a normative discipline where normative rules are consistently and continuously embedded in behavioural systems. It is often argued that theoretical propositions in Islamic economics are value judgements based on the Islamic sources of knowledge, which are not amenable to scientific analysis. The empirical methods, used for verification and falsification purposes, may provide however, useful insights on systematic deviations from ideal economic behaviour. The evidence can be used, in turn, in the design of corrective measures that adjust individual code of conduct and institutional behaviour in order to converge toward an ideal economic system. The validity and reliability of a particular Islamic economic theory can, thus, be scientifically assessed in or to formulate sound economic policies. In the realm of economic methodology, these arguments reflect the classical distinction between positive and normative economics and about the role of the discipline in describing and explaining behaviour or in shaping it. It is an important distinction given the existing arguments by Weisskopf (1971, p. 183), inter alia, about the "necessity for economics to include normative elements in its universe of discourse." Thus, if the intellectual efforts of Muslim scholars are meant to merely describe, explain and assimilate what economic agents do rather than advocate what they should do, then it is inevitable to ask what marginal contributions can Islamic economics can possibly bring to the universal discourse about economic problems without promoting ethical behaviour and economic justice. If the overriding objective of theorising and testing does not lie in the derivation of the organizing principles of an ideal economy and formulation of sound policies based on normative behavioural rules, then it is legitimate to ask what exactly Islamic economics is all about.

Central to criticism about the scope and methodology of Islamic economics is the notion that by virtue of its epistemological foundations, rational thinking should be guided by revelation, not reason separated from faith. It may be argued, as suggested by Muhammad Akram Khan (2013, p. 70), that it is still possible to develop the discipline by distinguishing the human from the divine, which is not part of economics but theology because it is "eternal, immutable and given." This distinction implies that "Islamic economics does not reject rationality in decision making. It only extends the meaning of rationality to include human well-being both in this life and in the hereafter. It does not reject maximization of utility as normal behaviour but redefines the meaning of 'utility'. Utility in Islamic parlance encompasses gain in the hereafter as well. It does not contradict the fact that human beings behave in self-interest, but it extends the meanings of self-interest, which could also include spiritual uplift, philanthropic spending, work for the well-being of one's family, neighbours and society at large, and so on. Economic analysis should integrate these wider meanings of self-interest."

Thus, the argument is that the conventional meanings of rationality, utility maximization, and self-interest can be semantically redefined or technically augmented in order to allow for model building consistent with metaphysical beliefs and moral convictions. Semantically however, it is difficult to extend the meaning of "self-interest" *ad infinitum* without conflating it with "social interest." It is possible to dispense with semantic exercises through the imposition of normative rules that constrain self-interest, such as the mandatory charity *zakat*, which is not just an act of self-interest in the purification of individual wealth, but a religious obligation toward society that lies beyond the boundaries of self-interest. Technically also, as noted by Kenneth Boulding (1969, p. 6) in *Economics as a Moral Science*, "There are no mathematical or conceptual difficulties involved in inter-relating utility functions, provided that we note that it is the perceptions that matter." The question remains as to whether semantic amendments to model assumptions that allow for bounded self-interest or utility function, for instance, can solve the problems of economic theory without abandoning its secular construct. The approach lends itself to criticism on the grounds that the mere integration of Islamic values does not render a secular paradigm Islamic. In this respect, Timur Kuran (1989, p. 170) argues that Islamic economics fails to provide a well-defined and operational analytical method, and "where efforts are made to give it analytical power, it loses much of its Islamic character."

It is not clear, indeed, how to proceed when the overriding principles of conventional economics stand in sharp conflict with the maxims of Islamic economics.

It is difficult, in light of these conceptual contradictions, to evade capture into a secular paradigm where positive economics takes precedence over the normative approach mandated by the Islamic worldview. It is not clear how to accommodate the economic postulates of resource scarcity and unlimited wants in the realm of Islamic economics, which regards relative scarcity as result of maldistribution, and the pursuit of self-interest only as subservient to social interest. It is noted in this respect that Hossein Askari et al. (2015, p. 36) consider the notion of scarcity in Islam from three complementary levels. First, the evidence from *Al-Qur'ān* implies that in absolute terms, there is no scarcity at the macro-global level because all creation is made in "exact measures."[2] The second dimension refers to relative scarcity caused by inequalities in the distribution of resources and income. The third dimension is represented by "existential scarcity" due to the finite conditions of human beings, which implies that, in the words of Walter Weisskopf (1971, p. 23, italics in original), the resources that "are ultimately scarce are *life, time* and *energy* because human finitude, aging and mortality." Thus, scarcity is an economic phenomenon that can be encountered at the micro-level because of unlimited wants, greed, selfishness, and economic injustice leading to unfair distribution of resources. Poverty as such, is the result of inequities in the distribution of resources, and wasteful consumption, rather than absolute scarcity or shocks to the production and distribution functions. Corrosion of trust in public policies may, thus, be the outcome of a reticence and unwillingness to wear one's heart on one's sleeve and openly discuss beliefs, sentiments, and perceptions about social and economic problems, including normative behaviour.

No amount of semantic engineering, theorizing, and empirical testing in Islamic economics can solve the problems of poverty, hunger, and destitution, when it embraces the conventional paradigm where poverty is regarded as the outcome of resource scarcity and individual choice. According to Masudul Alam Choudhury (1998, p. 133), a word of caution is warranted as Muslims economists' affinity for prediction and falsification within the received wisdom of neoclassical economics may culminate in unintended consequences. He argues that "In such a mould of thinking, no new contributions can be made respecting the substantively epistemological *praxis* of Islamic scientific order. The consequence will then be a pitiful methodological nicety without meaningful content; or it will be a defective scientific, empirical and institutional development in the framework of 'Islamic economics'." It is further argued that a petrified scientific pursuit cannot offer genuine solutions within its own distinctive model to the human predicament. Conventional economics is, according to Friedrich Hayek (1940), the subject of criticism for a slavish imitation of the methods and language of physical or natural sciences. And it may be argued that the very charges of scientism and abuse of reason apply with equal force to the development of Islamic economics.

The difficulties of formulating scientific statements and the dearth of empirical literature in Islamic economics should not lead to the conclusion that an ideal economic system cannot exist in Islam. Likewise, it is not possible to dismiss the early work on Islamic economic thought for fear, as noted by Muhammad Baqir As-Sadr (1982 [1994], p. 8), that the discipline "would be exposed to the charge of claiming that Islam was ahead of western thinkers in the scientific creation of the political economy."

The notion that the relationship between Islamic economics and conventional economics is one of rivalry or rebellion is a false problem. Independent of universal wisdom, it is a duty on Muslims to seek evidence from the authentic sources of knowledge in order to extract the organizing principles of an ideal economy. The fears and misconceptions are irrelevant to the more serious debate about the optimal path for the development of Islamic economic thought. There is no doubt that the organizing principles for an ideal economy derived from *Al-Qur'an* and *As-Sunnah* will benefit humanity, but the question of whether Islamic economics, with its present dependencies on human knowledge again, can enrich conventional economics is another issue. The benefits of integrating economic theories to examine the behaviour of a *homo economicus* disinclined to sacrifice self-interest, and a *khalifah economicus*, economicus are not obvious since the latter is an agent empowered by the Creator both economically and spiritually to perform responsibilities toward humankind, earth and the rest of creation, which can only be assumed through the process of self-purification rather than self-interested behaviour. It is not clear why a distinction between self-interest and bounded self-interest should be made either if the descriptive methodology has little bearing on theoretical predictions, and policy implications for the operation of economic institutions and behaviour of economic agents in an ideal economy. Thus, if in the conduct of economic analysis, Muslim economists should discern the divine from the human on the grounds that the former is part of theology, not economics, and the teleological character of economic behaviour should not be explained by the theomorphic nature of man, then attempts at developing Islamic economics based on an altered worldview of Islam are meaningless. The dilemma faced by Muslim economists in integrating two conflicting visions of reality cannot be resolved within the paradigm of conventional economics because descriptive and prescriptive methodologies belong to different realms of discourse.

Theoretical Doctrine Between Analytical Rigour and Practical Relevance

It is also argued that despite the growing literature, Islamic economics does not offer a body of doctrinal arguments. For instance, Muhammad Akram Khan (1991, p. 260) argues that "[m]ost of what is written consists of general principles, and that too within the framework of an ideal Islamic economy which does not exist anywhere. Only some of its ideas have found a place in the real world partly because its potential is not widely known." There is, indeed, a clear lack of theoretical models in Islamic economics, and a genuine risk that new economic ideas with insufficient theoretical modelling may fade away. But the argument applies to conventional economics as well. Paul Krugman (1995, p. 6), argues that it is possible, indeed, for broad economic insights that are not assimilated in models to draw the attention of scholars, but their impact is bound to be temporary if they are not "codified in a reproducible –and teachable –form." Given the tendency for economists to dismiss what has not been formalized, "the influence of ideas that have not been embalmed in models soon decays."

There is no doubt that general principles constitute the foundations of economic theory, and that efforts to define the maxims should precede the development of a theoretical doctrine in Islamic economics. The natural question arises as to whether it is the absence of consensus about the general principles themselves that is hindering the formalization of Islamic economic thought into a consistent theoretical doctrine. It is difficult to build a robust theoretical doctrine when Muslim scholars are consumed with intellectual disputes about the meanings and extended meanings of self-interest and rationality, and about the postulate of scarcity or abundance. However important these issues are, they can be resolved with reference to authentic sources of knowledge rather than fallible human "wisdom." It is not clear, either, whether theoretical doctrines should judged by the level of analytical rigour or relevance to the real economy. In this respect, Blaug (1992, p. 167) recognizes the trade-off between rigour and relevance, and notes that "if we argue in favor of a market economy compared to a command economy because of the dynamic characteristics of a competitive regime in fostering technical dynamism and cost-cutting innovations, and perhaps even political freedom to match economic freedom, our argument is anything but rigorous; it is, however, extremely relevant."

Thus, when Muslim economist argue against predatory capitalism and command economy, and in favour of an ideal exchange economy based on the organizing principle of risk-sharing, which ensures financial stability and shared prosperity, the arguments are anything but rigorous, however they are certainly relevant in addressing the chronic ailments of the economy. Intellectual efforts to conceive an ideal Islamic economy be subjected to the same standards of academic judgement applied to Adam Smith's arguments about a competitive economy with an invisible hand, which are anything but rigorous. In fact, the general principles of conventional economics were derived for a similarly imaginary competitive economy that evolved over several centuries but did not exist at the time Adam Smith wrote his seminal treatise. Thus, the principal failure of Muslim countries to develop vibrant economic systems based on economic justice and risk sharing should not be laid at the door of Muslim scholars alone. It is clear that not everything practiced in the Islamic world is Islamic, and particularly in relation to economic issues. Departure from Islamic practice in many aspects of social, economic and political life reflects a collective failure, not just of Muslim economists, to recognize the truth about the divine, truth that is evident from clear gnostic signs written in the horizons ($\bar{a}f\bar{a}q$, the heavens and earth), and in all human souls (*anfus*). It is a failure to recognize that sacred knowledge is not meant to be superseded by human knowledge. Whether the neglect is deliberate or accidental is not our concern here, but the reality is that there is no possibility of developing a genuine discipline of Islamic economics without recognizing the hierarchy of existence and the superiority of the sacred over the profane.

Thus, Islamic economics lends itself to wide criticism ranging from inconsistent doctrinal arguments to inexistent scientific statements. In its current form, Islamic economics is a disjointed and incoherent discipline, and it is not so sacrosanct as to be protected from candid criticism. It would certainly benefit from genuine efforts to take stock of past achievements, or lack thereof, and correct its course of action. Attempts at arranging and sorting out the arguments of an intrinsically normative discipline into a descriptive one, are bound to fail because they are epistemologically inconsistent and therefore meaningless.

While conceding to the fact that an ideal Islamic economy does not currently exist anywhere, protracted efforts to define the maxims of Islamic economics should not be regarded as attempts to construct abstract make-believe worlds. As argued by Muhammad Baqir As-Sadr (1982 [1994], pp. 8–9), the conviction of some scholars that the "Islamic economy is nothing but a myth and a mere figment of the imagination" may be the result of a failure to distinguish between economic science and economic doctrine. It is the latter that provides the overall framework for an ideal economic system, upon which the science of Al-Iqtiṣād can develop testable propositions. Thus, while recognizing the laborious task of Muslim economists in rethinking Islamic economics, a belief that the development of a coherent discipline of Al-Iqtiṣād based on the authentic sources of knowledge is unwarranted because no such a thing as an ideal Islamic economy is possible, would be an intellectually disabling belief.

The Contentious Relationship Between Religion and Economics

The question of whether human thought should be governed by faith or reason is a false dichotomy because, arguably, both are necessary and complementary. Historically however, the relationship between economics and religion has been unnecessarily antagonistic and contentious. John Kells Ingram (1888, p. 241) concurs with the views of physiocrats, in relating economics to natural sciences including physics and biology, but he also insists that "the science must be cleared of all the theologico-metaphysical elements or tendencies which still encumber and deform it. Teleology and optimism on the one hand, and the jargon of 'natural liberty' and 'indefeasible rights' on the other, must be finally abandoned." Thus, religion, which provides answers to metaphysical issues related to the fundamental nature of reality, is often regarded as the source of fallacies and misconceptions. But it might be useful to note also that religious belief has played a significant role in the development of modern economic thought. In its "Statement of Principles," the American Economic Association, which was founded in 1885, explicitly recognizes the complementary roles of the Church, state, and science in addressing social problems.[3]

Given this contentious relationship, it is important to understand the contents and discontents of religion in order to consider arguments about the usefulness or futility of bringing it into the universe of discourse about economic life. Western philosophers and anthropologists consider religion as a set of empirically irrefutable "beliefs," "convictions," and "ideas," with positive and negative heuristics of do's and do not's that should be either eliminated or allowed to evolve over time. *Religio* can refer to piety and life according to God's will, though the term *"novas religiones"* or new religions and alternative spirituality is used also in reference to fresh superstitious dreads. The word *religion* is derived from the Latin term *religio*, whose root meaning is to *bind*.[4] As argued by Seyyed Hossein Nasr (2000, p. 1), religion stands for "that which binds man to the truth." Islam is referred to as the religion of truth in *Al-Qur'ān* (48:28), "It is He Who has sent His Messenger with Guidance and the Religion of Truth."

The Arabic term *"dīn"* or *"deen"* oft-used with reference to religion is also stated in *Al-Qur'ān* (3:19) "Verily, the religion [din] of God [Allah] is Islam." Its root meanings are acknowledgement, natural inclination, submission, and judgement. The true religion of Islam, ad-din al-haq, is the perennial religion, religio perennis, as noted by Seyyed Hossein Nasr (2000, p. 20), who argues that "[t]here is only one doctrine of Unity which every religion has asserted and Islam came only to reaffirm what has always existed and thus to return to the primordial religion which was at the beginning and will always be, the eternal *sophia*, the *religio perennis*." Because human beings are endowed with the qualities of will, intelligence, and speech, and because they are by nature forgetful and thus imperfect, divine guidance with a primordial religion or *"ad-din al-hanif"* is an absolute necessity.

The cardinal doctrine about the ultimate nature of Reality is the unity of Being or "*Wihdat Al-Wujūd*," which precludes the existence of two completely independent orders of reality or being. In this respect, Syed Muhammad Naquib Al-Attas (2005, p. 11) argues that from the perspective of Islam, a worldview cannot be reduced to the mind's view of the physical world, nor can it be confined either to man's world of sense or sensible experience in this world based on social, political, and cultural exposures. He notes that it is incorrect to confine the meaning of Islamic worldview to the view of Islam about the universe, as conferred by the Arabic phrase <u>Nadhrat Al-Islam lil-Kawn</u> "because, unlike what is conveyed by *nazrat*, the worldview of Islam is not based upon philosophical speculation formulated mainly from observation of the data of sensible experience, of what is visible to the eye; nor is it restricted to *kawn*, which is the world of sensible experience, the world of created things." The basic argument is that "Islam does not concede to the dichotomy of the sacred and the profane; the worldview of Islam encompasses both *al-dunyā* and *al-ākhirah*, in which the *dunyā*-aspect *must* be related in a profound and inseparable way to the *ākhirah-aspect*, and in which the *ākhirah*-aspect has ultimate and final significance"[5] (italics in original). Thus, given the clarity with which the inseparable concepts of *al-dunyā* and *al-ākhira* are explained in divine texts and Prophetic tradition, the concept of worldview in Islam is anchored in authentic knowledge that cannot be the subject of philosophical conjecture, inference, or speculation.

To cast doubt over the cardinal doctrine of the unity of being and forget the theomorphic nature of man is to forget both the grandeur and pettiness, the significance and triviality of what he can be. Man is given the liberty to lead a life of illusion as a purely earthly creature in the Promethean mode of existence, pursuing the dominance of nature, which would ultimately lead to the destruction of the ecological balance and natural order. Alternatively, he has also liberty to bear the inner reality of a theomorphic man following religious laws to fulfil his cosmic and social responsibilities by preserving harmony in this world. It is the rebellion of the Promethean against the theomorphic during the Renaissance period and forgetfulness of the original nature "*fitrah*" that prevents man from attaining higher states of consciousness and from pursuing objectives in life that lie beyond those confined to a rational animal.

The rationalistic worldview and substitution of the theomorphic with promethean are the result of the process of secularization, which as argued by Syed Muhammad Naquib Al-Attas (1993, p. 20), does not have its roots in the Christian doctrine, but in the Western interpretation of Christian faith. Thus, "it is not the fruit of the Gospel, but it is the fruit of the long history of philosophical and metaphysical conflict in the religions and purely rationalistic *worldview* of Western man" (italics in original). Indeed, Western thought conceives modern man as prisoner of his own senses, focused solely on the unsatiated gratification of bodily senses. It is noted that secularization, which promotes a Promothean mode of existence, is at odds with seminal philosophical arguments. The father of modern philosophy René Descartes (1596–1650) argued in *Les Principes de la Philosphie* (1644 [2009]), that there is an organic unity in the principles of philosophy, which is likened to a tree with metaphysics as the root, physics as the trunk, and all other sciences as branches, including the principal ones of medicine, mechanics, and morality. Thus, Descartes acknowledged the importance of metaphysics in the tree of knowledge and of morality as the culmination fo wisdom, notions that are alien to secularism. He also regarded as principles of philosophy the notions that "we are not the cause of ourselves, but that it is God, and therefore there is God," and that "we must believe all that God has revealed, even that which is beyond the reach of our mind."[6] Thus, it is difficult to develop solid philosophical foundations for secularism without undermining the validity of Descartes principles about the existence of reality and divine revelation.

Historically however, secularism is associated with the development of rationalism in the thirteenth century as well as the movements of experimental science and humanism over the Renaissance period in the sixteenth century. The Renaissance humanism, in particular, emphasizes the predominant role of science and reason over all sources of knowledge including divine revelation. It has its roots in the word *humanitas*, which reflects the human virtues of benevolence, fortitude, mercy, and compassion, among others. Secularism, however, manifested itself in the gradual departure from philosophical questions about the nature of reality and being to issues related to human conscience and freedom of thought. The emphasis on individual judgement and experience usurps the place of sacred knowledge and metaphysics. It is the philosophy of agnostic humanism, which is based on the centrality of human experience, that constitutes the principal force driving secularisation throughout the nineteenth century, and to this date.

In this respect, Seyyed Hossein Nasr (2007, p. 143) notes that historicism, defined as the secularization of Christian doctrine about the march of time, "played an important role in creating a consciousness, within the new man, of his position in history considered as the secular flow of time rather than his position in the face of eternity." By emphasizing the notion that man can riddle himself of the burden of divine doctrines and rediscover himself in each encounter with a changing reality, secularism epitomizes a rupture between the sacred and the profane, between the metaphysics and sciences, and between the root and trunk in Descartes' tree of knowledge. Thus, a rationalistic worldview of the Western man, as noted above by Al-Attas, is a *de facto* desacralization of knowledge and substitution of a theocentric worldview with multiple anthropocentric ones. The end product of secularization is historical relativism.

Secularization is about the release of man from religious and metaphysical control over reason. It may be argued that the French notion of *laïcité*, which is the outcome of a conflict with the Catholic church, is a form of secularism that does not outlaw religion, but it does exclude religion from public affairs. In this respect, René Viviani (1863–1925) insisted that neutrality is not appropriate, the *laïcité* movement is firmly committed to a world of irreligion. The movement succeeded in extracting human conscience from faith, and "with a magnificent gesture, has turned off in heavens lights that will never be turned on again."[7] The separation of faith and reason resulted in the secularization of virtually all branches of scientific knowledge as well as the cultural, political and social aspects of life. Secularization became the undisputed paradigm based on the marginalization of religion into the "private sphere." But there remain complex issues related to political secularization, which precludes private beliefs in public life, and social secularization, which seeks irreligiosity in everyday aspect of social life, including how people relate to and interact with each other socially, and how society shapes its own value system. The complexity of the secularization process emanates from the unsurmountable difficulties in defining and maintaining a neat demarcation line between private life and public life. The resulting loss of the sense of the sacred is also conducive to a loss of the sense of permanence.

Given the difficulties in sustaining a dichotomy between the profane and the sacred, and given the transformation of the metaphysical question of "being" into one of "becoming" with reality reduced to a temporal process of evolution, there may be expectations about serious attempts to preserve the primacy of divine knowledge, and reconcile faith with reason. However, the depletion of sacred knowledge was not confined to modern interpretations of Judaism and Christianity as it eventually spilled to Islamic doctrine in an intellectually defeated and corrupted Muslim world. As noted by Abdur Rahman Ibn Khaldun (1332–1406) in his seminal work *Al Muqaddimah*, or *Prolegomenon, Introduction to History* (1377 [2005], p. 116) "the vanquished always want to imitate the victor in his distinctive characteristics." Part of the reason is that the soul always recognizes perfection in superior beings to whom it becomes subservient, either out of respect or for the erroneous assumption that subservience is not due to the weakness of the vanquished but the perfection of the victor. It is concluded that "if that erroneous assumption fixes itself in the soul, it becomes a firm belief."[8]

A belated call by some Muslim critics for the Islamization of Knowledge, as an anti-thesis of secularization, is not meant to enforce a non-rational form of wisdom, but to restore the primacy of sacred knowledge, reinstate the metaphysical order and consolidate the harmony between faith and reason. Taha Jabir Al-Alwani (1990) suggests that the Islamization of Knowledge may be regarded as a cultural and intellectual project aimed at restructuring the Muslim mind to generate knowledge consistent with the primary sources of knowledge about the truth, namely divine revelation *wah'y* and existence *wujūd*. Taha Jabir Al-Alwani (1995) further argues that Islamizing knowledge should be understood as "an intellectual and methodological outlook rather than as an academic field, a specialization, an ideology, or a new sect." In this respect, Syed Muhammad Naquib Al-Attas provide different perspectives about the notion of Islamization of Contemporary Knowledge *aslamat al-ma'rifah* as he argues that *al-ma'rifah* defined as the *a priori* knowledge acquired from innate experience cannot and need not be Islamized. Syed Muhammad Naquib Al-Attas (1993, pp. 44–45) defines Islamization as "the liberation of man first from magical, mythological, animistic, national-cultural tradition opposed to Islam, and then from secular control over his reason and his language. The man of *Islām* is he whose reason and language are no longer controlled by magic, mythology, animism, his own national and cultural traditions opposed to *Islām*, and secularism. He is liberated from both the magical and the secular world views." It is the liberation of the spirit or soul, which ultimately leads to physical and spiritual life in harmony with nature and all other beings. It is the liberation from subservience to physical desires and needs, and from the concept of man, defined according to Emile Durkheim (1858–1917), not as a spiritual but physical being driven only by material needs, leading to injustice, and conflict with nature and other beings.[9] Since reason is a projection of the Intellect (*intellectus*), Islamization is the liberation of reason from secular constraints to function in harmony with the Intellect. The Attasian definition of Islamization implies that it is a process driven not so much by *evolution* as by *devolution* to the original and primordial nature *al-fitrah*, which is a higher timeless ahistorical state of being independent of environmental conditions.

Thus, answers to the question of whether man needs religion in the organization and conduct of economic life depend on whether metaphysical questions are given primacy over secular ideas in understanding the nature of reality and the meaning of life. Certainly, the secularization of political and social life, including economic activities is inconsistent with the Islamic worldview. As argued by Abbas Mirakhor (1987, p. 251), it is in *Al-Qur'ān*, which provides the primary documentary source to search for Islamic economic ideas, and it is therein that lies the evidence that "the teleological character of economic behaviour is the result of the theomorphic nature of man." This is where Islamic economic doctrine parts way with inconsistent advocacy for religious-based solutions to global environmental problems and secular remedies to global poverty and financial instability. From the Islamic perspective, it is not possible to accept an economic system where the prosperity of some depends on the poverty of others and destruction of nature. As vicegerents on earth, the wholistic mandate of true believers in Islamic faith is to diligently serve justice in every single aspect of life, including a harmonious relationship with nature, and the promotion of economic and social justice.

Despite its wholistic and consistent worldview, there are unfounded claims that, as with democracy, Islam and economics cannot and should not be mixed. The alleged toxicity, it is often asserted by secular Muslim minds as well, derives from the potential damage that medieval religious thought can inflict on modern socio-economic systems and inhibit economic growth. In his analysis of the reasons why the Western world grew rich and the Middle East did not, Jared Rubin (2017, pp. 2–3) argues that there is no evidence that Islam *per se* is anti-growth, anti-Western, and anti-democratic. It is tempting, indeed, to ask the question of whether the burden of blame for the relative poverty, decadence, and poor governance in the Muslim world should be laid at the door of Islam. He notes that "it is impossible to avoid this question, even if it may be offensive to some; it is simply bad science to reject a hypothesis because it is offensive." He develops the objective argument, however, that "even if one accepts the idea that religious doctrine matters for economic performance, the facts simply do not line up. The histories of these regions in the millennium prior to industrialization do not align with the idea that Islam is antithetical to economic growth. The most important fact to account for in *any* theory of why the modern economy was born in Western Europe and not in the Middle East is that the Middle East was ahead of Europe economically, technologically, and culturally for *centuries* following the spread of Islam. From the seventh through twelfth centuries, Islamic empires dominated Western Eurasia. For its first four or five centuries, Islam was associated with *positive* economic growth" (*italics in original*). These historical insights are consistent with the central arguments advanced also by Murat Çizakça (2011) in his seminal work on *Islamic Capitalism and Finance* that, it is not Islam *per se*, but the cumulative effects of path dependency caused by persistent deviations from Islamic economic system that explain the dismal economic performance of Muslim countries. There is ample historical evidence, indeed, that the economic system in place from the seventh to thirteenth centuries advanced the closely related notions of protection of property rights, contract enforcement, and governance that have yet to be universally accepted in modern economic discourse.

Since Islam, per se, is neither anti-growth nor anti-development, the burden of blame for the lack of economic development should be laid, logically and for the sake of good science, elsewhere. As argued earlier, the answer lies in complete or partial neglect of the very economic principles that generated positive growth for many centuries. It lies with a complete or partial devotion to a secularization process that brought neither balanced economic growth, nor economic stability, but financial instability, poverty, and destitution. It is a blind secular approach based on a conflated espousal of religious sentiments without religion. An attempt to develop Islamic economics on secular foundations by adopting Islamic values without Islam is, indeed, an exercise in futility. If Islam is deemed to be irrelevant to the organization of an ideal economy, then Islamic values should have no bearing on the explanation of economic phenomena or the development of economic doctrine.

As with other branches of knowledge, Islamic economics is often portrayed as a project in progress. But as it does not wear an air of completeness, it may have very well grown into a pseudo-discipline that is not so much wrong as meaningless. In its current form, it is a universe of discourse that may intermittently stimulate curiosity and debate, but without being firmly rejected or wholeheartedly accepted, it would be swiftly dismissed as irrelevant to the serious problems of economic life. Thus, the most important challenge for Muslim economists is to recognize the optimal path for the development of Islamic economics as a coherent discipline firmly anchored in its unique Islamic worldview. The choices are patently clear. It is either that it remains firmly rooted in a secular framework that separates faith from reason and deconsecrates

Islamic values, or that it reclaims its place within the authentic paradigm of an Islamic worldview where it can embrace both the sacred and the profane and find its ethical compass and coherence with the truth.

ISLAMIC LAW AND ISLAMIC JURISPRUDENCE

Islamic economics is a discipline that serves, essentially the conscience of Muslims, by promoting an ideal economic system, the general principles of which are premised upon the maxims of Islamic law.[10] Islamic law, as defined by Mustafa Ahmad Al-Zarqa (2014, p. 9), "is a compilation of commands, rules of the creed and practical deeds that Islam obligates their implementation to achieve its reformative goals in the society." Consistent with Al-Attasian definition of Islamization, the primary reformative goal is to liberate the human mind from the slavery of imitation and superstitions. The primary purpose is to transform also the individual both morally and psychologically in order to prevent the prevalence of desires and greed over mind and duty. These intellectual efforts are consistent with the purposes of Islamic law, which aims at the transformation of society as a whole in order to ensure justice, order, public security. Thus, the intellectual creed, spiritual worship, and judicial legal system constitute the three pillars of Islamic law, which in turn, provides the basis for Islamic economics.

As such, Islamic jurisprudence, or *Al-Fiqh* which represents knowledge about *As-Shari'ah* or the immutable rulings of Islamic law ordained in *Al-Qur'ān* and *As-Sunnah*, is not an end in itself but a means to an end. Variations in *Usul Al-Fiqh*, the methodological principles and pre-requisites for the extraction of rules based on *As-Shari'ah* such as consensus (*ijma'*), analogical deduction (*qiyas*), and Arabic grammatical rules in understanding the meaning of the primary sources of *Al-Qur'ān* and *As-Sunnah*, may result in different rulings. A proper understanding of the immutable rulings by Muslim jurists, whose judgement depends also on expertise in *Usul-Al-Fiqh*, is essential for the extraction of rules and regulations that guide human beings in the conduct of spiritual life and social activities in constantly changing environments. Thus, though the terms Islamic law and Islamic jurisprudence tend to be used interchangeably, *As-Shariah* should not be confused with *Al-Fiqh*. However important the role of Islamic jurisprudence can be, it remains a means to an end, and as such, it cannot guide Islamic law, because fallible corpus juris cannot guide infallible divine text. It is the latter that should, under all conditions, take precedence and exert authoritative control over the former.

Insofar as Islamic economics is concerned, Muslims believe that the end has always been the realization of an ideal Islamic economic system governed by justice. The objective of Islamic law is not to burden people with strict rules and behavioural norms but to organize the economy in ways that achieve balance between rights with responsibilities and promote harmony between private pursuits and social interest. It is important for Islamic law to accommodate changes in the society, and it is thus, inconceivable that Islamic jurisprudence or *fiqh* remains an immutable body of legal rulings. As noted above, only Islamic law is immutable, Islamic jurisprudence is not. And as argued by Mohammad Hashim Kamali (2000, p. 82), "when a particular ruling no longer attains its underlying purpose and rationale, it should be changed and substituted with a suitable alternative. To do otherwise would mean neglecting the objective of the Lawgiver (*maqāsid al-sharīᶜ*) and the purpose of His law. To make *fiqh* accommodate with the realities of society is at once the essence and principal task of *ijtihād*. It is a collective duty (*fard kafā'i*), on all of those qualified to make a contribution, to initiate the necessary changes to *fiqh* and thereby help to keep the *Shari'ah* a relevant and viable force for the Muslim community." Thus, *ijtihād* or the intellectual effort to arrive at new rulings in Islamic jurisprudence necessitated by the emergence of unprecedented issues in the society should rest on the fundamental postulates of *As-Sharī'āh* contained in the primary sources of *Al-Qur'ān* and *As-Sunnah*.[11] Given the primacy of divine law, no ruling with established roots in *As-Sharī'āh* requires consistency with the conventional wisdom of secular legal systems because certitude can only be gained from sacred knowledge.

The main schools of Islamic jurisprudence, including the *Maliki*, *Hanbali*, *Hanafi*, and *Shafii*, among others, have derived corpus juris with legal maxims and accommodative rules that has no parallel in the history of the law. However, as argued by Jonathan Ercanbrack (2015, p. 5), "Islamic law, in particular rules concerning commerce, has not been a functioning legal system for over 150 years." Part of the reason has to do with the imposition of state law on Muslim populations during the European colonial era, but attempts to reintroduce Islamic law after independence have been resisted in the name of modernity. The fact that many

Muslim countries have discarded Islamic law at the end of the nineteenth century and continue to do so to this date, does not mean that Islamic economics should grow outside the realm of Islam and independently from Islamic law and Islamic jurisprudence.

Given the universality of the message of Islam, the notion that Islamic economics must serve the needs of humanity at large should not be a matter of concern. The *raison d'être* of Islamic economics, which should not be overlooked, is to establish the organizing principles and policies regulating an ideal economy that serves the conscience of Muslims. It does not exclude others, however, from sharing economic prosperity on the basis of the risk-sharing principle. Islamic economics sets the agenda for the organization of a just economic system for the well-being of all humanity. Indeed, as noted by Abbas Mirakhor (2016), both Muslim and non-Muslim residents are active elements of the same Ummah or society according to the preamble of the *Constitution of Medinah*, which constitutes the first written social contract in the history of humanity. It is a declaration of rights for all citizens, independent of religious beliefs, ethnic backgrounds or skin colours. It is a constitution that preserves the rights of minorities and protects them against discriminatory treatment, oppression, prosecution, and structural economic disadvantage. It is a social contract that stands in sharp contrast with the present-day dehumanizing treatment of economic migrants and crisis in inter-faith relations.

Thus, Islam is not an ethno-centric, time-dependent, and geographic-bounded religion. Given the universality of its message and recognition of universal rights, there is no reason to bend Islamic law or swing its pendulum toward extremes in directionless agitation to give undue prominence to new secular ideas about diversity, equality, globalism, and liberalism, *inter alia*. The Islamic corpus juris of rulings on standard contracts to facilitate production and exchange that accommodate social change and economic uncertainty is a testimony to the fact that the immutable Islamic law provides solutions to all humanity at all times. Accommodative Islamic jurisprudence is arrived at through reasoning by analogy or syllogism *qiyas*, assessment of public interest *maslahah 'ammah* and conditions of necessity, but the canons of Islamic law resist combination with secular norms.

The Secularization of Islamic Law

The principal objectives of Islamic law, it is usually argued, is the protection of human welfare, including faith, life, intellect, lineage, and property. According to Abu Hamid Muhammad Al-Ghazali (1058–1111), it is the protection of these five elements through the pursuance of benefit *maslahah* and prevention of harm *mafsadah* that constitutes Allah (swt)'s purpose in revealing the divine law *Shari'ah*. Since the purpose of divine law lies primarily in the promotion of justice, there are legitimate concerns about attempts to alter Islamic jurisprudence to serve vested interests in the name of legal modernism and the globalization of ideas and knowledge. For Muslim scholars aware of the dangers of pitting modern *fiqh* against classical *fiqh*, the answer is obvious. Mustafa Ahmad Al-Zarqa (2014, p. xxxiii) argues that the substitution of classical *fiqh* developed by successive generations of devoted and diligent scholarship with foreign jurisprudence and legislation that detaches Muslims from their beliefs, is "a declaration of bankruptcy rather than borrowing."

A corollary question arises as to whether the secularization of the *Shari'ah* was in fact facilitated by concerted efforts to undermine classical fiqh with the establishment of public welfare *maslahah 'ammah* not as a means to base legal rulings but as the source of Islamic law. Aharon Layish (1978, p. 263) argues that the modernist movement in Islam has failed to reshape Islamic doctrine, but the creation of new legal devices, such as the eclectic mechanism *takhayyur* or combination of legal elements from different schools of thought and patching *talfiq*, has been instrumental in undermining the classical *fiqh*, and paving the way to "intensive parliamentary secular legislation." The aim of legal modernism is to construct, particularly with issues of *mu'amalat* or interractions between people, *waqf* and personal endowments, a new jurisprudential edifice by borrowing different elements from various schools of Islamic jurisprudence to produce legal rulings that promote *maslahah 'ammah* or socially desirable outcomes.[12] It is, thus, argued that many statutory laws disguised as rulings firmly rooted in the *Shari'ah*, are in fact purely secular.

The secularisation of Islamic law is also driven by the transformation of the *Shari'ah* role in the legal system from the jurist's law to the statutory law, which is valid only within defined jurisdictions. A turning point is represented by the departure from *fiqh* through the enactment of codified legislation, where the codification of commercial law, for instance, allowed for interest-based transactions. The introduction of the judicial practice of the Supreme Constitutional Court underscored these significant transformations, as judicial decisions handed down by *Shari'ah* courts ceased to be binding. Indeed, decisions by lower courts confirming the prohibition of interest are more likely to be overturned by the Supreme Court, asserting thereby the primacy of commercial practice and customs as the most important source of law. The incremental decline in the role of Islamic law is evident in the reduction of *as-Shari'ah* to the status of customary law, and the transformation of Islam as a religion into personal belief system. Part of the reason behind the nationalization of endowment *waqf* properties is the control of financial resources in order to deprive Muslim legal scholars from their independent status and undermine their authoritative role in the *Shari'ah* discourse, paving thereby the way to the emergence of new elites of malleable secular legal experts.

Without any of the three pillars of Islamic law, including the intellectual creed, spiritual worship, and judicial legal system, it is impossible for Islamic economics to set the agenda for the organization of an ideal Islamic economy. It is impossible for such an agenda to be implemented and for the Islamic economy to radiate out with secular minds, weak spirits, and secularized legal systems.[13] Given its roots in the worldview of Islam, Islamic economics is not meant to grow in every direction, driven by unwarranted alterations of Islamic law in alignment with secular legal systems. It is difficult to confess ignorance to the truth that ends cannot justify the means, and that Muslim economists should extract economic principles and implement economic policies with reference to Islamic law as "the" not simply "a" source of Islamic economic thought. The distinction is important because if Islamic economics is to accommodate *hybrid* legal systems, it should be more appropriately referred to as *hybrid* Islamic economics. Similarly, if Islamic economics is based indeed on secular law, it would be nothing more than an oxymoron of "*Secular*" Islamic Economics.

ISLAMIC LAW OF TRANSACTION AND ECONOMIC DEVELOPMENT

Unlike the divine sources of knowledge including *Al-Qur'ān* and *As-Sunnah*, it is not possible to regard Islamic jurisprudence to be quite so sacrosanct as to remain immune to criticism for reasons related to the secularization of legal minds. It is imperative to rethink the important role of Islamic jurisprudence in the development of Islamic economic thought and the organization of an ideal economy. In this respect, Mohammad Hashim Kamali (2000, p. 2) argues that Islamic commercial law constitutes one of the most important fields of Islamic studies. Research on legal issues related to commercial transaction or *fiqh mu^{c}āmalāt* is essential for the generation of wealth and economic development in Muslim countries. There is evidence that Arab societies were pioneers in the history of commerce in terms of forward trading and use of commercial papers, preceding other parts of the world by several centuries.[14] The issuance of commodity coupons (*sukūk al-badhā'i^c*) by the government to its employees instead of the pay during the early Umayyad rule can thus be regarded as government debt. The sale of *sukuk al-badhā'i^c* or warehouse receipts before maturity is also akin to the contemporary concept of futures contracts. Thus, it is noted that the "reason that this kind of commercial practice –and certain other related ones such as the letter of credit (*hawālah*), bills of exchange (*safātij*) and promissory notes (*ruq^c al-sayārifah*)– found acceptance so early in the history of commerce is due to Qur'anic approval of deferred liability transactions, that is the concept of *mudāyanah* (see *Al-Qur'ān* 2:282) and the explicit validation of forward sale (*salam*) in the *Sunnah* of the Prophet Mohammed (*saa*).

Despite these pioneering practices, Islam still stands on the receiving end of criticism that as a source of backwardness and ignorance, it merely makes promises of economic prosperity that it does not live up to. It is often argued that Islamic law and its administration cannot promote the development of modern capitalism. Tony Huff (1999, p. 15) argues that by eliminating risk in business, Islamic law does not facilitate modern capitalist entrepreneurship. He further contends that Muslim countries cannot follow the economic development path to fulfil the expectations for shared prosperity and better life without jettisoning "virtually all aspects of Islamic law that relate to business and commercial activities." It is rather fashionable to claim without hard evidence that a secularization of Islamic law is a prerequisite for capitalism and economic development in the Muslim world, as suggested by Timur Kuran (2011, pp. x–xi), who argues that Islamic law was by no means a static construct, but "in certain areas critical to economic modernization, change was minimal" at a time when the West made transition from medieval to modern economic institutions. Unfounded claims that Islamic law are the source of economic retardation are, to say the least, misguided and inaccurate. There is a failure to distinguish between Islam as a religion, and Islam as a civilization, between sacred knowledge and secularized reason, and between Islamic law (*As-Shari'ah*) and Islamic jurisprudence (*Al-Fiqh*). Also, Murat Çizakça (2011, p. xiv) makes the strong argument about Islamic capitalism of the classical age, which some sincere Muslims may find irksome "was an economic system derived basically from the *Al-Qur'ān* and Prophetic traditions." The bulk of Islamic jurisprudence, which is deemed now the source of economic retardness, was laid down, in fact, by merchants who firmly believed in free markets, and refuted interference in the price discovery process. The Islamic legal principles and guidelines in matters related to exchange and commerce were defined earlier by the tradition of the Prophet (saa), a merchant who went about in market-places for a living, and the righteous Caliphs, Abu Bakr As-Siddiq and Uthman ibn 'Affan, businessmen who traded in cloth and cereals, respectively.[15] Thus, if as suggested by Bagehot (1880, p. 5), Political Economy can be defined as the science of business, then it is a historical truism to suggest that the legal foundations of political economy and the science of business were established through the development of commercial law and business practices in early Muslim societies.

Thus, while objective scholarly criticism of Islamic law and commercial practices is acceptable, a meandering of historical truth is not. Islamic law is not just the translation of the needs of society but a reflection of its ideals as well. It is unthinkable that a *corpus juris* of Islamic rulings, which covers all aspects of life in every detail, and has no precedent in the history of law, is deemed to be irrelevant to the regulation of modern life, including commercial transactions and economic activities. Nicholas Forster (2006) notes that there is neither a Christian law of contract nor a Christian law of property but "unlike Christianity in which law is secular," there does exist a body of laws in *As-Shari'ah* dealing with commercial matters. The French Code de Commerce, which exercised a strong influence on the promulgation of commercial law in several parts of the world has no religious roots. As suggested by Joël Monéger (2004), neither the philosophy of Enlightenment nor the spirit of the French Revolution made noticeable contributions to its development. "This code of merchants owes more to the Ancien Régime, and in particular Colbert, the great minister of King Louis XIV in the 17th century, to the need for order and to the anger of the emperor after the repeated bankruptcies of suppliers to the army, than to a vision of the business world that would emerge under the effects of the Civil Code and social mutations." It is further argued that the three French codification of commercial law, including the *Code Savary* in 1673, Napoleonic *Code de Commerce* in 1807, and *Commercial Code* in 2000, suffer from fundamental flaws, in that they either merely recognize the law of yesterday and ignore the reality of present times, or do not capture the course of commercial development in the future.[16] As such, French legislators tend to enact new rules in the field of commercial law without integrating them into the existing code. It is noted also that the current efforts to promote a European Business Code as a vector of economic, fiscal, and social convergence are opposed by several Member States on the grounds that "codification is a 'French specificity' that should not be brought at the level of the Union."[17]

Thus, the adoption or rejection of secular law by secular societies remains a sovereign decision. While Muslim leaders with secular minds may be inclined to succumb to external pressure, resistance by faithful Muslims to the secularization of Islamic law is not a matter of choice. The fact that Islamic jurisprudence developed, centuries ahead of others, a rich body of forward-looking commercial law recognizing the impact of economic uncertainty and risk, and dealing with the sources of informational asymmetry and ambiguity, should be a matter of pride, not shame. The *Al-Qur'ān* includes many verses of legal content and exemplary behaviour of the Prophet (*saa*) as trader is beyond doubt. Islamic law retained some Pre-Islamic Arabian customs that do not contravene the maxims of *As-Shari'ah*, others were abrogated or modified. Given the principle of permissibility as the norm, the objective of the Islamic legal system does not lie in the dissolution of cultures and fragmentation of cultural identities but in the reform of customary practices in order to serve an ideal economy that would benefit a stable and prosperous society.

As argued by Richard Potz (2011), the influence of Islamic law on the European legal system is both territorial given the history of Muslim rule in parts of Europe, and factual, particularly in commercial law given the existence of common economic interests. As the debate continues also on the European adoption of theoretic-methodological concepts, there is also new evidence about the origins of the common law. For instance, John A. Makdisi (1999) argues that "the legal institutions of the common law fit within a structural and functional pattern that is unique among western legal systems and certainly different from that of the civil law. The coherence of this pattern strongly suggests the dominating influence of a single preexisting legal tradition rather than a patchwork of influences from multiple legal systems overlaid on a Roman fabric. The only problem is that no one preexisting legal tradition has yet been found to fit the picture." It can be, thus, argued that the single coherent "preexisting legal tradition" is none but Islamic law. Indeed, the principal institutions that helped create the common law in the twelfth century for the first time in English history, including the contract law regulating the transfer of property ownership, property law protecting possession as a form of property ownership, and the trial by jury in the settlement of disputes, have their common roots nowhere but in Islamic legal tradition. The parallel "preexisting" Islamic institutions of *'aqd*, *istihqaq*, and *lafīf* constitute the precursors for English contract, assize of novel disseisin, and trial by jury, respectively.

There is also earlier evidence from Abraham Udovitch (1962) who suggests that the European partnership agreement of *commenda*, which was instrumental in the expansion of Mediterranean trade in the tenth and eleventh centuries, has its origins in Islam law. Further evidence is provided by Ron Harris (2020) who notes that the sophisticated *commenda* has its origins in the Arabian Peninsula, known in Islamic jurisprudence as *mudhārabah*, *qirādh*, or *muqāradhah*. It is neither a loan agreement nor an employment contract as it combines several functions within a single legal-economic institution with payoffs determined *ex post* depending on the realization of profits or losses. The profit-loss-sharing agreement predated the Italian *commenda*, which was emulated through commercial connections into other Mediterranean cities including Marseille and Barcelona. There is also scattered credible evidence pointing to the use of *qirādh* contracts by Indian maritime merchants, including Muslim Gujarati merchants trading with Persia and Arabia. There are also historical links between *qirādh* and the commercial institution of *ortaq* which extends from Persia to China. The singular term *ortoy*, which means "merchant partner," appears in the ninth-to-eleventh-century Uyghur sources related to Turkic trade networks. The evidence lends support to the argument that it is Muslim Turkish or Persian merchants who introduced the partnership model to Mongolia and China in the twelfth or thirteenth century, with further extension into Central Asia through the expansion of the Mongolian empire. As historical facts speak for themselves, Islamic legal rulings and practices were passed on through the ages with wide acceptance by diverse societies and cultures because of their innovative properties and ability to accommodate risk, which is inherent to all commercial transactions and economic activities that span time and space. The *fiqhi* process of *ijtihād*, which reflects intellectual efforts by qualified Muslim jurists to understand Islamic law, *Al-Shari'ah*, ensures that new rulings are necessitated by the observed or anticipated alterations and modifications in the space-contingent and time-dependent means caused by social and technological change. Islamic law does not discourage production, commerce, industry, entrepreneurship, and investment but it upholds the sanctity of private ownership, risk sharing, and freedom of contract with mutual consent and forbids deception, duress, fraud, impediments to trade, and other forms of injustice. Thus, of corrupt reputation, Islamic law has none to repair, and of borrowed legislation, there is none to redeem.

Despite the historical evidence of significant contributions to legal systems around the world, the dramatic change in current thinking from innovation to imitation through allegedly innocuous borrowing of secular ideas from secular legal systems under the banner of the secularization of Islamic law or Islamization of financial practices is fatally compromised. It is vain, indeed, to seek an Islamic counterpart for every species of commercial and financial contracts used in conventional finance. Driven by a desire to portray a modern image of the discipline, attempts to advance Islamic finance by reconciling Islamic law with secular practices are equally misguided. Murat Çizakça (2011, p. 4) argues that, even from the perspective of pure cost-benefit analysis, the *Shari'ah*-compliant approach to Islamic finance suffers from a dilemma pertaining to the inherent contradiction of improving efficiency at higher costs. If the objective of emulating conventional instruments is to derive efficiency gains, he argues, then the current emphasis of the Islamic finance industry on Arabic nomenclature and certification by *Shari'ah* experts are bound to increase rather than decrease costs. More serious criticism is levied by Timur Kuran (1989, p. 162) about the use of financing methods equivalent to interest-based transactions in the Islamic finance industry. Part of the reason for the conflated practice may have to do with a lack of expertise in assessing investment opportunities, and aversion toward risk-sharing finance which may ultimately lead to more losses than profits. There is also fear that less risky but more profitable customers might find better financing opportunities for borrowing at lower costs, and parallel fear that only more risky customers with higher likelihood of losses might be interested in profit-loss-sharing financing modes.

A recognition of public welfare *maslahah 'ammah* as the *de facto* source of Islamic law rather than a means to arrive at new legal rulings may have influenced the issuance of legal rulings that permit *Shari'ah* arbitrage and recalibration of the *modus operandi* of conventional finance and banking. Mahmoud El-Gamal (2006, p. 44), notes that legal stratagems and ruses *hiyal*, which merely involve the formal adherence to classical contract conditions, such as in the contract of same-item sale-repurchase *bay' al-'ayyinah* represent a clear violation of Islamic law. The mere adherence to form in the design of repurchase agreements is regarded as an elaborate and disguised attempt to circumvent the prohibition of interest or *riba*. Classical Islamic jurisprudence is clear on the impermissibility of such practices. As argued by Ibrahim Ibn Musa Abu Ishaq Al-Shatibi (1320–1388), compliance to the law is not about adhering to the form while squandering its substance. Also, Ibn Qayyim al-Jawziyyah (1292–1350) defined *hiyal* as the subtle management of aspects of a legal transaction in ways for which they were not intended. As the established principle in Islamic law is that (*a'māl*) based upon intentions (*niyyāt*), it is important to recognize the sale-repurchase contract as a means toward an end, and that the end can hardly be the transfer of ownership of the underlying asset. Given these clear classical Islamic rulings, innovation in Islamic finance should not be confused with blind imitation, adding the prefix "Islamic" to impermissible interest-loaded practices. As noted by Muhammad Ayub (2007), there is no obligation that financial innovation must engineer an Islamic finance product for each and every conventional instrument. The free-riding on conventional finance is in fact facilitated by an addictive reliance on borrowing from secular legal systems and secular institutions. It is incumbent on *fiqh* scholars, Islamic finance practitioners, and *Shari'ah* boards to ensure that Islamic financial services remain in conformity with the tenets of Islamic law, not merely in resemblance to its form.

As *Shari'ah* arbitrage is allowed to take various forms through the apparent use of nominate agreements and selective compliance with the requirements of classical contracts, there are growing concerns that the essence of the "Islamic jurisprudence" which provided innovative solutions to complex commercial needs in the past, is being altered beyond recognition to serve the narrow interests of the modern Islamic finance industry. There are diverging views on the future relationship between Islamic jurisprudence and Islamic finance. Mahmoud El-Gamal (2006, p. 45) expresses the hope that, at least in the short term, the "focus on form does not exclude consideration of economic substance entirely." It is further hoped that modest increments in substance may serve as catalysts for the long-term development of a "viable modern Islamic jurisprudence." With strong hopes, however, there are also real fears. Murat Çizakça (2011) argues, in contrast, that unless it develops its own genuine Islamic financial instruments, "Islamic finance will continue being an imitation of conventional finance, always one step behind it, with the result that the clients of the industry will lose hope that it will ever provide a hope of a bona fide alternative to conventional finance." The fear, indeed, is that the unwarranted and repeated recourse to legal stratagems and concealed forms of agreements would become an established trait, akin to the pursuance of individual desires, whims, and self-interest. It is irrational to adopt Islamic rulings meant to legitimize behavioural traits, which can only undermine the credibility of Islamic institutions and the stability of Islamic financial systems that are crucial in the organization of an ideal Islamic economy.

Thus, it is difficult to argue that Islamic jurisprudence and Islamic economics have evolved over the past centuries on the basis of authentic Islamic teachings and philosophy. There is, indeed, little evidence that the former has genuinely evolved and stronger evidence that the latter has been seriously compromised. It is important for Muslim legal scholars and economists to grasp the reality that there is no merit in intellectual attempts to fit secular ideals and ideologies into Islam. Secularization, as a philosophical program concerned with secular life and secular destiny, can only sever the connection of the consciousness of Muslims with the Islamic worldview. It contributes to intellectual confusion and error in knowledge. In a secular scheme of things, it is impossible to identify legal maxims or economic principles that can be truly Islamized either. The *Impossibility Theorem*, introduced in another chapter of this book, implies that given the radical differences in metaphysical, philosophical, and epistemological foundations, attempts at grafting secular ideas and Islamic principles one onto the other are bound to fail. Thus, it seems that for now, Islamic jurisprudence and Islamic economic thought, which used to go hand in hand, are both leaning against the wind.

Notes

1. For further evidence on the significant contributions of Muslim scholars in refutation of the Schumpeterian Great Gap, reference can be made for instance to Hamid S. Hosseini (2003), among others.

2. Reference is made to *Al-Qur'ān* (54:49), which reads "Verily, all things have We created in proportion and measure." Thus, the notion of absolute scarcity is rather inconceivable from the Islamic perspective of the unity of creation.
3. Reference can be made to the Statement of Principles of the American Economic Association (1887), which reads "Article III. 3. We hold that the conflict of labor and capital has brought into prominence a vast number of social problems, whose solution requires the united efforts, each in its own sphere, of the church, of the state, and of science." In a statement by its secretary, Richard T. Ely argued that "we wish to accomplish certain practical results in the social and financial world, and believing that our work lies in the direction of practical Christianity, we appeal to the church, the chief of the social forces in this country, to help us, to support us, and to make our work a complete success, which it can by no possibility be without her assistance" (American Economic Association, 1887, p. 18). See also Richard T. Ely (1910) for further insights on the history of the foundation and earlier days.
4. See for instance, Benson Saler (1987)'s examination of the etymology and definition of religion, where he notes that there are "two candidates from which *religio* may have derived: *legere*, 'to gather together', 'to arrange', a proposed derivation that we associate with Cicero, and *ligare*, 'to tie together', 'to bind', a possibility entertained by Lucretius and favored by the Christian writers, Lactantius and Tertullian."
5. It is also noted that Syed Muhammad Naquib Al-Attas (2005, p. 11) further argues that the perverse use of the Arabic phrase *nazrat al-islam li al-kawn* in contemporary Muslim thought is indicative of the unwarranted reference and undue influence of the modern, secular Western scientific conception of the worldview as confined to the world of sense and sensible experience.
6. Reference is made to Descartes (1644 [2009], p. 266 and p. 100), "*nos non a nobis ipsis, sed a Deo factos, eumque proinde existere*" [Part 1, *art.* 20], and "*credenda esse omnia quæ a Deo revelata sunt, quamvis captum nostrum excedant*" [Part 1, *art.* 25], respectively.
7. It is noted, however, that opponents to secularism *à la française* argue that the maxim of *laïcité*, which rests on the separation of religion from real life, is restrictive of the freedom of belief.
8. *Al Muqaddimah* constitutes a multidisciplinary approach to several fields of study including sociology, philosophy of history, ethnography, and political economy.
9. See for instance, Jamil Farooqui (1998, p. 199) argues that "Durkheim's concept of man as a being differs from that of Islam in the sense that he ignores the human urge and search for truth. When he explains individual

conscience, he highlights those individuality traits that emerge from physical craving and organic structure. He completely ignores the human's psychic, intellectual and spiritual needs, which are just as important as the former."
10. It is noted that in English, the phrase Islamic law is used to refer invariably to the *Shari'ah* and *Fiqh*. The distinction should be made however, between the former which is based on divine revelation, and the latter which represents its understanding by legal experts. The primary sources of *Shari'ah* are *Al-Qur'ān* and *As-Sunnah*, defined as the tradition of the Prophet Muhammad (*saws*) including his sayings and conduct. Islamic jurisprudence or *fiqh* is the result of intellectual legal insights *corpus juris* by various schools of thought (*Madhāhib*), scholars and judges through independent reasoning *ijtihād* and issuance of legal opinions *fatawa* to accommodate specific rulings *ahkam* to the changing needs of the society.
11. With respect to the principles of judgment, reference can be made to Mustafa Ahmad Al-Zarqa (2014, p. 41), who noted that "In the letter of Caliph 'Umar ibn Khattab to Abu Musa al Ash'ari (may Allah be pleased with them) while guiding him to the principles of judgment and its ideal method, the Caliph wrote: '*Use your brain on matters that perplex you and to which neither the Qur'an nor the Sunnah seem to apply. Know the similitude and weigh the issues accordingly. Follow that which is the closest to Allah and most resembling to the truth*'" (italics in original).
12. Reference can be made to previous efforts toward legal modernism driven by Muhammad 'Abduh, and Muhammad Rashid Rida, among others.
13. Reference is made, for instance, to *Al-Qur'ān* (2:256) "let there be no compulsion in religion: truth stands out clear from error."
14. Mohammad Hashim Kamali (2000, p. 2) notes that "[i]t is particularly interesting to note that soldiers and government officials during the early Umayyad rule (late seventh century/first century Hijra –when many of the leading Companions were still alive) were issued commodity coupons (*sukūk al-badā'i^c*) in lieu of the pay. Imam Malik has thus stated in his *Muwatta'* that *sukūk al-badā'i^c* found currency among people and they were brought and sold prior to maturity."
15. See *Al-Qur'ān* (25:7) which addresses the disdainful remarks of the disbelievers about the mundane life of the Prophet Muhammad (*saws*) "And they say 'mockingly', "What kind of messenger is this who eats food and goes about in marketplaces 'for a living'?"
16. The three codes referred to in Joël Monéger (2004) are the Colbert Ordinance introduced in 1673, the Napoleon Code of Commerce enacted in 1807, and the current Code de Commerce in application since 2000. He argues that "none of these codes met its objectives. As a result, their usefulness for practitioners remains in question. Legislators themselves do

not pay attention to them, passing new bills in the field of commercial law but not incorporating them into the existing code."
17. Reference can be made to the article by Philippe Dupichot (2021) on the efforts to craft a common European business law for Member States of the European Union.

References

Ahmad, A. R. Yusri. 2002. "Methodological Approach in Islamic Economics: Its Philosophy, Theoretical Contribution and Applicability." In *Theoretical Foundations of Islamic Economics*, edited by Habib Ahmed, 20–60. Jeddah: Islamic Research and Training Institute, Islamic Development Bank.
Al-Alwani, Taha Jaber. 1990. "The Reconstruction of the Muslim Mind: The Islamization of Knowledge." *American Journal of Islamic Social Sciences* 7: 453–457 (translated by Yusuf Talal DeLorenzo).
Al-Alwani, Taha Jaber. 1995. "The Islamization of Knowledge: Yesterday and Today." *American Journal of Islamic Social Sciences* 12: 81–101 (translated by Yusuf Talal DeLorenzo).
Al-Attas, Syed Muhammad Naquib. 1993. *Islam and Secularism*. Kuala Lumpur: International Institute of Islamic Thought and Civilization.
Al-Attas, Syed Muhammad Naquib. 2005. "Islamic Philosophy: An Introduction." *Journal of Islamic Philosophy* 1: 11–43.
Al-Zarqa, Mustafa Ahmad. 2014. *Introduction to Islamic Jurisprudence*. Kuala Lumpur: IBFIM,
American Economic Association. 1887. *Publications of the American Economic Association*. Vol. 1. Baltimore: John Murphy & Co.
Askari, Hossein, Zamir Iqbal, and Abbas Mirakhor. 2015. *Introduction to Islamic Economics: Theory and Application*. Singapore: John Wiley & Sons.
As-Sadr, Muhammad Baqir. 1982 [1994]. *Iqtisādunā—Our Economics*, 2nd ed., vol. 2, Part 1. Tehran, Iran: World Organization for Islamic Services.
Ayub, Muhammad. 2007. *Understanding Islamic Finance*. West Sussex: Wiley.
Bagehot, Walter. 1880. *Economic Studies*. Edited by Richard Holt Hutton. London: Longmans, Green and Co.
Blaug, Mark. 1992. The Methodology of Economics: Or How Economists Explain. (2nd ed., Cambridge Surveys of Economic Literature). Cambridge: Cambridge University Press.
Boulding, Kenneth E. 1969. "Economics as a Moral Science." *The American Economic Review* 59 (1): 1–12
Chapra, Umer. 1990. "What is Islamic Economics." Islamic Development Bank Prize Winner's Lecture Series No. 9. Jeddah, Saudi Arabia: Islamic Research and Training Institute.

Choudhury, Masudul Alam. 1998. "Why Cannot Neoclassicism Explain Resource Allocation and Development in the Islamic Political Economy?" In *Studies in Islamic Political Science*. Springer, Palgrave Macmillan.

Çizakça, Murat. 2011. *Islamic Capitalism and Finance*. Cheltenham: Edward Elgar.

de Nemours, Pierre Samuel Dupont. 1879. *Physiocratie, ou Constitution Naturelle du Gouvernement le Plus Avantageux au Genre Humain*. Dupont des Sociétés Royales d'Agriculture de Soissons & d'Orléans.

Descartes, René. 1644 [2009]. *Les Principes de la Philosophie* (in French). Paris: Librairie Philosophique, J. Vrin.

Dupichot, Philippe. 2021. "Designing a Common European Business Law." Revue Européenne du Droit, December.

El-Gamal, Mahmoud A. 2006. *Islamic Finance: Law, Economics, and Practice*. New York: Cambridge University Press.

Ely, Richard T. 1910. "The American Economic Association 1885–1909." *American Economic Association Quarterly* 11: 47–111.

Ercanbrack, Jonathan G. 2015. *The Transformation of Islamic Law in Global Financial Markets*. Cambridge: Cambridge University Press.

Farooqui, Jamil. 1998. "Durkheim's Concept of Man and Society: An Analysis." *Encounters Journal of Inter-Cultural Perspectives* 4 (2): 181–204.

Forster, Nicholas H. D. 2006. "Islamic Commercial Law: An Overview (I)." Revista Para El Analisis del Derecho.

Haneef, Mohamed Aslam Mohamed. 1997. "Islam, the Islamic Worldview, and Islamic Economics." *IIUM Journal of Economics & Management* 5: 39–65.

Haque, Ziaul. 1992. "Nature and Methodology of Islamic Economics: An Appraisal." *The Pakistan Development Review* 31: 1065–1075.

Harris, Ron. 2020. "The Commenda." In *Going the Distance: Eurasian Trade and the Rise of the Business Corporation, 1400–1700*, Chapter 5. Princeton and Oxford: Princeton University Press.

Hasan, Zubair. 1998. "Islamization of Knowledge in Economics: Issues and Agenda." *IIUM Journal of Economics and Management* 6: 1–40.

Hasanuz Zaman, S. M. 1984. "Definition of Islamic Economics." *Journal of King Abdulaziz University Islamic Economics* 1: 49–50.

Hayek, Friedrich. 1940. "Scientism and the Study of Society: Part I." *Economica* 9: 267–291.

Hosseini, Hamid S. 2003. "Contributions of Medieval Muslim Scholars to the History of Economics and Their Impact: A Refutation of the Schumpeterian Great Gap." In *A Companion to the History of Economic Thought*, Chapter 3. Malden, MA: Blackwell.

Huff, T. E. 1999. "Introduction." In *Max Weber and Islam*, edited by T. E. Huff and Schluchter Wolfgang, 1–52. New Brunswick: Transaction Publishers.

Ibn Khaldun, Abdur Rahman. 1337 [2005]. *Al Muqaddimah*. Translated by Franz Rosenthal. Princeton: Princeton University Press.
Ingram, John Kells. 1888. *A History of Political Economy*. Edinburgh: Adam and Charles Black, Ltd.
Islahi, Abdul Azim. 2014. *History of Islamic Economic Thought: Contributions of Muslim Scholars to Economic Thought and Analysis*. Cheltenham, UK: Edward Elgar.
Kamali, Mohammad Hashim. 2000. *Islamic Commercial Law*. Cambridge: Islamic Texts Society.
Khan, Muhammad Akram. 1991. The Future of Islamic Economics. *Futures* 23 (3): 248–261.
Khan, Muhammad Akram. 2013. *What Is Wrong with Islamic Economics? Analyzing the Present State and Future Agenda*. Cheltenham: Edward Elgar.
Krugman, Paul. 1995. "The Fall and Rise of Development Economics." In *Development, Geography, and Economic Theory*, 1–29. MIT Press: Cambridge Massachusetts and London England.
Kuran, Timur. 1989. "Islamic Economics and the Islamic Subeconomy." *Journal of Economic Perspectives* 9: 155–173.
Kuran, Timur. 2011. "The Long Divergence: How Islamic Law Held Back the Middle East." Princeton and Oxford: Princeton University Press.
Layish, Aharon. 1978. "The Contribution of the Modernists to the Secularization of Islamic Law." *Middle Eastern Studies* 14: 263–277.
Makdisi, John A. 1999. "The Islamic Origins of the Common Law." *North Carolina Law Review* 77: 1635–1739.
Mannan, Muhammad Abdul. 1970. *Islamic Economics: Theory and Practice (A Comparative Study)*. Lahore: Muhammad Ashraf Publisher.
Mirakhor, Abbas. 1987. "The Muslim Scholars and the History of Economics: A Need for Consideration." *The American Journal of Islamic Social Sciences* 4: 245–276.
Mirakhor, Abbas. 2016. "Seyed Kazem Sadr, The Economic System of the Early Islamic Period: Institutions and Policies." *Journal of Economic and Social Thought* 3: 458–466.
Monéger, Joël. 2004. "From the Colbert Ordinance on Trade to the 2000 French Commercial Code: A Reflection on the Potential of Economic and Commercial Law to be Codified." *Revue Internationale de Droit Economique* 2: 171–196.
Nasr, Seyyed Hossein. 2000. *Ideals and Realities of Islam*. Chicago: ABC International Group, Inc.
Nasr, Seyyed Hossein. 2007. *The Essential Seyyed Hossein Nasr*. Bloomington, IN: World Wisdom, Inc.
Potz, Richard. 2011. "Islam and Islamic Law in European Legal History." *Europäische Geschichte Online*.

Rubin, Jared. 2017. *Rulers, Religion and Riches: Why the West Got Rich and the Middle East Did Not*. New York: Cambridge University Press.

Sadr, Seyed Kazem. 2016. *The Economic System of the Early Islamic Period: Institutions and Policies*. New York: Palgrave Macmillan.

Saler, Benson. 1987. "*Religio* and the Definition of Religion." *Culture Anthropology* 2: 395–399.

Udovitch, Abraham. 1962. "At the Origin of the Western Commenda: Islam, Israel, Byzantium?" *Speculum* 42: 198–207.

Weisskopf, Walter. 1971. *Alienation and Economics*. New York: E. P. Dutton & Co.

CHAPTER 4

Ethics of *Iqtiṣād*

Ethics seek to develop moral conduct based on a set of values that determines what is intrinsically right or wrong for a given society.[1] How these ethics are derived from the values is subject to diverse sources and theories. Ethical behaviour is also subject to factors such as religious beliefs, the stage of moral development of the society, personal morals and values, family influences, peer influences, and life experiences of individuals or societies.[2] Every system of thought, ancient or contemporary, religious or secular, contains moral norms prohibiting their violation. In one form or another, in one degree or another, their sanctity is affirmed by all cultures and societies. One such example is the universality of the Golden Rule.

For a long while, economists have resisted linking economic theories to ethics, but as economic activities and financial markets advance and the complexity of economic choices increases, it is becoming necessary to incorporate ethical concepts such as honesty, fairness, integrity, trust, and cooperation into mainstream financial economics in more explicit form. Because economic activity involves a complex nexus of interactions economic processes such as production, exchange, and consumption, economic choices have an essential ethical dimension.[3] Aragon (2014, p. 17) calls the phenomenon of ignoring the ethical dimension "moral muteness" and observes that some ethical issues "are transmuted into less morally charged terminology, for example, by referring to financial

© The Author(s), under exclusive license to Springer Nature Switzerland AG 2023
N. El Maghrebi et al., *Revisiting Islamic Economics*, Palgrave Studies in Islamic Banking, Finance, and Economics, https://doi.org/10.1007/978-3-031-41134-2_4

manipulation as 'income smoothing,' lying as 'cheap talk,' or theft as 'rent seeking.'"

Vast research in financial economics on the economic consequences of imperfect information is actually dealing with ethical issues underneath expected behaviour and, therefore, has an ethical dimension embedded in the relevant theories. Two major concepts, moral hazard and adverse selection, are the foundation of several advanced economic and financial theories such as agency costs theory and signalling theory. The classic example of unethical behaviour such as dishonesty and information asymmetries in economics is that of Akerlof's (1970) "lemons" model, in which information asymmetries would lead to market failure when agents are expected to be dishonest. The dual conditions for market failure (that is, information asymmetries and dishonesty) suggested by Akerlof's model reflect the key link between economic value and ethics. **This necessitates that the assumptions about the moral character of economic agents could provide a deeper analysis of their economic behaviour.**[4]

Growing Critic of Conventional Economics' "Moral Muteness"

The gaping inequality, stagnant incomes, large unemployment, string of crippling crises, huge growth of government and consumer debts, and a host of other ills consequent to the operation of present form of capitalism have seriously challenged faith in the system. The widely held perception of selfish, greedy, and harmful business has created a regime uncertainty where, as many argue, there is doubt if the system can be saved from itself or is even worth saving. There can be little doubt that the repeated financial and economic crises and their aftermath demonstrated a fundamentally massive moral failure that has, in turn, caused a moral panic that there is a systemic assault upon human dignity, trust, contracts, and property, all of which constitute fundamental elements of the institutional structure of societies.

The question pertinent to the debate is whether it is the system that has morally failed or the people who operate in the system who have lost their moral and ethical moorings. Compelling arguments have been made that it is the system's moral failure when it creates incentive structures that unleash greed, selfishness, and self-centeredness by removing legal and regulatory restraints on behaviour of finance and business. In these circumstances, conditions are created for Gresham effect to allow bad ethics to drive good ethics out of the market.

The early social thinkers of the seventeenth and eighteenth centuries were fully aware of the very close ties between economics and ethics as many of them actually studied both ethics and political economy. This list includes Jeremy Bentham, David Hume, John Locke, John Stuart Mill, and Adam Smith. These thinkers were concerned about the key question of how one should live and what actions and conduct will be good for society. It is worth noting that Adam Smith, considered the father of Western economics, wrote his book *The Theory of Moral Sentiments* some decade and a half before his other treatise *The Wealth of Nations*. An argument has been made that the proposition discernible from *The Wealth of Nations* regarding the workings of market capitalism must be placed within the institutional framework of *The Theory of Moral Sentiments*, which provides the mooring for them. The decoupling of the two books, in effect, cuts off economics and finance from the ethics of the system envisioned by Smith.[5]

Many leading modern-era economists and thinkers have also voiced serious concerns about the ethical void in prevailing economic thinking. One proponent, Amartya Sen, argues that the distancing of economics from ethics has impoverished Welfare Economics and also weakened the basis of a good deal of descriptive and predictive economics and that economics can be made more productive by paying greater and more explicit attention to ethical considerations that shape human behaviour and judgement. In other words, greater morality can lead to greater efficiency and productivity.[6]

Sen (1987) further raises a very valid concern by questioning why economics gradually shook off its early interest in ethical issues to follow the problem-solving approach of engineering. Williamson (1993) observes that traditional economic theory has developed an analytical framework or methodology that focuses on analytical thinking, formalism, measurement, etc. which is considered unsuited to the analysis of economic choices driven by personal feelings or emotions since such decisions cannot be easily transposed to the straitjacket of quantitative goals. One plausible explanation for such a phenomenon is that during its early stages of development of economics as a social science, it could not be left behind in formulating behavioural issues through quantitative models. The intellectual appeal of physics and engineering during the industrial revolution was too strong to be ignored. In addition, the idea that the limits on resources could be overcome by advanced production means gave priority to tackling poverty over other considerations.[7]

Several important questions have been raised which need addressing to understand the complex relationship between the spheres of ethics and economics. First, does capitalism as a system need ethical conduct to overcome its deficiencies? As pointed out by several prominent social scientists, positive social externalities like trust, loyalty, justice in future dealings, and truthfulness, which define the broad concept of "ethical behaviour," are very much needed to tighten the loopholes in the prevailing practice of the market-based economic system.[8]

In practice, economists carrying out analyses of trust, honesty, fairness, and altruism have worked within the framework of the standard model for decision-making under uncertainty which is dominated by the quantitative model with the objective of maximizing utility. Hence, economists have used quantitative measures of satisfaction for the subject to assess the benefits of concepts of being truthful, helping others, or comparing with a reference group. This approach has been criticized for its many flaws, e.g. in the expected utility framework, prudence may be interpreted as risk aversion and thus not reflecting the reality.[9]

The capitalist system's ability to spontaneously deliver the optimal amount of ethical behaviour is questioned by many such as Arrow (1974) who argues that nothing guarantees this. Given that ethical behaviour has all the characteristics of a positive externality, basic economic theory would suggest that the amount privately supplied will not be optimal. Although everybody prefers to deal with honest, trustful, and compassionate partners, under certain circumstances, there will be incentives for individuals to create private benefits. Therefore, capitalism creates the conditions for the emergence of ethical behaviour but does not guarantee to reach the optimal level.[10]

In short, the view held by many inside and outside the profession is that the problem with economics is its model of man; the Max U approach robs the discipline of its "grand vision." A number of Adam Smith scholars see in the totality of his work a unified grand design. The Theory of Moral Sentiments and Lectures on Jurisprudence provides the moral rules, the institutional scaffolding[11] within which the economy described by The Wealth of Nations is embedded. It is compliance with the rules prescribed by the "Author of Nature" that assures balance in the economy. Recoupling the economy with the ideas in The Theory of Moral Sentiments could help cure conventional economics of its flatness.[12]

Research in various areas such as experimental, behavioural, cognitive, and evolutionary economics, as well as neuroeconomics, has produced evidence of the need to reform the concept of "economic man." It is also heartening that the inclusion of social capital, alongside labour, physical capital, and human capital, is no longer questioned. One wonders how long it will take before "moral capital" is also introduced as another element of the production function.[13]

META-ETHICS OF *IQTIṢĀD*

It is essential that the epistemological roots of moral thoughts, rules, beliefs, and motivation to act right or wrong defining meta-ethics of a system are understood before any framework of ethics for a discipline within that system is developed. In Islamic civilization, economics was never divorced from religious ethics having roots in the Noble Qur'an itself in which discussion of what is now known as *Iqtiṣād* or economics is almost always combined with ethics. The most famous classical Islamic work with this term in its title, that is, *al-Iqtiṣād fī'l-i 'tiqād* by al-Ghazzālī, deals with faith and theology and not with what we call economics today. From the point of view of traditional Islamic thought, *Iqtiṣād* or economics as an independent science is not even considered a legitimate intellectual discipline and is inseparable from ethics.[14]

Before any discussion on the ethics of Islamic economics or *Iqtiṣād* is undertaken, it is necessary to develop an understanding of the Islamic conception of the nature of man and his relationship with the Creator seeking answers to questions such as who man is, what the purpose of his life on earth is, what is his role in the society, and where he is going? The foundation of ethics in Islam is based on core tenets such as oneness of creation, role of man, upholding justice, preserving rights, and others which are briefly discussed below.

Unity of Creation

One of the core and fundamental axioms of Islamic ideology is the belief in the Unity and Oneness of the Creator (*Tawhid*), a corollary of which is the unity of the creation, particularly the unity of mankind. The axiom of Unity and Oneness of the Creator requires one to believe that all creation has only one omniscient and omnipresent Creator—*Allah* (swt)—who has placed man on this earth to pursue his own felicity and perfection.

Further, it becomes incumbent upon each believer to believe that the orbit of man's life is much longer, broader, and deeper than the material dimension of life in this world.

The axiom of the Unity is not only that the Creator is One, but that all His creation constitutes a unity as well. The *Qur'an* calls attention to the fact that despite all apparent multiplicity, human beings are fundamentally of one kind; they were created as one being (*nafs*) and will ultimately return to *Allah* (swt) as one (*nafs*) as well. The *Qur'an* says:

> Neither your creation nor your resurrection is possible other than as one united *nafs*. (31:28)

In a series of verses, the *Qur'an* exhorts man to take collective and unified social action as well as to preserve and protect the collectivity from all elements of disunity.[15] These and many other verses order human beings to work hard toward social unity and cohesion, construct their societies, and preserve and defend that unity. Unity and social cohesion are so central among the objectives of the *Qur'an* for mankind, that it can be argued that all conducts prohibited by Islam are those that ultimately will lead to disunity and social disintegration. Conversely, all righteous conducts prescribed by Islam are those that lead to social integration, cohesiveness, and unity. As a result, Islam is a call to collectivity and has given collectivity an independent personality and identity, which will be judged on its own merits or demerits separately from the individuals that constitute the collectivity. The final judgement on individual actions will have two dimensions, one as the individual and the other as a member of the collectivity.

Model of Man[16]

The concept of "man" in Islam is different from the typical concept of man assumed by the conventional economics. In Islam "man" is at once the servant of God—Allah (*al-ʿabd*) and His vicegerent on earth (*khalīfat Allāh fī'l-ard*.) He is not an animal that happens to speak and think but a being who possesses a soul and spirit created by God as the crown of creation (*ashraf al-makhlūqāt*).

The unique position of man among all created order stems from the fact that he has been designated as *Allah*'s vicegerent on earth. This designation is a Divine trust which bestows on man particular responsibilities and accountability which are composed of developing his own potentialities and, concomitantly, struggling for the creation of a just and moral social order on earth. To discharge the responsibilities with which he is charged, man is provided with the material and extra-material means to assist him in discharging his duties. First, he has been endowed with a theomorphic nature composed of the powers of cognition, intellect volition, and speech to recognize and accept *Allah* (swt) as the Supreme Creator. Through his intelligence and will, man can discern and then choose between right and wrong, between just and unjust, between true and false, and between the real and the illusory. Although this power of discernment has been imprinted on his soul, to help man remember his purpose and his responsibilities, he is provided with guidance and remembrance in the form of the *Qur'an* and with reminders in the persons of the prophets as well as other human beings, to show him the "right path."

Such a model of man incorporates a spiritual and moral framework that values human relations above material possessions. In this way, man is concerned about not only the material needs but also about establishing a balance between its material and spiritual fulfillment as a human being.

Justice and Equilibrium

The concept of justice in Islam is the aggregation of moral and social values, which denotes fairness, balance, equilibrium, and temperance. Its implication for individual behaviour is, first of all, that the individual should not transgress his bounds and, secondly, that one should give others, as well as oneself, what is due. Such a concept of ʿ*adl* (balance and justice) calls for overall harmony throughout the universe. The central Islamic values are the welfare of society and socio-economic justice. Any injustice perpetrated by individuals against other humans and against the rest of creation is ultimately an injustice to the self. Allah (swt) Loves justice; it is a central part of His Universal Love. Humans must live a life that is just and must stand up to and eradicate injustice wherever they find it.[17]

Preservation of Rights

Ethics in Islam can be best understood in light of principles governing the rights of the individual, society, and state; the laws governing property ownership; and the framework of contracts. Islam's recognition and protection of rights are not limited to human beings only but encompass all forms of life as well as the environment. Each element of Allah's (swt) creation has been endowed with certain rights and each is obligated to respect and honour the rights of others. These rights are bundled with the responsibilities for which humans are held accountable. The *Shari'ah* offers a comprehensive framework to identify, recognize, respect, and protect the rights of every individual, community, society, and the state. Islamic scholars and jurists have defined and codified detailed principles identifying these rights.[18]

The importance of being conscious and mindful of the rights of others, human or nonhuman, and the significance of discharging the responsibilities associated with such rights is reflected by the following saying of the Prophet (pbuh):

> So, give to everyone who possesses a right (*kull dhi haqq*) his right.

The term "right" (*haq*) denotes something that can be justly claimed or the interests and claims that people may have been granted by Islamic law or the *Shari'ah*. The majority of *Shari'ah* scholars and jurists hold that similar to physical property, rights are also property (*al mal*) because, like physical property, which has beneficial uses and can be possessed, rights also have beneficial uses and can be possessed. Rules defining property rights in Islam deal with the rights of ownership, acquisition, usage and disposal of the property. Any violation of these rules is considered a transgression and leads to disruption in the social order.

Internalization of Virtues

A virtue is a good trait of character, so well-entrenched in an individual that it influences which actions he or she wishes to take. In a deeper sense, cultivation and internalization of any virtue has spiritual significance. It is considered a meeting point between divine perfection and human life and therefore stands midway between the Creator and moral imperatives. It is virtue, as the ideal prototype, which gives men their scale of moral values and their standards of behaviour, and virtue must take precedence over morality, defining and determining it.[19] Virtue has a twofold aspect, relating to man himself and to man as a member of society. Like a tree, virtue has a root and a trunk from which, however, there grows a branch where the fruit ripens. The tree is now and always one and the same, but the branch and the fruit are to the tree what virtue is to the human collectivity.[20]

The attitude of soul that would actualize virtues must needs transform itself, on a lower, earthly plane, into norms and rules, and become a set of standards serving as the functional aspect of morality. Virtue is immutable, universal, absolute, and beyond space and time. On the other hand, morality which is subordinate to virtue is the link binding earth to heaven. If this link is lost, morality and law become a collation of expedient rules with no underlying authority.[21]

Virtues-based ethical theory of Islam can be summarized simply as internalizing virtues and set of rules specified by the Creator for the well-being and welfare of humans.[22] This set of rules and virtues applies to all aspects of human life without any exception. The adoption and internalization of these virtues ensure justice. Once the virtues are internalized and behaviour becomes compliant with the rules, then morality, ethics, and justice all are obtained. This is why Allah (swt) points to the role of the Messengers and Prophets as to read His book of rules to people, cleanse them, then teach them the wisdom behind the rules in the book and then induce them to establish interpersonal justice (*qist*).

Respecting and Protecting Environment

Axioms such as the unity of creation and preservation of rights humans have the responsibility toward actions that could degrade or destroy the environment. Gross ignorance as a leading cause of the ongoing environment crisis, which scholars believe can be alleviated if the global community begins to recognize the multiple states of being that are possible within the environment.[23]

VIRTUE-BASED ETHICS OF ISLAM

Virtue ethics theory—the study of moral character—has been an important strand in moral philosophy for literally thousands of years but has received little attention from contemporary economists.[24] The ethicists who rely upon a theory of virtue ethics have a rich history of philosophical thought from which to draw, though theories of virtue with specifically commercial applications are fairly recent.

The importance of virtues is recognized in almost all religions, traditions, and writings of philosophers. For example, in his Summa

Theologica, St. Thomas Aquinas (1225–1274), praised the intellectual virtues of wisdom, justice, temperance, and fortitude. In the early years of capitalism, Adam Smith (1759) recommended prudence, i.e. "wise and judicious conduct," as the "most ennobling of virtues."[25] Several other modern thinkers—David Hume, Samuel Smiles, Robert Solomon, and Deirdre McCloskey—base their writings on application of virtue to economic activities.[26] Discussion on ethics in Islam was dealt with extensively since the early history of Islam and the discussion surrounded around cultivating and internalizing virtues which would lead to ethical actions.[27]

Throughout Islamic history, different scholars have compiled sets of virtues based on various verses of the Qur'an and have identified virtues that would constitute an ethical act.[28] Emphasis was laid on internalizing virtues individually or collectively such that the person or the collectivity is a living manifestation of the virtues as opposed to doing them out of necessity. One important early work is by Abu Ali ibn Mohammad ibn Ya'qub Miskawayh (born 320 AH, died 421). His work is considered to have influenced the thinking of leading thinkers such as Al-Ghazali and Nasiruddin Tusi on this topic. Subsequently, the discussion mainly took place while developing principles underlying legal axioms. For example, scholars such as Al-Ghazālī (2005) dealt with the ethics of earning and living as he dedicated one full chapter in his classical work Iḥyā' 'Ulūm al-Dın (Revival of Islamic Sciences).[29] He identifies the virtues of justice, truthfulness, and benevolence as the main ethical values that must be internalized by agents in any economic activity.

Within an Islamic context, the term most closely related to ethics in al-Qur'an is khuluq (خُلُق) Arabic for moral character and trait, plural akhlāq (أخلاق) but there are other terms to describe the concepts of morals or positive values such as khayr (goodness), birr (righteousness), qist (equity), 'adl (balance and justice), haqq (truth and righteousness), ma'ruf (known, approved), and taqwa (piety). Allah (swt)[30] uses the same word khuluq in describing the Prophet's (saas)[31] behaviour and character (al-Qur'an, 68:4). These virtues were fully manifested through the character of the Prophet (saas), who is the role model to follow for the believers. The Prophet (saas) is reported to have said that he was sent for the purpose of perfecting the noblest of morals (مكارم الأخلاق).[32] The Qur'an (3:104) lays the broad foundation of the preferred character of humans to (a) do what is good; (b) be righteous; and (c) forbid and refrain from what is wrong.[33] After a broad classification of desirable behaviour is prescribed, the Qur'an (49:13) states, "The noblest of you in the sight of God are the best of you in conduct."

Recognizing the importance of good character traits or virtues alone is not sufficient unless one understands a subtle and strong relationship between the intentions, actions, and outcomes. In the Islamic concept of ethics, there is an emphasis on virtue, intention, action, and the outcome as a basis for judging whether an act is ethical or not. Although intention or *niyya* of an action plays a critical role in determining the legal aspect of the action, Islam recognizes the moral significance of intention in advocating sincerity of intent (*iḫlāṣ*). Each virtue is judged in light of the intention behind the practice of the virtue. The distinction between having the intention to serve humanity and the betterment of society as opposed to achieve personal gain could make an action ethical or unethical.

The nexus of virtues, intention, action, and outcome defines a framework of ethics that goes beyond legal or juridical ethics that focus exclusively on actions. For this reason, Kamali (2011) emphasizes that a jurist needs to go beyond the mere legal requirement of the validity of a contract to include discussion on the higher objectives (*maqāsid*) of Shari'ah to deem the contract ethical. This means going beyond the form and including the substance in evaluating the validity of any contract. Zilio-Grandi (2015) articulates that the Islamic conception of ethics dependent on virtues covers a much broader discipline than the restricted juridical understanding of the practice and, therefore, finds virtues behind every example of good conduct and not merely behind behaviour answerable to the Islamic law.

To summarize, Islam's framework of ethics is chiefly concerned with internalizing "good character traits," which must be exemplified in actions. **Being is preferred over doing**. The relationship between virtues, intentions, and actions lays the foundation of ethical behaviour such that virtue-based ethics have a logical priority over juridical ethics. Actions driven by good intentions and in the spirit of the practice of virtues would become ordinary behaviour that is not only ethical but is internally consistent in terms of intent, means, and outcomes. The result is ethical outcome of actions in the best interest of the individuals, society, and the whole creation. Islam's conception of virtue-based ethics differs from the conventional virtue ethic theory such that the axioms defining meta-ethics provide all necessary ingredients with a complete incentive system and associated rules which ensure social and economic justice for all.

Here is a brief discussion of key virtues worthy of possession by a believer as advocated by Islam.

Truthfulness and Integrity

Being truthful and keeping one's word are the core traits of a true human being. This is further emphasized particularly in reference to an economic agent who is truthful in his/her dealings.[34] A true believer or *Mu'min* is expected to be honest in dealings, have a strong commitment to his or her word and speak truth. The ultimate case of commitment to truthfulness is that one is expected to be truthful while giving evidence, even if it is against himself or herself. An honest and truthful trader is given tidings of blessings from the Creator while in the absence of these traits, any economic activity would be devoid of any blessings.

Trustworthiness

Islam places a strong emphasis on trust and considers being trustworthy as an obligatory personality trait.[35] At a philosophical level, the role of man on earth is to act as vicegerent or trustee of the Creator. The root of the word for "trust" (*amānah*) is the same as that for "belief" (*īmān*), for *Qur'an* insists that a strong signal of true belief is faithfulness to contracts and promises. It makes clear that performing contractual obligations or promises is an important and mandatory characteristic of a true believer.[36]

Honesty

The virtue of being honest in any economic or social transaction is the very basic character trait of a believer. The Qur'an binds faith and action through righteous deeds as inseparable. The Prophet (saas) explicitly declared honesty an article of faith as he said that there is no faith for one who lacks honesty.[37] Honesty does not only come from being truthful but requires avoidance of vices for worldly gains. There are several vices that are discouraged greatly when one is engaged in business transactions. Examples of such vices are purposefully deceiving others, engaging in cheating and fraud, and willfully holding or manipulating information pertaining to the transaction. One full chapter of the Qur'an is dedicated to manipulating weights and measures and giving short measures such as the act of giving short measures while demanding full measures from others. The chapter emphasizes the grave consequences of such behaviour.[38] The Qur'an also makes reference to the community of the Prophet Shu'ayb (sws), which was known for engaging in deceitful business practices, especially the manipulation of weights. Consequently, the community was destroyed for its persistence in deceit.

Goodness and Excellence (Ihsān)

The virtue of *Ihsān*, meaning benevolence, goodness, and excellence, is recognized in the Qur'an as well as in the sayings of the Prophet.[39] The concept of *Ihsān* is the embodiment of goodness and excellence in interaction and conduct at the personal, organizational, and societal levels. As a projection of goodness, it practically and spiritually encompasses mercy, justice, forgiveness, tolerance, and attentiveness. The concept of *Ihsān* is much broader than simply being good to others but includes striving for excellence in goodness so much so that one is willing to go beyond what may be expected under norms to achieve the welfare of fellow humans, the community, or the society.

Compassion and Generosity

Compassion (*rahma*) is a virtue that is greatly desired and admired. Compassion is stressed in the Qur'an as the basic attribute of God and all humans are expected to practise and exhibit it. Compassion calls for showing mercy, kindness, and passion toward others in all economic and social matters. One application of compassion is leniency in economic transactions in case of hardship and feeling the pain and suffering of others.[40] Leniency is especially encouraged with respect to debtors who are in difficult conditions provided that they made sincere efforts to meet their obligations.[41]

Cooperation and Solidarity

Islam seeks to guide man to direct individual action and responsible participation in economic affairs in a manner that commits him to solidarity and cooperation, resulting in a dynamic and growing economy.

Thus, the individual is made accountable for the moral effects of his social actions, including those in economic affairs, so that his own inner personal-spiritual transformation and growth is bound to the progress of the community.

Mindfulness of Vices or Unethical Practices

Virtues and vices are two faces of the same coin. Each virtue has implicit an opposite in the form of a vice that is a negative character trait to be avoided as it would lead to unethical behavior. For example, whereas truthfulness is a virtue, deceitfulness would be a vice. Whereas internalization of virtues is to be admired, the act of avoiding vices itself would become a virtuous act.

Prudence and Humility[42]

The role of man as vicegerent (*khilāfah*) of the Creator carries a very heavy responsibility to act with prudence because any violation of this trust itself would be unethical. Prudence calls for restoring balance in managing and utilizing resources to optimize the benefit and welfare of all. Prudence is an essential virtue for those who are in the position of leadership or management. Utilization of resources whether scarce or abundant, requires careful management keeping in mind the well-being of the community and the society. Wasting of resources is strongly condemned in Islam and no one is authorized to destroy or waste God-given resources.[43] Several externalities including sustainable development could follow if the vice of wasting resources is overcome. Whereas wasting resources is condemned, having excessive control on resources and not spending or utilizing for good causes is equally condemned.[44]

Humility is a valuable virtue considering that a person should be fully conscious of the state of humans with respect to the Creator. Being humble is appreciated and arrogance is considered the worst of vices. Arrogance is particularly disliked due to it being the root cause of many other evils. Spiritually, arrogance signifies man's claim of having better knowledge than the Creator and therefore, developing a sense of overconfidence and superiority with respect to other humans. History is witness to the destruction of civilizations or leaders due to arrogance.

Ethical Dimensions of *Iqtiṣād*

Ethics are embedded in the core principles of Islam and each rule prescribed has explicit or implicit ethical dimensions reflecting its adherence to core values and virtues. The philosophical foundation underlying the development of legal rules as well as its objectives (*maqasid*) is based on Islam's core virtues and values ensuring ethical outcomes. Following the rules will set the standards of an overall ethical behaviour for individuals, firms, communities, the state, and society. This defines a perimeter by sanctioning immoral and harmful activities with the objective to achieve the overall welfare of the society as a whole. The perimeter defined by the rules becomes the limit beyond which ethics would be compromised. As long as one is rule-compliant, there would not arise any question of any unethical behaviour.

Whereas discussion of ethical dimensions of *Iqtiṣād* or Islamic economics[45] is a very wide topic and is covered by earlier discussion in this volume in the contexts such as economic and social justice, redistributive justice, production, exchange, distribution, consumption, market rules, etc., in this section we limit the discussion to financial transactions and impact on the financial system with the objective of avoiding repetitiveness.

Ethics of Risk-Sharing

Two fundamental features of any financial transaction in Islam are the prohibition of interest in any form and the prohibition of excessive risk-taking (*gharar*). Each prohibition has embedded values and virtues defining its ethical dimensions. For example, prohibition of interest is characterized by the virtues of preservation of property rights and condemnation of economic and social exploitation. In the case of prohibition of excessive uncertainty and risk (*gharar*), a transaction can be declared null and void in considerations of fairness and justice, as *gharar* in a transaction may cause injustice and loss of property to one or both of the parties.[46] Prohibition of *Riba* (interest) and *gharar* (excessive risk due to information asymmetry) leads to risk-sharing instead of risk transfer in financial transactions which has system wide implications making the system standing on sounder ethical grounds.[47]

Islam endorses risk-sharing as the preferred organizational structure for all economic activities, and in fact the most comprehensive application of risk-sharing that goes beyond anything put forward by modern economic theories. In addition to the prohibition of interest-based contracts, Islam requires mandatory risk-sharing with the poor, the deprived, and the handicapped based on its principles of property rights. Risk-sharing in economic and financial transactions as advocated by Islam is embedded with several virtues such as justice, fairness, inclusion, solidarity, protection of rights, etc., and is void of vices such as deceit, expropriation, exploitation, and repression. The most meaningful human progress is achieved when all distinctions on the basis of race, colour, income, wealth, and social-political status are obliterated to the point where humanity, in convergence with the Qur'anic declaration (Qur'an, 31:28), truly views itself as one and united. It can be argued that implementation of Islamic finance will promote maximum risk-sharing, thus creating the potential for enhanced social solidarity.[48]

Here we provide select features of risk-sharing finance and argue that risk-sharing in economic and financial transactions when practised with other virtues would lead to an ethical and responsible financial system.

Risk-Sharing Prevents Exploitation

Interest-rate-based debt contracts are instruments of risk-shifting, risk shedding, and risk transfer, which are considered exploitative when compared to risk-sharing finance. Different rationales have been given for the prohibition of interest but each reaches the same conclusion. Property rights rationale of prohibition argues that in interest-based debt contracts, the creditor acquires property rights claim on the debtor, equivalent to the principal plus interest and whatever collateral may be involved, without losing the property rights claim to the money lent, which violates the property rights principles of Islam.[49] Other rationales for the prohibition of interest (*ribā*) include the prevention of economic exploitation among the transaction parties, which is contrary to the core values of economic and social justice. Since in Islam, money could only be a medium of exchange or measure of account rather than a commodity, paying rent for the use of money is not recognized unless money is converted to capital subject to a return. Therefore, money-renting is forbidden as it opens the door to potential exploitation and violates the spirit of social justice because it shifts all the risk from the financier to the borrowers and leads to imbalances in wealth and income distribution in society.

Efficient Allocation of Resources by Discouraging Over-Financialization of the Economy

When risk transfer is combined with high leverage, the growth of interest-based debt contracts and their pure financial derivatives—those with little or no connection to real assets—outpace the growth of the real sector, leaving the liabilities in the economy a large multiple of real assets needed to validate them. This phenomenon is called "financial decoupling" or "financialization" whereby finance is no longer anchored in the real sector. The result is financial instability leading to frequent crises.[50] Reinhart and Rogoff (2009) have cataloged the high frequency of historical occurrences of crises in the conventional interest-based system and have clearly shown that all crises, whether classified as currency or banking crises, have been at their core a debt crises.

An interest-based or risk-shifting financial system invariably creates a divergence between the real sector and the financial sector of the economy. The conventional fractional banking system allows multiple amounts of money to be created out of a given amount of bank deposits received, facilitating and enhancing the process of debt creation. The development of complex financial derivatives has resulted in credit expansion outpacing the growth of the real sector of the economy. As layer upon layer of securitization decouples the connection between the financial and real sectors, an inverted credit pyramid is created to the extent that the liabilities of the economy become a large multiple of real assets needed to validate them.[51] Additionally, such a system is characterized by mismatched maturity and values of the asset and liability structure of the balance sheets of banks. These institutions borrow short and lend long. When subjected to asset price shocks, the liability side of the balance sheet is very slow to adjust, while the asset side adjusts rapidly. Both mismatches create a potential for instability that can spread rapidly through contagion. The result can be an increase in the frequency, contagion, and severity of financial and economic crises.[52]

By prohibiting renting of money and encouraging trade financing, financial instruments facilitate direct financing of the real economy and therefore promote the allocation of resources to the real sector. Although debt obligations are created in the financial system, such obligations are the results of the sale or lease of real assets through the sale and lease-based modes of financing. The objective is to impose a fiscal discipline on individuals and firms to allocate financial resources to the real sector according to their capacity to pay back. In this process, any financial transaction which has no social value and is speculative is removed from the system so that the society as whole benefits from economic growth, stable banking, and financial system, and preserves the loss of GDP due to repeated crises.

Reduced Information and Agency Problems

An important performance dimension of risk-sharing finance, in general, and of Islamic finance in particular, is whether it is more or less vulnerable than conventional finance (which relies heavily on debt finance) to principal–agent and informational issues. Agency issues arise because of asymmetric information between agents (entrepreneurs) and principals (investors) and the possibility that the agent's utility maximization may not maximize the utility of the principal. The question is whether Islamic contracting (with risk-sharing) is better suited to solving this contractual dilemma through its reliance on risk/reward sharing under conditions where interest-based debt financing is prohibited. In the presence of informational problems such as asymmetric information (where only one side of the contract, usually the agent, has information not available to the other parties) there is a transaction cost as well as a cost of monitoring the agent's activities and the project(s) to be taken into account.

It could be plausibly argued that in Islamic contracts, asymmetric information issues would be minimized. This assertion is supported by the strict rules governing contracts, exchange, and trade. Such rules with the exercise of virtues such as justice, truthfulness, and trust by economic agents would reduce information asymmetry to a minimum. These include the need for written contracts that stipulate terms and conditions fully and transparently, the direct and unequivocal admonition that commitments to the terms and conditions of contracts must be faithfully carried out, and the strong emphasis on trust, cooperation, and consultation. Ethics governing market behaviour also create incentives—both positive and negative—to enforce honest, transparent, and compliant behaviour on the part of participants. Hence, risk-sharing contracts designed under Islamic rules would mitigate informational problems and could be better structured than interest-based debt contracts with incentives to maximize both parties' expected joint rewards.[53]

Preserving Sustainable Growth and Welfare Through the Stability of the Financial System

While, in our opinion, Islamic finance would be inherently stable because it is structured on a foundation of equity and asset-based financing and risk-sharing, conventional finance, a debt-and-interest-based system, has proven to be unstable. Recent historical analysis has demonstrated that all financial, banking, and currency crises are, at their core, a crisis arising from debt.[54] The main reason for the stability of risk-sharing system is the fact that when production is financed entirely by risk–return sharing or asset-based or equity finance, in the case of rapid changes in the price, assets, and liabilities both move in the same direction simultaneously—thus the financial structure adjusts in tandem on both sides of the ledger. A number of analytic models have investigated the adjustment process and have demonstrated the stability of Islamic finance in response to shocks as well as the growth implication of such a system in closed and open economy situations.[55]

An important feature of these models was the assumption of 100% reserve banking based on the understanding of bank deposits as a safekeeping operation firewalled from the risks involved in investment operations, i.e. the so-called two-window model. This feature of requiring banking depository institutions to hold 100% reserves against demand deposits removes two sources of instability associated with conventional interest-based, fractional reserve banking. The nonavailability of interest-based financial transactions and 100% reserve banking eliminate the ability of the financial system to create money out of thin air and impairs the ability to leverage an asset base into much larger liabilities.[56]

Encourages Anti-fragility of Financial System for Sustainable Economic Development

Because of four important characteristics: mutuality, commitment, horizontal governance, and common good objective, a risk-sharing financial system will be anti-fragile and less prone to frequent shocks. A risk-sharing contract mutually commits the participants to share resources, risks, and rewards. Because everyone has "skin-in-the-game," the governance structure will, most likely, be horizontal rather than vertical providing agility, flexibility, and greater accountability in the management and operations of the venture subject of the contract. Moreover, all participants work to gain the most out of the operations of the contract since they all stand to gain from effective, efficient, and productive outcomes. Due to these characteristics, risk-sharing resolves the issues of moral hazard associated with the principal–agent problem since the parties to the contract are functioning as both. As well, in a risk-sharing system where financing is being provided by shareholders, there is no incentive to withdraw financing when there may be a potential downturn as there would be in a risk-transfer system. Similarly, during the upside, financing would be available commensurate with increased productive activities only, unlike the risk-transfer system that provides greater credit during the boom and withdraws credit during the bust phases of the business cycle.[57] Hence, risk-sharing reduces or eliminates the procyclicality of finance. Also important is the fact that in the absence of a rentier class, risk-sharing finance improves income and wealth distribution thus reducing inequality.

Fight Against Financial Repression
It is clear that the nexus of fractional reserve banking, credit creation, debt creation, and leverage leading to financial crises is the cause of financial instability and fragility. The evidence for this process is the massive debt build-up in the world economy estimated to be US$50 trillion during the period of run-up to the 2007–2008 crisis. After the financial crisis of 2007–2008, many books and articles appeared focusing on the dangers of "excessive debt"[58] without realizing that the culprit is the mispricing of financial resources attributable to the interest rate mechanism. If there is an eternal proposition of economics, it is that mispricing of any resource gives rise to disequilibrium and misallocation of that resource. Excess debt is a clear indication that financial resources are not priced to reflect their opportunity costs. Financial repression, the deviation of the "administered" interest rate from the "market" interest rate, leads to market distortions, thus discouraging saving, investment, and economic growth. To the extent that neither the financial sector nor the governments are paying the true opportunity cost of financial resources, there is financial repression. It has existed and will continue to exist until and unless reforms force true "liberalization" of markets where prices all reflect opportunity costs.

Islamic finance addresses this mispricing and its consequent misallocation of financial resources through its requirement of materiality that financial resources must be used directly in production, a one-to-one correspondence between the financial sector and the real sector of the economy. This means that the rate of return to finance is determined by its productivity in the production sector rather than predetermined by policy or the monopoly power of rentiers. Islamic finance rules out maturity, value, and balance sheet asset–liability mismatches that create the dynamics of volatility. The result would be an anti-fragile and robust financial system by requiring risk-sharing among participants in transactions each of which will have to have "skin-in-the-game." Consequently, financial resources receive their true opportunity cost in a market-determined process where these resources are priced according to their most productive use. This process puts an end to financialization, financial repression, and excessive reliance on financial activities on speculation.

Enhances Cooperation Among Economic Agents
There is an important moral dimension to risk-sharing in Islam as it strengthens social solidarity by enhancing cooperation among all economic agents, which would also go some way in easing the coordination problem in the economy.[59] When the risk is spread by means of risk-/reward-sharing contracts, closer coordination is forged between the real and financial sectors of the economy. Risk transfer by means of interest-based debt contracts, in contrast, weakens that linkage. Nobel laureate Professor Robert Shiller, an advocate of risk-sharing, argues that risk-sharing has much to contribute to the growth of economies and to social solidarity. As an instrument for social integration, risk-sharing enhances human interaction and brings humanity closer to unity by requiring humans to share the risks of life with one another. In his words, "Massive risk sharing can carry with it benefits far beyond that of reducing poverty and diminishing income inequality. The reduction of risk on a greater scale would provide substantial impetus to human and economic progress."[60]

Enhances Financial and Social Inclusion
Risk-sharing is a contractual or societal arrangement whereby the outcome of a random event is born collectively by a group of individuals or entities involved in a contract, or by individuals or entities in a community. In a company, all shareholders share in the risk inherent in the operations of the company. At the community level, a family or a nation shares in the risks affecting the well-being of the family or the nation. Therefore, Islam's conception of risk-sharing is in part so designed to promote social solidarity by encouraging finance to play an integrating role in humankind. This form of finance would be inclusive of all members of society and all entities, especially the poor, in enjoying the benefits of

economic growth, and to bring humankind closer together through the sharing of risk.

BUSINESS ETHICS

The topic of business ethics is vast and has been dealt with throughout the history of Islam. Discussion ranges from the ethics of work, ethical treatment of workers, maintaining the ethical relationship between employees and employers, business and customers, business and stakeholders, and finally business and society at large including the environment. An exhaustive discussion is available in the literature on this topic but here, we would like to touch upon select aspects of the topic.[61]

Based on the set of virtues that are to be internalized by individuals, businesses, and corporations, a framework of business ethics in Islam is drawn. Whereas the character traits of individuals are easy to understand and explain, the application of similar traits to businesses or legal entities such as corporations is not straightforward. Businesses and corporates are the sum of the character traits of the individuals managing and running the businesses. There is a need to develop a character of business entities that emulates the desirable moral character of individuals. Therefore, a business entity should also strive for internalizing virtues of justice, preservations of rights, commitment to contracts, transparency, and fairness. Once businesses adopt such core virtues and avoid associated vices, their practices and actions would be considered ethical.

The virtue of truthfulness is the cornerstone of conducting ethical business where decisions are made in a transparent fashion and full disclosure is made to internal and external stakeholders. A business transaction void of transparency or willful misinformation may give the business monetary benefits, but such a transaction will not only be considered void of any blessings but also subject to accountability on the Day of Judgement. The virtue of trustfulness would require both parties to a business transaction to be transparent and have full disclosure on all aspects of the transaction including the terms of the contract, quality of the product or services subject to exchange, and the terms and the modes of payment. Truthfulness or transparency also enhances trust between the parties and in the market and in all fairness, each party expects full transparency and disclosure regarding the transaction.

Business ethics in Islam provide recognition and protection of the rights of stakeholders to the business under the virtues of preservation of rights, honouring of explicit and implicit contracts, mutual trust, and just treatment. These virtues define the ethical framework of acknowledging stakeholders' due rights and granting a voice in the governance framework of businesses.[62] A firm in the Islamic economic system can be viewed as "nexus-of-contracts" whose objective is to minimize transaction costs to maximize profits and returns to investors subject to the constraints that these objectives do not violate the property rights of any party whether it interacts with the firm directly or indirectly. In pursuit of these goals, the firm honours its obligations to explicit and implicit contracts without impinging on the social order. This perspective incorporates the stakeholders' role in its view of the firm and supports the recognition and protection of their rights.[63]

Business leaders or managers carry significant responsibility on their shoulders. First and foremost, a manager is expected to carry the best of character or virtues in conducting business and be accountable to superiors, subordinates, and stakeholders. Deteriorating values and ethics of top business leaders witnessed during the financial crisis are testimony to the importance of business leaders internalizing ethical behaviour rather than focusing on personal interest and greed. A good business leader ought to possess virtues of truthfulness, trustworthiness, striving for excellence, being conscious of the rights of all stakeholders, and acting in prudence.

A business leader should be truthful about financial statements, products being sold, and business practices. A business leader is expected to reflect the virtue of trustfulness in his/her conduct. Such trust has different dimensions. Whereas at one level, he/she is entrusted with the responsibility of managing the wealth of shareholders, at another level, internal stakeholders such as employees have put their trust in the expectation of fair treatment. Thus, it becomes the responsibility of the leader to maintain a fair balance and be conscious of the responsibility and accountability of this trust.

Leaders who are fully conscious of their responsibilities, limitations, and obligations as expected in Islam could never fall into a behaviour that would promote arrogance, ignorance, greed, deceitfulness, non-transparency, and delinquency. Islam governs the behaviour of leaders at least no less stringently than those of individuals. Although each member of society is expected to exhibit high moral values in the observance of contracts and covenants, many scholars are of the view that these requirements apply with even greater force to the actions of leaders. Therefore, a breach of faith on the part of a leader is more heinous in its nature and more serious in its consequence than a similar breach by an ordinary individual. A business leader is to exhibit the virtue of humility rather than arrogance.[64] Arrogance is considered a vice to be avoided because arrogance could lead to impairment of judgement to the point that one could violate the virtues of justice and preserving the rights of others. Arrogance has been known to be the cause of downfall not only of businesses but even of civilizations.

Finally, Islamic scholars have maintained that humans have the responsibility toward actions that could degrade or destroy the environment. As "regents," or trustees, humans are ordered to act preemptively and reactively to natural resource-related environmental events. Indisputably, enjoining environmental protection and discouraging its degradation are covered by this capstone rule of Islamic teachings. Therefore, it is incumbent on businesses in the Islamic perspective to ensure that their actions do not lead to degradation of the environment and all efforts are made to protect the environment either through individual business or collectively through collaboration across the industry. Business leaders and stakeholders including shareholders or owners should be proactive in the preservation of the environment as expected by Islamic virtues.

Conclusion

Religions have much to contribute to righting the wrongs of conventional economics by making available coherent and logically consistent alternative postulates and models ensuring ethical outcomes.[65] Based on the moral philosophy of Islam aimed at promoting economic and social justice and enhancing solidarity among communities, internalization of rules and virtues of Islam determine all facets of an economy ranging from the rules of market conduct, production, consumption, distribution, and redistribution. Ethics embedded in the prescribed rules and principles guarantee ethical outcomes in economic activities.

Risk-sharing in financial transactions and other forms of risk-sharing in Islam have a rich ethical dimension that fills the gaps observed in the prevailing economic system. Risk-sharing minimizes the exploitation inherent in an interest-based or risk-transfer system, leads to efficient allocation of limited resources, reduces typical information asymmetry and agency problems in economic dealings, enhances cooperation and solidarity in the societies, and promotes financial and social inclusion. A rich framework of business ethics leads to strong governance, transparency, and prudent leadership.

NOTES

1. Morals, values, and ethics are related and are interlocking concepts. Whereas morals refer to specific, articulated rules, values refer to the underlying aesthetic valuation or determination of those rules, and ethics refer to the practice of determining which rules should or should not be adopted. For example, the moral "you should feed the hungry" could be accompanied by the value "relieving suffering is good" and underpinned by an ethics that suggests that "those who have more than enough should share with those that do not have enough." The three have something of a symbiotic relationship, which can lead to confusing results if the purpose of one is obfuscated.
2. Rizk (2008).
3. Vranceanu (2005).
4. Aragon (2014).
5. Mirakhor and Alaabed (2013).
6. Chapra (2008).
7. Vranceanu (2005).
8. Vranceanu (2005).
9. Vranceanu (2005).
10. Vranceanu (2005).
11. "Scaffolding" is used by Douglass North (1990) to signify the institutional infrastructure (rules of behavior and their enforcement characteristics) of an economy.
12. Mirakhor (2014).
13. Mirakhor (2014).
14. Nasr (2017).
15. The verses emphasizing the principle of unity include: "And indeed this is my straight path therefore follow it—and do not follow other ways because that will lead to disunity amongst you" (6:153) "Grab hold of the rope of Allah collectively and do not disunite" (3:103) "Cooperate with one another unto righteousness and piety and do not cooperate with one another unto unrighteousness and enmity" (5:2).
16. See Nasr (1968). Available online at http://www.studiesincomparativereligion.com/public/articles/Who_is_Man-The_Perennial_Answer_of_Islam-by_Seyyed_Hossein_Nasr.aspx.
17. Iqbal and Mirakhor (2017).
18. Imam Zayn al-Abidin's treatise on rights, "*Risalat Al-Huquq*," covers a full spectrum of rights in Islam. For example, the right to one's property

(*al-mal*) means that one takes it only from what is lawful and spends it only on what is proper. The right of the associate (*khalit*) is that one neither misleads him, nor acts dishonestly toward him, nor deceives him. The right of the adversary (*khasm*) who has a claim against one is that, if his claim is valid, one gives witness to it against oneself. Ali Ibn al-Hussein (1990).

19. Lindbom (1975).
20. Lindbom (1975).
21. Lindbom (1975).
22. Iqbal and Mirakhor (2017).
23. Nasr (1968) was one of the earliest modern-day scholars to warn about the environmental crisis. His seminal work The Encounter of Man and Nature: The Spiritual Crisis of Modern Man published in 1968 remains one of the earliest writings on the environmental crisis by any conventional or Muslim writers.
24. Bruni and Sugden (2013).
25. Vranceanu (2005).
26. Heath (2013).
27. Significant discussion and analysis of the positions of the Qur'an and the Sunnah on morality and ethics were provided by the 4th Caliph Imam Ali (AS) in his book, *Nahjul Balaghah*, and by his grandson, Imam Zayn al-'Abedin (AS) in his book, *Risalah al-Huquq* (Treatise on Rights), which also included the *Risalah Al Huquq* (Treaties on Rights) covering moral and ethical behavior toward others according to the Qur'an and Sunnah. See Ali Ibn Abu Talib (1973 [1988]) and Ali Ibn al-Hussein (1988).
28. For example, Ali (2014) quotes Al-Mawardi's list of 10 virtues, which included capacity to reason, sound faith, knowledge, forbearance, generosity, adherence to accepted custom, righteousness, patience, thankfulness, and flexibility as virtues that could deem an act ethical.
29. This classical work dedicated a full chapter on the ethics of earning and living (Kitāb al-Ādāb al-Kasb wa al-Ma'āsh). Musa (2011).
30. Use of the term (swt) with Allah denotes "Subhanahu wa ta'ala" meaning "Glory to Him, the Exalted" as a sign of reverence.
31. Use of the term (saas) with the mention of the Prophet denotes "SallaAllah o 'Alayhi wa Aalihi wa Salaam" meaning the graces of Allah (swt) be upon him, and peace as sign of reverence.
32. Musnad Ahmad Ibn Hanbal, No: 8595.
33. Qur'an (3:104), "Let there arise out of you a band of people inviting to all what is good, enjoining what is right, and forbidding what is wrong: they are the ones to attain felicity."
34. A well-known saying of the Prophet is that "the truthful merchant [is rewarded by being ranked] on the Day of Resurrection with prophets, veracious souls, martyrs and pious people" (Tirmidhi, No: 1130).

35. Prophet (sws) was called a trustworthy (الأمين) person even before he was chosen to be a Prophet by Allah (swt).
36. There are various verses on the virtue of being trustful. For example, *al-Qur'an* (8:27) states "O you believers! Do not betray Allah and the Messenger, nor knowingly, betray your trusts." Also, see, *al-Qur'an* (2:58; 2:283; 12: 52; 23:1–8; and 42:107, 125, 143, 162, 178, 193).
37. Badawi (2013).
38. Qur'an (83:1–3) "Woe to those that deal in fraud. Those who, when they have to receive by measure from men, exact full measure, but when they have to give by measure or weight to men, give less than due."
39. In a famous saying of the Prophet also known as hadith of *Ihsān*, when asked "what is goodness?", He replied: "that you worship God as if you see Him, for if you see Him not, surely He sees you" (Rahman 1996).
40. The Prophet is reported as saying, "May Allah's (swt) mercy be on him who is lenient in his buying, selling, and in demanding back his money [or debts]" (Bukhari, No: 1934).
41. Kamali (2011). The Prophet (saas) said, "Truly the best of people are those who are best and most courteous in their demand for repayment." He takes a strong position that for those who take unfair advantage and procrastinate in their repayment of obligations, their conduct is tantamount to oppression (*zulm*) that falls outside the scope of lenient treatment.
42. Qur'an (4:36–37) "God loves not the arrogant, the vainglorious (nor) who are niggardly, enjoin niggardliness on others..."
43. Rice (1999). She gives the example of the 1st Caliph after the Prophet, Abu Bakr, who instructed not to kill indiscriminately or to destroy vegetation or animal life, even in war and on enemy territory, as an example of high ethical standards and the virtue of protecting the environment. She argued that if these were the standards in wartime, there would be no question of any waster or destruction during the time of peace.
44. Qur'an (6:141) "...and do not waste [God's bounties]: verily, He does not love the wasteful."
45. For in depth analysis of ethical issues in Islamic economics see Iqbal and Mirakhor (2017) and Mirakhor et al. (2020). For discussions of ethics and Islamic economics during early emergence of Islamic economics in modern times, see Naqvi (1981, 1993, 2003).
46. Kamali (2011). *Gharar* refers to elements of uncertainty in contracts that expose one or both of the contracting parties to risk. *Gharar* can also be caused by doubt or ignorance of one or both of the parties over the existence, quality, deliverability, or other material attributes of the subject matter of contract. The question whether risk taking in transactions amounts to *gharar* often depends on its scale and magnitude.

47. For in-depth discussion on risk-sharing aspect of Islamic economics and finance, see Askari et al. (2010).
48. Mirakhor (2007), Iqbal and Mirakhor (2011), and Askari et al. (2009).
49. Mirakhor (1989).
50. Menkoff and Tolksorf (2001), Epstein (2006), and Palley (2007).
51. Mirakhor (2011).
52. Askari et al. (2012).
53. Khan and Mirakhor (1987), Haque and Mirakhor (1987), and Presley and Sessions (1994).
54. See Reinhart and Rogoff (2009).
55. Khan (1987), Mirakhor and Zaidi (1988), Khan and Mirakhor (1987), Mirakhor (1990).
56. Krichene and Mirakhor (2008) and Mirakhor and Krichene (2009).
57. See, Stiglitz (1988).
58. See for example, Turner (2015).
59. See Mirakhor and Askari (2010, pp. 158–170), and Mirakhor (2010, pp. 8–19).
60. Shiller (2003).
61. For an in-depth discussion on business ethics, see Iqbal and Mirakhor (2017).
62. Iqbal and Mirakhor (2004).
63. Iqbal and Mirakhor (2004).
64. See Qur'an (17: 36–37) "Do not be arrogant in one's claims or beliefs: And pursue not that of which thou hast no knowledge; for every act of hearing, or of seeing or of (feeling in) the heart will be enquired into (on the Day of Reckoning). Nor walk on the earth with insolence: for thou canst not rend the earth asunder, nor reach the mountains in height."
65. Mirakhor (2014).

References

Akerlof, George A. 1970. The Market for 'Lemons': Quality Uncertainty and the Market Mechanism. *The Quarterly Journal of Economics* 84: 488–500.

Al-Ghazālī, Abū Hāmid Muḥammad ibn Muḥammad. 2005. Kitāb Ādāb al-Kasb wa al-Ma'āsh. In Iḥyā' 'Ulūm al-Dīn , ed. M.S. Muḥammad, 1st ed. Cairo: Dār al-Bayān al-'Arabī.

Ali Ibn al-Hussein, Zayn Al 'Abidin. 1988. *The Psalms of Islam*. Translated by William C. Chittick. Oxford: Oxford University Press.

Ali Ibn al-Hussein, Zayn Al 'Abidin. 1990. *Risalat Al-Huquq, The Treatise of Rights*. Translated by William C. Chittick. Qum: Foundation of Islamic Cultural Propagation in the World.

Ali, Abbas, J. 2014. *Business Ethics in Islam*. Cheltenham: Edward Elgar.

Aragon, George A. 2014. *Financial Ethics: A Positivist Analysis.* New York: Oxford University Press.
Arrow, K. J. 1974. *The Limits of Organization.* New York: W. W. Norton.
Askari, Hossein, Zamir Iqbal, and Abbas Mirakhor. 2009. *Issues in Islamic Finance and Economics: Progress and Challenges.* Singapore: Wiley.
Askari, Hossein, Zamir Iqbal, Noureddine Krichene, and Abbas Mirakhor. 2010. *The Stability of Islamic Finance.* Singapore: Wiley.
Askari, Hossein, Zamir Iqbal, Noureddine Krichene, and Abbas Mirakhor. 2012. *Risk Sharing in Finance.* Singapore: Wiley.
Badawi, Jamal, A. 2013. "Islamic Business Ethics." The Fiqh Council of North America.
Bruni, Luigino, and Robert Sugden. 2013. "Reclaiming Virtue Ethics for Economics." *Journal of Economic Perspectives* 27 (4): 141–164.
Chapra, Umer. 2008. "Ethics and Economics: An Islamic Perspective." *Islamic Economic Studies* 16 (1 and 2): 1–24.
Epstein, G. 2006. *Financialization and the World Economy.* New York: Edward Elgar.
Haque, Nadeem U., and Abbas Mirakhor. 1987. "Optimal Profit-Sharing Contracts and Investment in an Interest-Free Islamic Economy." In *Theoretical Studies in Islamic Banking and Finance*, edited by Mohsin S. Khan and Abbas Mirakhor. Houston: Institute of Research in Islamic Studies Books.
Heath, Eugene. 2013. "Virtue as a Model of Business Ethics." In *Handbook of the Philosophical Foundations of Business Ethics*, edited by Christoph Luetge, 109–129. Dordrecht: Springer.
Ibn Abi Talib, Ali. 1973 [1988]. *Nahjul Balaghah: The Peak of Eloquence.* Translated by Sayed Ali Reza, 1973, reprint of 4th Edition, published by Tahrik Tarsil, Qur'an Inc., 1988, New York.
Iqbal, Zamir, and Abbas Mirakhor. 2004. "Stakeholders Model of Governance in Islamic Economic System." *Islamic Economic Studies* 11 (2): 43–63.
Iqbal, Zamir, and Abbas Mirakhor. 2011. *An Introduction to Islamic Finance: Theory and Practice.* Singapore: Wiley.
Iqbal, Zamir, and Abbas Mirakhor. 2017. *Ethical Dimensions of Islamic Finance: Theory and Practice.* New York: Palgrave.
Kamali, Mohammad Hashim. 2011. "Ethics and Finance: Perspectives of the Sharīʿah and Its Higher Objectives (Maqāṣid)." 8th Kuala Lumpur Islamic Finance Forum (KLIFF), 3–6 October 2011.
Khan, Mohsin S. 1987. "Principles of Monetary Policy in an Islamic Framework." Paper prepared for the International Institute of Islamic Economics, Islamabad, Pakistan.
Khan, Mohsin S., and Abbas Mirakhor, eds. 1987. *Theoretical Studies in Islamic Banking and Finance.* Houston: Institute of Research in Islamic Studies Books.

Krichene, Noureddine, and Abbas Mirakhor. 2008. "Resilience and Stability of the Islamic Financial System: An Overview." IFSB Public Lecture, Islamic Financial Services Board.

Lindbom, Tage. 1975. "Virtue and Morality." *Studies in Comparative Religion* 9 (4): 227–235.

Menkoff, Lukas, and Norbert Tolksorf. 2001. *Financial Market Drift: Decoupling of the Financial Market from the Real Economy?* Heidelberg and Berlin: Springer-Verlag

Mirakhor, Abbas. 1989. "General Characteristics of an Islamic Economic System." In *Essays on Iqtiṣād: The Islamic Approach to Economic Problems*, edited by Baqir Al-Hasani and Abbas Mirakhor, 45–80. Silver Spring, MD: Nur.

Mirakhor, Abbas. 1990. "Equilibrium in a Non-interest Open Economy." *IMF Staff Papers* 37 (2), published in *Journal of King Abdulaziz University: Islamic Economics* 1993 (5): 3–23.

Mirakhor, Abbas. 2007. *A Note on Islamic Economics*. Jeddah: Islamic Research and Training Institute (IRTI).

Mirakhor, Abbas. 2010. "Whither Islamic Finance? Risk Sharing in an Age of Crises." Paper presented at the Inaugural Securities Commission Malaysia and Oxford Centre for Islamic Studies—Roundtable on Developing a Scientific Methodology on Shariah Governance for Positioning Islamic Finance Globally, March 15.

Mirakhor, Abbas. 2011. "Epistemological Foundation of Finance: Islamic and Conventional." Keynote address presented at the Foundations of Islamic Finance Conference Series, Kuala Lumpur, March 8–10.

Mirakhor, Abbas. 2014. "The Starry Heavens Above and the Moral Law Within: On the Flatness of Economics." *Economic Journal Watch* 11 (2) (May): 186–193.

Mirakhor, Abbas, and Alaa Alaabed. 2013. "The Credit Crisis: An Islamic Perspective." Global Islamic Finance Report (GIFR), Edbiz Consulting Ltd, London.

Mirakhor, Abbas, and Hossein Askari. 2010. *Islam and the Path to Human and Economic Development*. Foreword by Ali Allawi. New York: Palgrave Macmillan.

Mirakhor, Abbas, and Noureddine Krichene. 2009. "The Recent Crisis: Lessons for Islamic Finance." *Journal of Islamic Economics, Banking and Finance* 5 (1): 9–58.

Mirakhor, Abbas, and Iqbal Zaidi. 1988. "Stabilization and Growth in an Open Islamic Economy." IMF Working Paper No. 88.

Mirakhor, Abbas, Zamir Iqbal, and Seyed Kazim Sadr. 2020. *Handbook of Ethics of Islamic Economics and Finance*. Berlin: De Gruyter Oldenbourg.

Musa, Muhammad Adli. 2011. "Islamic Business Ethics and Finance: An Exploratory Study of Islamic Banks in Malaysia." Paper presented at the 8th International Conference on Islamic Economics and Finance, Doha, Qatar, December. Center for Islamic Economics and Finance, Qatar Foundation.
Naqvi, Syed Nawab Haider. 1981. *Ethics and Economics: An Islamic Synthesis.* Markfield, Leicestershire: The Islamic Foundation.
Naqvi, Syed Nawab Haider. 1993. *Development Economics: A New Paradigm.* New Delhi: Sage.
Naqvi, Syed Nawab Haider. 2003. *Perspectives on Morality and Human Well-Being: A Contribution to Islamic Economics.* Markfield, Leicestershire: The Islamic Foundation.
Nasr, Seyyed Hossein. 1968. "Who Is Man? The Perennial Answer of Islam." *Studies in Comparative Religion* 2 (1) (Winter): 31–48.
Nasr, S. Hossein. 2017. Foreword. In *Ethical Dimensions of Islamic Finance: Theory and Practice*, edited by Zamir Iqbal and Abbas Mirakhor. New York: Palgrave.
North, Douglass. 1990. *Institutions, Institutional Change and Economic Performance.* Cambridge: Cambridge University Press.
Palley, T. J. 2007. "Financialization: What It Is and Why It Matters." Working Paper no. 252. Annandale-on-Hudson, NY: The Levy Economics Institute.
Presley, John R., and John G. Sessions. 1994. "Islamic Economics: The Emergence of a New Paradigm." *The Economic Journal* 104 (424): 584–596.
Rahman, A. R. 1996. "Administrative Responsibility: An Islamic Perspective." *American Journal of Islamic Social Sciences* 3 (4): 497–517.
Reinhart, Carmen, and Kenneth Rogoff. 2009. *This Time Is Different: Eight Centuries of Financial Folly.* Princeton: Princeton University Press.
Rice, Gillian. 1999. "Islamic Ethics and the Implications for Business." *Journal of Business Ethics* 18: 345–358.
Rizk, Riham Ragab. 2008. "Back to Basics: An Islamic Perspective Business and Work Ethics." *Social Responsibility Journal* 4 (1/2): 246–254.
Sen, Amartya. 1987. *On Ethics and Economics.* Oxford and New York: Basic Blackwell.
Shiller, Robert J. 2003. *The New Financial Order: Risk in the 21st Century.* Princeton, NJ: Princeton University Press.
Smith, Adam. 1759 [2002]. *The Theory of Moral Sentiments.* Cambridge: Cambridge University Press.
Stiglitz, Joseph E. 1988. "Why Financial Structure Matters." *Journal of Economic Perspectives* 2 (4): 121–126.
Turner, Adair. 2015. *Between Debt and the Devil: Money, Credit, and Fixing Global Finance.* Princeton: Princeton University Press.
Vranceanu, Radu. 2005. "The Ethical Dimension of Economic Choices." *Business Ethics, the Environment and Responsibility* 14 (2): 94–107.

Williamson, Oliver. 1993. "Calculativeness, Trust, and Economic Organization." *Journal of Law and Economics* 36 (1): 453–486.
Zilio-Grandi, Ida. 2015. "What God Loves: The Qur'an and Islamic Ethics Proceedings." QLAMA: The Qur'an Between Late Antiquity and Middle Ages: Form, Structure, Comparative Studies, QLAMA, Siena May 22, in corso di stampa.

CHAPTER 5

The Crisis of Civilization and the Problem of Knowledge

Centuries of steady loss in economic power, social decadence, and political instability have left the Muslim world in a pathetic state of misery, anguish, and despair. The projection of the golden age of the world of Islam in the Muslim mind is nothing more than a bit of memory. For reasons not fully understood in the midst of intellectual wilderness and confusion, it is perhaps easier to attribute the monumental demise to external forces of suppression than to seek explanation from internal weaknesses inhibiting coherent thought and action. From Malek Bennabi's perspective, colonization is a logical consequence of weak, inept, and thus, *colonizable* societies. As a precondition to the alienating process of colonization, *colonizability* is a state of affairs of a despiritualized society in which knowledge is driven by confusion and scepticism rather than wisdom aligned with the Islamic worldview.

It is irrational to overlook Muslims' shortcomings in the rush to attribute blame for the loss of economic power that made the colonial years a reality. It is even easier to impart criticism, out of intellectual laziness, at Islam as a religion that embraces tradition, backwardness, and anti-modernism. There is, however, more complexity to the truth that needs to be addressed. There is no truth in the conclusion drawn from the two premises that, first, the Muslim world is economically weak, and second, that Islam is the prevalent creed, that therefore Islam represents an obstacle to economic development. There is no substance to this line of argument, which ignores the fact that secularized Muslim minds are disoriented minds incapable of organizing an ideal Islamic economy. It is difficult, indeed, to hold Islam responsible for the outcome of secular ideas and secular economic policies.

If the economic success in more distant history is attributed to strong allegiance of Muslims to Islam, it is only fair to consider economic failure as the result of weaker allegiance to the same truth. The response to a crisis of civilization may, however, follow different modes of thinking. As argued by Seyyed Hossein Nasr (1993, p. 119), there may be a reversion to the authentic sources of knowledge, *Al-Qur'ān* and *As-Sunnah*. Alternatively, there may be attempts at reforming and reconstructing Islam to accommodate change or to wait for the end of life on earth. In a sense, it is a clear choice for Muslims between reverting to truth, eclipsing that very truth, and subscribing to a conspiracy of silence. It is inconceivable that Islam, a religion established in perfection by Allah *swt*, is deemed, by secular minds devoid of basic Islamic knowledge, to be a creed of obscurantism, preventing inquiry and reform and carrying the seeds of its own destruction. It is impossible to provide viable solutions to the economic problems in Muslim societies when the Islamic worldview is suppressed or eliminated from Islamic economic thought. A secular mind is more concerned about filling empty niches in an inherently unstable economic system than in organizing an ideal economy.

The impossibility theorem proposed in the next chapter implies that grafting secular ideas onto Islamic economic thought or Islamic values onto conventional economics is not viable. The argument that an effective response to the crisis of civilization can only be achieved through a sincere reversion to the truth with a paradigm shift toward *Al-Iqtiṣād* principles drawn from *Al-Qur'ān* and the tradition of the Prophet (saa) is not a narrative created in a vacuum. It is imperative that the foundations of economic thought be shifted away from "scientific materialism," which dominates conventional economics, as well as the present universe of discourse called Islamic economics. A sincere reversion to the spiritual, intellectual, and social capital, which derives from the unique worldview of Islam, is a pre-requisite to economic revival in Muslim societies. It is possible to extract the principles for the organization of an ideal economy and explain its institutional structure from *Al-Qur'ān* and *As-Sunnah* using terminology that is familiar to minds versed in present economic and legal systems in order to navigate the social pressures and maze of rules and regulations. The use of conventional terminology together with Arabic terminology for the sake of clarity in the explanation of the Qur'anic vision of the economy should not be construed as an embrace of conventional economics.

A Brief Biography of Muslim Philosophers and Social Critics Over the Past Century

It is impossible, indeed, to avoid the problem of knowledge in any serious attempt to understand the crisis of civilization. Reference is made in this chapter to a group of philosophers and social critics who provided over the past century and a half, articulate and analytic criticism of the Western philosophical foundations of Economics. Dr Muhammad Iqbal has a treatise specifically addressed to Economic Science (*'Ilm al-Iqtiṣād*), as does Malek Bennabi in his work on the Conditions of Renaissance (*Shurūṭ Annahdha*) and Muslim in the World of Economics, among others. This collection of seminal works summarizes the philosophical, analytic, logical, and critical views of their authors as they address how Muslims should return to *Al-Qur'ān* to find solutions to their economic problems. Economic issues are also dealt with in detail in Sa'eed Nursi's Magnum Opus interpretation (*tafseer*) of *Al-Qur'ān* in Letters of Light (*Risalat Annur*). Al-Shaheed Sayyid Muhammad Baqir as-Sadr provided the most comprehensive view of the structure of the economy as envisioned in *Al-Qur'ān* in Our Economy (*Iqtiṣāduna*). Also, Dr Syed Muhammad Naquib Al-Attas and Dr Seyyed Hossein Nasr provide further insights with a collective emphasis on the notion that Al-Qur'ān is the fountainhead of ideas for every generation to conceive and implement its vision for future societies and economies. The consistent insights from these scholars reinforce the notion that it is impossible to graft the Islamic and secular worldviews one onto the other. In light of the critiques of conventional economics and Islamic economics provided in previous chapters, it is impossible to construct a consistent body of Islamic economic thought with either the inadequate processes of secularization or Islamization. In the greater scheme of an Islamic worldview, these approaches to the development of Islamic economic thought are not sustainable.

Muhammad Iqbāl (1877–1938) whose poetry in Urdu, Arabic, and Persian is rich in literary and intellectual content, is considered to be among the greatest of the modern era. He is often referred to as Allama Iqbāl with reference to his scholarship and status of poet *par excellence*, philosopher, social commentator, and politician, and to his revolutionary intellectual work on the history of Islamic thought, economics, science, philosophy of religion, and public policy. He used poetry as the main medium to express his various insights and participated in philosophical and political discourse through letters to political figures of his era. Another contemporaneous scholar Sa'eed Nursi (1877–1960), also known as Wonder of the Age (*Bediuzzaman*), is considered as one of the most influential scholars of Islam in modern Türkiye. Apart from his deep knowledge of religious sciences, he also mastered positive sciences by acquiring proficiency in mathematics, physics, chemistry, and astronomy. Having lived through an age of successive geopolitical crises in Türkiye and the world in recent history, and the rest of the world, Nursi articulated an intellectual response to the transformative events of world war, the disintegration of the Ottoman Caliphate, the birth of the Republic of Türkiye, Western colonization of the Muslim world, bifurcation of the world into communist and capitalist camps, and rise of the movements of materialism and atheism. Such a unique period in human history had a consequential effect on Nursi's thought, writings, and approach to education.

Malek Bennabi (1905–1973) is a social philosopher who is considered perhaps the first social scientist the Muslim world has produced since Abdurrahman Ibn Khladun (1332–1406). His logical approach to the study of human civilization focuses on the identification of universal principles that govern the rise and fall of civilization. He is the first to distinguish the concept of "colonizability," which distinguishes the internal factors of the Muslim world's dilemma of backwardness from the external factors related to colonization. His work written in Arabic and French has not received the scholarly attention it merits until the 1980s, and more recent English translations of his treatise on civilization have contributed to a better understanding of his significant intellectual insights. Also, As-Shaheed Sayyid Muhammad Baqir as-Sadr (1935–1980) is regarded as one of the most prominent writers on Islamic Philosophy and Economics. The seminal treatises on Our Philosophy (*Falsafatuna*) and Our Economics (*Iqtiṣāduna*) and Lessons in Islamic Jurisprudence extensive insights on the tradition and historical development of Islamic literature as well as valuable original insights on these interrelated fields of knowledge from one of the leading thinkers in the Muslim world over the past century.

Finally, reference is made to the seminal work on Islam and Secularism by Syed Muhammad Naquib Al-Attas, who introduced and defined the concept of Islamization of knowledge as the liberation of man from secular control over his reason to attain the original state of *fitrah* in harmony with the state of being and existence. There are also insights from Seyyed Hossein Nasr, another proliferate scholar in the history of Islamic philosophy, science and civilizations. His collection of work on Knowledge and the Sacred, Islamic Cosmological Doctrines, Islamic Art and Spirituality, A Muslim's Guide to the Modern World, and Ideals and Realities of Islam, among others, is inclusive of deep insights that address the intellectual challenges faced by Muslims in the modern world. It is not difficult to identify the problem of knowledge as the common thread that permeates across the seminal work of the above eminent scholars. From the history of Islamic thought, theory of civilization, and Islamization of knowledge, the central argument is that knowledge cannot be separated from faith and true belief, and that Islam does not subscribe to the secular dichotomy between the religious and profane, and between the spiritual and temporal in its philosophy of life. Thus, from the perspective of these earlier scholars and social critics, the disorder and chaos faced by the Muslim world can only be the result of confusion in knowledge about Islam and its worldview. As it is impossible to accommodate Islam within the ideals of secular minds, or to graft the Islamic worldview onto secular ideas, it is imperative to reaffirm the nature of knowledge and its true sources, in order to project justice in all spheres of responsibility and rebuild the socio-intellectual foundations of Islamic civilization.

THE DETERMINANTS OF SHIFT IN ECONOMIC POWER

Malek Bennabi (1903–1973) argues that Ibn Khaldun's theory of the rise and fall of civilization is inspired by the psychological factor of solidarity or group feeling (*"asabiyyah"*). Even as the dimension of civilization seems to be reduced to the scale of dynasty and royal authority, the transitory aspect of civilization reflects the inner workings of organic phenomena. The cyclical aspect of civilization is the result of the shifting dynamics based on the determinants of economic and the opposite factors of regression and decadence, which represent the force of inertia of any civilization. In his arguments about the notion of cycle, Bennabi (1954, [2006], p. 7) defines civilization as a "whole whose phases are not independent: in a biological process these are the causes of life and death—internal contradictions—that lead the being to its full development and then to its final disintegration. In the social order this fatality is limited or rather conditioned, because the direction and the term of evolution depend on the psycho-temporal factors on which an organized society could, in a certain measure, act by regulating its life and pursuing certain ends in a coherent manner."

Thus, as noted also by Ibn Khaldun (pp. 112–113), the evolution toward the making of royal authority and power depends on leadership based not only on solidarity or group feeling, but also on strong commitment to moral values such as faithfulness to obligations, and respect of religious law. In contrast, movement in the opposite direction toward loss of power, influence and decadence depends on moral weakness and commitment of sins and acts of transgression. The complete loss of political virtues is conducive to the destruction of royal authority, providing thereby an opportunity for others to cultivate new group feelings based on respect for religious law and the promotion of justice. It is, therefore, the emergence of true or false leadership and moral values that determines the direction of movement toward the establishment or demise of a political order. Similarly, with respect to the social and economic order, it is the virtues and vices that leadership reflects in the exercise of authority and promotion of justice or injustice that regulate social and economic life and determine the paths toward social harmony and economic prosperity or social instability and economic decadence.

During the critical phase of disintegration and decadence, the scale of values is, according to Bennabi (1954 [2006], p. 9) "reversed, and frivolities, then, appear as great things. And when such reversal takes place, the social edifice not being able to hold out solely on props of technique, science and reason must collapse, because the soul alone allows humanity to soar. When the soul makes default, it is the fall and the decadence, for all that loses its ascending force, could not but descend, pulled down by an irresistible force." As a means of material development rather than a finality, science does not constitute a substitute for conscience. It is the soul that determines the direction of movement, and the forces of economic power, regression, and decadence should be understood in terms of their relationship with "this unique source of human energy, that is the faith." The decay and fall of civilization become inevitable when the inner workings of the soul are weakened. Bennabi (1954 [2006], p. 92) further argues that as soon as the necessary equilibrium between spiritual and material forces and between finality and causality is lost in one direction or another, vertical fall becomes a certainty. These equilibrium conditions imply that the "Muslim civilisation lost its equilibrium the moment it ceased to observe the just relation between science and conscience, between the material factors and the spiritual order, thus, foundering in pure metaphysical anarchy and maraboutic chaos that have formed its decadence." The relics of Muslim civilization attested by the remains of villages, monuments, and architectural sculptures are, indeed, reflective of stregnth of faith followed by weakness. It is not possible for Muslim societies therfore, to aspire for civilizational renaissance without a reversion to the unique source of knowledge and strength.

Faith is the catalyser of human action, but when it loses its significance and is rendered irrelevant to the determination of individual action and to the promotion of justice, it ceases also to promote civilization. It is the end of a cycle of bio-historical synthesis. Faith, as argued again by Bennabi (1954 [2006], p. 10), "becomes the faith of the devotees who withdraw themselves from life, fleeing from their duties and responsibilities like all those who, since Ibn Khaldun, have taken refuge in *marabutism*." Social escapism, it is argued, cannot solve the civilizational problems of Muslim societies because it renders all social forms of interaction static. If faith is regarded as a means to achieve individualistic spiritual uplifting only by repudiating worldly life, it ceases to serve as the catalyser of social values, and human interaction. The conditions for renaissance a renaissance, thus, become increasingly difficult to achieve when the necessary equilibrium between spiritual and material forces is lost, and the linkage between finality and causality is severed. As argued by Seyyed Hossein Nasr (2000, p. 17), "Islam, in fact, being the religion of Unity, has never distinguished between the spiritual and temporal or religious and profane in any domain." Secularism is incompatible with Islam, a belief system based on Unity which does not recognize the dichotomy between the religious and the profane, and consitutes an ideal way of conduct in all spheres of life without exception.

It can be also argued that faith has been also at the foundation of Western civilization, which developed as a cycle of bio-historical synthesis based on sociological heredity similar to biological inheritance. It is apt to quote here the arguments by Al-Attas (1993, p. 134), who writes that Western civilization is a "civilization that has evolved out of the historical fusion of cultures, philosophies, values and aspirations of ancient Greece and Rome; their amalgamation with Judaism and Christianity, and their further development and formation by the Latin, Germanic, Celtic and

Nordic peoples. From ancient Greece are derived the philosophical and epistemological elements and the foundations of education and of ethics and aesthetics; from Rome the elements of law and statecraft and government; from Judaism and Christianity the elements of religious faith; and from Latin, Germanic, Celtic, and Nordic peoples their independent and national spirit and traditional values, and the development and advancement of the natural and physical sciences and technology which they, together with the Slavic peoples, have pushed to such pinnacles of power."

Thus, the importance of faith, based on Judaism and Christianity, in the rise of Western civilization is undeniable. It is further argued that Islam also has contributed significantly to Western civilization in the fields of knowledge, rational thinking, and scientific inquiry. At present however, the foundations of knowledge and faith that define the equilibrium conditions of civilization are inherently unstable. Under the present conditions, it is impossible for the certainty of religious knowledge and faith to be fused with the speculative nature of secular philosophies. It is impossible to conflate evolutionary and conflicting doctrines without creating a dualism in worldview that obscures the finality and purpose of Islamic and secular civilizations. It is also noted that the element of faith, which played a role in the emergence of Western civilization, started to fade away during the period of the *European Renaissance* in the fifteenth and sixteenth centuries. It was a period that marked a growing disinterest in Christianity as a revealed religion, and it was followed by three centuries of *Enlightenment*, where religious faith was eventually suppressed by positivist faith, scientism, and a blend of secular philosophies that replaced faith with reason.

Given the insatiable quest for economic power and nostalgic desire to revive old civilizations, it is the moulding of faith and sociology of knowledge that determine the fate of such endeavours. From the purely sociological perspective, civilization can thus be regarded, with reference to Bennabi (1954 [2006], p. 7), "as a numerical series following its course in similar but non-identical terms. Thus appears an essential notion of history: the *cycle of civilisation*. Each cycle is defined by certain psycho-temporal conditions proper to a social group: it is a 'civilization' in these conditions. Then the civilisation migrates, shifts its abode, transfers its values in another area. It thus perpetuates itself in an indefinite exodus, through successive metamorphoses: each metamorphosis being a particular synthesis of man, soil and time" (italics in original). Civilization is conceived as a numerical series in the sense that it follows certain patterns of evolution in transitory stages. It may collapse in certain places over a certain period of time only to migrate toward alternative spaces with different psycho-temporal conditions and historical fusions of faith, philosophies, values, and cultures. Thus, the problem of each society is intrinsically that of its own civilization, which cannot be advanced by simply imitating or borrowing ideas from the cultural milieu of another civilization. As noted by Sherif (2018, p. xx), Bennabi's theory of civilization is not about the accumulation of things but about the construction of an edifice and architecture with the temporal interaction of material resources and ideas. The idea that serves as a catalyst to the civilizing process is the product of the creation by the society of its own means to meet its own ends, and achieve its own civilisational aspirations. Given these conceptual constraints, it is impossible for a civilization to shift abode across societies that share the same ideas, same psycho-temporal conditions, and same worldviews.

Thus, the forces responsible for the rise and fall of states and dynasties, and for the emergence, regression, and decadence of civilizations are not limited to sociology and politics alone. The cyclical phases are the product of spiritual, philosophical, and material conditions. Since the metamorphosis can be regarded as a synthesis of man, soil, and time, the problem of civilization poses the problems of man, soil, and time, respectively. It is, however, the fundamental problem of man that determines the commencement and end of the civilizing process. It is man's thought and action that determine the migration of civilization and its shift in abode from soil to soil as well as its historical movement through time. It is impossible to understand the cycle of civilization, and patterns in the numerical series without considering the problem of man, which is intrinsically the problem of knowledge because man's thoughts and actions emanate from the authoritative worldview that projects the vision of ideal civilization.

The Problem of Knowledge and Intellectual Challenges

The problem of man is a problem of knowledge because it is the knowledge that shapes thought, which in turn drives both individual and collective action across time and space. The danger is that thought, which has the power to inspire action, can also inhibit and paralyze it. The infusion of alien concepts into the Muslim mind, which result in confusion and error in knowledge, imply also the severance of the relation between faith in the realm of the heart and its outward confirmation and manifestation in the action of the body. As argued by Malek Bennabi (1954 [2006], p. 45), "the absence of a direct relation between thought and action implies blind, incoherent action and results in a subjective appreciation of facts—in their over-estimation or under-estimation. In the modern Muslim world, it has given birth, on the one hand, to a psychosis of the 'easy thing' that leads to blind action, and on the other, to a psychosis of the 'impossible thing' that paralyses action." Thus, part of the reason for the decadence of Muslim societies is the dangerous thought that it is impossible to do anything because of ignorance, that it is impossible to become aware of the state of ignorance because of poverty, and that it is impossible to overcome this dilemma because of colonialism. It is the internal psychosis of colonizability that renders the external forces of colonialism and the state of colonization inevitable.

A consistent argument is also presented by Sa'eed Nursi, whose primary concern, as noted by Yucel (2017), by Voll (1999) and Yucel (2017), among others, was with the conditions for renewal and reform based on the analysis of the internal causes the decline of the Muslim world rather than external factors such as colonialism. Also, according to Al-Attas (1993, pp. 104–105), it is the "internal elements whose germs were evident in the early periods of Islam," that constituted the principal causes of the gradual decadence of the Muslim world, which rendered Western colonization possible. It is the status of colonizability that allowed the colonization of a significant part of the Muslim world since the seventeenth century, and continues to prevail with the projection of Western worldview and ideologies in the Muslim mind. The prevailing confusion of knowledge in the Muslim mind is the natural outcome of educational systems that perpetuate the loss of adab, the discipline of mind, body, and soul, and inculcate secular ideas that suppress Islamic thought and action.

The Muslim world is indeed, according to Malek Bennabi (1954 [2006], p. 40), a mixture of inherited residues from the post-al-Muwahhid epoch, Reformist and Modernist currents. Life, he argues, "does not analyse; it integrates. When the elements available are compatible and assimilable, it makes a synthesis of them; if they are heteroclite and disparate, it makes of them a syncretism, an accumulation, a chaos." Similar arguments about the impossible synthesis of conflicting worldviews are presented by other eminent scholars, such as Seyyed Hossein

Nasr (1993, p. 125), who notes that virtually all Western schools of thought, philosophies, and ideologies of the past centuries, including egalitarianism, existentialism, evolutionism, positivism, progressivism, and socialism, were endorsed to one extent or another, by scholars and followers in the Islamic world. There were even attempts at synthesizing some elements of Western thought with the Islamic worldview. "Many elements drawn from leftist ideologies have penetrated into the Islamic world in the garb of expressions taken from the language of the Quran and Hadith as well as of classical Islamic thought. Some have even tried to transform Islam as a religion into a leftist ideology." It is clear that given the inorganic nature of these currents of secular ideologies, it is impossible to project them onto the unique worldview of Islam.

The problem of knowledge is further complicated by the wrong belief held by some reformists and modernists that Islam and modern sciences are incompatible. It was mostly the rise of positivism, materialism, and secularism in the nineteenth century in the Ottoman Era that drove some Muslim scholars to interpret Islamic disciplines from the perspective of Western rationalism. Cognizant of the importance of the philosophical challenges, Sa'eed Nursi demonstrated that Islam and modern sciences can be indeed consistent with each other through a coherent understanding of the foundations of belief. As argued also by Al-Attas (1993, p. 120), it is imperative to discern the Qur'anic meaning from the Western concept of rationalism. As the rationalism derived from the Western concept of *ratio*, is different from the Qur'anic concept of the intellect *al-'aql*, which functions in accordance with the spiritual organ of cognition *al-qalb*, it is obvious that the attempt by modernists to "'rationalize' Verses of the Holy Al-Qur'ān they find convenient to their purpose in line with the theories and findings of modern science," is an exercise in futility.

From the Islamic perspective, modern movements aimed at reforming the divine law rather than human society constitute also an anomaly, according to Seyyed Hossein Nasr (2000, p. 89). Also, Al-Attas (1993, p. 112) contends that "not a single one of the so-called Modernists and Reformers of our times, including those who masquerade as 'ulama' barely reaches the lowest level of the great 'ulama' of the past and men of spiritual discernment who contributed so much to the knowledge of Islam and the Islamic world view." Indeed, a secular mind unable to comprehend the essence of the Islamic worldview and the immutable laws that bind thought to action cannot be expected to "reform" individual thought based on the sincerity of purpose and conscious action. As argued by As-Sadr (1982 [1994], p. xxvii), it is rather the firm belief that "Islam is the expression of its very self, the sign of its historical personality and the key to its former glory" that provides the basis for intellectual efforts to fight backwardness and promote development. These efforts can only be successful "if the method is adopted from Islam and if a framework for the starting point is taken from the Islamic system."

Thus, the advocacy of early Muslim philosophers and social critics for the modernization of Islam should not be confused with the attempts by some modernists at the modernization of Islam. The manifest failure to draw a clear line of distinction between these inherently contradictory processes is indicative of the severity of the crisis of knowledge in the Muslim world. As noted by El-Mesawi (2008, p. 250), "Bennabi ascertains, ersatz ideas, whether advocated in the name of authenticity or borrowed from the cultural world of another civilization in the name of modernization, are no more than carriers of a specific genre of viruses that ultimately erode the very moral, cultural, and material foundations of a society." Indeed, Islam rejects secular ideas because they are alien to its worldview in every respect, but the Muslim world has succumbed to a secularization process that produced, over many centuries, a state of confusion and error in knowledge. In the aftermath of the demise of the Muslim North-African Berber Caliphate of Al-Muwahhidun, it is a post-Almohad mind that emerged, a mind that suppresses the Islamic worldview and cannot grasp "anything except what is futile, absurd and even deadly." It is a mind where dead ideas attract deadly ones that poison the true faith, and inhibit purposeful thought and action.

A belief that knowledge is essential to the formation of thought implies also belief in sacred knowledge from the authentic sources of Al-Qur'ān and Prophetic tradition and in the immutability of the principles contained therein. It is important to guard against the desacralization and demeaning of Islamic teachings through the agency of semantic gymnastics, fickle principles, and mutable concepts from volatile secular ideologies. As argued again by Bennabi (1954 [2006], p. 41), the meaning of things can be either the one we attribute to them, or that given to us by themselves, or that others might want to give us. And the danger is that the meaning of Qur'anic concepts conveyed to us through divine revelation and demonstrated through Prophetic tradition lose their significance. It is difficult to develop Islamic economic thought, which defines the guiding principles for the organization of an ideal economy, on sound basis if it becomes captive to the meaning of things given to us by others rather than that derived directly from Islamic sources of knowledge. When historical and relativist interpretations of the meanings of truth and justice take precedence over their meaning in *Al-Qur'ān*, the fountainhead of true knowledge, then it is falsehood and injustice driven by inconsistent thought and action that are bound to prevail in all aspects of social and economic life.

Earlier insights from Muhammad Iqbāl reflect similar concerns about the assimilation of heteroclite elements resulting in syncretism and chaos. He argued that the movement toward rationalism in Europe had become the greatest hindrance to man's ethics because its idealistic systems were built on pure reason, devoid of the "fire of living conviction which personal revelation alone can bring." For Muslims, on the other hand, the "spiritual basis of life is a matter of conviction for which even the least enlightened man… can lay down his life." Thus, man's ignorance of his role in the universe and the potentialities within lead to certain fears which hinder his spiritual and ethical progression. He firmly believed in making man conscious of his self and channeling this realization into a source of power free of fear. The highest stage of man's ethical progress is reached when he becomes absolutely free from fear and grief. The object of Islam is to free man from fear and instead transform him into a unit of force with the will to struggle through ethical progress to attain the highest spiritual levels. Ultimately, this must be the object of all human activity.

The problem of knowledge, as argued by Al-Attas (1993, p. 107), is a problem of loss of *adab* toward Allah *swt* because knowledge should be approached, like all other acts of worship *'Ibādāt*, with complete humility, caution, and reverence. Thus, *adab* is a precondition of knowledge, and the loss of *adab* is conducive to confusion and error in knowledge. Indeed, as a result of the residues of incoherent secular currents and state of syncretism and chaos in knowledge, "many important concepts pertaining to Islam and the Islamic world view have lost their transparency and have become opaque" (Al-Attas 1993, p. 127). The corruption of knowledge results also in loss of justice, which is the cause of the social decadence and demise of Muslim civilization. It is the emergence of false leaders who lack the basic understanding of the nature and purpose of knowledge, and who subscribe to secular conceptions of justice, that is conducive to the perpetuation of ignorance and injustice, and thus, the crisis of civilization.

Given the nexus between knowledge and adab, it is difficult to address the problem of knowledge without structured educational systems that inculcate *adab* and correct knowledge to future generations. Kenneth E. Boulding (1983, pp. 9–10) argues that it is important to understand the dynamics of the "noosphere," which reflects the quantity and quality of human knowledge. Since human knowledge is confined primarily in the minds of human beings subject to death or "final denouement" as biological organisms, it is imperative that education facilitates the transfer of knowledge "from decaying older minds into decaying younger ones. This means that the noosphere itself, as a total body of knowledge, does not have to decay." The inevitable question arises as to whether the imparting of knowledge should be based on secular ideologies or on a hierarchy of knowledge that gives primacy to sacred knowledge, which considers both the spiritual and material life, and to *adab*, which in the words of Al-Attas (1993, p. 150) represents "the spectacle (*mashhad*) of justice as it is reflected by wisdom; and it is the recognition and acknowledgement of the various hierarchies (mariitib) in the order of being and existence and knowledge, and concomitant action in accord with the recognition and acknowledgement."

The purpose of education, thus, is not to inculcate any form of knowledge, but to inculcate adab because "the purpose of seeking knowledge is to inculcate goodness or justice in man as man and individual self." In this respect, Iqbāl also questioned the value and effectiveness of conventional approaches to education and prevailing systems which he considered to be not conducive the required character building or transformation to achieve goodness and progress. He cast serious doubts on the role of education in shaping the ethics of man and collectivity. He concluded that "the ethical training of humanity is really the work of great personalities, who appear time to time during the course of human history. Unfortunately, our present social environment is not favorable to the birth and growth of such personalities of ethical magnetism." Jalal (2009) notes that consistent with later arguments by Amartya Sen about the Capability Approach, Iqbāl focused on the notion that an education system that has no bearing on capacity building and the inculcation of Islamic moral values, is absolutely worthless. It is further argued that an educational approach oriented toward capability-building should seek the development of good character and avoid the treatment of human beings as machines.

Since the principal objective of education in Islam is to nurture a man of intellectual and spiritual discernment, Sa'eed Nursi developed also his own methods of teaching by combining positive sciences with Islamic disciplines. According to Nursi, wisdom stems from the combination of the conscience, which is illuminated by the religious sciences, and the mind, which is illuminated by positive sciences. Ayub (2020) notes that Nursi "believes that knowledge, education and faith form not only the prime ingredients for renewal of civilization but the integration of the three provide the platform for development and perfection. This linking of knowledge (*ilm*) with faith (*iman*) forms the core of Nursian model of education system." Thus, Nursi's methodology of teaching reflects a firm belief that educational reform is the principal remedy for the ongoing ignorance and backwardness of the Muslim community, and the viable solution to the economic social, and political problems faced by the Muslim world over the past centuries.

Consistent Perspectives on Economic Development and Economic Justice

Since the problem of civilization is not so much the problem of soil or the problem of time, as the problem of man, it is important to comprehend the nature of man's knowledge, which drives thought, and ultimately defines action. The three essential resources and factors of civilization are available in all societies in the world, but it is the conception and methodological approaches to solving these interrelated problems that differ. Man's action on soil and organization of time, whether on an individual or collective basis, provides the foundations for social and economic activities. As noted by Benlahcene (2011, p. 43), Malek Bennabi regards man as the primary device of society among the three structural elements of civilization. He writes that for Bennabi, "Man is the central force in any civilizing process and without him the other two ingredients are of no value. Man is the driving force behind development and progress or backwardness and decline." Thus, economic action can only be driven by economic thought, which is itself the product of knowledge. Since knowledge is not neutral, as argued by Al-Attas (1993, p. 133), it is imperative to derive the guiding principles for the organization of an ideal Islamic economy from the true sources of knowledge rather than from Muslim minds dominated by secular worldviews.

Thus, a paradigm shift toward *Al-Iqtiṣād*, a discipline concerned with the derivation of the organizing principles of an ideal economy, derived from authentic sources of Islamic knowledge, *Al-Qur'an* and *As-Sunnah*, is warranted. A shift is imperative because alternative approaches to the development of Islamic economic thought suffer from the confusion and error in knowledge derived from secular worldviews. As with conventional economics, there are several strands of methodological approaches within the universe of discourse called Islamic economics. The question inevitably arises as to whether the Islamization of Economics, which involves a synthetization of Islamic *Maqasid* or Islamic Morality with Economics, offers a serious path to sustainable economic development. There is compelling evidence from earlier scholars that the vision for an ideal economy is not the product of imagination but certainty in the authentic sources of knowledge. There are, however, residues of incoherent secular currents, partly reflected in the universe of discourse known as Islamic economics that slip into syncretism and chaos. As it is impossible for heteroclite and disparate parts to produce a consistent body of knowledge, Muslim societies with a genuine desire to reorganize the economic system and sow the seeds of lasting renaissance, should seek knowledge within an unperturbed universe of Islamic knowledge to rediscover the guiding principles of *Al-Iqtiṣād* paradigm of Islamic economic thought.

The rich intellectual legacy of earlier Muslim scholars includes insights about the organization of an ideal economic system based on the Islamic worldview, which is distinct from variants founded partially or entirely on secular beliefs. Baqir As-Sadr (1982 [1994]) argues in *Our Economy* (*Iqtiṣāduna*) that although Islam does not address economic phenomena from a scientific perspective, it does influence economic events and their ramifications for social organization by defining the responsibilities and functions of man, who constitutes the generator and pivot of economic events. It recognizes man as the principal actor who should be moulded with the spiritual and intellectual perceptions of Islam and its worldview. As-Sadr regards the process of economic development not merely as development programs legislated and implemented by governments but as a process in which all members of the community believe and participate. Thus, the economic doctrine of the society, or its political economy, is a view of the direction and course that society decides to follow in organizing economic life and solving practical problems. A collective doctrine, it is further argued, is one that nurtures in the individual a deep consciousness about the responsibilities toward society. It is a doctrine that does not deprive man of the consciousness about the ultimate destiny in Islam and remembrance of the soul's Covenant with its Creator.

Al-Iqtiṣād can thus be defined as an economic doctrine concerned with the organization of an ideal economy based on principles derived from Islamic sources of knowledge. A distinction is clearly made between conventional economics and the universe of discourse called Islamic economics, as Baqir As-Sadr (1982 [1994], pp. xliii–xliv) further argues that "when we use the words 'the Islamic economics,' we do not mean by that directly 'economics' because economics is a relatively new science and because Islam is a missionary religion and a way of life, its real job is not the pursuit of scientific studies... Rather, we mean by 'the Islamic economics': the economic doctrine of Islam which embodies the Islamic system in the organization of economic life."

Hence, while science and doctrine differ with respect to the method and objective of inquiry, their subject matter and spheres of inquiry remain the same. The subject matter of Islamic economics is the organization of an ideal Islamic economy where justice prevails in all aspects of economic life. The social order of Islam, as argued by Al-Attas (1993, p. 66) is one that promotes justice ('*adl*) to the individual as spirit and physical being as well as to the society. The individual contributes to the community in the same way that other members strive, according to their own capabilities, to fulfil their responsibilities with sincerity of purpose.

The notion that justice by itself is not a scientific idea constitutes an important insight from Baqir As-Sadr (1982 [1994], pp. 9–10), who argues that when justice combines with an idea, it profoundly marks it with a doctrinal pattern that discerns it from scientific thinking. It may be argued that part of the reason is that justice means a harmonious state of affairs where everything is situated in its proper place. To do wrong is injustice not just to others but to one's own soul as well. Since the conditions of harmony are not limited to the equilibrium relations of man with others but with the condition of man in relation to his self as well, the elements of human conduct and behaviour are hardly amenable to formal scientific inquiry.

Thus for instance, the iron law of labour, he further contends, is a proposition that does not determine whether bare sustenance wages coincide with justice or not. As argued by Thomas Leslie (1879, p. 36), the two questions of what is right and what motivates man to do right are not philosophically distinct, "according to the theory of an innate sense of right and wrong which assumes that every man's conscience informs him of his duty." It is, thus, for the man of spiritual and intellectual discernment to prevent injustice according to the Qur'anic concept of intellect *al-ʿaql* and spiritual organ of cognition *al-qalb*.

The related issues of freedom and equality are also addressed by Muhammad Iqbāl, who was an untiring advocate for a revitalization of Islam's ethical ideals in society. From the Islamic perspective, freedom is conducive to ethical and virtuous behaviour, which ultimately benefits society. Iqbal (1908) argues that the main ethical ideal in Islam, therefore, is to empower man with the correct knowledge to overcome fear and insecurity. It is the ceaseless effort towards the realization of ethical norms that instils in man a sense of responsibility and increases his awareness about the duty to do good and promote justice. Once fear is substituted with a sense of human personality, virtuous behaviour and respect for others will ensue. Whereas virtues are the source of empowerment and strength, evil acts weaken society. Thus, rule compliance can be achieved through righteousness (*birr*), which represents the highest virtue, as defined in *Al-Qur'ān* (2:177).

Also, Muhammad Iqbāl examined the notion of self-interest and the rights of individuals versus society. It is thus argued that the interests of the individual as a unit remain subordinate to the interests of society, which represents an integrated body that should project to the outside world a firm belief in the worldview of Islam and its moral principles. Social interest is a logical principle that regulates and limits the liberty of the individual to pursue self-interest. The dignity of individuals and the equality of humanity entail egalitarian social, political, and economic governance. There is in Islam, absolute equality of all members of the society. As piety is the only benchmark to differentiate among people, social distinction should be determined only on the basis of good character and virtue, not privileged class, colour, or caste systems. Man can, thus, be liberated to pursue his spiritual and material life according to the teachings of *Al-Qur'ān* and tradition of the Prophet (pbuh).

The emerging imbalance in social order is also a matter of concern because it undermines the conditions of real economic and social development of mankind. Social justice cannot be achieved unless the primary sources of social injustice are addressed such as human deprivation and impediments to economic freedom, which have multidimensional effects on human life social injustice. These impediments are not only conducive to reduced productivity but they affect also the individual level of self-esteem the levels of self-esteem leading to the destruction of spiritual values. For the sake of social justice, it is imperative to promote economic prosperity, but individual wealth creation should not be pursued at the cost of social welfare, resulting in pervasive social injustice. Uncontrolled greed and lust for wealth can undermine the conditions for harmonious and sustainable societies. Therefore, just economic development and wealth creation sould not be divorced from social, cultural, and political considerations.

In *The Treatise on Iqtiṣād* in *Risale-i Nur* collection, Sa'eed Nursi (1995) addresses economic issues from the Islamic perspective with direct reference to *Al-Qur'ān*. The focus is placed on consumer behaviour in relation to wastefulness and prodigality. It is argued that Allah's (*swt*) creation is for a purpose, and the fulfillment of these duties should be pursued without wasting resources. Man is entrusted with resources, which ultimately belong to the Creator of all things, and since the transfer of the right of ownership is temporary, the endowment cannot be construed as conferring absolute freedom and right to waste resources. The root verb *qasada* of the term *Iqtiṣād* confers also the meaning of harnessing resources for meaningful purposes without wasting. As noted by Aydin (2016), Nursi admonishes the behaviour of consumers in modern economies for not acting in compliance with the *Iqtiṣād*-driven rules of behaviour in the following terms: "O wasteful, prodigal, wrongful, unjust, dirty, unclean, wretched man! You have not acted in accordance with the *Iqtiṣād*, cleanliness, and justice that are the principles by which the whole universe and all beings act, and are therefore in effect the object of their anger and disgust."

Nursi proposes also a six-dimensional framework for human well-being and development including hope, truthfulness, love, solidarity, freedom, and generosity. It is, thus, argued that the demise of Muslim societies can be explained by six ailments, including despair and hopelessness in social life, lack of truthfulness in social and political life, predominance of enmity over love, lack of awareness about spiritual bonds among believers, widespread despotism, and pursuit of self-interest. It is important to provide proper remedies through educational systems that impart correct knowledge to prevent the sense of doubt and insecurity. It is also imperative to promote individual freedom and ensure social order in both the spiritual and material spheres in order to alleviate poverty and prevent the decline of moral values.

These views are consistent with the arguments advanced by Muhammad Iqbal (1904 [2004]) in his work on *'Ilm al-Iqtiṣād* and addressed in further work by Chaudhri (2002) and Saeed (2002) among others, that the study of economics is required to alleviate poverty, and that nations that fail to improve social and economic conditions are destinated to decay, decadence, and destruction. The views of Iqbal on poverty are discussed in related work by Tahir (2002), inter alia, where it is noted that Iqbal argued that the eradication of poverty and deprivation is essential for the flourishing of collective morality and moral consciousness in society. As the precarious conditions of poverty are deemed to be associated with problems related to feudalism and growing populations, he advocated land reform to free peasants from oppressive feudal landlords, and the effective use of human resources to eliminate poverty. A failure in the optimal use of resources would, thus, exacerbatethe problem of poverty. He further argues that from the Islamic perspective, it is a fundamental human right to be free from poverty. Thus, he writes that "after a long and careful study of Islamic Law I have come to the conclusion that if this system of Law is properly understood and applied, at least the right to subsistence is secured to everybody."

The problem of poverty is also addressed by Sa'eed Nursi, who advocates the adoption of measures to balance the needs of society based on the available resources. It is important to provide a correct definition of the needs and wants, because mainstream economic thought is driven by the maxim of infinite needs and scarce resources. A clear distinction is, thus, made between actual needs, which can be met through the economic use of resources according to the *Iqtiṣād*-based principles, and desires, which are rather endless. Further insights about the relationship between the sources of sustenance, and individual needs and desires are also provided. There is no assumption about resource scarcity as it is clearly argued that the means to sustain life on earth and meet the physiological needs of human beings are provided by Allah swt. As noted by Bakkal (2017), Nursi regards the legitimate sources of livelihood to be inclusive of industry, agriculture, and trade, whereas an imbalanced reliance on civil and military services for sustenance purposes would be detrimental to society because of a decrease in the capacity to generate wealth. Also, the wasteful use of resources to meet desires is conducive to substantial harm to the society.

Call for Paradigm Shift in Islamic Economic Thought

The economic insights provided by the eminent Muslim thinkers may overlap with certain economic principles espoused by contemporary scholars in conventional economics. They project, however, a unique spiritual dimension and sense of justice that are immutable because they derive from a distinctively wholistic Islamic worldview. It is on this Islamic worldview that Islamic economic thought should rest its foundations. It is clear from this collection of work by eminent Muslim social critics over the past century that a shift from the current dominant thinking to *Al-Iqtiṣād* is a matter of necessity not choice.

In the universe of discourse of conventional economics, economic doctrines change and the threat to the dominant paradigm, as noted by Robert Skidelski (2020, p. 144), "comes not from empirical anomalies, which can usually be insulated as 'puzzles' to be worked on, but from changes in world-view, which make the puzzles seem intolerable. A mismatch develops between the institutional map of the science and the problem which needs to be solved. A crisis develops when more and more practitioners occupy themselves with the solution of the anomaly, which resists solution by means of the paradigm. Ultimately a new paradigm is suggested. This is resisted by other members of the community but slowly wins them over. The revolution is completed when a younger generation takes over." It is not clear, however, whether a new paradigm can necessarily be embraced by younger minds because, as noted by Jack Wiseman (1991, p. 150), the dominant paradigm may sustain the *status quo* through various means of resistance, including the control of established outlets of publication, mutual citations, and other instruments to control power structures. Thus, criticism of well-established theories can be dismissed as irrelevant or trivial if the arguments for a new paradigm are not well articulated and persistently sustained over a sufficient period of time.

In this respect, John Kenneth Galbraith (1987, p. 283) argues that vested intellectual commitment to established belief constitutes also a powerful constraint since those who stand to benefit from the *status quo*, indeed, resist change. It is difficult for economists to relinquish beliefs assimilated during long hours of education, advocated through years of research, and imparted to generations of students to admit error and confusion in knowledge. Thus, as noted by Pencavel (1991, p. 153), there are two separate but closely related classes of issues in the discussion about the state of economics, including the state of the profession, and the state of ideas. However, the social context, which includes the state of the profession, and in which the discussion among economists takes place is bound to influence the assessment of the state of ideas, and thus the emergence of new paradigms. The argument about the importance of the social context is also manifest in the argument by Thomas Leslie (1879, p. 227) that the structure of the economy is the result of a long evolution marked by continuity and change, which is governed not just by economic factors, but also by the "history and the general laws of society and social evolution." It is the social, political, industrial, moral, and intellectual forces that shape also the structure of the economy, and in turn, the emergence, acceptance or rejection of new ideas.

Again, Galbraith (1987, pp. 1–2) argues that economic ideas are necessarily the product of their own time and place. The same line of argument is present in John Kells Ingram's (1888, pp. 3–4) contention that the emergence of economic doctrines and their contents are the product of the prevailing practical conditions, needs, and tendencies of the corresponding epochs. It is argued that every thinker is a child of his time, whose thinking is necessarily influenced by the social milieu in which he lives and interacts with others. While the influence of practice on theoretic inquiry imprints the latter with positive character, it tends also "to produce exaggerations in doctrine, to lend undue prominence to particular sides of the truth, and to make transitory situations or temporary expedients to be regarded as universally normal conditions." Thus, the danger is that economic doctrines that echo man's physical and material experience are made with complete neglect of man's spiritual existence.

The real danger, in the words of Malek Bennabi (1955 [2021], p. 25) is for Muslim scholars to lose the ideological struggle. He argues that in the same way that respiration regulates life in the individual body, it is ideology that regulates life in the social body, the ambitions of which can only be realized through the satisfaction of three necessary conditions related to the states of tension, integration, and orientation. It is impossible for a disintegrated society with a poor level of efficacy to achieve its aspirations. The ideological struggle lies in the recognition that even when the conditions of tension and integration are fulfilled, it is crucial that orientation is set in the right direction. Therefore, it is imperative to understand the modus operandi of internal and external forces that may influence the capacity of society to achieve its vision, economic or otherwise, by suppressing its tension, undermining its integration, and annulling its orientation. The objective of the ideological struggle is to correct the orientation because however high the tension and solid the integration can be, nothing sensible can be achieved when the direction of travel is wrong. This is, precisely, the overriding message of this book, which calls for rethinking Islamic economics and reorienting it away from secular ideas towards its authentic sources of knowledge.

Thus, when the vision and orientation are correctly set, the optimal method for the organization of economic life, as argued by Baqir As-Sadr (1982 [1994], p. xli), cannot be left for arbitrary choice. It is a decision that is necessarily defined by a balance of ideas and concepts based on spiritual and material factors. Hence, a paradigm shift in the universe of discourse called Islamic economics is only necessary if the emergence and choice of ideas take place in disconnection with the Islamic worldview. A paradigm shift is warranted when there is a continued preoccupation with secular ideas that distort the vision of an ideal Islamic economy. There is indeed, something seriously wrong with Islamic economics when it finds itself plagued with the very problems of conventional economics. As with the latter, the possibility of a paradigm shift in Islamic economics depends also on whether the dominant paradigm has the capacity to resist change and sustain the *status quo*. It may be argued that given the loss of *adab* and humility in the acquisition of true knowledge, which constitutes a serious obstacle to the admission of errors, a status quo is more likely than a paradigm shift.

However, as suggested also by the *Impossibility Theorem*, which is explained in more detail in the next chapter, it is now clear that the current paradigm of Islamic economics is not viable. It is not viable because it offers a secular philosophy for the organization of the economy that is, in *esse* and in *posse*, discernible from conventional economics only by a number of innuendos. There is no rationale for resistance because a *status quo* can only retard the organization of an ideal Islamic economy that serves the whole humanity. Relative to conventional economics, Islamic economics should be cut from a different cloth, driven by a different worldview, governed by different rules of behaviour, and aspiring for a different economic system. This is precisely the vision of *Al-Iqtiṣād*, advocated for by the eminent Muslim philosophers and social critics referred to in this chapter and the principal message of the present book.

Thus, the consistency of the profound insights presented in the intellectual work of the above eminent scholars over the past one-and-a-half centuries is reflective of a shared concern for the demise of the Muslim world, a shared belief in the Islamic worldview, and a shared recourse to the true sources of knowledge. It should not be surprising, hence, that these influential scholars were capable of discerning the internal causes of weakness and decadence from the external factors of colonization. It is not surprising that at critical crossroads of history, they issued the same call to awaken, abandan secular ideas, and revert to the authentic sources of knowledge. It is impossible to solve the chronic problems of fragile economies and fragmented societies without solving the problem of knowledge. It is impossible to change economic reality with the secular mind of corrupt leadership and scholarship that advocate confusion and error in knowledge. It is impossible to organize an ideal economy without the *adab* of knowledge that nurtures man of integrity, piety, and spiritual and material discernment that can promote justice. It is the same awakening call that is issued in this humble work, for a paradigm shift in Islamic economics that can pave the way for the renaissance of Muslim societies.

References

Al-Attas, Syed Muhammad Naquib. 1993. *Islam and Secularism*. Kuala Lumpur: International Institute of Islamic Thought and Civilization.

As-Sadr, Muhammad Baqir. 1982 [1994]. *Iqtiṣāduna—Our Economics*. 2nd ed., vol. 1, Part 1. Tehran: World Organization for Islamic Services.

Aydin, Necati. 2016. "The Tawhidi Paradigm and the 'Moral Market' from Nursi's Perspective." *Al-Shajarah* 21 (2): 157–191.

Ayub, Sheikh Javaid. 2020. "Integrating Secular and the Sacred Branches of Knowledge: Bediuzzaman Said Nursi's Perspective." *Katre International Human Studies Journal* (9) (June): 223–236.

Bakkal, Ali. 2017. "Bediuzzaman Said Nursi s Original Insights on Economy." *Katre, Uluslararasi Insan Arastirmalari Dergisi* 2 (3): 7–13.

Benlahcene, Badrane. 2011. *The Socio-Intellectual Foundations of Malek Bennabi's Approach to Civilization*. London and Washington: The International Institute of Islamic Thought.

Bennabi, Malek. 1954 [2006]. *Islam in History and Society*. New Delhi: Kitab Bhavan [translation by Asma Rachid of Vocation de l'Islam, in French, Paris: Edition du Seuil, 1954])

Bennabi, Malek. 1955 [2021]. *Textes sur la Lutte Idéologique- Pour Mieux Comprendre la Guerre Invisible*. Preface by Sadek Sallam. Ermont: Héritage.

Boulding, Kenneth E. 1983. "The Optimum Utilization of Knowledge—Some Central Concepts." In *The Optimum Utilization of Knowledge*. Boulder: Westview Press
Chaudhri, Fateh M. 2002. "Economic Vision of Allama Iqbal." *The Pakistan Development Review* 41 (4) (Part II, Winter): 983–987.
El-Mesawi, Mohamed El-Tahir. 2008. "Religion, Society, and Culture in Malik Bennabi's Thought." In *The Blackwell Companion to Contemporary Islamic Thought*, edited by Ibrahim M. Abu-Rabi, 213–256. Malden: Blackwell.
Galbraith, J. Kenneth. 1987. *Economics in Perspective: A Critical History*. Boston: Houghton Mifflin.
Ingram, John Kells. 1888. *A History of Political Economy*. Edinburgh: Adam & Charles Black.
Iqbāl, Muhammad. 1904 [2004]. *Ilm al-Iqtiṣād* (repr. Lahore: Sang-e-Meel).
Iqbāl, Muhammad. 1908 [1955]. *Islam as an Ethical and a Political Ideal: Iqbal's Maiden English Lecture*. Edited by S. Y. Hashimy, 53–101. Lahore: Orientalia.
Jalal, Ayesha. 2009. "Freedom and Equality from Iqbal's Philosophy to Sen's Ethical Concerns." In *Arguments for a Better World: Essays in Honor of Amartya Sen*, vol. II, edited by Kaushik Basu and Ravi Kanbur. Oxford: Oxford University Press.
Leslie, Thomas Edward Cliffe. 1879. *Essays in Political and Moral Economy*. Dublin: Dublin University Press Series.
Nasr, Seyyed Hossein. 1993. *A Young Muslim's Guide to the Modern World*. Kuala Lumpur: Islamic Book Trust.
Nasr, Seyyed Hossein. 2000. *Ideals and Realities of Islam*. Chicago, IL: ABC International Group.
Nursi, Said. 1995. *The Flashes Collection*. translation from Turkish. Sözler Neşriyat. Istanbul.
Pencavel, Jean. 1991. "Prospects for Economics." *The Economic Journal* 101: 81–87.
Saeed, Khawaja Amjad. 2002. "Economic Philosophy of Allama Iqbal." *The Pakistan Development Review* 41 (4) (Part II, Winter): 973–982.
Sherif, M. A. 2018. *Facets of Faith—Malek Bennabi and Abul A'la Maududi*. Kuala Lumpur: Islamic Book Trust.
Skidelski, Robert. 2020. *What's Wrong with Economics?: A Primer for the Perplexed*. New Haven: Yale University Press.
Tahir, Pervez. 2002. "Poverty, Feudalism, and Land Reform—The Continued Relevance of Iqbāl." *The Pakistan Development Review* 41 (4) (Part II, Winter): 967–972.
Voll, John Obert. 1999. "Renewal and Reformation in the Mid-Twentieth Century: Bediuzzaman Said Nursi." *The Muslim World* 89 (3–4): 245–259.

Wiseman, Jack. 1991. "The Black Box." *The Economic Journal* 101 (404): 149–155.
Yucel, Salih, 2017. "Is Islam an Obstacle to Progress in the Modern World? The Responses and Analysis of Said Nursi." *Australian Journal of Islamic Studies* 2 (1): 59–75.

CHAPTER 6

Islamization of Economics? An Impossibility Theorem

In the run-up to the twenty-first century, there were calls from outside and inside the economics profession for fundamental changes in the underlying philosophy of the discipline. This call intensified as the concern for environmental degradation for which economics and its existence (ontology), its value system (axiology), its knowledge claim (epistemology), its purpose (teleology), and its methodology were held responsible for worsening environmental and human conditions. Thomas Berry characterized such conditions: "In the twentieth century, the glory of the human has become the desolation of the Earth. And now, the desolation of the Earth is becoming the destiny of the human. From here on, the primary judgement of all human institutions, professions, programs, and activities will be determined by the extent to which they inhibit, ignore or foster a mutually enhancing human-Earth relationship."[1]

Calls for "the rapid implementation of new systems of economics, finance and governance"[2] that go "beyond the calculating, self-interested, individual to take account of community, compassion, and cosmos," and for the reform or complete abandonment of Economics became vociferous after the 2007/2008 Global Financial and Economic Crisis. Since then, proposals have emerged focusing on the need for a paradigm that includes a new human–earth relationship, based on trusteeship, as well as a new philosophical/ethical foundation. Our contention in this book is that *Iqtiṣād*—*Al-Qur'ān's* vision of how the economy is to be arranged—provides such a paradigm with a radically different philosophical foundation from that of Economics to the point that makes grafting of one onto the other Impossible. As is well-known, the latter emerged out of a historical experience peculiar to the European civilization yet claimed universality due to the powerful global hegemony of the Western scientific, cultural, intellectual, military, political, and economic dominance. As a result of this development, an attitude, a habit of thought, took shape in much of the non-industrial part of the world that the Western thought, seen as the engine of modernity, had all the answers to the problems facing these societies. Regarding the slow pace of economic growth and development as a serious challenge, these societies looked to the West for solutions. The period witnessed a widespread movement toward the adoption and implementation by these societies of Economic models and policies designed by Western and Western-dominated institutions.

Scholars, philosophers, and social critics in these regions warned of the follies and adverse consequences of indiscriminate and uncritical adoption and implementation of models and policy recommendations designed and developed based on a system of thought with philosophical and historical foundations radically different from those of host societies. The period also witnessed the beginning of the age of Muslim awakening out of which emerged brilliant and influential philosophers, scholars, and social critics deeply concerned with the plight of Muslim societies who issued clarion calls to awaken and return to the sacred sources of knowledge, primarily Al-Qur'ān in search for genuine solutions to the chronic problems they were facing. They argued that *Al-Qur'ān* offered more appropriate and, often, more efficient solutions to contemporary challenges of Muslim societies, including economic problems. While they had different styles of presentation, each framed their views relying primarily on *Al-Qur'ān* and the *Sunnah* of the Honoured Messenger (saa), and each, to different degrees, focused on challenges facing Muslim societies including issues of social justice, poverty, income distribution, and conditions of economic prosperity. Each scholar believed that it is possible to order a spiritually rich, materially comfortable, and socially stable collectivity that satisfies the necessary and sufficient conditions specified in the Qur'an. They also believed that the Noble Messenger (saa) had operationalized the vision of such a society provided by the Qur'an during his lifetime in Medinah society, functioning as its temporal authority (*Waliyul-Amr*, as in Verse 55: Chapter 5).

During the last 100 years or so, scholars who wrote in Arabic, Turkish, Persian, Urdu, and other languages of the Muslim world, referred to the way resources were managed in accordance with the guidance of *Al-Qur'ān* on *Iqtiṣād* which translators rendered as "Islamic economics" in English. In the 1960s, for example, as-Sayyid as-Shaheed as-Sadr called his famous book "*Iqtiṣāduna*" or "Our *Iqtiṣād*," by which he meant to present the authentic system of management of resources of a Muslim society according to the rules specified by *Al-Qur'ān* and distinguished it from the then two dominant systems of socialism and capitalism. He presented also the philosophical underpinning of the system in his other famous book "Falsafatuna," translated as "Our Philosophy" which he then compared with the philosophical foundation of the other two dominant systems. Whereas this latter translation was straight forward, and the title of the book easily mapped into its English translation without causing ambiguity and confusion, the former title's translation into "Our Economics" did not. When in the late 1970s, Muslim scholars trained in Economics began to discuss Islam's approach to the management of resources and write about the subject in English, they used the term "Islamic economics." By the early 1990s, a paradigm emerged called "Islamic economics," with its own distinguishing characteristics that differentiated it, in substance, from *Iqtiṣād*. One of the ambiguities of the term "Islamic economics" is that it is not quite clear from the title which "economics" is to be "Islamized." There is a wide spectrum of types of "economics" within the universe of discourse called "economics." Even within the Islamic economics universe of discourse, there is a spectrum of proposals. Some argue for "Islamization" of economics by incorporating Islamic *maqāṣid* into "economics" while others suggest "Islamization" via incorporating "Islamic morality" into economics.

There are also those who use "Islamic economics" as translation of "Iqtiṣād," the authentic notion of a discipline that deals with the management of resources within Muslim societies according to the rules prescribed in *Al-Qur'ān*. Excluding the latter notion, the question remains which "economics" is meant in the Islamization project? In the opening chapter, reference was made to a thoughtful presentation of "Islamic economics" which argued for Islamization by modification of some of the axioms of "economics" and incorporation of Islamic morality into that body of knowledge. From the content of the discussion of that proposal, it appears that the body of knowledge which is to be Islamized is that of the dominant paradigm referred to as "Orthodox" or "Neoclassical" economics. In the hope for clarity of the discussion here, this latter proposal will be identified with the capital letter "E," as "Economics," and "Islamic Economics" to differentiate it from "Unorthodox economics," on the one hand, and "*Iqtiṣād*," on the other. References were also made in that chapter to these three distinct paradigms together with a discussion of some of their distinguishing features. This Chapter attempts to briefly discuss the two polar cases of *Iqtiṣād* and Economics hoping thereby to clarify whether there is any basis upon which an intermediate paradigm between these polar cases can be envisioned legitimately. To avoid repetition of the philosophical terms in the rest of the Chapter, it is helpful to provide brief definitions for the terms at the outset of the discussion hoping that the reader will be able to relate the contents of discussion to the meanings of terms.

A Brief Note on Key Philosophical Terms

Metaphysics deals with the ultimate nature of reality as it is and not as it appears. It asks what Reality is and by what criteria will the Real be known? Reality is defined as immutable, permanent, and uncaused. Metaphysics studies the belief about some fundamental concepts such as the existence of phenomena and their properties, causality, space, time, life and its purpose, and others. Causality is an important topic in Economics, particularly in Econometrics. According to metaphysics, the universe is constituted by material, immaterial, seen, unseen, things that exist and things that potentially exist, space, time; all referred to as "events," or things that have existence and are subject to change. Alternatively, it may be said that the universe is composed of all events that were, are, and will be in the future, but how and why? Metaphysics suggests that events exist because they have causes. These causes existed before the events and are themselves effects of precedent causes that brought them into existence. There is therefore a chain of causation employed in "causal reasoning," a crucial element in the structure of modelling in Econometrics.

A question metaphysics asks is whether every event in the universe has a cause? Determinism answers that there is cause or a chain of causation that precedes any event in the universe; there are no uncaused events. An implication of this position raises the question whether determinism can accommodate human free will since, according to determinism, every event has a cause that also includes the exercise of human free will. If so, then determinism negates the latter with serious implications for human moral responsibility. Indeterminism alternatively holds that some events have no causes and are not subject of a chain of causation, including human free choice such as choosing among preferences corresponding to the rational choice theory of Economics. Indeterminism however leads to a question that has implications in Economics, if the choice is uncaused and simply follows the precepts of rational choice theory, in what sense is the choice free? And in what sense can individuals be responsible for their choices. Neither of these methods provides an effective answer to the questions and their implications.

Ontology focuses on the nature of "being," the origin of phenomena, and the question of existence of things. It addresses arguments relating to the meaning of existence, of "beingness," and the question of what do things that exist have in common? Do they share one substance that differentiates between what exists and what does not? Materialism argues that what has existed, all that exists and will exist share one substance: Matter. Idealism, on the other hand, holds that the one essential element events share is "mind." That is, the substance that constitutes reality is "mental" not physical. However, the question of whether there is only one cosmological "Mind" or multiple individual "minds" is contested among ontological idealists. A third type of ontological position is that of the dualists who argue that everything in existence is either physical or mental. The body is physical and can be perceived as such having all the relational properties that are possessed by material things. But there are also conceivable mental entities free of physical properties. They are not limited by physical constraints. Both the physical and mental entities exist in the universe. A third alternative, pluralism, holds that there are more than two substances that things that exist share. Over the past three decades, the question of the ontological foundation of Economics has become a hotly contested subject in which some economists have argued that Economics has failed to live up to its own standards of scientific respectability. It has insisted on "mathematical-deductivist" methodology that has reduced the explanatory and predictive ability; two characteristics that define science and scientific method. It is an ontology that falls far from that which relates social science to social realities.[3]

Epistemology concerns the nature of knowledge and claims about knowledge. It investigates questions of what is knowledge? how is it acquired? how is it validated and justified? There is a close relationship between ontology and epistemology. For example, questions of the origins of Economic theories, their relations to reality, the origin of the assumptions of theories and their explanations and justifications, their application to socio-economic reality, laws derived from these theories, and many other questions that relate to both the ontology and epistemology of Economics. Often Economic theories do not state explicitly their ontological, epistemological, or other philosophical dimensions in their presentations. Nevertheless, these philosophical issues lurk in the background of these theories.

Philosophy itself defines knowledge as true, justified belief. A belief can be held "*a priori,*" meaning that it is held without the need of sensory experience, or "*a posteriori,*" a belief held after experience. Among "*a priori*" ideas, some may be "innate." These are ideas inborn in humans rather than experienced or received, whose origin cannot be demonstrated experientially. They are implicit in the self or in the psyche of individual humans, such as the belief in a Creator. While in the Western tradition the origin of the concept of innate ideas or beliefs is traced to the seventeenth century and Rene Descartes, *Al-Qur'ān* refers to *Fitrah*, the innate, primordial nature which Allah swt has endowed to humans upon which the idea of Supreme Creator, Sustainer, and Nurturer is imprinted.

Belief is the essential aspect of knowledge, but it cannot become knowledge unless it is true, and the truth is supported by justification. Justification is the process by which the relationship between a belief and the external world is demonstrated. When a belief is justified, to be true, it is considered knowledge. While Economics, by and large, seems to have acquiesced to this proposition, in philosophy its acceptability is contested. Some philosophers, called the dogmatists, argue that it is possible for a belief to become knowledge through sensory experience. These philosophers, Empiricists, argue that humans attain knowledge through experience while others, the Sceptics, argue that human sensory and cognitive abilities are too limited to justify belief as true and elevate to knowledge. Among the empiricists, there is a group of philosophers, the Foundationalists, who argue that it is possible to acquire knowledge by inference from a basic true, justified belief. According to these philosophers, the inferential and basic beliefs—those that are justified by direct experiential evidence—provide the "foundation" of knowledge acquisition. Axiology investigates the value structure of phenomena, beliefs, and systems of thought. It is also noted that the axiology of Economics includes, inter alia, values such as efficiency, profitability, self-interest, and others. Each economic system of thought has its own axiology.

Also, methodology investigates the procedures, principles, rules, ways, and means by which researchers and scholars validate knowledge about phenomena. Finally, teleology investigates knowledge about phenomena by reference to their purpose.

Economics: Its Etymology and the Evolution of Its Definition

Etymologically, economics is said to be from Greek "Oikos" and "nomos." The former means household and the latter means "managing;" Oikonomia meant the management of household and its resources. Xenophon is said to have named one of his treatises, Oikonomikos, in which he discussed the frugal and judicious ways the resources of a household, a family, a tribe was managed. Xenophon was, according to Leshem,[4] the first to define "oikonomia" as the prudent management of the household frugally, maintaining a balance between too much and too little effort to generate a surplus. Generally, it appears, Greek philosophers, like Plato and Aristotle, had a teleological view of economic activities as instrumental in generating happiness and well-being for members of the society. They saw the economy as embedded in the entire societal structure, much as Karl Polanyi[5] had observed in the twentieth century. Greeks' teleological view of economic activities as the frugal mangement of household resources prevailed in the European societies and found a new articulation by Christian scholars during the Middle Ages through the intermediation of Muslim scholars whose books were by then brought from Spain and countries of the Middle East to the rest of Europe and translated into Latin.[6] The teleological view of economic activities expressed by Plato and Aristotle was restated by Scholastics as purposeful activities aimed at gaining felicity in the Hereafter. Scholastic thought is characterized by a close relationship between ethics, theology, and economics. Epistemologically, philosophers in the tradition of scholasticism believed there was an organic unity of knowledge with a strong reliance on metaphysics and transcendence.[7] Aided by the availability to the Scholastics of Latin translation of the works of Aristotle and other Greeks along with commentaries of Muslim scholars, the thirteen and fourteenth centuries marked a great leap in scientific knowledge without decoupling from metaphysical and transcendental orientation of the time.

New ideas regarding the role of money, as a medium and as a standard measure, exchange, value, markets, prices, and economic justice emerged in these two centuries. Joel Kaye asserts that the scientific advances of Scholastics—particularly their vision of nature and its dynamic workings using mathematics, geometry, and logic in the analysis of nature based on their observation of monetized society—provided the basis for scholars and researchers from Copernicus to Galileo to further science.[8] The fourteenth and fifteenth centuries were times of catastrophes, disasters, and crises. The period was marked, inter alia, by the great famine of 1315; Black Death of 1348; collapse of Italian banking; long lasting, large-scale, and highly costly wars; fall of Constantinople; and the weakening of Papacy and the Holy Roman Empire, all of which brought about sweeping changes represented by the emergence of the Renaissance (meaning rebirth) in fifteenth–seventeenth centuries. The traumas of the period lead to the emergence of an axiology that reoriented the value system in Europe away from metaphysical and transcendent and toward physical and worldly teleology.

In reaction to these traumas, it is the pursuit of wealth during this period that defined economic activities, an expected outcome of the crippling influence of stresses consequent of previous adverse developments. Major dimensions of the philosophical foundation of Economics—materialism, individualism, and secularism—had their birth in this period as did Mercantilism, the idea that nations should pursue wealth accumulation (preferably gold) through trade policies and colonization. The seeds that were sown during the Renaissance were nurtured and supplemented by ideas during the Enlightenment period, seventeenth and eighteenth centuries, following the Renaissance and the Protestant Reformation in which the roots of Economics strengthened. The period witnessed the birth of scientific method, empiricism, aggressive anti-religion sentiments—thought to have been prompted by reactions to religious wars, inquisition, and heresy trials—scepticism, rationalistic vigour (which insisted on replacement of inherited religious authority by "reason"[9]). The anti-religion sentiments of the period, the growth of scientific rationality resulting from the scientific revolution that took place[10] between the time of Copernicus' theory of heliocentrism[11] (1543) and Newton's Principia Mathematica (1687), and the prestige bestowed upon physical sciences led to the rejection of metaphysics and any idea of transcendence. Peter Gay (1973) argues that the thinkers of this age were aggressive in their criticisms against religion in general and Christianity in particular. They were intent on destroying all things religious and metaphysical. "The world that religion had shaped for so long was—in the philosophes' language—prey to the wild beasts of fanaticism and enfeebled by the poisonous fruits of the tree of superstitious."[12] The thinkers of the age were "intent on improving, and, if necessary, even inventing, science of man. Their work in psychology, sociology, and political economy, had this practical aim: These were disciplines that, once mastered, would help to make humanity freer, richer, more civilized than before."[13]

To the extent that Economics emerged from the historical, cultural, religious, socio-political experience of the Renaissance and the Enlightenment peculiar to Europe, it could not claim the global acceptability and applicability of its model achievements. Above all, the historical account of the evolution of Economics indicates no commonality with Islam to justify the eclectic understanding that "Islamic Economics" wishes to create. Be that as it may, during the Enlightenment period, crucial building blocks of Economics developed including, inter alia, the concepts of self-interest,[14] utility and its measurement and its influence on human economic behaviour, the notion of equilibrium, the operations of markets, the abandonment of the moral foundation of political economy, and the emergence of the idea of science of Economics independent of political economy. The teleology, however, remained the pursuit of wealth until Jeremy Bentham (1748–1832) discovered the concept of utility in the writings of David Hume (1711–1776) who in his: A Treatise of Human Nature refers to the concept of "utility" as a source of pleasure.[15] Hume claims that: "The chief spring or actuating principle of the human mind is pleasure or pain... moral distinctions depend entirely on certain peculiar sentiments of pain and pleasure... whatever mental quality in ourselves or others give us a satisfaction... is of course virtuous; as everything of this nature, that gives uneasiness, is vicious."[16]

Having borrowed the concepts of pleasure-pain and utility, Bentham proceeded to advocate for Utilitarianism and Hedonism philosophies. In hindsight, it appears this was a momentous development in the evolution of Economics. The influence of utilitarianism and hedonism on Economics continues, in one form or another, in this discipline. It was a watershed in changing the teleology of Economics from preoccupation with wealth to maximization of utility and minimization of disutility. Hedonism claims that pleasure and pain are the prime motivators of humans who seek to maximize the former and minimize the latter. Pleasure and pain, Bentham asserted, were humans "Sovereign masters." Bentham defined utility as the property of objects that produce pleasure, benefit, or happiness; disutility produces pain, evil, and unhappiness. Utilitarianism argues that society must implement policies according to the principle of greatest happiness for the greatest number of members to ensure the widest possible distribution of pleasure while minimizing pain for the society.[17] Bentham went further to argue that utility is measurable and suggested that this can be done either cardinally, through direct quantitative measurement, or ordinally, through rank-ordering of bundles of goods by consumers through introspection.

The year 1871 represents another important watershed in the history of Economics as William Stanley Jevons (1835–1882)[18] and Carl Menger (1840–1921)[19] independently advanced Bentham's contributions. This was the beginning of what became known as the Neoclassical Economics later to be named as Orthodox Economics. Menger appears to be the first author who changed the name political economy as he titled his book "Principles of Economics." He accepted Bentham's position that utility motivated human economic activity and argued that utility drives the demand for products and hence its value contrary to the classical economists who believed that cost of production determines value of products. Further, Menger argued that consumers behave in the market to maximize their utility. Jevons too accepted Bentham's ideas that humans behave to maximize their pleasure (utility) and minimize pain (disutility) and therefore their behaviour in the market is purposeful in that it is aimed at maximizing utility. These authors made explicit the idea of diminishing marginal utility which was hinted at without much discussion by Bentham.

Leon Walras (1834–1910) and Alfred Marshall (1842–1910) produced works that provided the capstone to the Neoclassical Economics. The teleology of Economics changed in the hands of these two thinkers who gave the markets—populated by self-interested participants and in which the forces of supply and demand interact freely—the crucial role of allocating resources. Marshall's contribution showed how equilibrium is achieved in individual markets, hence, the name "partial equilibrium analysis," while Walras' contribution focused on the overall market equilibrium, therefore, "general equilibrium." Influenced by his mentor, Leon Walras, Vilfredo Pareto (1848–1923) focused on the operations of the market, its equilibrium, and its function as resource allocation mechanism. He showed that optimal allocation of resources is achieved when it is no longer possible to make someone better off in allocating resources without making someone else worse off. This principle became known as Pareto-optimal allocation and formed the foundation of welfare economics. These five thinkers—Jevons, Menger, Walras, Pareto, and Marshall—are considered the architects of the Neoclassical Economics. In their hands, the axiology of Economics was constituted by utility, wealth, prices, demand, supply, and equilibrium. Thereafter, intellectual activities in Economics became theorizing about various dimensions of economic activities based on the works of these thinkers. Collectively, their works became the bulwark of intellectual support for capitalism in the twentieth century.

Economics: Its Definition and Method

It is helpful to remember that among the wide spectrum of a field of study or a universe of discourse, called economics, the concern here is with the dominant paradigm that is given the label of "mainstream," or "orthodox," or "Neoclassical," or simply "Economics." Books on the history of economic thought suggest that the origin of Economics traces back to the 1870s and the "marginal revolution." The definition of economics went through several transformations. During the eighteenth century, the focus of the discipline was on wealth. John Stewart Mill (1806–1873) considered that economics was a science that dealt with the generation and distribution of wealth. Marshall, in his textbook, Principles of Economics, published in 1890, defined the subject as the study of mankind in in the ordinary business of life. It examined, according to Marshall, the individual and social behaviour connected to the ways and means of acquiring and using the material need of well-being. In the closing decades of the nineteenth century and concurrently with the mathematical works of the marginalists, especially Marshall, Walras, and Pareto, serious attempts were made to present and structure economics as a science. Prior to these attempts, the word "science" used by some thinkers like Mill in attachment with political economy, included an underlying philosophy that related social sciences to physical sciences. Later attempts to use the label "economic science" focused on methodology to argue that economics is as much a science as physics or other natural sciences because it too uses the "scientific method" supported by the philosophy of positivism.

In continuation of the discussion of the basic point that "economic science" was the result of the peculiar socio-economic-cultural and religious experience of Europe, it is noted that the philosophy of positivism that granted economics its scientific pretensions began with David Hume (1711–1776). His aggressively antireligious attitude and rejection of metaphysics, that led to his empiricist-positivist philosophy, is best reflected in a set of questions he posed to readers of his book. He tells his readers to visit libraries and look at books on religious and metaphysics and ask themselves "Does it contain any abstract reasoning concerning quantity or number? No. Does it contain any experimental reasoning concerning matter of fact and existence? No. Commit it then to the flames: For it can contain nothing but sophistry and illusion."[20] Hume, having been influenced by the writings of John Locke and others before him, initiated the beginning of epistemological systems that were to come which influenced the evolution of economics. His work hints at the fact-value, positive–normative dichotomy which is still with "Economics," although within the universe of economic discourse, it is challenged.[21] Hume's work provided the basis for August Comte (1798–1857) who developed the epistemology of positivism in its contemporary form.

Perhaps the most important philosophy that cemented the epistemology of Economics was that of logical positivism developed by the Vienna Circle (1924–1936)[22] extending the ideas of positivism requiring verifiability through direct observation or logical proof for meaningfulness. Epistemologies such as those of theology, metaphysics, ethics, introspection, or intuition violate the verifiability criterion of meaning. They are therefore meaningless. A major problem of logical positivism is its confusion between epistemology and ontology since a lack of empirical evidence cannot be regarded as proof of non-existence. It confuses its model of reality with reality itself, as the absence of proof of existence of a phenomenon cannot be construed as proof of non-existence. [23]

Logical positivism too emerged out of another set of circumstances peculiar to Europe, specifically Vienna in the interwar period (Hands, 2001). Members of The Vienna Circle were philosophers and scientists united by their atheism and rejection of religiously based ethics. John B. Davis (p. 4) suggests that the Circle developed logical positivism "at a time in Europe when racist and nationalist ideas were regularly claimed to be scientific, and members of the Vienna Circle were among those personally exposed to violence and abuse in the name of such views." After their leader, Moritz Schlick was murdered in 1936, remaining members sought refuge and ended up in the UK and the US where they spread logical positivism.[24] In a few decades, this philosophy became dominant, influencing the emergence of the Austrian school of Economics (particularly the notion of spontaneous order). Most importantly, it influenced Lionel Robbins in developing the definition of Economics as the "science which studies human behaviour as a relationship between ends and scarce means which have alternative uses."[25] Robbins, with an emphatic insistence on the ontological argument of the "scientific nature" of the "science of Economics," relied on a concept coined by Schumpeter as "methodological individualism,"[26] with roots in the nineteenth-century discussions of individualistic theories of social formation in response to anti-individualistic, collectivist, philosophies that had gained prominence.[27] Methodological individualism holds the preferences, beliefs, and desires of individual human beings as the fundamental explanatory principle. The idea is premised on the rationality of human beings in that explanation of an individual's preference justifies her/his choice and that explanatory principle constitutes the principle of rational choice. During the period spanning the second half of the nineteenth and the twentieth centuries, Economics became an elaborate deductive system relying on formal logical-mathematical method.

Influence of logical positivism philosophy is quite evident in Robbins' strident opposition to inclusion of consideration of metaphysics, ethics, value statements or judgements, and, generally any non-positive epistemologies in Economics, thus, severely adhering to the fact-value, positive-normative dichotomy. In particular, he took a harsh stance against those, like Pareto, or Arthur Cecil Pigou (1877–1959), who, relying on marginal analysis, especially the law of diminishing marginal utility, argued for income redistribution that would result in increased total utility (or social welfare) for the whole society. Robbins argued that in Economic Science, interpersonal comparison of utility is a value judgement and therefore impermissible.[28] Defining Economics as a value-free science of how individual humans make decisions on allocating their scarce resources toward achieving some ends soon earned it the label of science of rational choice.[29] Moreover, Robbins insisted that Economics is not concerned with ends, implying that this "science" had no teleology. Economics, he says, "is entirely neutral between ends... it... should be clear therefore, that to speak of any end as being itself 'economic' is entirely misleading." The never-in-dispute, or even questioned, anchor of this definition is clearly the notion of scarcity, meaning there not being enough resources to satisfy unlimited wants. Thus, the axioms of scarcity[30] and unlimited wants are at the heart of Robbins' definition of Economics. While various textbook writers have different formulations of the definition, the fundamental ingredients of Robbins' definition are preserved. Logically, these axioms by themselves make Economics incompatible with *Al-Qur'ān's* vision of scarcity and the fact that humans are empowered not to respond to external impulses generated by whims (Hawā) or wants. There is even clear guidance from the *Al-Qur'ān* and Tradition of the Noble Messenger (saa) that when society is suffering massive poverty and destitution, needs too have to be carefully scrutinized to ensure surpluses are available to the needy.

Many consider Robbins' definition of Economics crisp and clear. However, some two decades earlier an Italian philosopher—seeped in the turbulent times of the last decades of the nineteenth and the early decades of the twentieth centuries, including encounter with fascism[31]—Benedetto Croce (1866–1952), articulated a pure vision of Economic science as a deductive system firmly grounded in human conscious (rational) action. He argued that as required from a science, all economic theorems are *a priori*. He rejected metaphysical, ethical, and transcontinental epistemologies. This also meant that Croce considered all instinctive, emotional, or other impulses that influence human behaviour as being outside the scope of Economics. Human conscious (rational) behaviour is "amoral," neither moral nor immoral, but based on legitimate utilitarian desire and hedonistic calculus on hedonistic calculus that what is economically useful is also pleasurable.[32] Geoffrey Mure (1893-1979) explains in *Retreat from Truth* (1958) that "Economic activity" is utilitarian, according to Croce, and the actions of the "Economic Agent" are that of an "egoist" who is "directed to the end of maintaining, expanding, and enjoying his own life as a singular individual ... who aims at getting ... something such that more there is for him the less there is for anyone else." He follows his own private individual end; "there is nothing moral or immoral in what he does." Axiologically, his actions or things he pursues are means only not ends and, as such, have no intrinsic value. Mure, commenting on the Economics' conception of an Economic agent, suggests an Economic Agent, suggests: "The only criterion of value which can be applied to his action is extrinsic: it is efficiency."[33] Croce, however, argues that utility is a value in Economics and indeed it is utility that forms the fundamental axiom of conscious human action. It is "an original and irreducible ... axiom according to which all men seek the greatest satisfaction with the least possible effort ... The economic axiom is a very general and purely a formal principle of conduct." Croce calls this axiom as the "Economic Principle," the logical foundation of Economics.[34]

While predating Robbins by three decades, Croce's definition of Economics is more crisp, unequivocal, clear, and, from a philosophical point of view, better grounded to allow for unambiguous characterization of Economics as the orthodox and dominant epistemology different from others within the spectrum of the economic universe of discourse. Croce defines Economics as grounded on the "Economic Principle": Economic man or "Economic Agent," in Croce's vocabulary, "seeks the maximum of satisfaction with minimum effort." Economics deals with conscious action of the Economic Agent in the here and now and is devoid of teleology, history, and any consideration of metaphysical, moral, ethical, or transcendental epistemology. As mentioned earlier, there is now considerable discussion on the need for clarity and reorientation of its ontology away from a mathematico-deductive to a more social-reality-oriented ontology. As Economics stands at the present, it is a deductive system in which—apart from some empirical content for its elementary axioms— its theorems, theories, and laws are all deductively derived. Croce asserts that its theorems and laws are like those of geometry; they have practical applications but do not rely on empirical verification for their validity. Economics, therefore, is pure science. Croce's contribution is immensely important and contains essentials of Robbins' definition and discussions long before Robbins published his contributions, yet Croce and his works in defining the pure science of Economics have been widely ignored.[35]

An important lesson of Croce for those who advocate Islamization of Economics through the introduction of Islamic morality is that, as he argues, Economic action is a condition of moral action but introducing moral action into Economics creates confusion, inconsistency, and breakdown of the fundamental Economic principle.[36] The clarity of Croce's definition and discussions of Economics allows a basis for comparison with *Iqtiṣād* to determine whether there is any justification for eclectic combinations that seem to be indicated by attempts at the Islamization Economics. Thus far, it is clear that Economics is a tree that grew out of a particular soil contaminated with its own peculiar and painful historical experiences not shared by the majority of the world's population. Economics is a response to that peculiar centuries-old experience, its only claim to universality is the hegemony and projection of military and economic power of countries that made its appearance and growth possible principally because it provided synergistically the intellectual justification for the ruling economic system, Capitalism. Not only the intellectual history of Economics but its philosophy contradicts major tenants and axioms of Islam from metaphysics through teleology. The radically different histories and philosophies seem to point toward the impossibility of grafting of these two polar cases one onto another.

Etymology,[37] Definition, and Philosophy of *Iqtiṣād*: An Introduction

Islam is a covenantal system of thought and action, meaning that all relations and behaviour are governed by a Primordial, formal, solemn, and abiding agreement between Allah swt and humanity at large. There are also mentions in *Al-Qur'ān* of other covenants between Allah and His Messengers, between Messengers themselves, and between and among humans. All covenants are entered into abiding by the terms and conditions of the original Primordial Covenant.[38] Such agreements specify each party's obligations relating to what is to be done and how, and what is to be avoided. Therefore, by acknowledging Allah swt as the Supreme Creator and Nurturer of all, humans have become signatories to that Primordial Covenant with clear provisions that govern human thought and action. The Principal of the Covenant specified these provisions in the form of rules that are prescribed in the *Al-Qur'ān*. These include rules that govern the management of the resources provided by The Creator to humans to facilitate the performance of duties and obligations resulting from the Primordial Agreement. Messengers have been appointed and given books of guidance throughout history to remind humans of these obligations. *Al-Qur'ān* is the Last and complete of these Messages sent along with the perfect human Messenger of The Creator to His Creation: Mohammad Ibn 'Abd Allah SallaAllah 'alayh wa aalih (saa).

As the Supreme Creator, Allah is the owner of all He has Created, including humans. The use of resources He has Created for humans are subject to rules that govern their distribution and uses for humans to enable them to attend to the ultimate teleology designated for them by Allah swt.[39] Collectivity of these rules constitutes the substance of the system of thought and action called *Iqtiṣād* whose etymology is derived from its natural habitat: *Al-Qur'ān*. Those who are faithful to the terms and conditions of the Covenant and are therefore rule-compliant, at least most of the time, are labelled as *Mu'minūn* (or *Mu'minīn* plural of *Mu'min*) whose root word is "*a-m-n*," security, meaning they have achieved a state of safety and security which trust in Allah swt affords them. That is, they have found a place within Allah's sanctuary of safety and security. This status grants them tranquillity and stability in their personal and social relationships. *Al-Qur'ān* indicates that, at times, a *Mu'min* slips in compliance with the rules.[40] Allah urges the faithful to repent and return to the path of full compliance. Those among the *Mu'minīn* who are, always and without exception, rule-compliant are those who are always conscious of the ever-presence of Allah. They are called *Muttaqūn*, those who are so intensely aware of the presence of Allah that always protect themselves against forgetfulness or unawareness by constant remembrance of Allah swt.[41] A society with a critical mass of these kinds of believers will achieve prosperity on earth and felicity in the hereafter.[42] From *Al-Qur'ān*, it becomes clear that *Iqtiṣād* is a collection of rules prescribed along with the ways and means of their implementation explicated by the Honoured Messenger (*saa*) as instructed by Allah swt.[43] The collection of rules themselves is referred to as The Book (*Kitāb*). When Allah swt ordains a rule to be followed, He refers to it as: "it is ordained upon you" (kutiba 'alaykum). Therefore, the Kitāb, *Al-Qur'ān*, is the collected presentation of all that has been ordained by Allah swt. Whoever complies with the rules prescribed by Allah swt is referred to in *Al-Qur'an* as *Muqtaṣid*, that is, one who abides by *Iqtiṣād*. Arabic dictionaries define a *Muqtaṣid* as someone who does what is prescribed and avoids that which is not permissible, meaning a rule-compliant believer.

The root of *Iqtiṣād* is "q-s-d," and five derivatives of it appear in *Al-Qur'ān*: *(1) Qaṣd* which means perseverance, determination, devotion aimed at staying the course one has chosen, for example, *Al-Qur'ān* refers to *Qaṣd as-Sabīl*,[44] meaning staying the course, remaining steady on the path, insisting on compliance with rules prescribed by Allah swt. Verse 9: Chapter 16, juxtaposes *Qaṣd as-Sabīl* to *Qaṣd al-Jā'ir* meaning the path of non-compliance, a path of injustice, path of instability, and unreliability. (2) (1) *Iqṣid*, an imperative to persevere, focus on the objective, or, alternatively, avoid extreme positions, rely on the golden mean.[45] (3) *Qāṣid*, an easy, straight, and trouble-free passage.[46] (4) *Muqtaṣid (masculine)* and (5) *Muqtaṣidah* (feminine) refer to rule-compliant individuals (male and female) or to a collectivity of people, *Ummah*, that share a common objective and follow a legitimate leader, an Imam.[47] Hence,

Islam envisions a close connection between an Ummah and its Imam so much so that an *Ummah* without an Imam is inconceivable. The Noble Messenger was the Imam of the Ummah Muslimah for whom he organized an *Iqtiṣād* based on the rules prescribed by *Al-Qur'ān*. To summarize, *Iqtiṣād* refers to the organization or management of resources provided by Allah swt in steadfast compliance with the rules prescribed by Him in pursuit of a balanced and blissful life here and hereafter. *Iqtiṣād* refers to a system of rules governing the use and disposition of resources as prescribed in *Al-Qur'ān*. As well, it refers to the discipline whose scholars and experts extract these rules, interpret their technical understanding, as temporally and spatially appropriate, determine policies to be implemented by legitimate authorities, and, finally, assess the results.

The initial model of *Iqtiṣād* was implemented by the Noble Messenger (saa) in *Medīnah* in accordance with the instructions of His Creator. *Al-Qur'ān's* Verse 2 of Chapter 62 explains the most important functions of the mission of the Messenger as: 1. Reciting[48] the Signs of Allah, introducing the hearers to the rules prescribed (the reference is to the Verses of the Book of Rules) along with underlining the fact of the necessity of compliance; 2. Cleansing the cognitive-perceptive-active abilities of the hearers in order to understand correctly the rules prescribed; 3. Teaching them how to comply with the rules; and 4. Explaining the wisdom, Hikmah, behind the rules ordained. The Blessed Messenger had performed these functions so perfectly that when he established the *Iqtiṣād* system, it had full popular support.[49] Once the *Iqtiṣād* system is set in place, the mission of the Beloved Messenger became one of encouraging the Muslims to establish social equity (*Qiṣt*) as ordained by Allah swt.[50]

Contemporary Muslim philosophers like Seyyed Hossein Nasr and Sayyid Naquib al-Attas and those of the older generation in the twentieth century, such as Said Nursi, Allamah Muhammad Iqbal, As-Shaheed Muhammad Baqir As-Sadr, and Mālek Bennabi, have thought deeply about the nature of metaphysical, ontological, epistemological, axiological, and teleological dimensions of relations of Allah and His Creation, including humans. They have explained the intricacies of these relationships in understandable philosophical terms.[51] Being fully familiar with the philosophy underlying Western economic thought, their advice was for the Muslim scholars to return to *Al-Qur'ān*, as explained in further detail in another chapter of this book, to structure a system that would manage resource uses according to the rules prescribed by Allah swt.

In its fundamental nature, *Iqtiṣād* derives its ontology directly from *Al-Qur'ān*. Once *Iqtiṣād* comes into being it has a sacred, not profane, presence. In concrete terms, it means that the collectivity adopting the system of *Iqtiṣād* will experience *Barakah*, multiple returns, whose operations have an unseen source. Phenomena like *barakah* point to a crucial difference, an unbridgeable difference between *Iqtiṣād* and Economics, their metaphysical underpinnings. Nasr explains that "metaphysic ... is the science of the Real, of the origin and end of things, of the Absolute and, in its light, the relative." As such, he suggests that metaphysics should be in the singular (Nasr, 1968, p. 81). Islam, Nasr asserts, has a wholistic, fully integrated view of the cosmos and "sees in the arteries of the cosmos and natural order the flow of divine grace or barakah." Humans are themselves channels of *barakah*. Nasr masterfully combines the metaphysics, ontology, epistemology, and teleology of Islam in a few short sentences. He explains that human purpose on earth is to gain knowledge to become The Universal and Perfect Human (*al-Insān al-Kāmil*), the perfect 'abd, perfect adorer of The Creator. Such a perfect human becomes "the mirror reflecting all the Divine Names and Qualities."

Nasr explains that humans are the crowning achievement of the process of Creation, and Allah's purpose in Creating humans is to have intimate knowledge of "Himself through His perfect instrument of knowledge that is the Universal Man." (Nasr, 1968, pp. 95 and 96). Allah swt has provided resources, the ways, and means to empower humans to remove all constraints, physical or otherwise, and barriers on their path of completion of this transcendental journey of becoming a perfect *'abd*, perfect adorer of Allah swt as exemplified by the Noble Messenger (*saa*). The ontology of the science of *Iqtiṣād* is its designation in *Al-Qur'ān* as a system of rules compliance which facilitates humans' epic journey toward achieving the perfect state as intended by The Creator. *Iqtiṣād's* purpose, its teleology, as a system is to aid humanity in its march toward the Absolute by demonstrating, through its epistemology, how they can liberate themselves and others from the bondage to the chains of base emotions and attachment to the world of matter. This liberation is crucial to the removal of distributional constraints and chokepoints that lead to maldistribution, poverty, and destitution that, in turn, slow or stop human celestial journey. Poverty, said the Beloved Messenger, is on the borderline of unbelief. Hence, achieving *qist* (equity) becomes the most important objective of *Iqtiṣād*. The rules of *Al-Qur'ān* governing the use of resources give primacy to distributional issues; an acknowledgement that the chronic problems of inequity and injustice that lead to poverty and destitution are caused by maldistribution rather than the paucity of resources.

Transcendental Nature of the Ontology and Epistemology of Iqtiṣād System

Iqtiṣād comes into existence when members of the society decide to manage the resources Allah swt has placed at their disposal according to the rules He has prescribed in *Al-Qur'ān*. It is incumbent on practitioners of *Iqtiṣād*, researchers, students, and scholars to extract the rules that govern the behaviour of each element of *Iqtiṣād*. And, based on this effort, it is possible to recommend policy actions that guide operations of the system of *Iqtiṣād*. The ontological underpinnings of *Iqtiṣād* as collections of rules governing behaviour of individuals and collectivities of humans in the use of resources originate in the fundamental axioms of Islam itself, all of which are metaphysical and transcendental in nature. Epistemology of *Iqtiṣād* accesses the teachings of *Al-Qur'ān* and the Beloved Messenger. As mentioned, an element of his appointment was to teach[52] the rules governing actions and behaviour as well as the wisdom (Hikmah) behind the rules. He (saa) taught that all rules and values in Islam rotate around the axis of *Tawheed*, the Unity, Singularity, and Uniqueness of Allah swt. Axiology of this system of thought teaches that actions and things have value if and only if they are pleasing to Allah swt. And teleology of an action of an individual is targeted at winning the approbation of The Creator.

As important and central *Tawheed* is to Islam's belief system, it is an abstract, cosmic, and purely transcendental expression that needs a vehicle to project onto the human plain of existence. *Al-Qur'ān* explains that Allah accomplishes this through the instrumentality of *Walāyah*,[53] a practical and widely familiar concept and process among humans. Its root is "w-l-y" (و، ل، ى). The word *Waliy* and its derivatives appear in *Al-Qur'ān* some 233 times indicating its importance. The semantic field of *Walāyah* indicates that it encompasses love,[54] help, assistance, protection, caregiving, and nurturing. The word *Waliy* applies bilaterally and reciprocally to relations between two things or two persons. It means that the two are so close that there is no space between them. Allah's *Walāyah* relationship with humans is unilateral. He swt is The Creator, Sustainer, Nourisher, Guide, and Lover of His Creation, including humans, and He is closer to humans than their jugular vein.[55] Fathers and mothers have unilateral *walāyah* relationship with their young children; reciprocity is not expected in this *walāyah* relationship. Humans have bilateral *walāyah* relationship with one another.[56] *Walāyah* of Allah is general and special. The former applies to the entire creation[57] while the latter applies to the rule—compliant.[58] This group is guided out of the darkness of bondage to anything non-Allah to a state of enlightenment where they perceive phenomena with the light of Allah swt. A crucial characteristic of this group is that they have no fear *(khawf)* of the future and no regret *(huzn)* about the past. *(huzn)* and have no fear of the future *(khawf)*. They are granted a place of certainty, safety, and security in the sanctuary which is the *walāyah* of Allah swt.[59] There is also a differentiation in terms of positive or negative walāyah. The former is the *Walāyah* of Allah and His Beloved Messenger, and those who are rule-compliant. The latter is the *walāyah* of al-Shaytan and his followers including, inter alia, those who reject Allah and His Beloved Messenger; the unjust and the iniquitous.[60] Enjoying the special *Walayah* of Allah swt is not possible without the *walāyah* of His beloved Messenger, achieved for those who follow the Messenger (saa).[61] That is those who are rule-compliant.

Walāyah of Allah swt is the manifestation, and theophany of the *Tawheed* on the human plane of existence as reflected best in Verses 32–44: Chapter 18, in a narrative which reveals the nature, meaning, and *Iqtiṣādi* implications of *walāyah*. The set of Verses tells the story of two neighbouring farmers with gardens of grapes, dates, and field of grains in conversation with one another about their gardens and fields. One is boastful about how he has made his two gardens and field productive and beautiful. He displays his pride in himself, his children, family, and tribe. He rejects Allah swt, and as a rule-violator, he boastfully claims that the riches he possesses will neither deplete nor perish. He also does not believe in the Day of Accountability. The other is humble, attributes everything to Allah swt, and admonishes the other that he must not reject his Creator. He warns his neighbour that he must acknowledge Allah swt as the One who created him from dust, the One who is responsible for his riches, his family, his tribe, and his garden and fields. Otherwise, he may find that someday, some natural but unexpected event will destroy his garden and his possessions. In the event, the neighbour rejects the advice, and entering his garden one day, he discovered all the fruits and grains which he was about to harvest destroyed. "Then he began to wring his hands for all that he had invested in his garden when all was now ruined.

He said to himself wish I had not associated partners with my Lord. He had no one to help him other than Allah, nor could he help himself. That is where the Walāyah rests with Allah, the True God."*Walayah of Allah.*" (Verses 42–44: 18). Being fully conscious of Allah swt and expressing gratitude for His Blessing has *Iqtiṣādi* implications as this narrative clearly demonstrates. As well, it demonstrates the phenomenon of testing that is repeatedly mentioned in various forms and formats in *Al-Qur'ān* as an epistemological instrument through which one gains knowledge of oneself as well as knowledge of the serious consequences of rule compliance and rule violation.

Iqtiṣād's ontology relates to the operations of different subsystems composed of institutions mentioned in *Al-Qur'ān* organized under the temporal authority of the Beloved Prophet in Arabia according to the walāyah system and prescribed rules in Al-Qur'ān. *Walayah* . These subsystems constitute a connected network, their unity and synchronized operations are governed by the energy of *walāyah* itself. This fully integrated network includes, inter alia: (1) Subsystem of reciprocity through *walāyah* relationships between and among members of the society[62]; (2) *Ṣadaqah*, a redistributive subsystem of transfer payments from the wealthy to those economically weak as a way to redeem the rights of the latter in the wealth of the former; (3) *Ukhuwwah*, fraternity, this subsystem reflects the imperative that those who believe in Allah swt and are rule-compliant are each other's brothers and sisters with the same mutual and reciprocal rights and responsibilities as between biological brothers and sisters[63]; (4) *Mawaddah*,[64] a subsytem of mutual support between those connected to one another through the Love of Allah swt; (5) *Dhil-Qurbā*, a subsystem of family members and network of close relatives for whom Allah swt Ordained love and support[65]; (6) *Takāful*; a subsystem of rights to mutual support among members of the society. An obligation arising from the tripartite *walāyah* of Allah swt, the mutual *walāyah* of those who are rule-compliant[66]; (7) *Hisbah*, an accountability and supervision subsystem including the hisbah of markets, the ontology of which originates in the all-important capstone rule of encouraging rule compliance and discouraging rule violation; (8) Administration of justice; (9) Defence and border protection; (10) *Bayt al-maal*, public treasury; (11) Markets; (12) Education; (13) Protection of orphans, poor, and destitute; (14) Provision of medical-health services; (15) Governance, the subsystem of *Uli al-Amr*; the office and functioning of legitimate authority in Muslim societies[67]; (16) the subsystem of work that includes rules governing the necessity of work for all able-bodied persons, employer–employee relations, fidelity, and reciprocity in the work place; (17) Social capital including trust, a subsystem which constitutes the glue that holds the entire system together.[68] (18) subsystem of production and consumption; and (20) the financial subsystem; savings, investment, and financial institutions. Space limitation does not permit coverage and discussion of the history of these subsystems. There are, however, numerous books covering the history of Muslim societies of Arabia, the Middle East, North Africa, Spain, and elsewhere from the eighth to twelfth centuries illustrate the organization and operation of these subsystems.[69] As well, coverage here of the network of rules that govern the operations of the *Iqtiṣād* system is constrained by space limitation, but interested readers can refer to relevant sources and discussion in other chapters of this book.[70]

Summary: An Impossibility Theorem

In line with the purpose of the book to make a case for a shift away from the thought system that argues for some grafting of Islamic ideas onto the discipline of Economics to "Islamize" it, this chapter considered some fundamental differences between the historical experiences and philosophical structures and methods of Economics and *Al-Qur'ān's* vision of how an economy is to be organized. Literature on Islamization suggests two major ways of grafting Islamic ideas onto Economics. First, it is proposed to modify the axioms of Economics to include moral/ethical teachings of Islam while the second argues for tagging onto Economics some *Fiqhi* principles, called the Objectives of As-*Sharī'ah* designed by some *Fiqh* Scholars or *Fuqaha* centuries ago, to develop Islamic Economics. Interpreting these attempts as efforts to establish a discipline combining Islam and Economics, this chapter argued that *Al-Qur'ān's* vision of the economy is so radically different from Economics that there is no basis to allow grafting of Islam onto Economics or Economics onto Islam. To make the argument, the chapter attempted to reach as deeply as possible into the historical and philosophical underpinnings of Economics to flesh out the major issues that make *impossible* the emergence of an Islamic Economics—a conception that proposes to graft dimensions of Islamic belief onto Economics—that would make logical sense and can guide policy toward solving the serious problems currently facing Muslim societies. The chapter also looked at *Iqtiṣād*, a paradigm derived from *Al-Qur'ān* and implemented by the Noble Messenger, that constitutes a polar case to Economics. The chapter attempted to show that metaphysically, ontologically, epistemologically, axiologically, and teleologically, the two polar cases are so radically different to rule out any grafting of one onto the other to structure a synthetic discipline called "Islamic Economics"—a term organically different from the case of translation of *Iqtiṣād* as "Islamic Economics."

The *impossibility* is also indicated by the fact that Economics is so strongly immunized against anything metaphysical, transcendent, moral, and ethical that even ideas coming from the inside of Economics are rejected without consideration. A case in point is the ideas on policies that would reduce income inequality through redistribution. The case was made by the leading Marginalists that provided a strong Economic case for policies that would have reduced poverty and income and wealth inequality, and, in doing so, would have increased social welfare. This was the idea coming from scholars such as Vilfredo Pareto (1848–1923) and Arthur Cecil Pigou (1877–1959) both committed to proclaiming the scientific character of Economics and its mathematico-deductive method, proposed, based on the concept of diminishing marginal utility, that income transfer from the rich to the poor would improve aggregate social welfare.[71] The proposal was soundly rejected. It was argued that this idea involved value judgement and interpersonal comparison of utility. That is, argued people like Robbins and later Economists, impermissible in the science of Economics. Clearly, any notion of introducing Islamic moral-ethical concepts into Economics would not seem logically permissible or acceptable either.

Islamic Economics implicitly assumes that Islamic morality-ethics can be grafted onto Economics because of their intrinsic values. But why should anyone who adheres to Economics and its Economic Principle (*à la* Croce-Robbins) have a compelling reason to accept Muslim economists' proposition when even the ideas initiated by "insiders" to enhance the welfare of the entire society are outright rejected. Even if one dismisses the idea of acceptability by Economists, the advocates of various "Islamization" proposals have yet to present a logically coherent and consistent case that adding ethics and morality into Economics would result in a solid foundation for arguing that this is how people should live. A case needs to be made by the advocates of Islamization by "moralization" of Economics or by those who argue for the adoption of Fiqhi positions to combine the "Objectives of Shari'ah" with Economics that it is possible to design and implement practical policies based on such proposals. An answer needs to be provided by advocates of these untenable arguments to the question of why should Islamization proposals that artificially graft Islamic ideas onto Economics be preferred to *Iqtiṣād*, a paradigm based on the immutable, consistent, sacred system of rules prescribed by Allah swt in favour of fallible, ever—changing, Fiqhi perceptions of the "Objectives of *as-Sharī'ah*" as demonstrated throughout the history of the concept from Juwayni to *Al-Ghazali*, to *Al-Shatibi* all the way to Ibn Ashur and to Taha Jabir Al-Alwani?[72] The list of Objectives has been expanded or contracted depending on the views of the scholar of Islamic Law, Faqīh, involved. It was expanded from 5 to 20 and contracted again to 5 then, to 3. Incredibly, the original list of the five (5) *maqāṣid* did not include the all-important Objective of "justice," which is explicitly emphasized in Al-Qur'ān, until the twentieth century when Ibn Ashur explicitly included it. Fiqh represents human fallible opinions as evidenced by the ever-changing menu of Objectives enunciated by *Fuqahāh* throughout history. By contrast, the rule-based system that is *Iqtiṣād* relies on immutable rules explicitly stated in *Al-Qur'ān*, the ultimate source of knowledge, and not on fallible human judgement. These rules are not purely abstract and theoretical but eminently practical and forcefully logical as they provide solid bases to design practical policies to address contemporary social problems.

Iqtiṣād is a theonomy that is structured—both as a system and as a guide for individuals—by rules prescribed intended to facilitate human celestial journey. Indeed, in consideration of the proliferation of papers, books, and articles on *maqāṣid*, Islamization, and Islamic moralization of Economics, a major concern is whether this preoccupation and obsession with proposals for paradigms that avoid dealing directly with *Al-Qur'ān* represents a phase of emergence of what Malek Bennabi called "infantile economics," paralleling the development of contemporary "Islamic finance." Malek Bennabi considered the development of such artifacts as resulting from Muslim infatuation with the economic achievements of the West and their desire to emulate the science and policies that made these achievements possible. The objective would be, as it has occurred in case of "Islamic finance," to divert the gaze of Muslims from looking at their celestial objectives toward looking at earthly *maslahah*-driven, profit and utility maximizing ends as indeed has happened to "Islamic finance" as a result of close cooperation of Muslim financiers, bankers, and *Fuqahāh*. There is a sense that the unwritten and unspoken infatuation permeates writings on "Islamic Economics," as it has in "Islamic finance," thus representing a regressive move after what appeared to have been Muslim awakening progressing over the last hundred years or so. To see this regressive move, consider that the turn of the twentieth century witnessed the publication of the first book in Arabic on Economics, by the Algerian Faqih Al-Shaikh 'AbdulQadir Al-Majawi Al-Tilmisani: Al-Mirsad Fi Masa'il al-Iqtiṣād, published in 1904 in Algeria. The author attempts to combine Islamic Fiqh with principles of Western Economics. The book displays the author's familiarity with Western economic writings as well as the economies of leading capitalist economies of the time. Confirming the point made by Malek Bennabi regarding Muslim "infatuation," the book explicitly expresses admiration for the economies and economic policies of Western countries. There is of course no reason not to acknowledge these economies and their economic policies provided one also takes seriously and critically the source of much of the Western wealth: colonialism and imperialism, especially considering that the book was written at the height of implementation of French Colonial policies.[73] Concerns expressed by Malek Bennabi and many Muslim philosophers, and social critics over the past many decades are in regard to using Islamic fiqh, ethics, and selective verses of *Al-Qur'ān* to justify Economics, and policies based on it, precisely because they are seen uncritically as the reason for the Economic progress of the West. This may well be the whole underlying and implicit justification for insistence on Islamization of Economics rather than adopting *Iqtiṣād* as a genuine and authentic Islamic paradigm to address issues related to the management of resources in Muslim societies and eradicate poverty, correct income and wealth maldistribution, and economic injustices gripping human societies. The danger is that the disaster, which is now Islamic finance, could be replicated by Islamization of Economics on the same Fiqh grounds that maslahah demands it.

Allah o 'A'lam.

Notes

1. Berry, Thomas, 2020. "Historical Mission of Our Time." Journeyoftheuniverse.org, November 24, 2020.
2. See, Ethics, Economics, Finance, and Governance for the Anthropocene. Third Draft of: A Working Paper of the Third Millennium Economy Project, 2014. Brooklyn, NY: Capital Institute.
3. See, for example, Lawson, Tony, 2009. "The Current Economic Crisis: Its Nature and the Course of Academic Economics." *Cambridge Journal of*

Economics 33: 759–777. On differences between the philosophy of science and that of social science, see, Rudner, Richard, S., 1966. *Philosophy of Social Sciences*. Englewood Cliffs, New Jersey: Prentice Hall.
4. Leshem, Dotan, 2013. "Oikonomia Redefined," *Journal of the History of Economic Thought* 35 (1): 43–61. See also, Lowery, S. Todd, 1998. "The Economics and Jurisprudential Ideas of Ancient Greeks: Our Heritage from Hellenic Thought," In *Ancient and Medieval Ideas and Concepts of Social Justice*, edited by S. Todd Lowery and Barry Gordon. Leiden: Brill.
5. See George Dalton, ed. 1968. *Primitive, Archaic and Modern: Essays of Karl Polanyi*. Garden City: New York: Doubleday.
6. Mirakhor, abbas, 2014. "Muslim Scholars and the History of Economics," In *Islam and the Challenges of Western Capitalism*, edited by Murat Cizacka. London: Edward Elgar.
7. Patriarca, Giovanni, 2021. "Introductory Reflections on Scholastic Economic Thought. From the Thomistic Approach to the Franciscans," *Iberian Journal of the History of Economic Thought* 8 (1): 81–92.
8. Kaye, Joel, 2014. *Economy and Nature in the Fourteenth Century*. Cambridge: Cambridge University Press.
9. It appears that the writers, philosophers, and intellectuals of the Enlightenment employed the ideas of "reason" and "rationality" in their vigorous polemics against organized religions.
10. On scientific revolution see, Cohen, H. Floris, 1994. *The Scientific Revolution: A Historiographical Inquiry*. Chicago: University of Chicago Press.
11. For an interesting article on this subject see, Ragep, F. Jamil, 2007. "Copernicus and his Islamic Predecessors: Some Historical Remarks," *History of Science* 14: 65–81. Ragep suggests that "…Copernicus borrowed much of the mathematics of his heliocentric system from Islamic astronomers."
12. Gay, Peter, ed. 1973. *The Enlightenment: A Comprehensive Anthology*. New York: Simon and Shuster, pp. 16–18. It is important to note that during this period, an idea of "natural religion" developed called Deism that while rejecting organized religions, believed the idea of a Supreme Creator—whose existence can be proven by rational thought through observations of the natural world—but refused the idea that such a Deity would interact with humans or interfere in their affairs. The idea was developed with a view toward Newtonian physics that the universe was created as a machine and set in motion by the Supreme Creator and governed by "natural law." Deists extended this idea to the social system. They believed in the immortality of the soul, Divine reward and punishment, and Devine Providence. Adam Smith is believed to have been a deist as was Thomas Paine, the author of the Age of Reason in the 1790s, referring to the Enlightenment period.

13. Ibid, p. 19.
14. For a historical account of the evolution of the concept of "self-interest," see, Rogers, Kelly, ed. 1997. *Self-Interest: An Anthology of Philosophical Perspectives.* New York: Routledge.
15. See, Hume, David, 1958/1888. *A Treatise of Human Nature.* Edited by L. A. Silby-Bigge. Oxford: Clarendon Press, p. 450.
16. Ibid, pp. 574–575.
17. Bentham, Jeremy, 1780. *An Introduction to the Principle of Morals and Legislation.* London: T. Payne and Sons, pp. 1–6, and 26–29.
18. Jevons, William Stanley, 1871. *The Theory of Political Economy.* Reprinted in 1957 by Kelly and Macmillan, Inc. New York.
19. Menger, Carl, 1871. *Principles of Economics.* Reprinted in 1981 by the New York University Press.
20. Hume, David, 1748/1999. *An Enquiry Concerning Human Understanding.* Oxford: Oxford University Press, p. 211.
21. See, for example, Davis, John B., 2013. "Economists' Odd Stand on the Positive-Normative Distinction: A behavioral Economics View," In *Handbook on Professional Economic Ethics: View from the Economic Profession and Beyond*, edited by G. DeMartino and D. McClosky. Oxford: Oxford University Press; also, Putnam, Hillary, 2002. *The Collapse of Fact/Value Dichotomy and other Essays.* Cambridge: Harvard University Press.
22. See, for example, Hands, D. Wade, 2001. *Reflection Without Rules: Economic Methodology and Contemporary Science Theory.* Cambridge: Cambridge University Press.
23. For critique of logical Positivism see, Joad, Cyril Edwin Mitchinson, 1950/2011. *A Critique of Logical Positivism.* Whitefield, MT: Literary Licensing LLC. Also, Zaman, Asad, 2013. "Logical Positivism and Islamic Economics." *International Journal of Economics, Management and Accounting* 21 (2): 1–18. For critique of empiricism, see, Mure, G. R. G., 1958. *Retreat From Truth.* Oxford: Basil Blackwell.
24. Holt, Jim, 2007. "Positive Thinking," In *The New York Review of Books*, December 21, 2007.
25. Robins, Lionel. 1932. *An Essay on the Nature and Significance of Economic Science.* London: Macmillan.
26. Schumpeter, J. A., 1909, "On the concept of social value." *Quarterly Journal of Economics* 23 (2): 213–232.
27. Udehn, L., 2001. *Methodological Individualism: Background, History and Meaning.* London: Routledge; see also, Oliveria, Thiago Dummont and Carlos Eduardo Suprinyak, 2018. "The Nature and significance of Lionel Robbins' methodological individualism." *Economia* 19 (1): 24–37.
28. Robbins, Lionel, 1938. "Live and dead issues in the methodology of economics." *Economica* 5 (18): 342–352.

29. Rational Choice theory has three fundamental axioms (or assumptions): (1) Completeness. Individuals have complete preferences, meaning that the individual can rank-order all available alternatives and that this order is transitive. (2) Preferences are stable. (3) Invariance principle argues that while a person making a choice between two alternative, availability of the third alternative is irrelevant in that it does not affect the choice between the first two options.
30. Note that scarcity is such a crucial assumption that the entire edifice of Economics depends on its validity. This means that if it is shown that resources humans need are not scarce but in fact abundant, Economics as a "science" collapses. Charles Eisenstein makes such an argument in his book: Sacred Economics. Berkeley: Evolver; as well, its arguments weaken considerable, if the word "want" is changed to "basic," or "essential" needs.
31. See, Korner, Axel, 2011. "The Experience of Time as Crisis. On Croce's and Benjamin's Concept of History," *Intellectual History Review* 21 (2): 151–169. Also, Roberts, D. D., 1987. *Benedetto Croce and the Uses of Historicism*. Berkeley: University of California Press.
32. Croce, Benedetto. 1914. *Historical Materialism and the Economics of Karl Marx*. Translated by C. M. Meredith. New York: Macmillan.
33. Mure, G. R. G., 1958. *Retreat From Truth*. Oxford: Basil Blackwell, pp. 20–23. See also, Mure, G. R. G., 1967. "The economic and the moral in the philosophy of Benedetto Croce." Lecture delivered before the Centre for the Advanced Study of Italian Society in the University of Reading, Tuesday 8 November 1966. Thanks are due to Professor Idris Samawi Hamid for making this paper available. Croce discusses his ideas on "Economic science" in his book: Historical Materialism and the Economics of Karl Marx published by Macmillan in 1914 some three decades before Robbins. He also devotes some 40 pages of his book, Benedetto Croce, 1913. The Philosophy of the Practical: Economic and Ethic. Translated by Douglas Ainslie. London: Macmillan, pp. 113–157.
34. See Chapter 2 of his book, Historical Materialism and the Economics of Karl Marx.
35. An exception is, Jankovic, Ivan, 2018. "Benedetto Croce as an Economist." *Cosmos and Taxis* 6 (1/2): 42–53.
36. See A. D. Lindsay "Introduction" to Croce' Historical Materialism and the Economics of Karl Marx.
37. 'Abd ArRazzaq BilAbbas has attempted an archeology of the term "Al-Iqtiṣād Al-Islami" in his article in 2014 "Al-Iqtiṣād Al-Islami: Hafriyyah Mustalah," Islamiyyah Al-Ma'rifah 78: 105–132.
38. See, for example, Verse 172: Chapter 7. All references to verses of the Qur'an will follow the convention used her; verse will be mentioned followed by the chapter.

39. See, for example, 56: 51.
40. See, for example, 2–3: 61.
41. See, for example, 102: 3; 136: 4; 35: 5; 119: 9; 70: 33; 28: 57.
42. See, for example, 196: 7.
43. See, for example, 2: 62.
44. See, 9: 16.
45. See, 19: 31.
46. 42: 9.
47. See, 66: 5 and 32: 31.
48. The semantic field of the verb "*Yatlow*: يتلو" is rather wide, see for example entries under the verb 'tlow' in Raghib al-Isfahani: Mufradat, or in Arabic-English Dictionary of Qur'anic Usage, by Elsaid M. Badawi and Muhammad Abdel Haleem, pp. 135–136, published in 2008 by Brill in Leiden, The Netherland. Other Arabic lexicons have even more expansive semantic field for this verb, see for example, Lisan al-Arab.
49. See, Sadr, Kazem, 2016. *The Economic System of Early Islamic Period*. New York: Palgrave.
50. See Verse 25: Chapter 57. See also S. M. N. Al-Attas, 2015, pp. 1–17.
51. See, for example: Nasr, S. N., 1968. *The Encounter of Man and Nature: The Spiritual Crisis of Modern Man*. London: George Allen and Unwin; also, see, Al-Attas, S. M. N., 2015. *On Justice and the Nature of Man*. Kuala Lumpur: IBFIM. Thanks are due to S. Dr. Adam al-Habshi for gifting a copy of this book.
52. See 2: 62.
53. Mirakhor, Abbas and Idris Samawai Hamid, 2009. *Islam and Development: The Institutional Framework*. New York: Global Scholarly Publication.
54. Ghazi, bin Muhammad bin Talal, 2010. "Love in the Holy Qur'an. Chicago: Kazi Publications". In the Foreword to this book, S. H. Nasr writes: From Divine Love, from God's Love for Himself, has issued all of creation, at whose centre resides man, and there has also emanated from that Love revelation to guide him to that love and through Love to Him who is not only the source of all love, but Love Itself. Let us recall that on of His beautiful names is Love or al-Wadud. Does not the sacred tradition (al-hadith al-qudsi) state, "I was a hidden treasure; I loved (*ahbabtu*) to be known; therefore, I created creation so that I would be known"?
55. See 16: 50 for example.
56. For more on Walayah see the excellent books of Professor Hamid on the subject. Hamid, Idris Samawi, 2011. *Islam, Sign & Creation: The Cosmology of Walayah*. New York: Global Scholarly Publications, and Islam, Station & Process: The Spirituality of Walyah, Published in 2011 by Scholarly Publications.
57. 9: 42, for example.
58. 62: 10, for example.

59. 257: 2, for example.
60. 107: 2; 28: 3; 55–56: 5; 119: 4; 63: 16; 51, 81: 5; 1–2: 60, for examples.
61. 31: 3, for example.
62. For a good analysis of reciprocity from economics point of view see, Serge-Christophe Kolm, 2008. Cambridge: Cambridge University Press. Many anthropologists believe that humanity could not have survived without cooperation, sharing and reciprocity. The Qur'an expresses the imperative of reciprocity in form of a question: "Is not the reward of Ihsan other than Ihsan?" While Ihsan is generally translated as "good doing," there is an incredibly astute Hadeeth of the Noble Messenger when asked the meaning of Ihsan, he is reported to have said that Ihsan means acting always as if you are in the presence of Allah, that you see Him because even if you do not see Him, He sees you. This is a definition of full rule-compliant behaviour of those who are in a constant state of consciousness of the presence of Allah.
63. For example, 10: 49.
64. 23: 42, for example.
65. For example, 177: 2; 36: 4; 26: 17.
66. For example: 71: 9; 72: 8.
67. See, for example: 44, 45, 47: 5 and 59: 4.
68. Ng, Adam, et al., 2016. *Social Capital and Risk Sharing*. New York: Palgrave.
69. For example, Al-Tabari, Abu Ja'far Muhammad ibn Jarir, 915. *History of Messengers and Kings*. Albany: State University of New York Press. Also, Al-Miskawayh, Ahmad ibn Muhammad. Tajarib Al-Umam (known as History of Ibn Miskawayh). Leiden: Brill, 1908–1924.
70. See for example, Darraz, Muhammad 'Abd Allah, 1950. Dustor Al-Akhlaq Fi Al-Qur'an (rules governing behaviour in the Qur'an). This book was written in French. It was translated into Arabic in 1973 by Dr 'Abd as-Sabur Shaheen and published by Al-Azhar Al-Shareef. The book is the first attempt by a Muslim scholar in contemporary history to extract all rules governing behaviour from the Qur'an and Sunnah. Also see extremely useful and helpful 5 volumes of a book on the subject, Al-Hakimi, M. R., Al-Hakimi, M., and Al-Hakimi, A., 1992. Al-Hayat. Tehran: Maktab Nashr al-Thaqafa Al-Islamiyyah. See also, Mirakhor, Abbas and Hossein Askari, 2017. *Ideal Islamic Economy: An Introduction*. New York: Palgrave.
71. This proposition came to be known as Pigou-Dalton Principle; see, Pigou, A. C., 1912. *Wealth and Welfare*. London: Macmillan; and Hugh Dalton, 1920. "The Measurement of the Inequality of Income." *Economic Journal* 30 (119): 348–361. In the last two decades there has been a renewed interest in Pigou-Dalton Principle, see for example, Anthony b. Atkinson and Andrea Brandolini, 2015. "Unveiling the Ethics

Behind Inequality Measurement: Dalton's Contribution to Economics," *The Economic Journal* 125 (583).
72. See, for example, Al-Ilwani, Taha Jabir, 2001. Maqasid Al-Shari'ah. Beirut: IIIT. Also, Kamali, Mohammad Hashim, 2014. Maqasid Al-Shari'ah Made Easy. Occasional Paper Series. Washington and London: IIIT.
73. The book was republished by King Abdulaziz University in 2014. See also, Jilali 'Asheer, 2011. "Al-Qira'ah Fi Al-Mirsad Fi Masa'il al-Iqtiṣād li Al-Shaikh Abdulqadir Al-Majawi Al-Tilmisani" Dirasat Islamiyyah 6 (3): 125–146. Shaikh Al-Majawi is enamoured with the economy of UK, the US, and, especially, France and their economic policies that among his last words of the book he claims: "...ان الدولة الفرنسوية جادة فى نفع العباد و تعليمهم و فتحت ابواباً لكل من يرومه". For a view that expresses close (nearly one-to-one) correspondence between Islamic Economics and Fiqh, see Muhammad, Yusuf Kamal, 1998. Fiqh Iqtiṣād Al-Suq: Al-Nashat Al-Khass. Cairo, Egypt: Dar Al-Nashr lilJami'at.

CHAPTER 7

Behavioural Norms and Institutional Structure of *Iqtiṣād*

The vexed questions about the norms of individual behavioural and institutional rules cannot be addressed without raising many strands of argument about moral philosophy and empirical demonstration. Insofar as the development of Islamic economic thought is concerned, these questions need to be settled if the structure of the discipline as a whole is to be sound. When confronted with normative problems, it is not beyond the wit of economists to offer elaborate devises that combine the rational maximizing behaviour of economic agents with normative value judgements. It is, however, difficult to arrive at distributive justice because the invisible hand theorem, which underlies the second welfare theorem of Pareto optimal allocation of resources achieved as the outcome of competitive equilibrium, is a theorem of positive economics not normative one. It is a theory that leaves out the difficult questions of property ownership, and the justice of the underlying distribution of endowments.

Thus, Islamic Economics shaped in the mould of conventional economic thought with a secularization process whose end product is historical relativism cannot promote economic justice. There is, indeed, fundamental unfairness in theories of morality-based utilitarianism and social contracts that provide distributional mechanisms but fail to promote just outcomes. Inconsistent social and economic policies are not conducive to justice in accordance with the primary conceptions of distributive justice by Aristotle or social justice by Saint Thomas Aquinas. The concept of justice, which is at the foundation of thriving economies and stable societies, has been, historically, defined by philosophy and religion, and increasingly so by economic thought. It is clear that it is difficult for Islamic economics to set an agenda for the organization of an ideal economy on the basis of changing conceptions of justice, 'adl which should be, in the words of Ibn Khaldun, the foundation of social organization and human civilization.

As argued in the previous chapters of this book, a paradigm shift to *al-iqtiṣād* is necessary because it precludes conflation and regime shifts between conflicting worldviews, and reinstates the importance of justice *al-mīzān* in keeping equity amongst mankind according to the Islamic worldview. A misguided approach to the construction of Islamic economics is conducive to the cumulation of methodological errors and policy mistakes. It is difficult to concur with the view that compounded doctrinal flaws and errors are inevitable because learning takes place by doing. Such a view cannot earn intellectual credence in the presence of authentic knowledge from the Qur'an and the tradition of the Prophet (*saa*) for the development of a stream of economic thought, *Iqtiṣād*, concerned with the organization of an ideal system based on economic justice. That unique stream of economic thought does not require a separate theory of justice. The system of justice is endogenous to Islam and it simply arises as the natural outcome of practices by rule-compliant societies. As argued by Muhammad Baqir as-Sadr (1982, [1994], p. 9) in *Iqtiṣāduna (Our Iqtiṣād)*, "justice by itself is not a scientific idea; so when it combines with an idea, it imprints it with doctrinal stamp and makes it distinct from scientific thinking." Thus, justice should not be simply regarded as the abstract expected outcome of solving the puzzle of optimal equilibrium based on the rationality postulate, utility maximization, perfect knowledge, and perfect competition. It is rather the doctrinal stamp that should imprint every practical aspect of social and economic life.

Thus, justice, which is inseparably mixed with Islamic economy, is too important to be forsaken in the pursuit of weak links between two conflicting worldviews. As argued in previous chapters, if Islamic economics is dissociated from the Islamic worldview, nothing of substance can render it discernable from conventional economics. It is further argued, in this chapter, that an ideal economy cannot be organized without behavioural norms and institutional structures that govern social interactions and economic exchange based on justice. The usual criticism about a lack of objectivity because economic thought is not necessarily contaminated with value judgements. It is important to seek justice (*'adl*) because it is closest to piety (*taqwa*), irrespective of the conceptual proliferation of the notions of justice and truth. To err is human, but in the words of Ali Ibn Abi Talib, (raa), "whoever seeks truth but misses it cannot be likened to that who seeks falsehood and achieves it." Thus, it is difficult for Islamic economic thought to occupy itself with partial truth and partial justice, when these notions constitute the core of its teaching. As the principles should be pursued for their own sake, it is impossible for a discipline that disowns its own conceptions of justice and truth and neglects its own set of normative behavioural rules to articulate its own agenda for economic justice and human development.

The contour of an ideal Islamic economy, or *Iqtiṣād* is, as succinctly described by Abbas Mirakhor and Hossein Askari (2017, p. 205), "one where everyone who is able works, using knowledge to combine with their own labour and the resources provided by the Creator, to produce goods and services for society. Economic, social, and political affairs are conducted with the goal of removing barriers to the progress of all humans and in full compliance with rules, including those governing property rights, market behaviour, exchange and trade, and contracts and trust. Knowing that they are responsible and accountable, individually and collectively, they invest allegiance in a legitimate authority to carry out their affairs, with the legitimacy of the authority established by rule-compliance." It is thus, important to note that *Iqtiṣād* is founded on a belief system, authentic knowledge, and rules-based behaviour, which ensure that man accepts the wisdom of Allah swt in all aspects of life in ways that positive propositions become essentially undiscernable from normative statements.

Iqtiṣād is about the recognition of the nature of being, dignity of work, sanctity of property, inviolability of covenants, and truthfulness in dealings. It is about the organization of an ideal economic system that is intimately connected to the Islamic worldview, rather than one subordinated to the system of morality and value-free judgements that depend on individual and social inclinations, self-interest, and utilitarianism. Thus, the principal purpose of this chapter is to explain the rule-guided human actions including norms of behaviour and institutional structure, which derive directly from the authentic sources of knowledge in Islam, and render thereby *Iqtiṣād* distinctively different from alternative sources of economic thought and reasoning, which rely on praxis, subjectivism, and notions about justice that may be just as likely to be false as true.

Etymology and Quranic Foundations of *Iqtiṣād*

Iqtiṣād is a collection of Islamic economic thought deriving from two streams of thinking, *ʿilm* or knowledge, namely jurisprudence or *fiqh*, and economic analysis, respectively. Whereas the development of *fiqh* depends on the cognitive abilities to deduce and extract rulings from the Qur'an and Prophetic tradition to regulate economic affairs, economic thinking is about understanding, predicting, measuring, and guiding the impact of *fiqh* rulings on economic reality. This line of argument implies that corpus juris is a pre-requisite for economic analysis, and that a distinction should be made between *fiqh* scholars concerned with eliciting legal rulings and economists devoted to the analysis of economic phenomena. The formation of legal opinion requires from jurists the possession of the appropriate knowledge and understanding about the principles of jurisprudence *usul ul-fiqh*, and the ability to make *ijtihād* through analogical reasoning.

The same argument applies to economists, who should possess the fundamental knowledge and understanding about the causal forces at work in the economic system in order to express an intellectually sound and informed opinion about the nature of economic phenomena. To argue that all opinions, on either of the legal and economic sides, carry the same weight cannot be helpful in distinguishing truth from falsehood. It is, thus, important that Muslim economists possess also a minimum understanding of the language and meaning of legal rulings, and that legal jurists understand those of economic opinions. It is not possible to keep legal rulings and economic opinions scrupulously out of sight from each other because they are both interested in understanding and regulating the same ideal economy. Thus, authoritative knowledge and expertise in *fiqh* and economic analysis are inseparable. The relation between the science of *fiqh* (*ʿilm al-fiqh*) and science of economics (*ʿilm al-iqtisad*) is not one of rivalry. None can be sufficient on its own in designing the institutional structure of an ideal economy, making inferences, and reaching policy decisions. The danger is that one discipline ignores the other because there is no benefit in legal rulings based on inaccurate economic knowledge and in economic opinions that contravene the tenets of Islamic law. It is this balanced mixture that sets Muslim jurists and economists with responsibilities beyond those of technocratic policy advisers because a normative discipline requires consistency between legal rulings and economic opinions for the organization of an ideal economy.

Thus, *Iqtiṣād* provides a paradigm for complementary and mutually enhancing sciences of *fiqh* and economic analysis aimed at achieving the Qur'anic vision of an ideal economy. It is a paradigm that does not rest on a contentious relation between religion and science, but on a consistent Islamic worldview that is distinct from the secular ideologies underpinning conventional economics. As argued in previous chapters, it is difficult to merely incorporate the maqasid of the Shari'ah or Islamic morality maqāsid or Islamic morality into the mould of conventional economics in order to develop a school of integrated economic thought called Islamic economics, the essence of which is unlike *Iqtiṣād* that is based solely on authentic sources of knowledge, by no means unambiguous. It is not clear, given the wide spectrum of conventional economic theory, which secular doctrines can be satisfactorily "Islamized" and corroborated as part of Islamic Economics. Neither the gap between economic reality and economic theory from conventional economics nor the confusion in knowledge and intellectual disorder in the universe of discourse called Islamic economics can be safely ignored. In contrast, *Iqtiṣād*, on the other hand, rests on the certitude of sacred knowledge, grounded in its natural habitat of the *Qur'an* and *Sunnah*. It is a paradigm that does not suffer from internal failures and contradictions, and to believe that the reorganization of the economy to serve justice is a utopian ideal would be an intellectually disabling belief.

Etymologically, there is no word for the term "economics" in classical Arabic because, as argued by Seyyed Hossein Nasr (1993, p. 204), it was never regarded in traditional civilizations as an independent discipline separate from ethics. Economics became "gradually both a scientific discipline and distinct activity of its own and in many areas it became divorced from ethics." Though the term *iqtiṣād* is commonly used in translation of the modern field of economics, it linguistically connotes a rich collection of notions in Arabic. As explained also in previous chapters, it is a noun derivative from the gerund *q-ṣ-d* or *qaṣada* قصد, which literally means "to mean" and "to intend." The Qur'an includes several derivatives, ranging from the noun *qaṣd* used in reference to remaining steady on the path, to the imperative *iqṣid* in an injunction to moderate the pace, and the adjective *qāṣid* to describe a moderate trip. The derivative noun *maqṣad*, which means aim and purpose, is also frequently used in the literature of Islamic economics in its plural form as in the objectives of

The Lawgiver (*Maqāṣid as-Shāri'*) and purposes of the law (*Maqāṣid as-Shari'ah*). Thus, the term *Iqtiṣād* is directly derived from the verbal root *iqtaṣada* اقتصد, with the feminine adjective *muqtaṣidah* appearing in the Qur'an (66:5) with reference to an *Ummah* or community persevering on the right path. It portrays a spiritual dimension as clearly manifested in the notion of *Moderation in Belief* or "*al-Iqtiṣād fil-I'tiqād*" explained by Abu Hamid al-Ghazali (1058–1111).

According to AlMajawi and Brihmat (1904 [2014], pp. 82–83), *Iqtiṣād* can be defined linguistically as "moderation in spending, as a degree between frugality and extravagance" and terminologically as "the measures intended to increase wealth in ways that require less efforts and yield more revenues to promote the means of comfort and luxury." But it is also noted that the relation between the social measures to the wealth of nations, or Political Economy, and individual measures to increase the wealth of individuals, *Personal Iqtiṣād*, is bound to be hostile in nature. It is argued that hostility between political economy and personal economy can be partly explained by difficulties in distributing wealth on equal basis and in proportion to human efforts given the competition of individuals, and "the dominance of the strong over the weak, and the rich over the poor, due to the disparity of power among individuals, especially financial power, so the strong grows stronger and the weak becomes weaker" (authors' translation from Arabic). This is a definition of *Iqtiṣād* that adheres to the view that part of the economy is hostile to another, which is not necessarily true because the overriding objective of *Iqtiṣād* should not be reduced to the pursuance of economic prosperity and standards of material comfort at the detriment of others. Given the human nature and potential conflict between public and private interests, the definition and promotion of justice should not be left to the whimsical arbitrariness of individuals or societies. It is imperative, indeed, that an ideal economy be founded on iqtiṣād-driven behavioural rules and institutional structure that balance the spiritual with the material, the eternal with the temporal, and the individual with the communal, in order to secure economic justice.

Thus, it is important to derive an appropriate definition of *iqtiṣād* that is consistent with the notion of justice and its epistemological and ontological foundations. As argued by Baqir as-Sadr (1982 [1994], pp. xliii-xliv), the word "Islamic economics" should be distinguished from "economics" because whereas the latter is a relatively new science, Islam is rather a way of life that cannot be reduced to the pursuance of scientific endeavour. *Iqtiṣād* can be defined as "the economic doctrine of Islam which embodies the Islamic system in the organization of economic life on the strength of the balance of thought this doctrine possesses and denotes and which is made up of the moral ideas of Islam and the scientific, economic or historical ideas which are linked with the problems of economics or the analysis of the history of human societies." This line is argument is shared also by Al-Daghistani (2022, p. 270), who contends that "*iqtiṣād* cannot mean only economy from a dominant modern understanding in its technical sense as a rational, accumulation-based, and profit-oriented process but as a human behaviour of providence, structured around the principles of moral uplift."

Iqtiṣād is intrinsically related to the notions of perseverance, moderation, and golden mean. It can be defined as the optimal use of resources provided by *The Creator* in accordance with rules that are prescribed by *The Lawgiver* in the *Qur'an* and operationalized by His Prophet to achieve felicity in this life and in the hereafter. As argued by Askari, Iqbal, and Mirakhor (2015, p. 31), the *Qur'an* is the fountainhead of all Islamic paradigms, and "the framework within which all relevant envisioned conceptions of reality find their source." The fundamental principles of *Iqtiṣād*, which provides a vision for an ideal economy, can only be derived from the Qur'an in order to be regarded as immutable rules both temporally and spatially. As it has its roots in the Qur'an rather than a secular mind, *Iqtiṣād* is neither a pure construction of the human mind as in Immanuel Kant's (1724–1804) conception of mathematics, nor a mental and abstract science concerned with conduct of economic man as in Mill's conception of political economy.

The immutability of the *iqtiṣād*-driven behavioural and institutional rules stems from the *Qur'an's* unique attributes of authenticity, timelessness, and inimitability. In contrast to other prophets who were given signs of wonders apart from divine revelation, Prophet Mohammad (*saa*) received the Qur'an itself as the greatest sign to provide guidance and assurance to mankind. The clarity and force of evidence in the Qur'an make the Qur'an itself its own proof, as argued by many scholars including Ibn Khaldun (p. 73). It is a divine revelation that cannot be produced by other than Allah swt, without any crookedness, or falsehood, and that is immune to alteration, deformation, and falsification. And so are the behavioural rules contained therein.[1] It is inconceivable that economic principles derived directly from the Qur'an as operationalized by Prophet (*saa*) suffer from the inconsistency and vagueness of secular paradigms. There is a real problem if the development of Islamic economic thought is conditional on the immutable rules were to be dismissed, either in whole or in part, as irrelevant in order to acquiesce to the demands of secular worldviews.

BEHAVIOURAL RULES AND THE PROMOTION OF ECONOMIC JUSTICE AND SOCIAL WELFARE

The Qur'an is by no means a rules-laden divine revelation, but by necessity, it is inclusive of a body of behavioural rules because faith should be reflected by consistent deeds. As argued by Al-Attas (1993, p. 72), "Islam is both belief and faith (*iman*) as well as submission in service (*islām*); it is both assent of the heart (*qalb*) and mind (*'aql*) confirmed by the tongue (*lisān*) as well as deed and work (*'amal*)." Thus, a distinction is made between *īman* as the system of belief, *Islām* as the acts of worship, and *ihsān* as the highest devotion to worshipping Allah *swt* as if one could see Him.[2] Thus, as a religion based on Unity or tawhid, Islam is not merely a system of beliefs and convictions without consequences but also a system of practices, values, and attitudes that are consistent with the Islamic worldview. There is no room, in Islam, for cognitive dissonance leading to a dichotomy between belief and practice. The existence of various levels of understanding and practice across Muslims is a natural outcome of differences in spiritual levels, and degrees of resolve and devotion, but there is only one Islam.

There is no room for individual conduct that blends truth with deception, benevolence with malevolence, and good with evil. The behavioural rules that are meant to resonate in the entire fabric of society and economic life are asserted in the *Qur'an* and operationalized by the Prophet (*saa*) with a level of clarity and consistency that leaves no room for errors of understanding and interpretation. The normative rules are not meant to bind individuals and institutions to specific bits of behaviour and neglect others at the risk of undermining economic justice. As the rules rest on a human conscience that is vitally linked to faith, they reflect a complete harmony between reason and intellect. It is a conscience that values rectitude and righteousness in all economic and social activities without exception. *Iqtiṣād*, thus, is not destined to paint only a partial picture of economic life where value judgements are eschewed, but an entire portrait where contractual freedom and risk sharing are embraced to serve justice in the entire economy.

It is because the conduct of economic activities is necessary to human sustenance and a pre-requisite to social life that the Qur'an includes several references to the primary concept of vicegerency (*khilāfah*) and the economic notions of subsistence (*ma'āyish*), sustenance (*rizq*), and building and settlement (*'imārah* and *isti'mār*). With respect to *khilāfah*, there are numerous references in the Qur'an to the notion that Allah swt decreed the creation of a vicegerent on earth.[3] Since this is a divine will, the meaning of vicegerency should not be the subject of doubt or misinterpretation. As noted by Al-Attas (1993, p. 39), "This does not mean that he should be presumptuous enough to regard himself as 'copartner with God in creation.'" The stewardship of the kingdom of nature is rather a trust (*amānah*) offered to the Heavens, the Earth, and the Mountains but they declined to assume it out of fear.[4] The placement of the burden of trust on humanity implies the necessity to live in harmony with nature and other creations.

It is undeniable that this harmony necessitates the promotion of justice in all aspects of life. This requirement is clearly reflected in Allah's injunction to Prophet Daoud (as) to judge between people in truth and justice based on the status of vicegerent on earth.[5] A failure to promote justice by following one's lust, desires, and whims is thus a failure to serve as vicegerent of Allah (*swt*). Though obedience (*tā'ah*) is a duty that flows directly from worship (*'ibādah*), which is the purpose of creation, disobedience on the other hand may follow from forgetfulness (*nis'yān*), which is also inherent to mankind. Indeed, man is honoured over many of Allah's creation, but he is called (*insān*) in reference to his behaviour and conduct, partly because he is ungrateful, hasty, impatient, miserly, and prone to forgetfulness (*nis'yān*), which derives from the same verbal root "to forget" *(nasiya)*. It is forgetfulness of the original state of harmony with that of all beings and existence (*fitrah*), and there is indeed no change in the pattern of creation and work of Allah swt.[6] As described in the Qur'an, the first human creation forgot the prior Covenant, and Allah swt found on his part no firm resolve.[7] Thus, forgetfulness as part of man's attributes of weakness, is conducive to a lack of resolve, and injustice in the fulfilment of the requirements of vicegerency *khilāfah*. The state of forgetfulness leads to the certainty of ignorance (*jahl*) and the tragedy of injustice (*dhulm*), which have no remedies in secular theories about knowledge and definitions of justice but in divine guidance and remembrance of man's ultimate purpose of existence and true relationship with his Lord.

Allah *swt* who placed man with authority on earth to fulfil the duties of *amānah* and vicegerency, would certainly provide the material means to fulfil the requirements of life.[8] By virtue of his very nature, man is in permanent need to satisfy both the spiritual and physiological demands. Indeed, Allah *swt* has provided the means of subsistence and sustenance through the subjection (*taskhīr*) of all creation on earth. The subjection of the seas is such that fresh and tender flesh and ornaments may be extracted, and ships may sail through by His command.[9] The spreading out of the earth like a carpet and heavens like a canopy, the setting of mountains firm and immovable, and the production of all types of bounties in due proportions implies the provision of adequate means of subsistence.[10] This subjection means that the means of subsistence are not provided solely for man's own sustenance but also for those whose sustenance man is not responsible.[11] It is a testament to the fact that Allah *swt* has subjected all creation and provided subsistence in due balance for the sustenance of mankind and other creation in order to seek of His bounties and be grateful. Given the divine provision of ample bounties and means of subsistence in due proportions for the sustenance of all creation, the perpetual conditions of food poverty and human hardship can only derive from man's forgetfulness, ignorance, and negligence of the duties of vicegerency. It is, indeed, difficult to reconcile the fact that the very resources made available in due proportions by divine will are also found to be in perpetual scarcity without conceding to the notion of man's complicit tempering of the cup with the salt of ingratitude and indifference, which are leading to economic injustice. Silence and wavering in the face of institutionalized injustice in the form of infringement on property rights, encroachment on the fundamental right to equal wage for work of equal value, and inequitable taxation, is tantamount to complicity and acquiescence. The absence of justice is conducive, among others, to the erosion of trust, which is an essential force in organizing social life and economic activities.

The Qur'an refers also to the notion of *isti'mar*, the conditions of settlement on earth, which is necessary also for the fulfilment of trust *Amanah*. Indeed, Allah (*swt*) created Adam and all mankind from soil, and settled them on earth from which the necessary nutrients for the human body can be extracted.[12] He decreed that Adam shall inhabit the earth, and the meaning of settlement is conferred by the Arabic terms *istimar* or *'umran*. The word *'imarah* conveys also the meaning of physical building, construction, and maintenance as implied by the divine decree that the masjids of Allah shall be maintained only by believers.[13] It implies also physical presence in the masjid for *'ibadah* purposes as in *'umra*, which literally means visiting populated sites. Ibn Khaldun uses the word *'umran* in a broader meaning than *hadhāra* (civilization) and *tamaddun* (city-dwelling), and distinguishes between *al-'umran al-hadhari* (urbanism and sedentism) and *al-'umran al-badawi* (bedouin civilization). Ibn Khaldun (1337 [2005], p. 91) argues that "differences of condition among people are the result of different ways in which they make their living. Social organization enables them to co-operate toward that end and to start with the simple necessities of life, before they get to conveniences and luxuries." Thus, *Iqtiṣād* can be, alternatively, defined as the organization of economic activities to achieve the conditions of *'umran* and social welfare.

The sign of ruin of *'umrān* or civilization is the prevalence of injustice, as argued by Ibn Khaldun, who defines justice as the placing of everything in its proper place and giving everyone his due. Al-Attas (1993, p. 76) also defines justice means "a harmonious condition or state of affairs whereby everything is in its right and proper place." This implies that with respect to man, justice means the condition or state whereby he is in the right and proper place, both in relation to his self and in relation with others. It is impossible to pursue a harmonious organization of the economy without the promotion of a system of justice where man lives in harmony with his self and with his environment. Thus, the settlement of man on earth was not to proceed without divine guidance about economic justice, legitimate ways of earning a living, and behavioural rules that govern all aspects of life and interactions of man with his environment. Indeed, if there were angels settled on earth living in peace and quiet, rather than error-prone human beings, Allah swt would have certainly sent an angel messenger nevertheless.[14] Prophets were sent to remind mankind about the prior Covenant with Allah swt. As norms represent standards of conduct that individuals are expected to adhere to, there is a need for a benchmark against which behaviour is compared and contrasted to. The benchmark model for Muslims is the Prophet *saa* who is described in the Qur'an as a man with an exalted standard of character (*khuluq adheem*).[15] As no obedience and loyalty to Allah *swt* can be conceived without obedience and loyalty to His Messenger, the only legitimate path to vicegerency is to emulate the Prophet's (*saa*) leadership in all spheres of societal life from the religious and spiritual to the political and economic aspects. Given the fact that the Prophet's (*saa*) experience is not one of an angel but that of a human being and merchant walking in markets, the behavioural rules that govern man's economic life can be directly drawn from the Prophet's conduct, which is perfectly consistent with the Islamic worldview.

Thus, the Qur'an indicates that for the purposes of '*umrān* and fulfilment of *amānah*, Allah swt secures the means of sustenance in due balance. Whether the provisions are made in abundance or limited proportions for individuals or communities at a particular point in time, is a matter for Allah swt alone to decide, as it is to Him that belong the keys of the heavens and earth.[16] It is to Him that belong also the keys of the unseen, as not even a leaf falls without His knowledge.[17] It is with His perfect knowledge of all things that He expands and restricts provisions to whoever He wills.[18] These bounties are not conditional on belief, or lack thereof, as they are provided to those who seek the transitory lusts of this life as well as those who seek the hereafter.[19] It is impossible to count the favours of Allah because they are innumerable, but man is rather given to injustice and ingratitude.[20] Indeed, man is created with an element of impatience, he tends to be unsettled when evil touches him and stingy when good reaches him, except those whose conduct is consistent with their covenants.[21] Thus, there is a tendency for man to regard Allah's testing with favours as an act of honouring and restrictions on subsistence as one of humiliation.[22] This is a secular view of individual life where a relentless struggle to climb the social ladder casts Allah's expansion and restriction of wealth and means of sustenance as an act of honouring or humiliation.

The alternative worldview on which *iqtiṣād* is founded, calls for the weight of conscience to bear within a greater scheme of things, where restrictions on bounties are meant to test patience, resolve, and resilience, and extensions to test empathy, altruism, and humility, in fulfilment of the responsibilities deriving from the Covenant *amānah*.[23] The argument that it is difficult to exhibit altruism in a heterogenous society would embolden attempts to steer Islamic economics from a discipline of normative behaviour to one of merely descriptive statements. The organization of an ideal economy based on *iqtiṣād* principles is based on the *tawhīd* worldview, which implies the unity of creation, and relies on conscious human action not hedonistic calculus based on social status, or ethnicity. It is Allah *swt's* wisdom that there are orders of hierarchy in human societies, with none composed of equal elements. If He so willed,

He could have made mankind one people, but they will not cease to dispute.[24] Thus, a man of discernment entrusted with the responsibilities of vicegerency can recognize the fact that heterogeneity is inevitable, and that endless disputes about social structure are just a distraction from the more important issues of social organization and from the duty to organize the economy in ways that serve justice to all.

The real honour or humiliation, thus, does not lie in increasing or diminishing wealth but in the conscious exercise of vicegrent duties of providing care, or lack thereof, for other members of the society, including the orphans and the poor.[25] The system of alms *zakat*, which is a pillar of distributive justice in *iqtiṣād*, is based on moderation and risk-sharing through the provision of a pre-determined share of individual wealth exceeding one's needs in sustenance of particular segments of the society. Indeed, righteousness cannot be achieved through an insatiate passion for wealth but with spending from what is most cherished.[26] Furthermore, there are many injunctions to follow behavioural rules related to moderate consumption and savings. The principle of moderation is clearly stated in the Qur'an in terms of avoiding conditions leading to one's hand becoming tied to the neck or overstretched in ways that lead to niggardness or destitution.[27] This fundamental principle of *iqtiṣād* stands in stark contrast to the maxims of consumer sovereignty and selfishness that underlie the development of conventional economics. The integration of secular maxims within a synthetic discipline called Islamic economics cannot be harmless because they are clearly inconsistent with the behavioural norms explained above. As these rules emanate from the Qur'an and Sunnah, they depend on a permanent covenant with Allah *swt* not on a mutable social contract a Social Contract, and unless Islamic economics abandons the grafting of secular maxims, it would remain entangled in secular worldviews. The Impossibility Theorem proposed in previous chapters, suggests that given the radically different worldviews and philosophical foundations, it is impossible to graft polar disciplines one onto another through the process of Islamization or secularization. Thus, *iqtiṣād*, which provides an organic and complete framework for Qur'an-based rules that govern the structure and functioning of an ideal economy, implies that grafting is an impossible exercise and a dangerous source of confusion, doubt, and scepticism.

Justice and harmony necessitate an ideal form of human social organization, which can be explained by the fact that, as noted by Ibn Khaldun (1337[2005], p. 45), "God created and fashioned man in a form that can live and subsist only with the help of food. He guided man to a natural desire for food and instilled in him the power that enables him to obtain it. However, the power of the individual human being is not sufficient for him to obtain (the food) he needs, and does not provide him with as much food as he requires to live." Given the differences in aptitude and nature of risks associated with the necessary seeking of livelihood, it is difficult for one person to satisfy his own needs without cooperation with others. Thus, man, as noted again by Ibn Khaldun (1337, [2005], p. 45), "cannot do without a combination of many powers from among his fellow beings, if he is to obtain food for himself and for them. Through co-operation, the needs of a number of persons, many times greater than their own number, can be satisfied." The recognition of cooperation and exchange relations, rather than threat relations, are central to economic activities is consistent with the definition by Boulding (1969, p. 14) of economics as "the study of that part of the total social system which deals with exchangeables." The emphasis on exchange implies that risk-sharing is important in organizing economic activities. This is also a clear departure from the classical definition of economics in terms of optimal allocation of scarce resources. As argued above, *iqtiṣād* discards the axiomatic treatment of resources as scarce, because it implies that the hands of Allah *swt* are tied up.[28] There is compelling evidence from the Qur'an that Allah *swt* provides both the necessary bounties in due proportions as He pleases through the subjection of all creation on earth as well as the means of subsistence.

Thus, while there are no limits to His bounties, it is also Allah's wisdom to exercise restrictions because unless the provisions are made in due measure, there is a potential for people to transgress beyond all bounds.[29] Thus, part of the reason for restricting provisions is the avoidance of mischief, transgression, and injustice. The history of mankind reveals, indeed, that cooperation is not the only means through which a division of labour and increased output can be achieved. There is also a tendency for threat and aggressiveness, which lead to injustice in the division of the economic pie. The wealth and income inequalities are reflective of fundamental problems related to property rights not only with respect to providers of labour and capital but also other members of society who cannot seek livelihood by themselves. With reference to Boulding (1969, p. 14) again, an exchange system of social organization differs from the integrative system based on one-way transfer of exchangeables, and most importantly from the threat system. A restraining influence is needed to ensure normative conduct, behaviour, and etiquette befitting the duties, qualities, and properties of vicegerents.

The restraining forces should be guided solely by a conscious urge to promote justice, in the economic sphere as well as in all other aspects of social life. It is a duty imposed on all Muslims without exception, simply because justice is the ultimate objective or *maqsad* of *Shari'ah* and because acts of injustice can be contagious, leading to the ruin of *'umran*. The requirement of enjoining good and prohibiting evil (*al-amr bilma'ruf wan-nah'i anil-munkar*) is a fundamental principle of behavioural norms, from which economic rules flow naturally. Both legal (*halal*) and illegal (*haram*) matters are indeed evident, and it is incumbent on Muslims to save their religion and honour by avoiding doubtful issues in between, of which many people may not be aware.[30] As the perseverance of a party on the right path is described in Qur'an as '*ummah muqtasidah*, it is important to understand *iqtisād* also in terms of compliance with Qur'anic ordinances and prohibitions related to economic life. It is further ascertained beyond doubt that compliance with divine law constitutes not just salvation in the hereafter, but also guarantee of enjoying happiness and economic prosperity in this life.[31]

Thus, *iqtisād* as a paradigm that offers normative prescriptions for the organization of an ideal economy cannot remain silent on normative rules of behaviour, which allow man to live according to the dictates of divine law. As the very meaning of *Islam* is to submit (*aslama*) to the Will of Allah swt, following the form of right religion (*millah*) of Ibrahim (as) and subsequent prophets, and since there is no compulsion in religion,[32] compliance with *Iqtisād*-based behavioural rules depends on the freedom of the rational soul, conscious of its Covenant with Allah, to do justice to itself. It is difficult indeed, to cultivate harmonious relations with others without harmony between man and his self, which cannot be achieved in turn without knowledge about the purpose of creation and existence. A collective doctrine, as argued by Baqir As-Sadr (1982 [1994], p. 8), is one that "cultivates in every individual a deep consciousness about the responsibility toward the society." This consciousness requires a constant reminder that the fulfilment of responsibilities cannot be achieved with ignorant imitation but with rational judgement deriving from the intellect, which lies in the spiritual organ of cognition, the heart (*al-qalb*). This implies that individual actions can be assumed to be ideally conducted in good faith in the presence of a deep consciousness that they will find favour with Allah swt and that they are not merely the outcome of a quest for individual happiness but in accord with collective welfare as well.

Thus, the rules of behaviour, which are often identified with the institutional framework can be useful, as argued by Askari, Iqbal, and Mirakhor (2015, p. 51), in achieving three objectives, including the reduction of cognitive demand on individuals in the face of uncertainty, the distinction between acceptable and unacceptable behaviour, and the rendering of individual actions more predictable. These rules imply that with full knowledge of the consequences of lawful and unlawful behaviour, individuals can be assumed to act with truthfulness and *bona fide*, and share a common sense of responsibility. The choices taken by individuals under conditions of uncertainty are bound to influence, directly or indirectly, the decisions of others, affect the level of trust and counterparty risk, and inhibit or facilitate coordination and exchange. It is important to note that though rules of conduct are often referred to as institutions, it is incumbent on public institutions to impose normative rules on individual behaviour and shape the social and economic relations between individuals. Thus, given the nature of man created with the conditions of forgetfulness, impatience, and inclination toward natural desire (*hawa*), there is indeed a need for a cautious exercise of restraining forces and for the alignment of institutional incentives that promote justice across time and space.

Criticism levied about the immutability of behavioural norms and their suitability for all human societies independent of time and space are misguided and unfounded. For instance, Kuran (1983, p. 353) argues that behavioural norms derived from a traditional seventh-century Muslim society are not appropriate for the development of modern economies because of differences in the perceptions of reality, intractability of altruistic behaviour, and free-rider problems, among others. While acknowledging the importance of norms, it is also argued that "the principal strength of the Islamic doctrine is also its most glaring weakness" because a normative system cannot be expected to provide "perfectly well-defined and clear constraints on individual economic decisions and to be applicable with equal force to all societies in all stages of development." It is not clear how initial arguments about normative behaviour are transformed, without strong evidence, from praiseworthy to blameworthy ones. It is an implicit subscription to the neoclassical view that positive rather than normative analysis should drive economic science. Indeed, the argument implies that economic man whose worldview is secular and whose behaviour is governed by self-interest and free-riding instincts rather than altruism and consciousness about social responsibility provides a more viable alternative. If, however, the behavioural norms derived from the *Qur'an* and *Sunnah* were to be substituted by the axiomatic rationality of economic man, then Islamic economics would have to abandon its Islamic worldview, and it would, thus, be deprived of its *raison d'être*.

There is a failure to understand the purpose of behavioural norms and the nature of their relationship with the institutional framework. Insofar as normative principles and institutional framework are derived from the Qur'an not from local customs, traditions, and habits, they are immutable and should stand the test of time. However crude and unsophisticated the economies of seventh-century Arabia may be, the normative principles were successfully operationalized by the Prophet *saws* in a society with diverse perceptions of reality and different worldviews. The reality is that even in the absence of the Prophet's (saws) teachings and demonstrative practices, criticism from "modernist" reformers would still be levied against abstract divine injunctions that have little bearing on economic life. It is irrational to abandon a tested system of consistent economic thought that avoids gaps in knowledge and generational crises of identity in the presence of evidence from alternative economic doctrines based on human experience, that is neither strong nor compelling. The reality also, is that, as argued by Kamali (2000, pp. 2–3), every human society guided by the same Islamic norms of behaviour preceded the rest of the world by many centuries in the inception of forward trading and in the issuance of commercial papers, which constitute an integral part of present-day financial systems. The reality, also, is that economies are always in a state of permanent change with technological advances affecting the terms of exchange and means of sustenance, but the behavioural and institutional principles that regulate change are immutable. Several aspects of economic life can, indeed, be instituted, altered, and improved through new policy and legislation, and this argument applies with equal force to an ideal economy, the organizing principles of which are derived from authentic sources of knowledge. As noted by Stiglitz (2017, p. 629), the critical norm that should be used in the assessment of policy changes is that "change is desirable only if it improves social welfare, taking into account the impacts on distribution. The objective of policy is not to maximize GDP." GDP is merely a measure of economic activity not human welfare, and as argued by Nutter (1968) also, it seems that output and growth in output have become ends in themselves. Indeed, the objective of economic and social policies is not to pursue different labyrinths of prosperity without adhering to the norms of equity and justice. Thus, it may be difficult for a secular mind in a secular society to understand the bare essentials of behavioural norms and institutional framework deriving from the Islamic worldview. And it is more difficult to establish the foundations of an ideal economy if Muslim scholars and jurists who have the ability to effect change by elucidating authentic knowledge and promoting justice, choose simply to resist it.

Institutional Framework of an Organic *Iqtiṣād*-Driven System

As noted above, there is a tendency to use the terms "rules of behaviour," "rules of conduct," and "institutions" interchangeably, but it may be useful to distinguish, hereafter, between normative rules and institutional structure. The distinction is important because it is for institutions to impose constraints on individual conduct that are consistent with the normative principles derived from the Qur'an and operationalized by the Prophet (saws). The role of institutions is to enforce the law and demand compliance with particular rules of conduct and human interaction. It is noted that there is a tendency to conceive institutions as the rules of the game in a society. North (1990, p. 3) defines institutions as "humanly devised constraints that shape human interaction." Also, Aoki (2001, p. 275) argues that "an institution constrains each agent's action choices through the beliefs implied by it," and further contends that in the absence of constraints, unenforceable laws cannot be qualified as institutions. It is noted that institutions differ from organizations, which are created, according to North (1990, p. 7), to take advantage of the opportunities determined by institutions in the society in accordance with the standard constraints of economic theory. However, as organizations evolve, they also transform institutions. It is the interaction between institutions and organizations that is conducive to institutional change, but economic theory plays an important role in creating opportunities, developing organizations, and changing institutions.

Thus, a distinction between rules of conduct and institutions may not be necessary when both the norms of behaviour and constraints are designed by the society, and economic theory is derived from a secular worldview. For an ideal *iqtiṣād* system however, this distinction is crucial because the normative rules of behaviour with respect to which institutional constraints are imposed, are derived from the Qur'an, not defined by the society. It is crucial that the constraints imposed by institutions are accompanied by a system of incentives that guides individual behaviour in consideration of social and economic choices. The definition and alignment of incentives depend, in turn, on the conceptions of man and society, and on the way in which a receptive mind (*'aql*) and heart (*qalb*) make logical interpretations of reality and choices based on belief in reward and punishment in the hereafter. It is clear that a paradigm shift cannot be based on a mixture of Islamic and secular worldviews, a blend of truth and falsehood, which leads to confusion and uncertainty about normative rules, shared beliefs, and institutional constraints and incentives. The ultimate objective of the institutional framework for an ideal *iqtiṣād* system is to achieve economic justice in the use and allocation of resources, production, and exchange, as well as in the distribution of income and wealth. Following the above discussion about normative behaviour, the focus is placed, hereafter, on the properties of the institutional structure, including the notions of property, contracts, markets, risk-sharing, wealth, work, cooperation, and competition.

Property and Property Rights

The organization of economic and social activities requires justice and harmony in human interactions. This can only be achieved with a recognition for all individuals of the fundamental right to property. It is possible to define property as a set of claims, powers, liabilities, and duties attached with an asset. An early theory of property rights from a Western perspective dates back to the seventeenth century's work about a normative theory of the creation of property rights by Locke (1680, p. 274), who argued that "Though the earth and all inferior creatures be common to men, yet every man has a property in his own person. This nobody has any right to but himself. The labour of his body, and the work of his hands, we may say, are properly his. Whatsoever, then, he removes out of the state that nature hath provided and left it in, he hath mixed his labour with, and joined to it something that is his own, and thereby makes it his property." He further contended that "government has no other end but the preservation of property." The line of argument that private property, which exists before government, derives from natural law and natural rights and that original appropriation occurs through labour, is shared to some extent by Adam Smith (1901 [2007], p. 129), who states in *The Wealth of Nations* that "The property which every man has in his own labour, as it is the original foundation of all other property, so it is the most sacred and inviolable."

These important insights are not new, however, since the institution of property rights has a rich and long history in Islam, which precedes the above intellectual insights by almost a millennium. The recognition of legitimate property rights to all human beings irrespective of faith, gender, or race, implies that Muslim women enjoyed, indeed, property rights centuries before women in Western countries in particular. There are also Qur'anic injunctions against eating up each other's property by false means, or using it as bait for the authorities to devour a portion of other's property knowingly.[33] It is incumbent also on guardians to provide orphans their property as soon as they are found to possess sound judgement in protecting their interests.[34] These rules represent a clear recognition of the important role of private property in the conduct of social and economic affairs. As noted by Mirakhor and Askari (2015, p. 80), there are three bases of private property in Islam. The first source of property includes property based on natural resources obtained from a combination of personal skills and technologies. It includes also income from self-made assets as well as assets acquired in exchange of the product of labour. The second and third sources include property acquired through transfer and inheritance from producers, respectively. Thus, whereas the first source of private property is consistent with the Lockean theory as it relates to personal abilities and effort, it is the second and third sources that provide the necessary basis for the rules of distributive justice to operate.

The notion of economic justice in *iqtiṣād* is founded on the fundamental principles that Allah swt is the ultimate owner of all resources, that the right of access to resources is universal, that no individual should be excluded from opportunities to combine mental and physical abilities with resources, that work is a primary source of property-rights claims, that claims can be transferred through gifts and-or inheritance, and that no other claims to property rights can be deemed legitimate. As noted by Mirakhor and Askari (2019, p. 193), "instantaneous property rights claims that do not result from labor or gifts, such as theft, bribery, gambling, rent on money or from prohibited activities, are not recognized as legitimate." Thus, distributive justice is concerned with economic relationships, which result, by their very nature, in the creation of property rights through combinations of resources and skills or in the transfer of rights among parties. As argued by Phelps (1991, p. 164), economic justice is related to relationships in terms of "collaboration in production, trade in consumer goods, and the provision of collective goods. There is typically room for mutual gain from such exchange, especially voluntary exchange." It is further argued that distributive justice is justice in the arrangements for the distribution of gains among participants in accordance with individual contributions, efforts, and opportunity costs. Given these definitions, it is still unclear, however, how economic justice can be achieved if property rights are regulated by economic theories, economic laws, and economic institutions that have no bearing on the promotion of justice. In this respect, Stiglitz (2017, p. 631) recognizes the impact of abuses of property rights and monopoly powers, and suggests that a weakening of intellectual property rights, and restrictions on abuses of monopoly powers in the granting of patents can improve not only the static efficiency of the economy, but also the ways in which the fruits of innovation are shared, and incomes are distributed.

These important insights are consistent with the argument proposed by Baqir as-Sadr (1982 [1994], pp. 9–10), and explained in other chapters, that justice is not a scientific idea but when it attaches itself to an idea, it transforms it into a doctrine that is intrinsically different from scientific thinking. Thus, the notions of private property, economic freedom, and prohibition of interest are connected with the Islamic doctrine of economics only because they are imprinted with justice. In contrast, economic laws usually expressed as scientific explanations of economic phenomena, are not imprinted with the seal of justice because they are mere descriptions of economic reality rather than normative rules driven by economic justice. For instance, the iron law of wages, which stipulates that labourers should be entitled to remuneration not exceeding the means of bare sustenance, alienates justice as a mere theory and a futile illusion that is irrelevant to policy formulation or justification. Thus, when economic laws and distributive justice belong to different realms, it is difficult to conceive laws aimed simultaneously at the protection of property rights and the promotion of justice.

In contrast, it is possible to conceive justice-imbued principles of property rights consistent with the Islamic worldview as argued by Askari, Iqbal, and Mirakhor (2015). It is crucial to acknowledge, first, the ultimate ownership of all property and assets rests with Creator of all things.

It is from the ultimate owner that a conditional right of possession is transferred to the collectivity of humans in order to fulfil the duties attached with their status of vicegerents on earth. This transfer establishes the right of collectivity to the resources provided as means of sustenance by the ultimate owner. Access to the natural bounties should be provided to all on the basis of equal opportunities in order for individuals to combine resources with human labour for the production of goods and services. The transfer of property created from the combination of labour and resources does not diminish the original rights of collectivity to the natural resources or goods and services. It is possible to derive two corollaries from the above fundamental principles. First, an individual is entitled to property rights only through the combination of resources with his/her own labour or through transfer from other individuals with the means of exchange or inheritance. Second, it is also crucial to recognize the immutability of property rights in the sense that the rights to property acquired through the application of creative labour on resources imply priority in the possession, use, and exchange of the goods and products, but do not annul the original property rights of the ultimate owner, the Creator, and Provider of all things.

In addition to the above principles, it is important to acknowledge the duty of sharing part of income generated from property given the nature of the trust covenant between the ultimate owner and trustee. The Qur'an explains the purpose of the duty of *zakāh* alms as purification of one's wealth from the right of others. It is not an act of favour or voluntary charity but an obligatory redemption of the rights of the poor and the needy, whose human dignity must be protected. The final principle imposes another limitation to property rights in the sense that the destruction, waste, squandering, and use of property for unlawful ends are prohibited. Thus, the Western conception of property rights as conferring to individuals an absolute freedom to dispose of property as he/she wishes is refuted from an Islamic perspective. The absolute ownership belongs rather to the Creator and Provider of all things, and transfer of resources to the collectivity of humankind is a matter of entrusting the responsibilities to rule according to His will and be just to all creation.

The above principles imply that an individual unable to work, for whatever reason, should not be denied the benefits of the original right granted to the collectivity to access the resources on the basis of equal opportunities. It is clear also that the primary sources of poverty and inequality lie in the existence of rules that restrict access to resource endowments and distort the exchange and transfer of property rights. Given the weaker or weakening mental or physical capabilities, the old and poor tend to be regarded as a burden to society because of their limited ability to contribute to society through creative labour. Whereas the focus is often placed on the protection of private property against the threat of government expropriation, rent-seeking through non-productive profit activities should be recognized as a violation of the property rights of others. Insofar as rent-seeking does not entail the application of one's labour to resources in order to create property rights, a claim on property rights accrued through the creative labour of others is clearly illegitimate. It may be argued that the notion of rent-seeking is intractable because it is based on subjective value judgements, and that conventional economics should be purged of any moral content if it aspires to the status of economic science. From the perspective of an ideal economy based on the *iqtiṣād* paradigm however, moral questions are central to the normative definition of an ideal structure of property rights, where relative individual rights are recognized, respected, and protected.

It is difficult, indeed, to abide by rent-seeking and interest-based arrangements in the absence of precise economic logic that justifies profit seeking activities. The very definition of rent-seeking as non-productive profit activities implies the appropriation of a share of property rights created by others without a commensurate exposure to the economic risks associated with the use of resources. The prohibition of interest in Islam can, thus, be justified by the absence of risk-sharing in the creation of property rights through the application of creative labour to original resources. The rent-seeking activities are not only distortive of the mechanisms of creation and transfer of property rights, but they are also the source of oppression and exploitation, income and wealth disparities, financial crises and economic recessions, and poverty amid plenty.

The central contradiction of capitalism, as argued by Thomas Piketty (2014, p. 571), is that "a market economy based on private property, if left to itself, contains powerful forces of convergence, associated in particular with the diffusion of knowledge and skills, but it also contains powerful forces of divergence, which are potentially threatening to democratic societies and to the values of social justice on which they are based." The destabilizing force does not lie, indeed, in human knowledge and skills, which can be applied to resources in order to create property rights, but in the capital, which is used to claim rights on income generated by others, without sharing the risks of economic activities, and without one's own creative labour. This implies that the existing property, or wealth accumulated in the past, is bound to increase at a higher rate than the growth rate at which the uncertain rights to property may accrue from creative labour. Thus, it is in a market economy where the structure of private property is distorted by interest rates that the private rate of return on capital is bound to remain significantly and persistently higher than the growth rate of income and output.

Thus, an ideal *iqtiṣād*-driven system should be based on this unique set of principles about property rights, which derive directly from the Islamic worldview. These principles do not rely on the relative views and changing beliefs of individuals and society, but reflect the unity of creation, the duties of vicegerency, the endowment of resources in due balance, and the provision of means of sustenance, including human intelligence and reason. It is impossible for Islamic economics to reorganize the economy in ways that alleviate poverty, reduce income disparities, and promote shared prosperity, without a structure of property rights conceived within the realm of justice. There is a need to redefine the rules governing the creation and transfer of property rights so that opportunities to access resources, including information, and intellectual property rights are available to all, and incomes are distributed on equitable basis.

Contracts and Contractual Obligations

It is clear from the discussion above that the conduct of economic activities requires cooperation and coordination among parties. In addition to the clarity with which the bases of property rights and rules of transfer should be defined in the realm of justice, transactions between parties should be also regulated accordingly. The institution of contract defines the time-dependent obligations that parties are expected to fulfil in order to achieve the ultimate objectives of the contract. There is a clear command to all believers, in the very first sentence of Chapter 5 of the Qur'an, to honour all contracts (*'ukūd*).[35] Any promise should be made with the serious intent to fulfil it because it carries an absolute obligation to honour it. The concept of contract is fundamental to Islamic law (*Sharī'ah*), which is contractual in essence. The original Covenant between man and Allah swt (*mīthāq*) is an acknowledgement by all human souls of Allah's Lordship, and it is a conscious and willing submission to Allah's Will and obedience to His Law during the course of man's life on earth.[36]

As argued by Attas (1993, p. 74), the man of Islam is bound ultimately by the Covenant that his soul has sealed with God, not by the social contract, "though he lives and works with the bounds of social polity and authority and contributes his share towards the social good and though he behaves *as if* a social contract was in force" (italics in original). This implies that an act of injustice against other individuals or against the society is a violation of the Covenant with God, and thus, an act of injustice against one's own soul by placing it in the wrong course. Thus, the fulfilment of obligations stemming from man's Covenant with God and man's agreements with others are inherently related. The Covenant with God is the dominant concept that lies at the core of the Islamic worldview of Being and regulates other aspects of man's life on earth both as an individual and as member of a collectivity. It is mandatory for both parties to an agreement to hold a genuine intent to enter into it, because the duty of rule compliance to contractual obligations applies to the relationship of humans to their Creator as well as to one another.

The institution of contact is governed, as with that of property rights, by a consistent set of principles that derive from the *Shari'ah's* perspective on contracts and contractual obligations. Following Kamali (2000), the permissibility of transactions and contracts (*ibahah*) is usually considered as the first principle of the law of contracts. The Islamic law of transactions (*fiqh al-mu'āmalāt*) implies that transactions are, by default, permissible unless there is evidence of clear prohibition. The rules of evidence operate in the opposite direction with respect to acts of worship and devotional matters (*'ibādāt*), where the basic assumption is prohibition unless there is evidence of clear validation. This reversal in the balance of evidence about legal validity and prohibition is reflective of in the nature of man's covenant with his Lord and his contractual agreements with others. Since the purpose of man's creation is *'ibādah*, acts of devotion from prayer (*salah*), fasting (*siyam*), regular charity (*zakat*), and pilgrimage (*haj*) to supplication (*doā*), and remembrance (*dhikr*) are predetermined by Allah swt, the true Object of Worship (*Ilāh*).[37] Innovation in worship is not permissible because acts of service are performed for the sake of Allah alone and approved by Him alone. In contrast, contracts between individuals are governed by the liberty granted to interested parties to provide informed consent. Permissibility is the rule because a mere presumption of prohibition in the absence of clear evidence of unlawfulness would impose unnecessary restrictions on the freedom of enterprise and innovation. Thus insofar as economic transactions are concerned, whereas there is no ruling on permissible matters, there is clear explanation in the *Qur'an* and the *Sunnah* regarding prohibitions.

It is Allah's wisdom that He gave clear guidance about the lawful (*halāl*) and the unlawful (*harām*), and remained silent about other matters. For those who understand the elaborated verses of the Qur'an, the question is asked, indeed, as to who has forbidden the adornments and pure means of sustenance that Allah has provided to believers in this worldly life.[38] There is also is clear message not to hold unlawful the good things that Allah has made lawful.[39] It is not for humans to falsely describe with their tongue this is lawful and this is unlawful, because this is the prerogative of the Lawgiver.[40] Thus in application of the principle of permissibility, it is not incumbent on parties to provide evidence on the permissibility of contractual agreements. The contract may thus be deemed valid provided that there is no clear text of prohibition. The permissibility rule covers a wider scope of economic transactions than the specific areas of prohibited transactions, facilitating thereby the functions of production, exchange, and transfer of property rights while ensuring justice in dynamic economic systems and dynamic economies and changing societies.

The second principle is the provision of ease and prevention of hardship. Again, there is clear evidence from the Qur'an that Allah *swt* intends to provide ease and not create hardship in the fulfilment of man's duties on earth, including matters of worship.[41] Allah (*swt*) did not impose any hardship in the religion.[42] A relief from specific duties is conditional on human ability, as there is no blame on the weak, or on the sick, or on those who have nothing to spend.[43] Indeed, Allah *swt* does not burden a soul beyond its capacity,[44] and does not wish to place man in hardship.[45] The Prophet *saa* reminded his companions that they have been sent to make things easy and not to make them difficult.[46] As argued by Kamali (2000, p. 71), the principle of provision of ease and prevention of hardship are usually regarded as part of the objectives of Islamic Law (*Maqāṣid as-Sharī'ah*). They are also intrinsically related to other legal maxims such as the notions that necessity renders the unlawful lawful, and hardship attracts alleviation, and when a matter narrows down, it should be widened. Thus, contractual stipulations included to facilitate the satisfaction of particular needs of contractual parties or prevent hardship in the fulfilment of their obligations are, in principle, valid insofar as the provision of ease and prevention of hardship do not alter the nature of the contract itself and violate its ultimate purpose.

It is natural that only lawful acts sanctioned by Islamic law may form the basis of an agreement. The freedom of contract (*hurriyat atta'āqud*), which constitutes the third principle, is thus, of a conditional nature. Indeed, it is usually argued that parties are at liberty to create a contract and define contractual obligations through mutual agreement, but the *effects* of the contract are rather determined by the *Shari'ah*. For instance, the terms of transfer of property rights in a sale agreement are determined by the *Shari'ah*, which protects the rights of both parties. A voidable stipulation (*shart fāsid*), which may be beneficial to one party, can be nevertheless invalidated by *Shari'ah* on the basis that it violates the purpose of the contract. Thus, stipulations that are neither valid nor voidable are deemed to be null and void (*bātil*), which implies that while the contract is upheld, the condition is completely disregarded.

The rationale behind these principles is to protect property rights, and ensure justice by avoiding the conditions where the freedom of contract implies entry into unchartered territory of potential abuse and contractual ambiguity. The essential requirements of a contract include the freedom to make an offer (*ījāb*) and that of providing acceptance (*qabūl*), but it is also important to prevent conflicts, abuse, fraud, exploitation, and injustice among parties. There are various views about the notions of risk, uncertainty, and ambiguity (*gharar*). A contract of sale may be deemed void and null depending on the degree ignorance and informational asymmetry about the terms of the contract, including the substance of the subject matter of sale by buyers or sellers. There may be, indeed, contractual conditions characterized by incomplete information about the available quantity, time of completion, prospects of delivery, and terms of payment, and in particular for contracts where payment or delivery occurs at a future date. Kamali (2000, p. 85) argues that in order for *gharar* to have legal consequences, it must be excessive not trivial, and directly affect the subject matter of contracts, among other conditions. However, certain types of fiduciary contracts such as cost-plus-profit sale (*murābahah*) can be deemed invalid independent of the degree of *gharar*. As noted above, justice demands rule compliance, and compliance requires, in turn, clarity about contractual terms, which in turn depends on the availability of accurate and timely information.

The fulfilment of contractual obligations requires also sincerity and truthfulness from both parties, who are expected to demonstrate faithfulness to contractual obligations in the face of increased economic uncertainty. Thus, it is important to recognize the fact that property rights are entrusted to man from Allah (*swt*), and that contractual obligations, which result in the transfer or creation of property through creative labour, are governed by *Shari'ah*, which has its foundation in the Covenant between Allah and man. As Allah (*swt*) does not fail in His Promise, it is incumbent on man to perform their own duties with the sincerity of purpose. It is incumbent on contractual parties to be faithful to each other, refrain from violating property rights, and respect the sanctity of mutual agreements.[47] This will increase the amount of trust among parties, which constitutes an essential element of the social capital in Islam. The terms of trust (*amānah*) and belief (*īman*) share similar verbal roots, and the linkage between trust, trustworthiness, and faith implies that believers are expected to be faithful to contractual obligations. A loss of trust between parties constitutes, however, a serious impediment to the negotiation of contracts and conclusion of agreements. In the absence of trust, the costs of contract monitoring are bound to rise, and complex mechanisms may be needed for the sole purpose of contract enforcement.

It is important to note also that the institutions of contract and trust are pervasive in Islam. Every single public office represents indeed, a contract between the holders of authority and the community, and if confidence and trust between the two parties wane, it is rather difficult to expect compliance with contractual obligations. Thus, while no person has the right to force appropriation or expropriation, it is also permissible for the society to exercise priority rights over private property if individual rights stand in conflict with collective interests. However, the absence of trust stemming from discriminatory treatment based on socioeconomic status, faith, or ethnicity can undermine the necessary process of coordination, which depends on the rules of cooperation. It is only when rulers remain faithful to their contractual obligations to discharge their duties with justice (*qist*) that they can expect the subjects to fulfill their own duties of obedience to leadership.[48] As noted by North (1990, p. 7), past attempts by rulers to devise property-rights mechanisms that serve their own interests were accompanied by higher transaction costs and inefficient systems of property rights. Indeed, it is the rulers, among Muslim communities, who neglected the basic principles of property rights and economic justice, leading to economic decay and fall of Islamic civilization. It is misguided leadership also that sanctioned merchant capitalism and allowed for various aberrations of property rights, resulting in economic injustice and increased income disparities. Thus, the blame is not to be laid on Islam, but on the door of generations of Muslims with secular minds who abandoned the teachings of the Qur'an and failed to internationalize its normative rules of behaviour. It should be laid, principally, at the door of Muslim rulers who gave precedence to secular economic systems over the ideal economy based on the *iqtiṣād* principles derived from the *Qur'an* and the *Sunnah*.

The notion that the poor economic performance of countries with Muslim majorities is due to the prohibition of interest lays the blame on the institution of contract. There is, however, compelling historical evidence from the development of business partnerships which constitute the foundations of capitalism, that it is perfectly possible to protect property rights for all contractual parties and engage in various economic activities, unhindered by interest prohibition. It may be argued that the economic system practised by the Islamic world during the period from the seventh to thirteenth centuries, is not a variant of "merchant capitalism" that predates liberal capitalism, but capitalism with moral foundations. A compelling case is made by Murat Çizakça (2011, p. 29), who argues that various business partnerships are perhaps the most important institutions that emerged in Islamic capitalism, which derives from the fundamental principle of interest prohibition. In the absence of interest (*ribā*), the question arises as to how to combine the key factors of production when capital, labour, and entrepreneurship are owned and supplied by different individuals. What is needed from the perspective of financiers who provide capital for entrepreneurs, is to conceive some form of reward for the risk exposure without violating the principle of interest prohibition. It is the innovative institution of business partnership that provided a viable solution to the important problem of protecting the interests of all parties, including the owners of capital. The rate of interest, which is pre-determined as a percentage of capital is substituted by the rate of return, which is determined on *ex post* basis depending on the outcome of business activities. It attributes the owners of capital with property rights in the form of financial claims on the net assets of the enterprise rather than fixed claims on the property rights of entrepreneurs based on the amount of capital supplied. Thus, business partnerships, based on the permissible contracts of exchange (*bay'*) and trade (*tijārah*), constitute an innovative form of contract designed to protect the property rights of all parties, including those of capitalists, without violating the principle of interest prohibition.

It should be emphasized that in addition to partnership contracts, it is the use of money and credit instruments that facilitated the emergence of Islamic capitalism more than a millennium before the institution of distorted predatory forms of capitalism in the Western world. It is noted that originally, the economy envisioned by Adam Smith invokes the notions of moral duties, benevolence, and sympathy, ordained by the Author of Nature to be internalized by market participants could well be an approximation of the Islamic vision of the economy, as argued by Mirakhor and Askari (2017, p. 74). In an ideal *Iqtiṣād*-driven system, business partnerships remain one of the most important institutions. Part of the reason is that this institution recognizes the impact of uncertainty on the outcome of private enterprise and all economic activities. It recognizes also the importance of risk-sharing in the organization of exchange relationships in the economy. It recognizes also the importance of protecting property rights and regulating the distribution of income among the financiers, entrepreneurs, and labourers. It can also provide the basis for the development of a market economy, where prices are determined through the free forces of supply and demand. Thus, the institution of markets that facilitate exchange provides the final linkage in an *iqtiṣād* system between the institution of property rights, and that of contracts.

Markets and Information

It is clear from the explanation above that the institution of contract derives from the institution of property rights in the sense that it allows parties to combine creative labour and resources to produce new property and distribute new property rights. It can be argued also that the institution of markets is a natural outcome of the two institutions of property rights and contracts in the sense that it allows for the transfer of property rights to third parties that were not necessarily involved in the initial creation of property. Thus, the raison d'être of goods and services markets lies in the institution of the contracts of exchange (*bay'i*) and trade (*tijārah*). In contrast, the rationale behind the existence of stock markets is the institution of business partnerships, which as explained above, results in the creation of financial claims for financiers, which can be traded with third parties.

The institution of markets is built upon the three pillars of property rights, contract and trust, as well as information, which can be useful in the elimination of ambiguity (*gharar*) and the reduction of uncertainty in the formation of expectations. It depends also on the balance between the right not to be harmed and the obligation not to harm others. Market prices are the result of the interaction between the forces of supply and demand. There is undisputable evidence about the development of free markets in Islamic economy, which derives from a firm belief that there should be no interference in the price discovery process. The imposition of taxes on market participants or market transactions was prohibited by the Prophet saws, who created also incentives for non-Muslims to encourage participation in market activities and trade irrespective of differences in economic status, ethnicity, or faith. As noted in Mirakhor and Askari (2017), the travelling non-Muslims were considered guests and non-market losses were guaranteed by the Prophet (*saa*).

The system of rules governing markets includes the removal of barriers to market entry and exit, and the elimination of restrictions on the free movement of goods, services, and resources across markets. It eliminates also restrictions on international trade in the form of taxation of imports and exports. The rules provide also clear definitions of the terms for the completion of trade transactions at future dates, and the state guarantee of enforcement of all contracts. There are also clear prohibitions of price controls, hoarding of commodities and productive resources as well as interference of third parties in the negotiation of contracts, interference with supply before market entrance, and collusion among market participants. The rules governing markets are based on the free and transparent flow of information regarding prices, quantity, and quality of goods, in order to guard against the conditions of ambiguity (*gharar*), which can invalidate the contracts of sale and spot trade in particular.

There is also historical evidence that since unhindered flow of accurate, complete, and timely information is crucial for market efficiency, and compliance with behavioural rules is important for its proper functioning, the office of market supervisor *muhtesib* was instituted to ensure compliance to rules and their internalization before market entry. The current prohibition of insider trading based on access to confidential information before public announcement echoes earlier Islamic ruling about market conduct prohibiting interference with the price discovery mechanism. The free flow of information and rule compliance are conducive to fair and just market prices, which imply the protection of property rights and the sanctity of contracts. Thus, the *muhtesib* plays a crucial role in strengthening the organic relationship between the institutions of property rights and contracts. Indeed, a failure to prevent monopoly practices, market manipulation, fraud, and any activities that undermine the functioning of market mechanism, is conducive to unfair prices, which weaken the incentives to invest and corrode the social capital of trust. These issues are of fundamental concern because increased uncertainty about the production and distribution functions has implications for the conduct of economic and social life.

Risk-Sharing and Shared Prosperity

A coherent doctrine of an ideal *Iqtiṣād* system cannot be conceived without understanding the impact of pervasive uncertainty on all aspects of economic life. Indeed, the institution of private property is based on the combination of resources with labour to create new property rights, but the outcome of this creative combination remains uncertain. Similarly, the institution of contract, which is based on the transfer of existing or newly created property rights among contractual parties, requires compliance with contractual obligations, but the outcome of business agreements remains uncertain as well. It is possible through the prescribed rules of conduct to render the behaviour of economic agents and contractual parties more predictable, but while the risks emanating from economic uncertainty can be reduced, they cannot be completely eliminated.

Thus, the organizing principle of risk sharing in *iqtiṣād* system reflects the contractual imperative that entitlement to property rights is conditional on exposure to the risk of loss and liability. Profit, it is usually argued, comes with liability, and higher returns are commensurate with higher systematic risk. No party to an agreement should be entitled to profit in the absence of liability to losses. Thus, the distinction is clearly made in the *Shari'ah* between lawful and unlawful profit. The economic rationale behind the prohibition of interest lies in the absence of liability under any state of the world. Uncertainty can be defined, indeed, as the existence of multiple possible states of the world that may occur in the future. It is possible, then, for the provider of capital to remain insulated from the adverse effects of uncertainty with contractual stipulations to the effect that liability for losses is waived under all contingencies. The charging of interest can, thus, be regarded as a claim for fixed income proportional to capital, independent of the outcome of economic activities.

From the Islamic perspective, the argument that exchange (*al-bay'i*) is like interest (*ar-ribā*) has been clearly refuted by Allah swt, who has permitted exchange (*al-bay'i*) and prohibited (*ar-ribā*) transactions. The reasons may be intrinsically related to differences in the nature of these transactions as governed by the institution of property rights.[49] The permissibility of the exchange of assets derives from the concomitant exchange of property rights from one party to another. In contrast, *ribā*-based transactions imply the exchange of cashflows today for larger amounts in the future, without the transfer of property rights over the principal from the lender to the borrower. The retention of property rights by the lender is also accompanied by a transfer, at the time of contract conclusion, of the property rights over the fixed income to the lender. As the risks of the transaction are completely borne by the borrower alone, there is a clear violation of property rights in interest-based debt transactions, which renders debt financing impermissible in Islamic finance. In contrast, equity financing is based on the principle of risk-sharing, where financiers assume the liability of losses and are entitled to pro rata income based on the return from business activities subject to economic uncertainty.

Financial instability is an essential feature inherent to all financial systems based on interest-bearing debt. It reflects a profound disconnect between the financial sector and the real economy. Indeed, debt accumulation and higher leverage allow the financial sector to grow independent from the growth rate in the real economy. It allows for the formation of asset bubbles through debt financing, which would ultimately burst leading to banking crises due to debt defaults. The risk of default should not be confused with economic risks because it is a by-product of contractual agreements. Indeed, the rate of return on capital is pre-determined in complete neglect of the reality that rates of return in the real economy can only be determined on ex post basis. The uncertainty about future demand and supply functions and disruptive technologies may lead to losses, resulting in the inability of borrowers to honour the obligations of interest-based contracts. The absence of liability for losses with respect to lenders under all states of nature is reflective of risk transfer to borrowers. In contrast, equity financing provides the contractual basis for the protection of property rights in the sense that a transfer of rights on future income is conditional on the realization of profits. In the absence of profits, there is no obligation to transfer property rights to financiers, and thus, unlike debt, there is no default in equity financing. Thus, the organizing principle of risk sharing in the iqtiṣād system, which of risk-sharing, which promotes equity rather than debt financing, shall strengthen the linkage between the financial sector and the real economy, and provide the basis for shared prosperity.

It is clear from the above discussion about Islamic capitalism that risk-sharing promotes economic justice and shared prosperity as it entitles the different owners of the factors of production to share the income from business activities on a fair and equitable basis. The principle of risk-sharing can also provide some insights into the central contradiction of capitalism, which has serious implications for income distribution. As argued by Thomas Piketty, there is compelling evidence that the rate of return on capital is persistently higher than the rate of growth of output and income. Whereas the rate of income growth depends on the outcome of the essential economic activities of production, exchange, and distribution, the rate of return on capital is function of debt or equity financing. Since the return on equity is, by definition, a positive function of the outcome of economic activities, it cannot conceivably exceed the rate of growth in income and output. This leaves debt financing as the only force of destabilization, as interest payments are fixed on *ex ante* basis, independent of the rate of return in the real economy. It is the transfer of property rights from entrepreneurs and workers to financiers that explains the persistently higher rates of return on capital. Thus, there should be no sanctity for interest-based debt agreements, which undermine economic justice and tilt the distribution of income in favour of financiers through flagrant violations of property rights.

It is the skewed distribution that implies conditions of plenty for a few and scarcity for the many, leading to poverty trap. As noted by Acemoglu and Robinson (2013, p. 454), there is a need to recognize the roots of world inequality and poverty in order to avoid pinning hopes on false promises such as foreign aid. Part of the roots of inequality stems from the central contradiction of capitalism, and serious attempts to eradicate poverty should start by understanding how the economic system functions, how money becomes not just the means of exchange but also the end of it, and how the property rights of the poor and working poor are persistently violated. It is the approval and even admiration of self-interest as an overriding assumption in economic models that sends an unmistakable message of alienation that the poor should be abandoned to their own fate. As poverty is regarded as a matter of individual choice and in the absence of benevolence, there are no genuine policy recommendations aimed at promoting economic justice. In the *iqtiṣād* system, the institution of *zakat* provides the poor with a non-negotiable property right and share in income distribution. Rather than accepting poverty as a predicament, it is important to provide the poor with some sense of empowerment and control over their own life. It is, thus, important to reinforce the institution of risk-sharing in every aspect of economic life in order to rebalance the distribution of property rights, which would equalize the distribution of income and wealth, and establish the foundations for shared prosperity.

Thus, in light of the above discussion, it is clear that the institutional structure of *iqtiṣād* vision of an ideal Islamic economy is composed of three layers. The first dimension is the institution of property rights, which represent a conditional right of possession granted from Allah swt, the Creator of all things and the ultimate owner of all property and assets. The second dimension is the institution of contracts, which governs the exchange and transfer of rights through mutual agreement, and in accordance with the duties and obligations prescribed by the Lawgiver. The third dimension is the institution of markets, which allows for the exchange and transfer of rights to third parties according to normative rules of market conduct that ensure fair prices and economic justice. The organic relationships between the different dimensions depend on compliance with the normative rules of behaviour at each level, as well as on a system of incentives that promote trust, information transparency, and risk-sharing. The three dimensions are sufficient to cover all types of economic activities, those undertaken on individual basis and under contractual agreements, as well as those involving third parties according to market transactions.

It is an institutional structure for an ideal economy that should be judged on the basis of the clarity and coherence of the rules governing the relationships between parties rather than human malpractices and distortions. It is impossible to build an ideal Islamic economy by insulating the institutional dimensions from each other, and arguing that the rules of compliance apply only to others. It is difficult, indeed, to protect property rights without an uncompromising equality before the law. It is difficult also to protect the freedom of agreement without prohibiting contracts that violate property rights. It is difficult also to preserve market integrity without unhindered access to information. It is impossible to promote an ideal Islamic economy without instilling a sense of responsibility, mutual trust, and risk-sharing, which allows for the sharing of economic prosperity.

Given the above behavioural norms and institutional structure of the *iqtiṣād* system, it is impossible to graft some Islamic institutional elements onto conventional economics in an otiose attempt to "Islamize" it, or to graft some value-neutral ideas onto *iqtiṣād* to "secularize" it. From the Western perspective, the prohibition of interest constitutes, as noted by Presley and Sessions (1994, p. 586), perhaps the most controversial aspect of Islamic economics, because the elimination of *ribā* would involve the rewriting of capitalist economics. The far-reaching implications of interest prohibition cannot be ignored, but it is a fond belief in the entire institutional structure and rules of behaviour derived from the *Qur'an* and *Sunnah* that would transform capitalist economics. Given the differences in philosophical foundations, however, it is difficult to suppress the intellectual and spiritual elements of Islam in order to secularize its economic thought, and it is futile to graft Islamic values and institutional structures onto conventional economics to develop a synthetic discipline from heteroclite and disparate elements.

It is important, indeed, to guard against grafting new ideas from neoclassical economics, which has a distaste for institutions. As noted by (Skidelski, 2020, p. 117), some economists "argue that business and other organizations are a transitional phase in the process of making markets more complete." While the shape of business enterprises and markets is bound to change in the knowledge economy, the existential problem of uncertainty will remain. It is important to reflect on the powerful forces that may shape the economic dynamics, such as digital technologies which affect the flow of information and communication. Given the changing nature of secular ideas and economic doctrines, it is difficult to make a synthetic discipline without a compromise of the Islamic worldview. *Iqtiṣād*, on the other hand, has its unique set of rules of behaviour and institutional structures that allow for the organization of an ideal Islamic economy.

The ideal Islamic economic system is flexible to accommodate the changing needs of society, including new production functions, new methods of delivery, new modes of payment, new markets, and new networks of markets, but the norms of behaviour and institutional rules that define the creation and exchange of private property and transfer of property rights are immutable. They are immutable not because Islamic jurisprudence is immune to the confusion and error that some Muslim scholars tend to diffuse, at the behest of secular peers or otherwise, in the interpretation of the sources of Islamic knowledge. They are immutable not because this corpus juris is the product of original intellectual efforts in commercial law and economic issues over centuries of devoted scholarship. They are immutable simply because they flow from the truth that the very Covenant that man sealed with the Lawgiver, is timeless, and thus not subject to discounting, devaluation, or depreciation.

NOTES

1. The Qur'an is described in the Qur'an itself as the absolute truth (*Alhaaqqah* 69:51), without any crookedness (*Az-Zumar* 39:28), or falsehood (*Fussilat* 41:42), and which cannot be produced by other than Allah swt (*Yunus* 10:37).
2. *Sahih Al-Bukhari* 50 Book 2, *Hadith* 43.
3. On the notion of vicegerency, reference can be made to the Qur'anic verse (*Al-Baqarah* 2:30) *"Behold, thy Lord said to the angels: "I will create a vicegerent on earth." They said: "Wilt Thou place therein one who will make mischief therein and shed blood? whilst we do celebrate Thy praises and glorify Thy holy (name)?" He said: "I know what ye know not.""* (*Al-Baqarah* 2:30).
4. Reference to the concept of trust (*amānah*) in the Qur'an (*Al-Ahzab* 33:72) as follows *"We did indeed offer the Trust to the Heavens and the Earth and the Mountains; but they refused to undertake it, being afraid thereof: but man undertook it;- He was indeed unjust and foolish."* (*Al-Ahzab* 33:72).
5. The status of vicegerency applies to all human beings including prophets, as stated in (*ṣād* 38:26) *"O David! We did indeed make thee a vicegerent on earth: so judge thou between men in truth (and justice): Nor follow thou the lusts (of thy heart), for they will mislead thee from the Path of Allah."*
6. The notion of fitrah refers to the pattern upon which mankind was created, as explained in (*Ar-Rum* 30:30) *"So set thou thy face steadily and truly to the Faith: (establish) Allah's handiwork according to the pattern on which He has made mankind: no change (let there be) in the work (wrought) by Allah: that is the standard Religion: but most among mankind understand not."*
7. On the notion of forgetfulness of the principal covenant, reference can be made to (*Taha* 20:115) *"We had already, beforehand, taken the covenant of Adam, but he forgot: and We found on his part no firm resolve."*
8. The linkage between the provision of means of sustenance and duties of vicegerency is clear from the following Qur'anic verse (*Al- 'Araf 7:10*)

"It is We Who have placed you with authority on earth, and provided you therein with means for the fulfilment of your life: small are the thanks that ye give!"

9. Reference can be made to *(An-Nahl 16:14)* "It is He Who has made the sea subject, that ye may eat thereof flesh that is fresh and tender, and that ye may extract therefrom ornaments to wear; and thou seest the ships therein that plough the waves, that ye may seek (thus) of the bounty of Allah and that ye may be grateful." and to *(Al-Jathiyah 45:12)* "It is Allah Who has subjected the sea to you, that ships may sail through it by His command, that ye may seek of his Bounty, and that ye may be grateful."

10. In this respect, reference can be made also to *(Al-Anbya 21:32)* "And We have made the heavens as a canopy well-guarded: yet do they turn away from the Signs which these things (point to)!" and to *(Al-Hijr 15:19)* "And the earth We have spread out (like a carpet); set thereon mountains firm and immovable; and produced therein all kinds of things in due balance."

11. There is evidence from the Qur'an that the means of sustenance are provided to all living creatures as in *(Al-Hijr 15:20)* "And We have provided therein means of subsistence for you and for those for whose sustenance ye are not responsible."

12. For instance, the notion of *isti'mar* can be understood from the Qur'anic verse *(Hud 11:61)* "To the Thamud People (We sent) Salih, one of their own brethren. He said: "O my people! Worship Allah: ye have no other god but Him. It is He Who hath produced you from the earth and settled you therein: then ask forgiveness of Him, and turn to Him (in repentance): for my Lord is (always) near, ready to answer.""

13. As with the notion of *isti'mar*, the term *'imarah*, which appears in the Qur'an, conveys also the meaning of building and settlement, as in *(At-Tawba 9:17)* "It is not for such as join gods with Allah, to visit or maintain the mosques of Allah while they witness against their own souls to infidelity."

14. It is clear from the Qur'an that Allah swt provides guidance for man in all aspects of life on earth, as in *(Al-Isra 17:95)* "Say, 'If there were settled, on earth, angels walking about in peace and quiet, We should certainly have sent them down from the heavens an angel for a messenger.'"

15. With respect to the qualities and character of the Noble Prophet *(saa)*, the Qur'an states in *(Al-Qalam 68:4)* "And thou (standest) on an exalted standard of character."

16. The Qur'an states that Allah swt provides provision to whomsoever He wills as in *(Ash-Shuraa 42:12)* "To Him belong the keys of the heavens and the earth: He enlarges and restricts. The Sustenance to whom He will: for He knows full well all things."

17. Reference can be made to the Qur'an on Allah (swt)'s perfect knowledge about everything, as in *(Al-An'ām 6:59)* "With Him are the keys of the unseen, the treasures that none knoweth but He. He knoweth whatever there

is on the earth and in the sea. Not a leaf doth fall but with His knowledge: there is not a grain in the darkness (or depths) of the earth, nor anything fresh or dry (green or withered), but is (inscribed) in a record clear (to those who can read)."

18. With respect to the notion that Allah (swt) provides sustenance in due balance, reference can be made also to *(As-Shuraa 42:12) "To Him belong the keys of the heavens and the earth: He enlarges and restricts. The Sustenance to whom He will: for He knows full well all things."*
19. The Qur'an states that bounties of Allah swt are not restricted to particular people, but extended to whom He wills, as made clear in *(Al-Isra 17:20) "Of the bounties of thy Lord We bestow freely on all- These as well as those: The bounties of thy Lord are not closed (to anyone)."*
20. The notion that the bounties of Allah swt are unlimited is clearly explained by the Qur'an in *(Ibrahim 14:34) "And He giveth you of all that ye ask for. But if ye count the favours of Allah, never will ye be able to number them. Verily, man is given up to injustice and ingratitude."*
21. It is incumbent on man, indeed, to strive despite the human characteristics of impatience and forgetfulness, to commit himself to norms of conduct consistent with the soul's covenant with the Creator. The Qur'an states in *(Al-Ma'arij 70:19–34)* that *"Truly man was created very impatient, fretful when evil touches him, and niggardly when good reaches him. Not so those devoted to Prayer, those who remain steadfast to their prayer, and those in whose wealth is a recognised right for the (needy) who asks and him who is prevented (for some reason from asking), and those who hold to the truth of the Day of Judgment, and those who fear the displeasure of their Lord, for their Lord's displeasure is the opposite of peace and tranquility, and those who guard their chastity, except with their wives and the (captives) whom their right hands possess,- for (then) they are not to be blamed, but those who trespass beyond this are transgressors, and those who respect their trusts and covenants, and those who stand firm in their testimonies, and those who guard (the sacredness) of their worship." (Al-Ma'arij 70:19–34).*
22. The Qur'an states that the provision and restriction of bounties is for testing purposes, as in *(Al-Fajr 89:15–16) "Now, as for man, when his Lord trieth him, giving him honour and gifts, then saith he, (puffed up), "My Lord hath honoured me." But when He trieth him, restricting his subsistence for him, then saith he (in despair), "My Lord hath humiliated me!""*
23. Another evidence about the wisdom behind restrictions of bounties is provided by the Qur'an in *(Al-An'am 6:165) "It is He Who hath made you (His) agents, inheritors of the earth: He hath raised you in ranks, some above others: that He may try you in the gifts He hath given you: for thy Lord is quick in punishment: yet He is indeed Oft-forgiving, Most Merciful."*
24. It is Allah (swt)'s wisdom that there are intrinsic differences between people and orders of hierarchy, as stated in the Qur'an *(Hud 11:118)*

"If thy Lord had so willed, He could have made mankind one people: but they will not cease to dispute."

25. There are clear Qur'anic injunctions to fulfil the obligations of every member of the society toward others, and to provide for the rights of the poor and needy, as stated in *(Al-Fajr 89:17–18)* *"Nay, nay! but ye honour not the orphans! Nor do ye encourage one another to feed the poor!"*
26. The relationship between faith and deeds is clearly explained in the Qur'an, as in *(Al-Imran 3:92)* *"By no means shall ye attain righteousness unless ye give (freely) of that which ye love; and whatever ye give, of a truth Allah knoweth it well."*
27. The Qur'an requires man to seek balance in all aspects of life, including moderate spending, as stated in *(Al-Isra 17:29)* *"Make not thy hand tied (like a niggard's) to thy neck, nor stretch it forth to its utmost reach, so that thou become blameworthy and destitute."*
28. The suggestion that Allah's hand is fettered, and that spending is limited, rendering thereby resources scarce, is strongly rejected in the Qur'an, as stated in *(Al-Ma'idah 5:64)* *"The Jews say: "Allah's hand is tied up." Be their hands tied up and be they accursed for the (blasphemy) they utter. Nay, both His hands are widely outstretched: He giveth and spendeth (of His bounty) as He pleaseth."*
29. There is, indeed, wisdom in Allah (swt)'s restrictions on bounties, as explained in the Qur'an *(Ash-Shura 42:27)* *"If Allah were to enlarge the provision for His Servants, they would indeed transgress beyond all bounds through the earth; but he sends (it) down in due measure as He pleases. For He is with His Servants Well-acquainted, Watchful."*
30. Sahih al-Bukhari 52, Book 2, Hadith 45.
31. There is clear evidence in the Qur'an that compliance with divine law and commitment to the cause of Allah (swt) is conducive to happiness in this life and the hereafter, as stated in *(Al-Ma'idah 5:66)* *"If only they had stood fast by the Law, the Gospel, and all the revelation that was sent to them from their Lord, they would have enjoyed happiness from every side."*
32. The notion that religious beliefs cannot be imposed against the will of people is clearly stated in the Qur'an, as in *(Al-Baqarah 2:256)* *"Let there be no compulsion in religion, truth stands out clear from error. Whoever rejects evil and believes in Allah hath grasped the most trustworthy handhold, that never breaks. And Allah heareth and knoweth all things."*
33. There are several Qur'anic verses that deal with economic injustice, including the violation of property rights, as in *(Al-Baqarah 2:188)* *"And do not eat up your property among yourselves for vanities, nor use it as bait for the judges, with intent that ye may eat up wrongfully and knowingly a little of (other) people's property."*
34. The protection of property rights applies to all, including weakly minded people and orphans, as stated in the Qur'an, in *(An-Nisa 4:5–6)* *"To those*

weak of understanding make not over your property, which Allah hath made a means of support for you, but feed and clothe them therewith, and speak to them words of kindness and justice. Make trial of orphans until they reach the age of marriage; if then ye find sound judgment in them, release their property to them; but consume it not wastefully, nor in haste against their growing up. If the guardian is well-off, let him claim no remuneration, but if he is poor, let him have for himself what is just and reasonable. When ye release their property to them, take witnesses in their presence: But all-sufficient is Allah in taking account."

35. There are several Qur'anic verses providing clear injunctions to fulfil covenants, including *(Al-Mā'idah 5:1)* "O ye who believe! fulfil (all) obligations. Lawful unto you (for food) are all four-footed animals, with the exceptions named: But animals of the chase are forbidden while ye are in the sacred precincts or in pilgrim garb: for Allah doth command according to His will and plan."

36. Reference to the original Covenant in the Qur'an can be found in several verses including *(Al-A'raf 7:172)* "When thy Lord drew forth from the Children of Adam—from their loins— their descendants, and made them testify concerning themselves, (saying): "Am I not your Lord (who cherishes and sustains you)?" They said: "Yea! We do testify!" (This), lest ye should say on the Day of Judgment: "Of this we were never mindful""

37. The Qur'an states in many verses, indeed, that all creation celebrate the praise of Allah swt in worship, as in *(Al-Isra 17:44)* "The seven heavens and the earth, and all beings therein, declare His glory: there is not a thing but celebrates His praise; And yet ye understand not how they declare His glory! Verily He is Oft-Forbear, Most Forgiving!"

38. It is for the Lawgiver, alone to decide about the lawfulness of the adornments and means of sustenance that He provided, as stated in the Qur'an, *(Al-A'raf 7:32)* "Say: Who hath forbidden the beautiful (gifts) of Allah, which He hath produced for His servants, and the things, clean and pure, (which He hath provided) for sustenance? Say: They are, in the life of this world, for those who believe, (and) purely for them on the Day of Judgment. Thus do We explain the signs in detail for those who understand."

39. There are also clear Qur'anic injunctions against the forbiddance of adornments that Allah swt has made lawful, as in *(Al-Ma'idah 5:87)* "O ye who believe! make not unlawful the good things which Allah hath made lawful for you, but commit no excess: for Allah loveth not those given to excess."

40. It is also noted that Allah (swt) has clearly defined the lawful and unlawful, and it is allowed for human beings to alter these distinctions, forging thereby lies against Allah swt, as stated in the Qur'an, *(An-Nahl 16:116)* "But say not—for any false thing that your tongues may put forth, "This is lawful, and this is forbidden," so as to ascribe false things to Allah. For those who ascribe false things to Allah, will never prosper."

41. The Qur'an provides many indications about the ease with which acts of worship can be carried, as with the duty of fasting during the month of Ramadhan, as stated in *(Al-Baqarah 2:185)* *"Ramadhan is the (month) in which was sent down the Qur'an, as a guide to mankind, also clear (signs) for guidance and judgment (between right and wrong). So every one of you who is present (at his home) during that month should spend it in fasting, but if anyone is ill, or on a journey, the prescribed period (should be made up) by days later. Allah intends every facility for you; He does not want to put to difficulties."*
42. There is, indeed, no hardship in seeking the pleasure of Allah *(swt)*, as indicated in the Qur'an *(Al-Hajj 22:78)* *"And strive in His cause as ye ought to strive, (with sincerity and under discipline). He has chosen you, and has imposed no difficulties on you in religion; it is the cult of your father Abraham. It is He Who has named you Muslims, both before and in this (Revelation); that the Messenger may be a witness for you, and ye be witnesses for mankind!"*
43. The fulfilment of duties in Islam is, indeed, function of individual abilities, but sincerity to Allah (swt) remains the principal condition for the acceptance of good deeds, as indicated in the Qur'an *(At-Tawba 9:91)* *"There is no blame on those who are infirm, or ill, or who find no resources to spend (on the cause), if they are sincere (in duty) to Allah and His Messenger: no ground (of complaint) can there be against such as do right: and Allah is Oft-forgiving, Most Merciful."*
44. It is clear that Allah (swt), the Just does not put obligations on anyone beyond his capacity, as stated in the Qur'an *(Al-Baqarah 2:286)* *"On no soul doth Allah place a burden greater than it can bear. It gets every good that it earns, and it suffers every ill that it earns."*
45. The Qur'an includes many injunctions to obey the commands of Allah (swt) to the best of one's capabilities, in every aspect of worship, even in preparation for prayers, as indicated in *(Al-Ma'idah 5:6)* *"Allah doth not wish to place you in a difficulty, but to make you clean, and to complete his favour to you, that ye may be grateful."*
46. Sahih Al-Bukhari Hadith 635.
47. The Qur'an includes several verses about the sanctity of covenants, including statements that Allah swt never fails in His promise, as in *(Az-Zumar 39:20)* *"But it is for those who fear their Lord. Those lofty mansions, one above another, have been built: beneath them flow rivers (of delight): (such is) the Promise of Allah: never doth Allah fail in (His) promise,"* and in *(Ar-Ra'd 13:31)* *"But the Unbelievers,- never will disaster cease to seize them for their (ill) deeds, or to settle close to their homes, until the promise of Allah come to pass, for, verily, Allah will not fail in His promise."* There is also Allah (swt)'s promise to be fulfilled about serving justice on the day of judgement, which is clear in *(Al-Imran 3:9)* *""Our Lord! Thou art*

He that will gather mankind together against a day about which there is no doubt; for Allah never fails in His promise.""
48. There is no doubt that obedience to rulers is not unconditional. The Qur'an in (An-Nisa 4:59) states, indeed, that *"O ye who believe! Obey Allah, and obey the Messenger, and those charged with authority among you. If ye differ in anything among yourselves, refer it to Allah and His Messenger, if ye do believe in Allah and the Last Day: That is best, and most suitable for final determination."* Also, Ali Ibn Abi Talib (raa) reported that the Noble Prophet (saa) said "there is no obedience to anyone if it is disobedience to Allah. Verily obedience is only in good conduct." (Sahih al-Bukhari 7257 and Sahih Muslim 1840).
49. The Qur'an makes a clear distinction between trade and usury as it states in *(Al-Baqarah 2:275)* that the one indulging in *riba* does not stand but stands one who is driven to madness, and *"that is because they say: "Trade is like usury," but Allah hath permitted trade and forbidden usury."*

References

Acemoglu, Daron., and James A. Robinson. 2013. *Why Nations Fail: The Origins of Power, Prosperity and Poverty.* London: Profile Books Ltd.
Al-Attas, Syed Muhammad Naquib. 1993. "Islam and Secularism," *International Institute of Islamic Thought and Civilization,* Kuala Lumpur, Malaysia.
Al Daghistani, Sami. 2022. *The Making of Islamic Economic Thought: Islamization, Law and Moral Discourse.* Cambridge, United Kingdom: Cambridge University Press.
AlMajawi AbdelKader., and Omar, Brihmat. 1904 [2014]. "AlMirsad fi Masaa'il AlIqtisad", (in Arabic) edited by Abderrazzak BelAbbes, University of King AbdulAziz Press.
Aoki, Masahiko. 2001. *Toward a Comparative Institutional Analysis.* Cambridge, MA: MIT Press.
Askari, Hossein, Zamir Iqbal., and Abbas Mirakhor. 2015. *Introduction to Islamic Economics.* John Wiley.
Baqir as-Sadr, Muhammad. 1982[1994]. "Iqtisādunā -Our Economics," *World Organization for Islamic Services,* Tehran, Iran, Vol. 2, Part 1, 2nd ed.
Boulding, E. Kenneth. 1969. Economics as a Moral Science. *The American Economic Review* 59: 1–12.
Çizakça, Murat. 2011. *Islamic Capitalism and Finance.* Edward Elgar.
Ibn Khaldun, AbdurRahman. 1337 [2005], "AlMuqaddimah," translated by Franz Rosenthal, Princeton University Press. Princeton New Jersey.
Kamali, Mohammad Hashim. 2000, "Islamic Commercial Law," *Islamic Texts Society.*
Kuran, Timur. 1983. Behavioral Norms in the Islamic Doctrine of Economics. *Journal of Economic Behavior and Organization* 4: 353–379.

Locke, John. 1680[1993]. *John Locke Political Writings*. Edited with Introduction by David Wooton: Hackett Publishing Company Inc., Cambridge.

Mirakhor, Abbas., and Askari Hossein. 2017. *Ideal Islamic Economy: An Introduction*. Palgrave Macmillan.

Mirakhor, Abbas., and Hossein Askari. 2019. *Conceptions of justice from earliest history to Islam*. New York: Palgrave Macmillan.

Nasr, Seyyed Hossein. 1993, "A Young Muslim's Guide to the Modern World," *Islamic Book Trust*, Kuala Lumpur.

North, Douglas, C. 1990, "Institutions, Institutional Change and Economic Performance," Cambridge University Pres.

Nutter, G. Warren. 1968. Economic Welfare and Welfare Economics. *Journal of Economic Issues* 2: 166–172.

Phelps, Edmund S. 1991. "Distributive Justice" In *The World of Economics*, edited by Eatwell, J., Milgate, M., Newman, P. The New Palgrave. Palgrave Macmillan, London.

Piketty, Thomas. 2014. Capital in the Twenty-First Century. Translated by Arthur Goldhammer. The Belknap Press of Harvard University Press. Cambridge, Massachusetts and London, England.

Presley, John R. G., and John, Sessions. 1994. Islamic Economics: The Emergence of a New Paradigm. *The Economic Journal* 104 (424): 584–596.

Skidelski, Robert, 2020. "What's Wrong with Economics? A Primer for the Perplexed," Yale University Press, New Haven, and London.

Smith, Adam. 1901[2007]. *The Wealth of Nations*. New York: Cosimo Books.

Stiglitz, Joseph. 2017. The Coming Great Transformation. *Journal of Policy Modeling* 39: 625–638.

Zingales, Luigi. 2015. "Presidential Address: Does finance benefit society?" *The Journal of Finance LXX*, (4): 1327–1363.

CHAPTER 8

Rethinking the Essence of Macroeconomic Policies in the *Iqtiṣād* Paradigm

There is mounting evidence that a synthesis of ideologies ranging from individualism and materialism to progressivism and evolutionism are at the roots of the current predatory economic system, which has given rise to severe economic and financial crises, income and wealth inequalities, and environmental degradation. It is difficult, however, to solve these problems without revisiting the philosophical and epistemological foundations of conventional economics. As argued in other chapters, attempts at Islamizing economics by grafting Islamic values onto a secular edifice are bound to fail as Islamic and secular worldviews are intrinsically irreconcilable. The Impossibility Theorem implies that the radical differences between the two polar cases at the metaphysical, ontological, epistemological, axiological, and teleological levels render the structuring of synthetic discipline called "Islamic economics" impossible. The combination or grafting of heteroclite and disparate elements does not make them a synthesis but a syncretism in the words of Malek Bennabi. The chronic conditions of extreme poverty and deprivation are *prima facie* evidence of syncretism and chaos. The lingering economic inequalities reflect, indeed, the impairment of the inner workings of justice in the organization of economic life. It is impossible to promote justice and solve the economic and social problems generated by income and wealth inequalities within the universes of discourse called economics, or secularized "Islamic economics" when new ideas about economic justice based on metaphysical, moral, and ethical arguments are entirely rejected.

Iqtiṣād, which offers an organically different approach to the organization of an ideal economy, offers new perspectives on the problems of income and wealth inequalities. Because its guiding economic principles are derived directly from an undisturbed universe of knowledge, the Qur'an and tradition of the Noble Prophet (saa), *Iqtiṣād* should not be regarded as a mere translation of "Islamic economics," a discipline that emulates conventional economics. It is a discipline that derives its principles from divine guidance, and seeks to maintain a just and careful balance between the scientific obligations to distinguish the true from the false, and moral obligations to discern the good from the bad and the right from the wrong. The conception of economic policies based on material and spiritual discernment within the Qur'anic framework of *Iqtiṣād* should promote economic justice in all aspects of social and economic life. *Iqtiṣād* should not be regarded as a patently value-laden discipline unable to establish an ideal economy and change the reality of economic life.

Thus, as a discipline that provides practical solutions to economic problems, *Iqtiṣād* does not lend itself to the argument that economic policies can be allowed to drift away from the pursuit of economic justice. Hence, the overriding objective of this chapter is to examine the issues of income and wealth inequality from the *Iqtiṣād* perspective of positive economics. No attempt is made, here, to formulate fiscal policies or to analyse the transmission mechanisms of monetary policies in the absence of interest rates. Though such policy issues are important in their own right, the focus is placed rather on the implications of risk-sharing and property-rights protection for distributive justice. It is argued that part of the reason for income and wealth inequalities lies in the prevalence of risk-transfer arrangements such as debt financing, which are conducive to economic injustice. In contrast, the organizing principle of risk-sharing ensures effective redistribution mechanisms, which represent a viable alternative to inherently unstable interest-based financial systems. Hence, the central argument advanced in this chapter is that economic policies cannot be neutral with respect to economic justice, and that risk-sharing can regulate the impulses of the real and financial sectors of an ideal *Iqtiṣād*-based economy with an integrated system of policies and structural patterns of behaviour that promote justice and avoid income and wealth inequalities.

The Nature of Economic Inequalities and Redistribution Proposals

It is often argued that the problems of economic inequalities and anaemic growth rates have been exacerbated by the onset of the US financial crisis and the new coronavirus outbreak. The bulk of the literature focuses on the adverse effects of persistent inequality on the economic, social, and political life as well as public finance. Apart from well-documented consequences of economic inequalities, recent evidence suggests that high levels of economic inequality are conducive to financial crises (Kumhof, Rancière et al. 2015; Rajan 2010; de Haan and Sturm 2016; Turner 2016) and lower economic growth (World Economic Forum 2017; OECD 2015; IMF 2017). Thus, addressing the problems of economic inequalities manifested by extreme poverty and unsustainable economic growth is of crucial importance in the promotion of economic justice. The concept of economic inequality suffers, however, from two misconceptions that are prevalent both in academia and among policymakers, and it is important to provide some clarity in order to understand the roots of economic inequality and develop viable solutions. Firstly, the concept of economic inequality is frequently confused with that of income inequality when it is rather wealth inequality that forms the main source of economic inequalities. Secondly, there is also a failure to recognize the economic rents stemming from interest-based financial systems as the main source of wealth inequality (Akin and Mirakhor 2019).

The first misconception that restricts economic inequality to the domain of income inequality obscures the fact that economic inequality rests principally on the existence of wealth inequalities. Wealth, which encompasses financial assets and real estate among others, can reproduce itself as a stock variable much faster than income, which is a flow variable. One important reason for focusing on income inequality is that mainstream economic theory assumes income inequality as the main determinant of wealth inequality since it defines wealth as the accumulation of income flows over time. However, the assumed relationship between income and wealth has weakened for the last few decades. Indeed, according to the World Inequality Lab (2021), the share of global income accruing to top 10% highest incomes has decreased over the past two decades, but both global and within-country distribution of wealth have deteriorated compared to income.[1] The share of wealth owned by the global top 0.01% has risen at a time when the global bottom half owns a mere 2% of total global wealth. The trends in the wealth distribution have dissociated from the trends in income distribution by making wealth inequality the main driver of economic inequality. It is clear that in the absence of stronger commitment to redistributive policies, these trends are bound to worsen.

The dissociation between wealth inequality and income inequality is related to the second misconception, which assumes that wealth inequality is a function of capital accumulation determined by income, meritocracy, and savings (Akin and Mirakhor 2019). However, there is compelling evidence that wealth inequality is driven by economic rents, not capital accumulation (Stiglitz 2015b). Today, the bulk of the wealth inequality is composed of "wealth residual," which can be defined as the increase in wealth without concomitant growth in capital (Basu and Stiglitz 2016). The concept of wealth residual is analogous to the Solow residual in the theoretical literature on economic growth. Solow (1957) suggested that only 13% of economic growth in the US could be attributed to the factors of production (labour and capital) whereas the rest was residual. As indicated by Stiglitz (2015b), exploitative economic rents are responsible for the formation of wealth residual, and in turn, wealth inequalities. It is also argued in the literature that interest-based debt contracts are the principal vehicles of exploitative economic rents and ensuing wealth residual (Akin and Mirakhor 2019; Maghrebi and Mirakhor 2015; Akin 2017).

Thus, it is important to understand the determinants of wealth residual in order to develop appropriate mechanisms for redistribution policies that address the problems of wealth inequality. The available redistribution proposals roughly fall into two strands, namely, asset-based and income-based redistributive policies. First, proposals for asset-based redistribution focus on the reallocation of the ownership of assets in order to narrow down the wealth gap between the rich and the poor. The redistribution policies directly aimed at reducing inequality consider the instruments to reallocate wealth per se. Historically, the objectives of asset-redistribution policies were pursued with the means of land reforms in Taiwan, Korea, and China, among others. Second, proposals for income-based redistribution focuses on mitigating income inequality based on the underlying assumption that income is the main driver of wealth inequality (Akin and Mirakhor 2019). Proposals under the income-based redistribution encompass "hard" income-based redistribution tools such as the taxation of income and wealth at higher rates. Studies by the OECD (2017) and the IMF (2021) argue that less distributive taxation and benefit systems represent important causes of worsening inequalities in the last several decades. The G7 proposal of a global minimum rate of corporate taxes is an example of "hard" income-based redistribution policies. There are also "soft" income-based redistribution proposals such as the proposal for shared prosperity pioneered by the World Bank (2016; 2020b).[2]

The "soft" school of thought take, as a matter of fact, the current distributions of income and wealth as given, and then focus on policies for equitable redistribution of additional income through various mechanisms such as public investment in health and education, financial inclusion, and insurance against risks. The working mechanisms underlying the proposal for shared prosperity leaves, indeed, the current concentration of wealth within the top percentiles intact and allows further economic rewards to accrue principally to high-wealth individuals, leading thereby to an endogenous increase in wealth inequality. The implementation of soft income-based redistribution tools may have adverse effects on wealth distribution such as perverse incentives in labour markets (OECD 2017) and investment decisions (Seshadri and Yuki 2004). The *status quo* conditions for asset inequality imply that the very governance structures, which give rise to inequality, remain intact too. Proposals aimed at addressing the pitfalls and weaknesses in income-based redistribution require wholesale changes in the rules of the game (Stiglitz 2015a), as well as changes in the underlying property-right claims such as the asset-based approach (Bowles 2012) and risk-sharing asset redistribution (Akin et al. 2020; Akin and Mirakhor 2019; Akin 2017).

THE LINKAGE BETWEEN WEALTH RESIDUAL AND INTEREST-BASED DEBT

There is mounting evidence that a significant part of wealth inequalities stems from wealth residual. As discussed by Aaminou and Akin (2020) and Akin and Mirakhor (2019), interest-based debt is an important determinant of wealth residual. The starting point in understanding the linkage between interest-rate mechanism and wealth inequality is the "fundamental inequality" $(r > g)$, where (r) stands for the real rate of return to capital and (g) for the growth rate of output and income. The fundamental inequality posits that the rate of return on capital is persistently higher than the growth rate of the economy, resulting in a rising relative share of capital income and greater wealth inequality. As argued by Piketty (2015b),

> [T]he rate of return on capital significantly exceeds the growth rate of the economy (as it did through much of history until the nineteenth century and as is likely to be the case again in the twenty-first century), then it logically follows that inherited wealth grows faster than output and income. People with inherited wealth need to save only a portion of their income from capital to see that capital grow more quickly than the economy as a whole. Under such conditions, it is almost inevitable that inherited wealth will dominate wealth amassed from a lifetime's labor by a wide margin, and the concentration of capital will attain extremely high levels—levels potentially incompatible with the meritocratic values and principles of social justice fundamental to modern democratic societies.

Jordà et al. (2019) show that rate of return to wealth is systematically higher than the economic growth rate in 16 advanced economies over the period from 1870 to 2015. Furthermore, the gap between (r) and (g) increased in the sub-period 1980–2015, which coincides with the era of increased financialization. The evidence is sample-independent as the fundamental inequality is found to be valid at least in the selected countries over both the full sample and sub-periods. Conventional economics suggests that the main source of wealth inequality lies in income disparities, mainly in the form of wage inequality and return to capital, both of which are linked to economic activities.[3] This theory implies that a convergence of the rates of return to wealth (r) and return to national income (g) toward each other would lead the fundamental inequality to disappear over time. Indeed, the basic relationship in the neoclassical economics is that the rate of return to capital is the rate of interest in the economy. The interest rate, according to this definition, is then the reflection of the marginal productivity of capital and economic growth (see Ljungqvist and Sargent (2012), and Wickens (2008) for textbook explanations of the concept of interest).

Thus, a natural extension of the relationship between interest rate and economic growth is that the rates of return to wealth (r) and return to national income (g) should theoretically converge, leaving no room for the fundamental inequality. The persistence of a gap between these two rates of return is evidence of the existence of artificial impediments to convergence, which result in extreme imbalances in income distribution.

These impediments are conducive to the formation of wealth residual and the exacerbation of wealth inequalities. Hence, the argument is made, hereafter, that interest-rate mechanisms are conducive to the formation of wealth residual through two main interrelated channels, namely, the quantity channel and the price channel.[4]

The Quantity Channel

The quantity channel refers to the distortive effects of interest-based debt contracts on wealth distribution due to the asymmetric terms of access to finance (quantity of finance) for economic agents with different levels of wealth. It can be argued that interest-based debt contracts allow for asset-rich individuals to benefit from financing sources at more favourable terms than asset-poor individuals. The asymmetric access to finance amplifies the wealth inequality by facilitating the perpetuation of economic rents for asset-rich individuals. The quantity channel operates mainly through two salient properties of interest-based debt contracts, namely the requirement of collateral and state-independent claims.

Collateral

In an ideal and frictionless economy, the contracts are complete and fully enforceable. A failure to meet these essential features of contracts has significant consequences on the behaviour of economic agents and their ability to benefit from financing sources. In case the contracts are complete and fully enforceable, it is the initial wealth that solely determines the budget constraints of economic agents without affecting their behaviour and contractual opportunities (Bowles 2012). In other words, both asset-rich and asset-poor economic agents have the same opportunity sets in their financial decisions. However, since incomplete and unenforceable contracts remain the norm rather than the exception, asset-poor economic agents cannot benefit from the same financing opportunities contained by the class of contracts available to asset-rich agents.[5] Thus, even if both asset-rich and asset-poor agents have the same budget constraints, differential contractual terms typically favour asset-rich agents.

The state-independent and fixed payments (principal amount plus interest installments) that borrowers owe creditors constitute the defining feature of credit contracts. From the perspective of the creditors, the existence of information asymmetries and high monitoring costs render financial contracts with state-independent payoffs more advantageous than other contractual agreements, such as partnership-type contracts. As explained by Buiter and Rahbari (2015):

> The issue of monitoring costs is intrinsically linked to the issue of asymmetric information between entrepreneurs and borrowers. The seminal work in this area is Townsend (1978). In his setup, information is asymmetric, as only the entrepreneur observes the state of the world (the success of his investment project) as a matter of course and provides the investor with a report. The outside investor has to pay a (fixed) monitoring cost to learn the state (in Townsend, 1978, this monitoring cost is deterministic, given a state), which is why this manifestation of asymmetric information is referred to as 'costly state verification'. Monitoring here can be thought of as the time, resource and opportunity cost of observing the actions of the firm, its financial position as well as the environment within which the firm operates. Monitoring costs can indeed be high as effective monitoring may require financial as well as operational expertise. But monitoring costs also include the costs associated with bankruptcy. Townsend (1978) showed that in such a setting a contract that features constant, state-independent payments from the entrepreneur to the investor and no monitoring in the 'good states' and a state-contingent payoff (equal to the value of the project minus the cost of monitoring) in the 'bad states' is 'optimal', defined as maximising the payoff or utility of the entrepreneur, subject to satisfying a reservation (or participation) constraint for the investor.

However, debt contracts with state-independent payoffs are "impossible contracts" simply because they are incomplete and unenforceable. These types of contracts are not incentive-driven under the axiomatic assumptions of conventional economics, such as self-interest and rationality. Since credit contracts do not include incentives to increase the borrower's promise to pay back the debt (truth-telling, non-speculative risk-taking, *inter alia*), the "rational" behaviour for borrower is not to avoid using debt but to avoid, to the extent possible, the payment of debt (Iqbal and Mirakhor 2017). A pledge by borrowers to assign assets as collateral is important for creditors to shift the parameters of an impossible contract and make it rather conceivable. Indeed, the collateral constitutes a crucial determinant of access to credit (Serra-Garcia 2010). However, the reality is that asset-poor agents typically do not have adequate assets to pledge as collateral. Bowles (2012) summarizes the effects of collateral on access to finance and the terms of contract as follows:

> The most obvious reason why an individual's amount of wealth influences the kinds of contract she can engage is that only those with sufficient wealth can undertake projects on their own account, that is, without borrowing. And among those who do borrow, those with more wealth borrow on better terms. This is because greater wealth on the part of the agent allows contracts which more closely align the objectives of principal and agent. This is the case, for example, when the borrower has sufficient wealth to post collateral or put her own equity in a project, and therefore has greater incentives to supply effort, to adopt the more prudent risk levels preferred by the lender (the principal), to reveal information to the principal, and to act in other ways that advance the principal's interests but that cannot be secured in a contract.

Thus, asset-rich agents have easier access to credit at more favourable terms even if their project is of lower quality compared to asset-poor agents. The lower expected income associated with investment projects undertaken by the latter gives rise to a wedge between (r) and (g), which amplifies the wealth inequality. A primary example of the effects of collateral on the formation of wealth is provided by real-estate markets, which constitute one of the most important investment vehicles for households. Asset-rich agents can purchase real-estate assets at more favourable conditions given their ability to provide higher collateral. As an investment class with high returns, the wealth stemming from real estate begets more wealth over time. On the other hand, asset-poor agents are left with the option to purchase real estate only upon the acceptance of debt obligations with high interest rates. The combination of high debt with low collateral increases the likelihood of debt defaults and financial crises, which are conducive to a significant loss of wealth for asset-poor agents, as posited by Mian and Sufi (2014), and Hintermainer and Koeniger (2015), among others.

State-Independent Payoffs

Collateral can be regarded as a "positive" selection mechanism that governs borrower's access to finance since it allows asset-rich agents to secure financing at relatively more favourable terms than asset-poor agents. On the other hand, state-independent payoffs represent a "negative" selection mechanism since asset-poor agents are required to service debt independent of the state of the world. With the prospects of economic growth, credit expansion allows asset-poor agents to over-borrow relative to their capacity to pay back. However, state-independent payoffs including debt principal and interest payments are conducive to financial stress under conditions of economic contraction. Thus, the reduced capacity to service debt independent of income generated under volatile economic conditions contributes to wealth inequality.[6] Buiter and Rahbari (2015, p. 151) explains that,

> [t]he academic literature has emphasized that debt, particularly when it is relatively large, can cause either underinvestment (the debt overhang problem of Myers (1977)) or excessive risk-taking. For the former (debt overhang), the presence of existing (relatively large) debt means an entrepreneur faced with a capital call for an investment project or considering a new (positive NPV) investment project, may refuse to invest because the capital injection (by reducing the probability of default) would also lead to a wealth transfer to the existing lenders. For the latter, the presence of debt coupled with limited liability aggravates the issue that equity has a convex payoff function: the equity owner is able to capture all of the upside (after costs, including debt service), but her losses are limited to losing her equity investment. Debt, particularly if it is large enough, can, therefore, systematically induce adverse behavioral distortions in the decisions of individual households and businesses.

Mian and Sufi (2018) posit that an excessive increase in household debt is closely associated with the severity of recessions and declines in real GDP growth, both of which have consequences for income and wealth distribution. A large increase in household debt leads to a sizeable decline in household spending during economic recessions because of debt defaults and loss of wealth. The reduced capacity of households to service debt leads to the problems of non-performing loans on the balance sheet of banks. These conditions result in liquidity problems, leading to credit contraction and credit crunch that affect investment in the real sector. At the same time, firms are likely to incur losses and become increasingly exposed to financial difficulties due to adverse demand and increasing unemployment. The financial problems faced by firms would ultimately reverberate on the balance sheet of banks as business activity declines further leading to banking crises and economic recessions. The government bailout of banks to reduce the likelihood of bank contagion and systemic risk, further exacerbate wealth inequalities by exposing borrowers and protecting lenders. Since households at the lower ends of income and wealth distributions have a higher marginal propensity to consume from disposable income, the adverse conditions stemming from credit crunch reduce also the ability of asset-poor agents to service the state-independent payoffs.

THE PRICE CHANNEL

The price channel refers to the ability of interest-based debt contracts to generate capital gains for the benefit of asset-rich agents. The source of wealth residual does not stem from differentiated access to finance as explained with reference to the quantity channel, but from differentiated rent (price) generated by the interest mechanism itself. The price channel mainly works through two sources of rent directly linked to the existence of the interest-rate mechanism, namely leverage and asset booms.

Leverage

It is the very nature of interest-based debt contracts that results in high leverage ratios where debt claims can reach levels multiple times of current output (Bezemer 2011). Leverage, which is typically measured as credit to GDP ratio, has tripled in advanced economies over the last several decades. In the two decades before the US financial crisis alone, the growth rate of credit volume was double that of the nominal GDP in many developed countries (Turner 2016). The same patterns can be observed in many developing and emerging economies. Such high growth rates of credit expansion are taking place independent of the rates of growth in the real sector. As highlighted by Turner (2016),

> credit growth appears necessary to drive the economies forward. But if that is really true, we face a severe dilemma. We seem to need credit to grow faster than GDP to keep economies growing at a reasonable rate, but that leads inevitably to crisis, debt overhang, and post-crisis recession. We seem condemned to instability in an economy incapable of balanced growth with stable leverage.

It is the expansion of credit by the banking sector independent of the economic activity in the real sector that allows for higher leverage rates. Most of the credit created by the banking system flows into consumption, financial investment, and purchase of existing assets rather than productive investment that allows for the optimal allocation of capital (Turner 2016). It is credit that allows the poor to borrow for consumption purposes and raise the levels of indebtedness, and thereby leverage ratios. As indicated by Mian and Sufi (2014), leverage was instrumental in increasing the capacity of low-income and middle-income classes in the US to cope with declining real wages and living standards. Meanwhile, leverage enabled asset-rich agents to further increase wealth by investing in higher income-generating assets such as stock and real-estate assets. In the absence of a structural change in income and wealth distribution, borrowing by the poor begets new borrowing, increasing thereby the levels of indebtedness and leverage. Thus, the perpetual indebtedness of asset-poor agents and increasing returns of asset-rich agents contribute directly to the generation of wealth residual and wealth inequality.

There are other effects of leverage on the formation of wealth disparities. Past some threshold level, borrowers may realize the severity of leverage ratios and reduce consumption and/or investment in order to secure solvency. Turner (2016) explains the process as follows:

> [W]hen house prices fall, borrowers suffer a fall in net worth, and the higher their leverage is, the greater the percentage loss they experience. With a 90% loan to value mortgage, a 5% fall in house prices wipes out 50% of the household's equity in their house. Faced with falling net worth, many households cut consumption. This follows in part from a simple 'wealth effect': when people feel less wealthy, they tend to consume less and save more. But it is amplified if debtors are worried that the fall in their net worth could go so far as to make them insolvent, facing them with the additional costs of bankruptcy, repossession, and the sale of their home at a fire sale price. Fear that default might make it impossible to borrow in the future (except at exorbitant rates) may also be an important concern. So when house prices fall, highly leveraged households focus strongly on reducing their debt levels—the household equivalent of the Japanese companies that Richard Koo analyzed—and their reduced expenditure depresses demand in the economy. But this reduction is not offset by increased expenditure on the part of net creditors elsewhere in the

economy: indeed, if asset house prices mean falling prices for credit securities, or concerns about bank solvency, net creditors may themselves reduce expenditure.

Thus, the wealth effect, described above, implies that asset-rich agents save their net worth during economic downturns whereas poorer agents are bound to lose disproportionally larger portions of their net worth. The principal effect of leverage is to exacerbate wealth inequalities by allowing the rich to benefit from more favourable access to credit in a world of volatile asset prices (Turner 2016). The requirements for collateral, inner workings of leverage, and the formation of asset bubbles and bursts are crucial factors that explain the formation of wealth residual and inequalities.

Asset Prices

The speculative activities leading to the formation of asset bubbles are facilitated by expansionary monetary policy and excessive supply of credit. The inherent instability of interest-based debt systems is the result of a growing disconnect between the financial and real sectors of the economy. The unlimited expansion of credit, reflected by higher leverage and unrestricted money creation, leads to upward pressures on asset prices, particularly in the markets for equity, housing, and commodities. The crux of the problem is that demand for goods and assets is not financed from existing incomes or savings, but by abundant credit. The buying pressures on assets are driven not only by speculators but also by rational individuals who contribute to asset price bubbles based on expectation of rising asset prices (Askari and Mirakhor 2015). The disconnection between the financial and real sectors is largely explained by the existence of interest-bearing debt and increasing leverage, fuelled by expectations of ever-increasing asset prices.

The vicious cycle of asset bubbles and bursts is indicative of the crucial role of volatile asset prices in the perpetuation of wealth inequality. Indeed, heterogeneous income and wealth groups benefit from asset bubbles and suffer from asset bursts differently. As highlighted by Turner (2016), *"superior access to credit in volatile economic circumstances has often been crucial to the accumulation of large fortunes."* There are typically two mechanisms that give rise to the formation of wealth disparities related to fluctuations in asset prices. First, asset portfolios differ across various income and wealth groups. Asset portfolios are more diversified and equity holdings are higher for top segments of wealth distributions. On the other hand, lower segments of wealth distributions are associated with portfolios biased toward fixed-income deposits (Domanski et al. 2016). As argued by Jordà et al. (2019) investment by higher wealth groups into real estate and equity markets is associated with historically highest rates of return. Second, the different financing opportunities available for asset-rich and asset-poor agents result in different levels of indebtedness and portfolio compositions. Leverage is found to be significantly lower for top segments of wealth distribution whereas lower segments are associated with higher indebtedness in relation to real-estate purchases.

Historically, capital gains in real-estate investment during periods of asset booms constitute the main component of the price channel. In contrast to equity, which is associated with a disproportionally smaller share in the middle and lower segments of wealth distributions relative to the top segment, real estate represents higher a share in the portfolio composition of middle and lower segments. The portfolio disparities can be explained by differences in net worth positions between the rich and the rest. Real estate is typically the most important asset for households, and the main mode of finance for real estate is represented by bank credit. Indeed, the composition of bank loan portfolios shifted over the last half century from productive investment activities to real estate (Turner 2016). Furthermore, the bulk of credit for real-estate investment represented the purchase of preexisting real-estate assets. Since the supply of land is fixed, more demand implies higher prices. When real-estate prices increase due to asset booms, a vicious cycle ensues as rising prices give impetus to further buying pressures, leading to even higher prices and increased buying pressures (Bacha and Mirakhor 2013). The formation of asset bubbles reflects upward movement in market prices independent of fundamental values. Asset bubbles have asymmetric effects on asset-rich agents, who tend to benefit from higher asset prices than the rest. It is the asset-rich agents who stand to benefit from easier access to credit on more favourable terms, which allow for the purchase of real estate as the momentum for rising prices becomes evident. In contrast, the conditions of ever-increasing real estate prices require, from the rest, more bank credit and higher collateral despite their lower net worth.

Thus, as the asset-rich agents gain disproportionally with the increase in asset prices, it is the highly leveraged poor who are exposed to larger losses as asset prices fall. The asymmetric effects are explained by the propensity for debt to exacerbate price falls because of the likelihood of foreclosures and the concentration of losses on heavily indebted households, leading to negative equity. Thus, depending on the extent of price falls, borrowers may be forced to absorb most of the losses, if not all, while rich lenders and investors in senior tranches in structured finance products may be entirely protected from losses through risk transfer to mezzanine or equity tranches, or through government bailouts. As a result, severe financial crises and recessions exacerbate the conditions of wealth inequality by further exposing borrowers and protecting lenders (Askari and Mirakhor 2015).

Risk-Sharing and the Notion of Wealth Residual

It was argued earlier that the persistent divergence of the return on capital (r) from the rate of growth in output and income (g) stems from the existence of impossible contracts based on interest-bearing debt, which constitute an important determinant of wealth residual. This argument reflects the importance of risk-sharing as an alternative to risk-transfer agreements, which are conducive to financial crises and wealth inequality. If the rate of return to wealth is determined *ex post* as a function of the outcome of economic activities rather than *ex ante* as fixed-income streams based on interest rates, the fundamental inequality ($r > g$) can be transformed into a form of cointegration relationship ($r = f(g)$), where the rate of return to wealth moves in tandem with the growth rate of the economy. As argued by Maghrebi and Mirakhor (2015),

> [s]ince the payoffs are contingent on the realization of a particular state of nature, the realized return on real investment is known only on ex post basis. The growth rate can be positive or negative depending on the realization of favorable or unfavorable states of nature. This implies that capital is not allowed to increase irrespective of growth rates, and that it is bound to decrease with negative growth.

The linkage between the rate of return to wealth and the growth rate of the real economy has the potential to address the problem of wealth residual. Hence, the organization of an ideal economy based on the *Iqtiṣād* principle of risk-sharing can provide viable solutions to the enduring crisis of income and wealth disparities. In order to understand the notion of risk-sharing and its relevance to mitigating wealth inequality, it is important to consider first the conceptual and semantic differences between risk, uncertainty, and ambiguity. As stated by Bartholomew (2008), risk is an indispensable ingredient to human life as it provides "*the richness and diversity of experience necessary to develop our skills and personalities.*" Since risk results from the diversity of human beliefs, expectations, freedom of choice, and free will, "*to forego risk is to forego freedom; risk is the price we pay for our freedom.*" The notion of risk reflects the possibility of loss, whether small or large, as well as the opportunity for profits stemming from human development and technological innovation.

It is rationality, according to standard assumptions of conventional economics, that guides human behaviour. The assumption of rationality implies that the formation of expectations by economic agents is constrained only by random errors given the probability distribution of outcomes (Erbas and Mirakhor 2013). This assumption implies an ergodic, stationary, stochastic world. In a non-ergodic world, the future is ontologically uncertain, and while systematic risks can occur, they can never be entirely predicted in advance (Davidson 2009). Frank Knight (1921 [1964]) argues that risk applies to situations in which the odds can be measured while the outcomes are not known a priori and that uncertainty applies to situations in which even the odds are not available. Thus, whereas risks with known probability distributions can be insured, uncertainty is not subject to insurance because there is no known probability distribution with prospective payoffs to be insured. There is, however, a semantic alteration of conceptual definitions in more recent research about probability theory, where uncertainty is substituted by "ambiguity," and refer rather to risk in its Knightian definition. The concept of ambiguity stems from the "impossibility of cognitive completeness," which is, in turn, explained by the absence of complete information (Askari and Mirakhor 2014). Since ambiguity renders decision-making almost impossible, patience and increased knowledge constitute the principal strategies for optimal decision-making (Erbas and Mirakhor 2013).

The relatively new fields of behavioural economics and the concept of bounded rationality proposed by Daniel Kahneman and Amos Tversky provided new insights about human behaviour under uncertainty (see Kahneman 2003; Kahneman and Tversky 1979). Kahneman (2003) suggests that the reactions of economic agents to risk in real-life situations differ from what the standard assumption of rationality predicts.

Kahneman models of human behaviour under risk are based on the proposition of framing effects and the prospect theory. The framing effects imply that ambiguity may be suppressed by individual perceptions in the sense that the same situations result in different outcomes due to differences in perceptions across economic agents (Kahneman 2003). This implies that reactions may differ as economic agents conceive the same situations differently based on their own perceptions. The way prospects are framed leads to different choices of the economic agents (Tversky and Kahneman 1981). The prospect theory, on the other hand, implies that an abrupt shift from risk-aversion to risk-seeking can be explained by changes in attitudes toward potential gains and losses with respect to reference points not necessarily defined by utility functions alone (Kahneman 2003). Part of the reason for the behavioural changes has to do with the endowment effect, status quo bias, and loss aversion, which are examined by Kahneman et al. (1991), Samuelson and Zeckhauser (1988) and Kahneman and Tversky (1988), respectively. These economic anomalies represent violations of the assumptions underlying the preference order in standard theory, either in terms of stability, symmetry, or reversibility. For instance, the loss aversion implies a tendency for agents to remain at the status quo when departure from current conditions is associated with unfavourable outcomes.

Thus, as summarized by Askari and Mirakhor (2014), the framing effects and the prospect theory provide some guidelines in addressing risk and understanding the importance of risk-sharing:

  i. when it comes to a choice between certain and uncertain gains, people generally prefer certainty even if the prospect of uncertain gains is objectively much larger than certain gains;
 ii. in choosing between certain and uncertain losses, people generally prefer uncertain alternatives even if the prospective loss is larger than the certainty case; and
iii. people generally overestimate small short-term risks and underestimate long-term risks.

It is important to note also that there are two main types of risk, namely, systematic and idiosyncratic risks (Rizvi et al. 2016). Systematic risk, including market risk and inflation risk, *inter alia*, is undiversifiable and thus, uninsurable by nature. It is possible to manage systematic risk at the macro level through institutional and policy measures, but it constitutes part of total risk that is impossible to eliminate. The idiosyncratic risks are limited to specific segments of the economy, including shocks to particular sectors, risks inherent to particular assets or markets, firm bankruptcies, and job losses. While idiosyncratic risks can affect economic agents, they remain diversifiable, and thus insurable.

Apart from the above classification of risks with respect to their systematic or idiosyncratic effects, it is possible also to examine alternative classifications of risk according to their distribution among parties. Contractual relationships involve risks that can be either transferred, shifted, or shared. Risk-transfer takes place in arrangements among intermediaries, depositors, and borrowers where risk is transferred from surplus units to deficit units (Bacha and Mirakhor 2013). The banking system is based on risk-transfer relationships between surplus and deficit units since the investment risk to depositors is transferred to banks, who in turn, transfer risk to borrowers. On the other hand, risk-shifting occurs when the burden of losses in financial transactions is laid at the door of third parties without prior consent (Mirakhor and Bao 2013). Risk-shifting is manifest during financial crises, where government bailouts of financial institutions are financed with public funds, giving credence thereby to criticism levied against the privatization of profits and socialization of losses. In contrast, risk-sharing reflects contractual or societal arrangements whereby the outcomes of random events are borne collectively by contractual parties (Askari et al. 2012). Risk-sharing is undertaken with the expectation that collective involvement and allocation of multiple resources and skills result in safety-in-numbers, risk diversification, and reduction of idiosyncratic risks. Instances of risk-sharing arrangements range from equity investment to participation in cooperatives and insurance against idiosyncratic risks.

Risk-sharing finance is an effective mechanism to address the problem of wealth inequality through the preclusion of economic rents, which constitute the main determinant of wealth residual. As opposed to risk-transfer and risk-shifting relations inherent to debt-based financial systems, risks are rather shared between parties. Risk-sharing prevents the realization of state-independent outcomes and shocks to the financial system as all parties to financial transactions are not only entitled to share profits but are also liable to bear losses. Moreover, risk-sharing finance does not contribute to the procyclicality of the financial system, which reflects the association between economic growth and recession with credit expansion and contraction (Rochet 2008). In contrast to debt financing, risk-sharing contributes to the stability of the financial system since the returns to financial contracts are not predetermined but dependent on the outcome of economic activities (Askari et al. 2010). The preclusion of procyclical financial systems results in the elimination of systemic risk, and the prevention of asset booms based on debt-fuelled speculative activities. Risk-sharing finance is not conducive to increased leverage because returns on financial assets are determined ex post as a function of returns in the real economy. It is noted also that risk-sharing finance does not necessarily require the provision of collateral since it is essentially based on partnership relations that preclude the risk of debt default. The salient features of risk-sharing finance prevent the perpetuation of economic rents and the formation of wealth residual. As argued by Mian (2013), it is the failure of promoting risk-sharing that constitutes a serious source of economic problems and financial crises, and thus income inequality.

Risk-Sharing Asset Redistribution

The notion of asset redistribution focuses on policy solutions to the lingering problems of wealth inequality based on asset rather than income redistribution. Historically, several forms of asset redistribution were implemented such as land reforms as well as inheritance and wealth taxation. More recent policy proposals for asset redistribution include the implementation of domestic and global wealth taxation. Given the narrow room for policy manoeuvre in the aftermath of the US financial crisis, and the fiscal impact of the disease outbreak, it is tempting for governments to seek alternative sources of revenues. In the absence of prompt economic recovery and sustainable growth, the taxation of top wealth percentiles may remain among the priority measures of policymakers. It may be argued that the essence of Thomas Piketty's proposal for a globally coordinated wealth tax, which would allow for sustainable investment in infrastructure and education (Piketty 2014; 2015a). It is the crucial problems of coordination and compliance that constitute the main challenges in implementing global tax proposals. It is noted, in this regard, that 130 countries have agreed in 2021 to impose minimum corporate tax rates of at least 15% as a first step in coordinating tax initiatives. However, the drive toward the globalization of finance competition to attract capital beyond borders, and the existence of tax havens have the potential to dilute the effectiveness of tax-oriented proposals for asset-based redistribution.

The current proposals for asset-based redistribution do not alter the nature of exchange relations in the economy governed by debt contracts. It is the debt-based contracts that inhibit growth-enhancing governance structures that are essential to the elimination of fundamental inequality.[7] It is because asset-poor agents cannot enter contracts available to asset-rich classes that they remain poor. The need for the former to accept fixed-income contracts rather than returns more in line with the opportunity costs of their resources. Fixed-income contracts impede productivity-enhancing behaviour, such as the full exertion of work efforts, provision of full information, and full cooperation. An important feature of fixed-income contracts is that productivity-enhancing behaviour cannot be embedded in contracts such as debt agreements, because of high monitoring costs. It is also argued that fixed-income contracts do not incentivize borrowers to elicit maximum levels of efforts, and that they lead to coordination failures (principle–agent problems) because of weaknesses in the incentives structure.

There are other important inefficiencies reflected by missed opportunities for potential entrepreneurs, investors, and innovators to contribute to economic activities and enhance productivity. There is, indeed, mounting evidence that asset-poor entrepreneurs are either excluded from credit markets or compelled to incur higher financing costs than entrepreneurs with higher levels of wealth. There is also evidence that asset-poor agents have higher rates of time preference as well as higher levels of risk-aversion (Lawrance 1991; Moseley 2001; Carney and Gale 2005; Hopkins 2018). In consideration of the economic costs of wealth inequality, Bowles (2012, 37) argues that,

> where contracts in financial markets are incomplete or unenforceable, individuals lacking in wealth are either precluded from engaging in a class of contracts that are available to the wealthy, or enter into these contracts on unfavorable terms. […] why an individual's amount of wealth influences the kinds of contract she can engage in is that only those with sufficient wealth can undertake projects on their own account, that is without borrowing. And, among those who borrow, those with more wealth borrow on better terms. This is because greater wealth on the part of the agent allows contracts which more closely align the objectives of principal and agent. This is the case, for example, when the borrower has sufficient wealth to post collateral or put her own equity in a project, and therefore has greater

incentive to supply effort, to adopt more prudent risk levels preferred by the lender (the principal), to reveal information to the principal, and to act in other ways that advance the principal's interests but that cannot be secured in a contract.

It is possible to consider alternative approaches to asset-based redistribution that do not involve hard radical redistributive policies, but critical changes in the design of contracts for economic exchange away from debt-based contracts toward skin-in-the-game agreements (Bowles 2012). There is, indeed, a class of contracts that are incentive-compatible, enhance productivity, and generate sustainable economic growth. The incentive-compatible contracts have the potential to rethink the relationship between principal and agent based on the ownership structure and information sharing. Asset redistribution, in effect, rewrites the rules of property-right claims by allowing agents to share the three crucial dimensions of property rights: (a) the right to control access to the asset; (b) the right to control the usage of the asset; and (c) the right to claim the residual income generated by the asset (Bowles 2012). A typical example of such contracts is the joint partnership agreement where ownership of an economic venture is shared between parties. Partners share the property-right claims jointly and have joint claims on the residual income of the venture as well. In this respect, Bowles (2012) further argues that:

> in contrast to income-based egalitarian strategies, which are rarely better than productivity-neutral (and often a lot worse), asset-based egalitarianism can in principle be productivity-enhancing. This is true both because it can implement more efficient distributions of residual clamancy and control rights and because redistributing assets addresses a major cause of unequal incomes, and thus gives greater scope for markets to do what they are good at: identifying losers—firms that fail to produce good products at competitive prices—and getting them out of the game.

Asset-based redistribution has the potential to enhance efficiency and effectiveness in the economy as each party to the contract is bound by skin-in-the-game conditions, reducing thereby the disparities between principle–agent differences. The existence of skin-in-the-game can also minimize the monitoring and supervision costs associated with the problems of information asymmetries. A direct consequence of skin-in-the-game conditions is that contractual parties have the liberty to choose investment projects with different risk-return profiles. Moreover, asset-based redistribution can create a reciprocal and trusting environment that strengthens social cohesion and solidarity. It reduces also income inequality without the perverse incentives that promote resistance to change in the case of income-based redistribution. The theoretical framework proposed by Bowles demonstrates the rationale for a preference of asset-based over income-based redistribution, but it does not provide clear guidance about the implementation of asset-based redistributive policies.

It is possible to refer to the risk-sharing principle of Islamic finance in order to understand the practical implications of asset-based redistribution. The Kuala Lumpur Declaration in 2012 by prominent experts in Islamic jurisprudence and Islamic economics contends that risk-sharing is the essence of Islamic finance (ISRA 2012). Risk-sharing in Islam is achieved mainly through three interrelated forms (Maghrebi et al. 2016):

i. redistributive institutions for risk-sharing such as *zakah*, *sadaqah*, *qard al-hasan* and *waqf*,
ii. intergenerational risk-sharing through Islamic inheritance rules, and
iii. risk-sharing financial instruments such as *mudaraba* and *musharakah*, *inter alia*.

With respect to redistributive institutions based on risk-sharing, *zakah* is the most important redistributive mechanism, and one of the five pillars of Islam. From the policy-making perspective, *zakah* constitutes a more effective instrument in the fight against wealth inequality than alternative proposals based on wealth taxation. A pre-determined rate applied to the portion of individual wealth beyond a given threshold *nisab* represents the legitimate share of asset-poor agents in the accumulated wealth of the asset-rich segment of the society.[8] It is interesting to note that the minimum *zakah* rate of 2.5% is rather close to the optimal rate of wealth taxation proposed by Piketty (2014). But in contrast to the challenges of implementing Piketty's proposal for global wealth taxation in terms of political viability, global coordination, rule compliance in discharging *zakah* is based on clear Qur'anic injunctions that apply to all asset-rich Muslims irrespective of race or ethnicity. There are also other forms of redistributive mechanisms such as the institution of *waqf*, or endowment which played historically an important role in the alleviation of poverty and the development of Islamic civilization. With respect to intergenerational risk-sharing, there are clear inheritance rules in the Qur'an and Sunnah that govern the transfer of wealth on equitable basis.

There is still room for further research on the design of financial instruments based on risk-sharing and on their usefulness for asset-based redistribution. Macro-market securities constitute a potential instrument of risk-sharing in public finance as they "*can allow people to mitigate risks to their income and countries to enhance international risk-sharing*" (Rizvi et al. 2016). These financial instruments resemble *sukuk* securities, which represent a primary mode of risk-sharing in Islamic finance. GDP-linked *sukuk* can be regarded as macro-market instruments based on sharing the country's economic output (Bacha et al. 2015; 2014; Ismath Bacha and Mirakhor 2017). GDP-linked *sukuk* can be useful instruments of asset-based redistributive policies aimed at mitigating wealth inequality. They present investors with the prospects of stable financial returns function of growth rates in economic output.[9] The issuance of sukuk provides an important alternative to debt-based instruments which promote, as discussed earlier, the procyclicality of the financial system. Also, sukuk instruments reduce the reliance of governments on public debt as they appear as equity in the balance sheet of the public sector. This allows also for the elimination of inherently regressive features of interest-bearing debt, which foster wealth inequalities.

Akin and Mirakhor (2019) provide the first quantitative analysis of risk-sharing as a mechanism of asset redistribution. The simulation model assumes that the public sector allows for the lowest 40% of the population to hold risk-sharing instruments but there is no secondary market in which households can transact GDP-linked *sukuk* in case of liquidity needs. Since GDP-linked *sukuk* constitute a substitute for the income class of transfer payments, households can allocate part of their income to the purchase of new risk-sharing assets. The evidence from the simulation analysis of income distribution suggests that secondary markets and other complementary institutions of income redistribution should be promoted in order to implement asset-based redistributive policies.

Thus, GDP-linked *sukuk* and similar variants, such as revenue-generating *sukuk* for infrastructure projects, constitute innovative forms of financial instruments based on risk-sharing as the fundamental *Iqtiṣād* principle for the organization of an ideal economy. However, there are practical issues in the use of risk-sharing mechanism for the purposes of asset-based redistribution that remain unanswered. Indeed, the theoretical model developed by Akin and Mirakhor (2019) assumes risk-sharing *sukuk* are made available to the bottom 40% in wealth distribution, but it is not clear how sukuk allocation and trading can promoted from the practical policy perspective. The purpose of the following sections is to explain some practical aspects of risk-sharing finance and its implications for asset-based redistribution.

Risk-Sharing Universal Basic Assets (RUBA)

The objective of *Iqtiṣād*, as a discipline aimed at elucidating the foundations of an ideal Islamic economy derived from Qur'anic and Prophetic injunctions, is to promote social justice through optimal exchange and redistribution mechanisms. The optimality of economic equilibrium and social stability is reflected by the alleviation and elimination of poverty, ensuring thereby decent standards of living for all segments of the society. Economic policies should ensure that individuals are entitled to adequate income and wealth levels to lead a decent life with human dignity. In line with the objectives of *Iqtiṣād*, the principal functions of the government are twofold, namely the provision of adequate infrastructure for education, security, welfare, public services, health and safety as well as the promotion of generational and intergenerational redistribution. These interrelated functions imply that members of the society have a collective responsibility for income and wealth redistribution through the transfer of surplus income and wealth toward the asset-poor agents. As noted earlier, *zakah* constitutes an important redistribution mechanism, but it should be supported by other distributive and redistributive policies. In addition to the functions of ensuring full employment and economic growth and stability, fiscal policies should be geared also toward the mitigation of shortfalls in redistributive mechanisms.

As economic benefits tend to accrue asymmetrically to asset-rich agents, current redistribution proposals, such as wealth taxation and shared prosperity, may not be sufficient to mitigate ever-increasing wealth inequality. It is important to examine novel mechanisms for asset-based redistribution founded on the *Iqtiṣād* principle of risk-sharing such as the risk-sharing universal basic assets (RUBA). The RUBA refer to macro-market securities for income generation, which are annually distributed either on unconditional or partly conditional basis to younger economic agents below a certain age. The salient features of these income-generating securities resemble those of the existing programs for Universal Basic Income (UBI), but they provide incremental advantages deriving from the risk-sharing principle.

The principal merit of the UBI scheme lies in the provision of regular and unconditional cash payments to all members of the society through government social programs. As noted by Standing (2017), it is a stable and predictable basic income that differs from the "*minimum income guarantee, which tops up low incomes to a given level, usually requiring complex means tests. And it is different from a negative income tax or tax credits, which are withdrawn as income rises.*" The UBI proposal is an old new notion dating back to the 1980s by some economists, philosophers, and social scientists in Europe, but it gained further interest among both academics and policymakers in the aftermath of the US financial crisis. The debate revolves around issues related to implementation plans and viability, but it focuses also on the role of the state and financial markets in promoting asset-based wealth redistribution.

At the foundations of the UBI proposals, there is an element of moral sentiments consistent with the holistic perspective of Adam Smith. Tony Atkinson (2011) notes that "*[UBI] is not just a form of redistribution; it is a moral statement.*" The recent interest in the UBI idea is indeed, reflective of an increasing awareness about the serious implications of wealth and income inequalities, which are accompanied by the erosion in social protection systems and safety nets in the face of automation, globalization, pervasive informality, and degradation in human capital (Gentilini et al. 2020). As indicated by Standing (2017):

> The growing interest in basic income partly reflects a recognition that current economic and social policies are producing unsustainable inequalities and injustices. The twentieth-century income distribution system has broken down, as globalization has swept forward, as 'neo-liberal' economics has done its work, and as the technological revolution has facilitated transformative changes in labour markets. One outcome has been a growing 'precariat', consisting of millions of people facing unstable, insecure labour, a lack of occupational identity, declining and increasingly volatile real wages, loss of benefits and chronic indebtedness.

Thus, the UBI is deemed not just as a poverty reduction program, but an economic right intrinsically related to the pursuit of social justice.

The UBI can be viewed also as a social dividend and a mechanism for income smoothing against the deterioration in purchasing power, particularly in the face of monetary policies based on inflation targeting and weak protection against diminishing real wages. Since the rationale for new redistribution schemes based on the UBI proposal is to reduce income inequality stemming from the formation of economic rents (Standing 2017), it constitutes mainly a relief mechanism against wage inequality. It is important to bear in mind, hence, that it addresses the issue of inequalities deriving from the formation of wealth residual on *ex ante* rather than *ex post* basis.

The feature of universality in the UBI proposals is justified by the problems of limited coverage from which the existing social protection schemes suffer. According to recent estimates from the World Bank, only 18% of the eligible population effectively receive some form of social assistance in low-income countries, and the small share increases only as the country becomes more developed (Gentilini et al. 2020). It is the limited awareness and unaffordable application costs that may explain the low rates of access to social protection schemes by the eligible segments of the population. As explained by Gentilini et al. (2020), the rationale for the UBI implementation rests on several arguments. First, the provision of unconditional cash payments to members of society that meet simple eligibility criteria, such as citizenship and age, minimizes the potential risks associated with exclusion and inclusion errors. Second, the universality feature may minimize also the impact of individual factors including ignorance, fear, stigma, or sense of humiliation. Third, the elimination of application and selection mechanisms is conducive to lower processing and settlement costs. Fourth, the schemes are not necessarily conducive to a loss in efficiency because universality weakens the disincentives for some segments of the population exceeding a certain income threshold to abstain from work and rely on social benefits alone. Fifth, from a political perspective, the UBI schemes are not necessarily repulsive to certain segments of the voting population as they benefit all voters independent of income and wealth distributions.

There are however, several arguments against the UBI proposal ranging from concerns about fiscal sustainability to labour market inefficiencies. It is thus argued that unconditional payments to all members of society would divert scarce resources away from the poor benefiting from the existing social programs. It is also argued that they are associated with disincentives from participation in the labour markets. However, the main concerns about the implementation of the UBI schemes derive from the increasing financial burden on government finances. The cost of regular payments to all eligible citizens can be significant by any budgetary measure. It may be possible to provide funding for the UBI policies through budget reductions in the existing social protection schemes or tax increases, but these fiscal options raise questions about their net long-term economic benefits and political support. The literature finds that a budget-neutral implementation of UBI schemes in many countries would benefit the asset-poor and reduce the existing burden on social protection programs (Gentilini et al. 2020).

The growing interest in the UBI proposals may be explained, in part, by the fact that the income distribution system of welfare states has rather broken down. The share of labour in the generation of national income has diminished due to many factors such as economic globalization, and technological change, as well as the rise in rentier income. It can be argued that the new social and economic conditions require new income redistribution mechanisms. However, the question remains as to whether even a fully implemented UBI would ensure that the desired reduction of wealth inequalities in particular would be achieved. Similar to the proposal of shared prosperity advanced by The World Bank, the UBI schemes do not address the fundamental sources of wealth inequality. As noted previously, the problem of wealth inequality has its root causes in the formation of wealth residual, and insofar as the underlying causes are not addressed, the problem of wealth inequality will persist. Thus, the implementation of the UBI proposals may be associated with perverse effects on inequality and poverty as the resources currently available to the most vulnerable segments of the society would be allocated to all members independent of income and wealth distributions.

Thus, in light of the above arguments and counterarguments about the UBI schemes, it may be argued that RUBA proposals are more consistent with the objectives of *Iqtiṣād*, and provide a more effective means to address the problem of wealth inequality, on an *ex ante* basis, in accordance with the principle of risk-sharing. Nevertheless, some features of the UBI mechanism can be useful in devising and implementing an effective RUBA framework. Part of the lessons drawn from the UBI proposals can be summarized as follows.

- As highlighted by Acemoglu (2019), the implementation of the UBI proposals can be prohibitively expensive unless accompanied

by deep cuts to other social safety nets or by significant increases in tax revenues. The lesson is that an effective asset-based redistribution mechanism should not create significant additional burden on public finances.
- The universality feature of the UBI schemes may result in deteriorating conditions for the most vulnerable and poorest segments of society as resources are reallocated to benefit all members of society, including the rich.
- The principal objective of the UBI proposals is to provide social protection against wage inequality resulting from failures of the welfare state. It is the more serious and urgent problem of wealth inequality stemming from the formation of wealth residual that should constitute the main focus of policymakers.
- It may be argued that relative to wealth inequality, income inequality is the lesser of two evils. The UBI idea cannot possibly solve the problems of increasing wealth inequality because it does not address the issue of wealth residual. Whereas a basic income sustained with regular modest amounts reinforces the status quo of "capitalism with baseline income maintenance," a basic capital grant with single large amount may lead to "capitalism with equal starts" that permits market-driven inequalities (Standing 2017, p. 8). The important issue, then, is not to limit the focus of policymakers on income maintenance alone, but on the necessity to address the market-driven inequalities as well.
- The argument of social justice used to justify the UBI proposals should be also reconsidered. In a world where contracts are incomplete and unenforceable, interest-based agreements constitute a serious source of injustice. As discussed previously,
    - (i) credit constraints may prevent high-quality projects from being implemented by the asset-poor,
    - (ii) credit-constrained agents can typically undertake projects associated with lower expected returns,
    - (iii) access to credit increases risk-taking by economic agents with higher expected returns, and
    - (iv) credit constraints on economic agents affect their degree of risk tolerance, which influences, in turn, their saving and investment decisions.

Given the above explanation, it should be noted that the UBI proposals provide the recipients with the imputed income endowment from government budgets or stock of capital, as in the case of the Alaska Permanent Fund, but do not entitle them with ownership of capital or asset itself. There is arguably a failure to address the root causes of the problem because wealth inequality is the direct result of not just lower income but also poverty in asset ownership. As argued by Skidelsky (2001), people need an asset or endowment to "start a business, or buy a house, or invest in their education or 'blow it'." Indeed, once people are entitled with ownership over income-generating assets, it is more likely than not, that the generated income will constitute a substitute for basic income. But it is important to understand also the nature of risk and decision under uncertainty, and the impact of opportunities for the creation of property rights on inequality.

Thus, the next section proposes a blueprint for the implementation of asset-based redistribution schemes founded on the *Iqtiṣād* principle of risk-sharing in Islamic finance.

Blueprint for the RUBA: Public Basic Asset Fund (PBAF)

It is possible, at this juncture, to propose a blueprint for asset-based redistribution derived from the *Iqtiṣād* principle of risk-sharing. A Public Basic Asset Fund (PBAF) can be established by the government as a citizen-trust endowment for young adults. The PBAF allows eligible participants to accumulate financial assets through direct investment into financial instruments based on risk-sharing. The channelling of funds into real investment allows the economy to thrive and the society to share risks and benefit from shared prosperity. Once the pre-determined eligibility conditions are satisfied, participants can allocate assets to predefined objectives based on their own needs and preferences, ranging from education and health to housing and entrepreneurship. Participation allows also for subsequent trading of PBAF shares in the capital markets.[10]

The salient feature of PBAF proposals is the reliance on investment vehicles based on risk-sharing finance. There are, however, similar initiatives such as the Child Trust Fund (CTF) program in the United Kingdom based on long-term tax-free savings accounts for children. It was a short-lived experiment, as the CTF program was announced in 2001, initiated in 2005, abolished in 2010 arguably for political reasons, and replaced by individual saving accounts in 2011. The CTF program provided children from birth until the age of seven with vouchers to which parents were allowed to add more funding subject to annual limits, but the main objective was to increase awareness about the importance of saving and management of personal finance. With relatively less emphasis on asset redistribution. Also, the Alaska Permanent Fund and the Norwegian Pension Fund represent similar initiatives in the sense that the revenues generated by these endowments are distributed as social dividends to eligible citizens. As indicated by Standing (2017), *"viewed as a rightful share of income flowing from our collective wealth, the social dividend approach is politically attractive since it would not require either dismantling existing welfare systems or raising taxes on earned income."*

In Malaysia, the Permodalan Nasional Berhad (PNB) scheme bears close resemblance to the PBAF proposal, and it is possible to draw lessons from the PNB experience for the adoption of PBAF as an effective mechanism of asset-based wealth distribution and economic development. The PNB initiative was established in 1978 and designed as a model for the creation and redistribution of wealth by entitling Malaysians to contribute individually toward economic development through investment opportunities in investment unit trusts.[11] As highlighted by the World Bank (2020a),

> [T]he intent was to increase equity ownership of Malays up to 30% of the total value of listed companies, as part of the NEP's aim of creating a share-owning class among the Bumiputera. The government created an institution designed to encourage Malay participation in corporations and to assuage traditional fears of losses given the risk averse nature of Malay society. The government also wanted to promote long-term investments and avoid speculative profit-making, envisaging PNB as a vehicle to both increase and sustain economic participation. The aim was to create a less disparate society with shared prosperity.

The PNB experience spanning several decades demonstrates the viability of financial instruments for asset-based redistribution driven by risk-sharing and dynamic capital markets. Given the large number of participants, it provides also strong evidence that it is indeed possible to reach many segments of the population including low-income classes, and provide opportunities for profitable long-term investment even for risk-averse households.

Thus, with reference to the various initiatives including the CTF program, Alaska Permanent Fund, the Norwegian Pension Fund, and the PNB, it can be argued that public funds providing social dividends can offer opportunities for large-scale redistribution mechanisms. Similarly, the Public Basic Asset Fund has a strong potential to offer a risk-sharing mechanism for sustainable and inclusive asset redistribution. The blueprint for the Public Basic Asset Fund proposal includes three main steps:

- Establishment of the Public Basic Asset Fund,
- Investment in risk-sharing instruments, and
- Trading of Public Basic Asset Fund shares in secondary markets.

Establishment of the Public Basic Asset Fund

As noted earlier, there are serious concerns about the implementation of the UBI initiatives because of its increased burden on public finances with higher taxation or other means of public revenues. In contrast, the PBAF proposal depends on the issuance of central (investment) deposits (CDs) to initialize the income-generating asset base. It should be noted, here, that public wealth funds can also be harnessed in resource-rich countries as a complement to the issuance of CDs. However, it can be argued that the CDs should be the main source of initial PBAF funding in order to promote public awareness about the importance of risk-sharing and shared prosperity.

The fractional reserve system weakens, indeed, the grip of central banks on money supply since banks can also create money through interest-based lending. Given the nature of debt financing based on promises of state-independent income, money created in the fractional reserve system constitutes one of the most important determinants of financial crises, and thus, wealth inequality (Hodgson 2013; Dietsch 2021; Colciago et al. 2019). As indicated by Al-Jarhi (1981), the adoption of full-reserve system would provide the central bank with exclusive power to control the money supply and contribute toward the reduction of wealth inequalities. However, monetary policies driven by lower interest rates or quantitative easing have rather exacerbated the problem of wealth inequality. As strongly argued by Standing (2017), *"the $4.5 trillion in QE by the US Federal Reserve was enough to have given $56,000 to every household in* *the country... Instead, QE has enriched the financiers, worsened income inequality and hastened the alarming oncoming crisis of underfunded pension schemes."*

Thus, it is not possible to rely on fiscal or monetary policies based on the interest-rate mechanism and debt financing. In this regard, Al-Jarhi (1981; 2020) proposes the adoption of CDs created by apportioning the total money supply between Islamic and conventional shares. Conditional on full-reserve banking system, the CDs can, thus, be used as investment funds to be placed in Islamic banks with Shariah-compliant modes of financing. It is argued, also, that the proceeds from central deposit certificates (CDCs), which are Shariah-compliant and tradable monetary management instruments, can be added to the CDs. It is important to note that, in contrast to the rate of interest, which is determined in the debt-based money market, the expected payoffs on CDs instruments depend on the rate of return in the real economy.

Thus, consistent with the arguments advanced by Al-Jarhi, the CDs instruments remain the principal source of funding in the establishment of PBAF initiatives, independent of the available natural resources. Since only a portion of money supply is replaced with CDs, leaving the total supply unaltered, and since PBAF certificates can only be used for risk-sharing investment in the real economy, there are limited concerns about strong inflationary pressures. These salient features stand in sharp contrast with the current UBI proposals where large-scale payments may trigger upward price dynamics. At first glance, the CDs proposal may be regarded as a non-viable and costly approach to asset-based redistribution. But on closer examination, it is the implementation of redistributive policies driven by risk-sharing finance rather than debt that hold better prospects for sustainable solutions to the problem of inequality.

Investment in Risk-Sharing Instruments

The establishment of the PBAF fund constitutes only the starting point in the implementation of RUBA proposals. What makes the fund income-generating and risk-sharing-based is how the initial funds are invested in the real economy. There are two main investment options for the RUBA fund:

- Real sector activity through Islamic banks
- Infrastructure investments

Al-Jarhi (2020) proposes that the CDs be placed with Islamic banks based on *mudharabah* mode of financing (trustee finance or passive partnership). The central bank places also some portion of the CDs annually to the Islamic banks through *mudharabah* contracts on the condition that Islamic banks can only use the allotted funds to invest in selected sectors, transactions, or modes of finance. At the end of the *mudharabah* contract, the realized returns are shared between the Fund and Islamic banks. As the funds are employed in financing investment activities in the real economy, the average rate of return to *mudharabah* contracts should reflect the realized returns in the real sector.

Another area for the effective allocation of CDs investment portfolios is the financing of infrastructure projects by the public sector. As indicated by Bacha and Mirakhor (2017), risk-sharing instruments are appropriate for development projects that generate stable revenues, such as tolled highways, railroads, mass rapid transit systems, and airports, among others.[12] Thus, there is a strong potential for using risk-sharing-based instruments to finance infrastructure projects in developing countries as an alternative to the debt-based borrowing. Thus, investment in infrastructure projects presents PBAF shareholders with the prospects of stable returns associated with lower risks, allowing thereby PBFA asset portfolios also to steadily grow over time.

Trading PBAF Shares in Secondary Markets

The principal objective of the PBAF proposal is to provide effective means for the asset-poor segments of society to benefit from revenue-generating assets and reduce wealth inequality. Hence, the definition of appropriate eligibility criteria for participation as PBAF shareholders constitutes a crucial part of the proposal. Similar to the Child Trust Fund (CTF) program in the UK and Baby Bonds proposal in the US, every child receives at birth a PBAF trust account, which accrues benefits that can be made available at adulthood. The sustainable growth of assets managed by PBAF funds through investment into the real economy and infrastructure projects should ensure stable income for trust account holders over time.

However, there is also a need to ensure that, in addition to clear eligibility criteria, PBAF shares can be liquidated with the same ease with which other financial assets can be disposed of. For the proposal to work, there should be matured secondary markets, where these income-generating financial assets can be bought and sold at informationally efficient market prices. The PBAF proposal requires that secondary markets are established within domestic equity markets because of the risk-sharing nature of these financial instruments. The PBAF shares can also be used as collateral to facilitate exchange relationships. In order to prevent the concentration of asset ownership, investors should not be allowed to hold a share of the total PBAF stock above a certain threshold. Ultimately, it is the free access to accurate and timely information about the performance of investment projects and the real economy that will determine the degree of efficient market pricing, and the trust of shareholders in the long-term viability of risk-sharing instruments as effective tools of asset-based redistribution.

In conclusion, the policy issues addressed in this chapter highlight part of the serious challenges faced in the design and conduct of fiscal and monetary policies based on debt financing and the mechanism of interest rates. It is clear that the chronic problems of income and wealth inequality cannot be solved with policy recommendations derived from conventional Economics. It is argued, indeed, that since interest-bearing debt contracts are "impossible contracts" based on promises of state-independent payoffs, they contribute toward exploitative economic rents, which are responsible according to Stiglitz (2015b), for the formation of wealth residual, and in turn, wealth inequalities. Thus, fiscal and monetary policies based on the very interest-rate mechanism, which promotes economic rents, cannot arguably be part of the solution to the problem of income and wealth inequalities.

It is important, thus, to rethink the essence of macroeconomic policies, and redesign more effective redistributive policies based on risk-sharing as an important *Iqtiṣād* principle in the organization of an ideal economy. In contrast to redistributive policies based on social protection and universal basic income programs, which tend to lay additional burden on public finances, risk-sharing addresses the problem of inequality on *ex ante* rather than *ex post* basis. It is noted that risk-sharing finance precludes, indeed, the formation of economic rents, which constitute the main determinant of wealth residual, and in turn, the problem of wealth inequality. Thus, asset-based redistributive schemes such as the Public Basic Asset Fund based on risk-sharing finance address the challenges faced by asset-poor segments of the society through the provision of opportunities for every child to accrue annual benefits until adulthood, from the returns to investment in the real economy and infrastructure projects. The rate of return on PBAF shares depends on the return on investment in the real economy rather than interest rates determined in the money markets.

Thus, it is important to reiterate the contention, made throughout this book, that *Iqtiṣād*, which provides a Qur'an vision of an ideal economy, is founded on radically different metaphysical, epistemological, philosophical, and moral foundations that make the grafting of conventional macroeconomic policies onto *Iqtiṣād*-driven redistributive policies based on risk-sharing impossible. The Impossibility Theorem implies that there is no basis for a synthesis of fiscal or monetary policies when the forces that govern the dynamics of an *Iqtiṣād*-driven economy do not depend on interest rates but on risk-sharing. The challenges of income and wealth disparities cannot be addressed with fiscal and monetary policies based on the same interest-bearing debt financing that is the crux of the problem of inequality. Hence, it is important to rethink the essence of macroeconomic policies, which should be responsive to the needs of risk-sharing finance and asset-based redistributive policies rather than steered toward debt-based financing that perpetuates economic rents, financial crises, economic recessions, and social injustice.

Notes

1. The statistics from the World Inequality Lab (2021) indicate a decrease in the top 10% of income distribution from 61% in 2000 to 55% in 2020, but the share of the global top 0.01% (composed of 520,000 individuals) rose from 7% in 1995 to 11% in 2021. With a mere 2% ownership of total global wealth, the average income of the global bottom 50% is estimated to be 38 times lower than the average income of the global top 10%.
2. According to the World Bank (2020b), "shared prosperity measures the extent to which economic growth is inclusive by focusing on household income or consumption growth among the population at the bottom of the income distribution rather than on the average or on those at the top."
3. It is important to distinguish between capital and wealth. Capital is relevant to productive activity while wealth encompasses capital, real estate, and other financial assets. For a comprehensive review of the difference between these two concepts and their implications on the inequality, see Akin and Mirakhor (2019).
4. The quantity and price channel are associated non-wealth residual component of the wealth inequality, such as income inequality and savings, as well. For instance, capital income depending on the interest rates has an effect on the income inequality part of the wealth inequality. However,

we assert that the bulk yet unexplored part of the wealth inequality is the wealth residual. Due to this fact, the quantity and price channels solely focus on the links that have an effect on the wealth residual.
5. As defined by Wang (2013, 63), *"complete contract is a contract in which the income-sharing rule is capable of handling all possible contingencies so that additional mechanism are unnecessary."*
6. It should be noted, here, that the existence of interest-based debt contracts gives rise to problems of limited access as well as unlimited access to credit. This implies that it is not just the quantity or pervasiveness of debt contracts, but the very existence of debt contracts that is the source of problems related to wealth and income disparities.
7. Bowles (2012) considers governance structure as productivity-enhancing "if the winners could compensate the losers (which would make the change Pareto improvement), except that the implied compensation need not be carried out or even be implementable under the informational conditions and other incentive problems in the economy."
8. *Nisab* is the minimum amount of wealth over which the payment of *zakah* becomes compulsory.
9. It might be argued that tying sukuk returns to GDP makes the returns more volatile and riskier. However, it is possible to redesign the rate of return mechanism to reduce the level of return volatility. For instance, there can be upper or lower bounds in the rate of return on GDP-linked sukuk. Theoretical studies and simulations of the behaviour of GDP-linked bonds indicate that a shift from conventional bonds to GDP-linked bonds can benefit high-debt countries in terms of increased macroeconomic stability and lower market volatility.
10. The entire OIC region, which includes the Middle East and North Africa, as well as Sub-Saharan Africa, most of Central Asia and South & South-East Asia, has a highly unequal wealth distribution. These conditions imply that the PBAF proposal for asset-based redistribution driven by risk-sharing finance can be relevant for the cooperation and coordination of OIC efforts toward the implementation of viable solutions to the problem of wealth inequality.
11. The total value of assets under PNB management in 2020 reached RM 322.6 billion, including more than 14.5 million accounts.
12. It is noted, in this respect, that around 30% to 40% of the government budgets in the OIC countries are devoted to development projects.

REFERENCES

Aaminou, Mohamed Wail, and Tarik Akin. 2020. "Risk-Sharing Finance and Inequality in a Benchmark Agent-Based Model." In *Handbook of Analytical Studies in Islamic Economics and Finance*, edited by Nabil Maghrebi, Tarik Akin, Zamir Iqbal, and Abbas Mirakhor. Berlin: De Gruyter Oldenbourg.

Acemoglu, Daron. 2019. "Why Universal Basic Income Is a Bad Idea." *Project Syndicate*, June 2019.

Akin, Tarik. 2017. "Financialization, Risk-Sharing and Wealth Inequality in A Stock-Flow Consistent Model." The International Centre for Education in Islamic Finance (INCEIF).

Akin, Tarik, Obiyathulla Ismath Bacha, Zamir Iqbal, and Abbas Mirakhor. 2020. "Risk-Sharing Asset-Based Redistribution in Public Finance: A Stock-Flow Consistent Analysis." In *Handbook of Analytical Studies in Islamic Economics and Finance*, edited by Nabil Maghrebi, Tarik Akin, Zamir Iqbal, and Abbas Mirakhor. Berlin: De Gruyter Oldenbourg.

Akin, Tarik, and Abbas Mirakhor. 2019. *Wealth Inequality, Asset Redistribution and Risk-Sharing Islamic Finance*. Berlin: De Gruyter Oldenbourg.

Al-Jarhi, Mabid Ali. 1981. *Towards an Islamic Monetary and Financial System: Structure and Implementation*. Jeddah, Saudi Arabia: The International Center of Research in Islamic Economics, King Abdulaziz University.

———. 2020. "The Islamic Macroeconomic Model: How to Apply It." In *Islamic Monetary Economics*, edited by Taha Egri and Zeynep Hafsa Orhan, 28–55. Oxford: Routledge.

Askari, Hossein, Zamir Iqbal, Noureddine Krichene, and Abbas Mirakhor. 2010. *The Stability of Islamic Finance: Creating a Resilient Financial Environment for a Secure Future*. Singapore: John Wiley & Sons.

Askari, Hossein, Zamir Iqbal, Noureddine Krichene, and Abbas Mirakhor. 2012. *Risk Sharing in Finance*, 1st ed. Singapore: John Wiley & Sons.

Askari, Hossein, and Abbas Mirakhor. 2014. Risk Sharing, Public Policy and the Contribution of Islamic Finance. *PSL Quarterly Review, Economia Civile* 67 (271): 345–379.

Askari, Hossein, and Abbas Mirakhor. 2015. *The Next Financial Crisis and How to Save Capitalism*, 1st ed. New York: Palgrave Macmillan US.

Atkinson, Anthony B. 2011. "Basic Income: Ethics, Statistics and Economics." Centre for Research in Economic Analysis, University of Luxembourg. https://www.nuff.ox.ac.uk/users/%0Aatkinson/Basic_Income Luxembourg April 2011.pdf.

Bacha, Obiyathulla Ismath, Ahcene Lahsasna, and Abdou Diaw. 2014. "Public Sector Funding and Debt Management: A Case for GDP-Linked Ṣukūk." *Islamic Economic Studies* 22 (1): 185–216. https://doi.org/10.12816/000 4135.

Bacha, Obiyathulla Ismath, and Abbas Mirakhor. 2013. *Economic Development and Islamic Finance*. Edited by Zamir Iqbal and Abbas Mirakhor. *Economic Development and Islamic Finance*. The World Bank. https://doi.org/10.1596/978-0-8213-9953-8.

Bacha, Obiyathulla Ismath, Abbas Mirakhor, and Hossein Askari. 2015. Risk Sharing in Corporate and Public Finance: The Contribution of Islamic Finance. *PSL Quarterly Review, Economia Civile* 68 (274): 187–213.

Bartholomew, David J. 2008. *God, Chance, and Purpose: Can God Have It Both Ways?*, 1st ed. Cambridge, UK: Cambridge University Press.

Basu, Kaushik, and Joseph E. Stiglitz. 2016. *Inequality and Growth: Patterns and Policy Volume I: Concepts and Analysis*. 1st ed. London, UK: Palgrave Macmillan UK. https://doi.org/10.1057/9781137554543.

Bezemer, Dirk J. 2011. "Causes of Instability: Don't Forget Finance." *Levy Economics Institute Working Papers No. 665*. https://doi.org/10.2139/ssrn.1808020.

Bowles, Samuel. 2012. *The New Economics of Inequality and Redistribution (Federico Caffè Lectures)*. Cambridge: Cambridge University Press.

Buiter, Willem H., and Ebrahim Rahbari. 2015. "Why Economists (and Economies) Should Love Islamic Finance." *JKAU: Islamic Economics* 28 (1): 139–162.

Carney, Stacie, and William G. Gale. 2005. Asset Accumulation Among Low-Income Households. In *Assets for the Poor: The Benefits of Spreading Asset Ownership*, edited by Thomas M. Shapiro and Edward N. Wolff, 165–204. New York, NY: Russell Sage Foundation.

Colciago, Andrea, Anna Samarina, and Jakob Haan. 2019. Central Bank Pilicies and Income and Wealth Inequality: A Survey. *Journal of Economic Surveys* 33 (4): 1199–1231. https://doi.org/10.1111/joes.12314.

Davidson, Paul. 2009. Can Future Systemic Financial Risks Be Quantified? Ergodic vs Nonergodic Stochastic Processes. *Revista De Economia Política* 29 (4): 324–340. https://doi.org/10.1590/S0101-31572009000400001.

Dietsch, Peter. 2021. Money Creation, Debt, and Justice. *Politics, Philosophy & Economics* 20 (2): 151–179. https://doi.org/10.1177/1470594X21999736.

Domanski, Dietrich, Anna Zabai, and Michela Scatigna. 2016. "Wealth Inequality and Monetary Policy." *BIS Quarterly Review, March*.

Erbas, S. Nuri, and Abbas Mirakhor. 2013. "The Foundational Market Principles of Islam, Knightian Uncertainty, and Economic Justice." In *Economic Development and Islamic Finance*, edited by Zamir Iqbal and Abbas Mirakhor, 93–130. Washington, D.C.: The World Bank. https://doi.org/10.1596/978-0-8213-9953-8.

Gentilini, Ugo, Margaret Grosh, Jamele Rigolini, and Ruslan Yemtsov. 2020. *Exploring Universal Basic Income: A Guide to Navigating Concepts, Evidence, and Practices*. Washington, DC: World Bank. https://doi.org/10.1596/978-1-4648-1458-7.

Haan, Jakob de, and Jan-Egbert Sturm. 2016. "Finance and Income Inequality: A Review and New Evidence." *DNB Working Paper No.530*. De Nederlandsche Bank.

Hintermaier, Thomas, and Winfried Koeniger. 2015. "Household Debt and Crises of Confidence." *IZA Discussion Paper No. 9409*.

Hodgson, Graham. 2013. "Banking, Finance and Income Inequality." *Positive Money*, no. October: 35.

Hopkins, ed. 2018. Inequality and Risk-Taking Behaviour. *Games and Economic Behavior* 107 (January): 316–328. https://doi.org/10.1016/j.geb.2017.11.007.

IMF. 2017. *Fiscal Monitor: Tackling Inequality. Fiscal Monitor*. Washington, D.C.: International Monetary Fund.

———. 2021. "COVID-19 Recovery Contributions." Washington, D.C.: International Monetary Fund.

Iqbal, Zamir, and Abbas Mirakhor. 2017. *Ethical Dimensions of Islamic Finance*. Cham: Springer International Publishing. https://doi.org/10.1007/978-3-319-66390-6.

Ismath Bacha, Obiyathulla, and Abbas Mirakhor. 2017. "Funding Development Infrastructure without Leverage: A Risk-Sharing Alternative Using Innovative Sukuk Structures." *The World Economy*, June, 1–11. https://doi.org/10.1111/twec.12512.

ISRA. 2012. Kuala Lumpur Declaration. In *The Second Strategic Roundtable Discussion ISRA-IRTI-DURHAM University*, 1–3. Malaysia: Kuala Lumpur.

Jordà, Òscar., Katharina Knoll, Dmitry Kuvshinov, Moritz Schularick, and Alan M. Taylor. 2019. The Rate of Return on Everything, 1870–2015. *The Quarterly Journal of Economics* 134 (3): 1225–1298. https://doi.org/10.1093/qje/qjz012.

Kahneman, Daniel. 2003. A Perspective on Judgment and Choice: Mapping Bounded Rationality. *American Psychologist* 58 (9): 697–720. https://doi.org/10.1037/0003-066X.58.9.697.

Kahneman, Daniel, and Amos Tversky. 1979. Prospect Theory: An Analysis of Decision under Risk. *Econometrica* 47 (2): 263–291.

Kahneman, Daniel, and Amos Tversky. 1988. "Prospect Theory: An Analysis of Decision Under Risk." In P. Gärdenfors & N.-E. Sahlin (Eds.), *Decision, Probability, and Utility: Selected Readings* (pp. 183–214). (Reprinted from "Econometrica," 47 (1979), pp. 263–291). Cambridge University Press. https://doi.org/10.1017/CBO9780511609220.014.

Kahneman, Daniel, Jack L. Knetsch, and Richard H. Thaler. 1991. Anomalies: The Endowment Effect, Loss Aversion, and Status Quo Bias. *Journal of Economic Perspectives* 5 (1): 193–206. https://doi.org/10.1257/jep.5.1.193.

Knight, Frank H. 1921 [1964]. *Risk, Uncertainty and Profit*. New York: Augustus M. Kelley.
Kumhof, Michael, Romain Rancière, and Pablo Winant. 2015. Inequality, Leverage, and Crises. *American Economic Review* 105 (3): 1217–1245. https://doi.org/10.1257/aer.20110683.
Lawrance, Emily C. 1991. Poverty and the Rate of Time Preference: Evidence from Panel Data. *Journal of Political Economy* 99 (1): 54–77. https://doi.org/10.1086/261740.
Ljungqvist, Lars, and Thomas J. Sargent. 2012. *Recursive Macroeconomic Theory*. Third. Cambridge, MA: MIT Press.
Maghrebi, Nabil, Zamir Iqbal, and Abbas Mirakhor. 2016. *Intermediate Islamic Finance*. Singapore: John Wiley & Sons Singapore Pte. Ltd. https://doi.org/10.1002/9781119191551.
Maghrebi, Nabil, and Abbas Mirakhor. 2015. "Risk Sharing and Shared Prosperity in Islamic Finance." *Islamic Economic Studies* 23 (2): 85–115. https://doi.org/10.12816/0015021.
Mian, Atif. 2013. "Monetary Policy and Macro-Prudential Regulation: The Risk-Sharing Paradigm." *Working Paper No. 713*. Central Bank of Chile.
Mian, Atif, and Amir Sufi. 2014. *House of Debt: How They (and You) Caused the Great Recession, and How We Can Prevent It from Happening Again* (1st ed.) Chicago: University of Chicago Press.
Mian, Atif, and Amir Sufi. 2018. "Finance and Business Cycles: The Credit-Driven Household Demand Channel." *Journal of Economic Perspectives* 32 (3): 31–58. https://doi.org/10.1257/jep.32.3.31.
Mirakhor, Abbas, and Wang Yong Bao. 2013. Epistemological Foundation of Finance: Islamic and Conventional. In *Economic Development and Islamic Finance*, edited by Zamir Iqbal and Abbas Mirakhor, 25–66. Washington, D.C.: The World Bank.
Moseley, William G. 2001. African Evidence on the Relation of Poverty, Time Preference and the Environment. *Ecological Economics* 38 (3): 317–326. https://doi.org/10.1016/S0921-8009(01)00184-7.
Myers, Stewart C. 1977. "Determinants of Corporate Borrowing." *Journal of Financial Economics*, 5, 147–175. https://doi.org/10.1016/0304-405X(77)90015-0.
OECD. 2015. *In It Together: Why Less Inequality Benefits All*. Paris: OECD Publishing. https://doi.org/10.1787/9789264235120-en.
OECD. 2017. *Bridging the Gap: Inclusive Growth 2017 Update Report*. Paris: OECD Publishing.
Moseley, William G. 2017. *Bridging the Gap: Inclusive Growth 2017 Update Report*. Paris: OECD Publishing.
Piketty, Thomas. 2014. *Capital in the Twenty-First Century*. Cambridge, MA: Belknap Press of Harvard University Press.
Piketty, Thomas. 2015a. Capital and Wealth Taxation in the 21st Century. *National Tax Journal* 68 (2): 449–458. https://doi.org/10.3386/w20871.

Piketty, Thomas. 2015b. Putting Distribution Back at the Center of Economics: Reflections on Capital in the Twenty-First Century. *Journal of Economic Perspectives* 29 (1): 67–88. https://doi.org/10.1257/jep.29.1.67.

Rajan, Raghuram G. 2010. *Fault Lines: How Hidden Fractures Still Threaten the World Economy*, 1st ed. New Jersey: Princeton University Press.

Rizvi, Syed Aun R., Obiyathulla Ismath Bacha, and Abbas Mirakhor. 2016. "Risk Sharing and Public Policy." In *Public Finance and Islamic Capital Markets*, 65–98. New York: Palgrave Macmillan US. https://doi.org/10.1057/978-1-137-55342-3_4.

Rochet, Jean-Charles. 2008. "Procyclicality of Financial Systems: Is There a Need to Modify Current Accounting and Regulatory Rules?" *Banque de France Financial Stability Review No:12*.

Samuelson, William, and Richard Zeckhauser. 1988. "Status Quo Bias in Decision Making." *Journal of Risk and Uncertainty* 1 (1): 7–59.

Serra-Garcia, Marta. 2010. "Moral Hazard in Credit Markets: The Incentive Effect of Collateral." *Tilburg University Working Paper*.

Seshadri, Ananth, and Kazuhiro Yuki. 2004. Equity and Efficiency Effects of Redistributive Policies. *Journal of Monetary Economics* 51 (7): 1415–1447. https://doi.org/10.1016/j.jmoneco.2003.10.006.

Skidelsky, Robert. 2001. "Asset Based Welfare." 2001. https://web.archive.org/web/20120307200422/http://www.skidelskyr.com/print/asset-based-welfare.

Solow, Robert M. 1957. Technical Change and the Aggregate Production Function. *The Review of Economics and Statistics* 39 (3): 312–320. https://doi.org/10.2307/1926047.

Standing, Guy. 2017. *Basic Income: And How We Can Make It Happen*. London: Penguin Books.

Stiglitz, Joseph E. 2015a. *Rewriting the Rules of the American Economy: An Agenda for Growth and Shared Prosperity*. New York: W. W. Norton & Company.

———. 2015b. "New Theoretical Perspectives on the Distribution of Income and Wealth among Individuals: Part III: Life Cycle Savings vs. Inherited Savings." *NBER Working Paper Series No. 21191*. Cambridge, MA.

Turner, Adair. 2016. *Between Debt and the Devil: Money, Credit, and Fixing Global Finance*, 1st ed. Princeton, New Jersey: Princeton University Press.

Tversky, Amos, and Daniel Kahneman. 1981. The Framing of Decisions and the Psychology of Choice. *Science* 211 (4481): 453–458. https://doi.org/10.1126/science.7455683.

Wang, Susheng. 2013. *Organization Theory and Its Applications (Routledge Studies in Business Organizations and Networks)*. 1st ed. New York, NY: Routledge.

Wickens, Michael. 2008. *Macroeconomic Theory A Dynamic General Equilibrium Approach*. New Jersey: Princeton University Press.
World Bank. 2016. *Poverty and Shared Prosperity 2016: Taking on Inequality*. Washington, D.C.: World Bank. https://doi.org/10.1596/978-1-4648-0958-3.
———. 2020a. "Malaysia Islamic Finance & Financial Inclusion."
———. 2020b. *Poverty and Shared Prosperity 2020: Reversals of Fortune*. Washington, DC: World Bank. https://doi.org/10.1596/978-1-4648-1602-4.
World Economic Forum. 2017. *The Inclusive Growth and Development Report*. Geneva: World Economic Forum.
World Inequality Lab. 2021. "World Inequality Report 2022."

CHAPTER 9

The Risk-Sharing Organizing Principle of *Iqtiṣād*

A paradigm shift toward *iqtiṣād* principles is necessary because society cannot hold together if fails to address risks inherent to all economic activities to ensure justice. The alternative is bleak because principles are indivisible and the consequences of risk transfer are dire. Risk sharing should not be confused with alternative attitudes toward risk, including risk transfer, which is conducive to recurrent financial crises, economic recessions, and increasing income disparities. Government bailouts of too-big-to-fail institutions using public funds to mitigate the risk of contagion during banking crises constitute an implicit shifting of private losses to third parties. A recourse to risk shifting to solve problems caused by risk transfer is a misguided approach that violates the basic principles of property-rights protection. In the resolution of financial crises, economic justice would be better served with risk-sharing arrangements such as debt-equity swaps seem to be systematically dismissed as impractical solutions.

Perhaps, it is easier to lament the accumulation of debt, explain the unpredictability of financial crises, and defend a *status quo* of fragile debt-based financial systems. It is arguably more difficult to redefine the role of financial intermediation, and risk diversification which does not eliminate aggregate shocks to the real economy, and restructure financial systems

© The Author(s), under exclusive license to Springer Nature Switzerland AG 2023
N. El Maghrebi et al., *Revisiting Islamic Economics*, Palgrave Studies in Islamic Banking, Finance, and Economics, https://doi.org/10.1007/978-3-031-41134-2_9

on the basis of risk sharing finance. It is easier to blame the depressingly common occurrence of crises on maturity mismatches, high leverage ratios, low interest rates, and lack of regulation. It is more difficult to hold non-traditional beliefs that defy conventional economic wisdom about the usefulness of interest-based debt and risk-transfer financial systems. As repeatedly argued by Reinhart and Rogoff, among others, the roots of eight centuries of financial folly lie in debt defaults and banking crises. It may be argued, thus, that no amount of banking regulation or debt ceiling can lessen the likelihood of the next crisis in debt-driven financial systems. Systemic risk may indeed, migrate from the banking to non-banking institutions as more securitized bank loans lie in the balance sheets of pension funds, insurance firms, and investment funds.

Thus, it is rather difficult to advance the agenda for an ideal economy based on iqtiṣād principles without understanding the causes of financial instability. Part of the reason for the recurrence of financial crises is the accumulation of debt through financial regulation and policies that entrenches expectations about fixed income and undermine risk sharing. Historical evidence about the regulation of interest on loans dates back to 1775 BC in the Babylon of Hammurabi, and though elaborate schemes were designed to eschew accusations of *de facto* interest structures, and despite the conditional hostility under the Jewish and Christian traditions, the rationale behind its clear prohibition in Islam is evidence of its timeless economic and moral implications. There are clear injunctions against interest in the authentic sources of knowledge, the Qur'an and the Sunnah, which leave no room for rapprochement between Islamic finance and conventional finance based on a compromise about interest-based arrangements. At *prima facie*, marginal deviations from an ideal economy based on risk-sharing may seem trivial and inconsequential, but on closer observation, the serious cumulative effects of interest-based transactions on economic justice and social stability should not be underestimated. Indeed, as interest-based debt and risk-transfer transactions become the norm, the notions of justice and morality, as well as the normative rules of behaviour would be redefined in order to accommodate new forms of rent-seeking practices.

The danger for Muslim societies is that silent acquiescence to a compromise with consciousness can ultimately lead to tolerance of a change in consciousness. The disintegration of consciousness would, in turn, render criticism of debt finance and inherently unstable financial systems irrelevant to the derivation of *Iqtiṣād* principles for the organization of an ideal economy from the *Qur'an* and *Sunnah*. Indeed, if interest is differentiated from usury and tolerated as a pre-requisite to the integration of Islamic finance with global finance, it would be impossible to enshrine its prohibition as an axiomatic principle of Islamic economic thought. As demonstrated in previous chapters, the Impossibility Theorem implies that a reconciliation between conventional economics and Iqtiṣād, which represents the ur'an's vision of ideal economy is not possible. It will be clear also from the present chapter that it is impossible to reconcile the organizing principle of risk sharing in Islamic finance with the theory and practice of conventional finance based on risk transfer. Thus, it is imperative that the economic rationale behind the prohibition of interest and other forms of risk transfer as well as the essence of risk sharing are well understood in order to avoid shifting the windows of morality to accommodate rent-seeking and eschew skin-in-the-game agreements. It is the organizing principle of risk sharing that ensures economic justice based on the *iqtiṣād*'s normative rules of behaviour and institutional structure. The failure to share economic risk is a failure to share economic prosperity, and to ensure safety in numbers. Given the impossibility to diversify aggregate shocks to the real economy, there remain the real prospects of widening income disparities, poverty, destitution, and social instability, which would leave economists and policymakers with.

Economic Uncertainty and the Notion of Risk

For the purposes of extracting the orgarnizing principles of an ideal economy, it is important to understand the notions of risk and attitudes toward risk, which in turn necessitate the examination of the impact of uncertainty on economic life. There is, indeed an irreducible amount of randomness in economic systems, where failure to predict the future cannot be simply explained by flaws and deficiencies in human knowledge. The complexity of social and economic systems derives from an amount of indeterminism even larger than biological systems. As noted by Kenneth E. Boulding (1987, p. 116), "Parameters change all the time. We are constantly passing from one region of time to another, and at the boundaries between them the parameters change… The failure of prediction can come either because we don't know what the parameters of the system are or because the parameters of the system change. We can imagine what celestial mechanics would be like if the planets were moved by angels who either did or did not like astronomers. I would no longer be a lovely constant, but would wobble all over the place, just like the propensity to consume, or the money supply, or even demand and supply curves."

Thus, it is rather difficult to view the economy as a predictable system, where the exact timing and extent of recessions can be foreseen with the same precision that eclipses can be expected based on accurate and stable parameters in celestial mechanics. Economies cannot be seriously described as predictable systems because economic parameters such as the propensity to consume, investor confidence, and market sentiment, among others, are notoriously unstable. The random arrival of new information and disruptive technologies may alter a variety of parameters related to skills, beliefs, and expectations. It is because parts of the economic system interact with others in dependable and undependable patterns that there is room for the system to grow in size and shrink unpredictably. Indeed, the economy, as a system, cannot be simply regarded as the sum of its parts, and if the rules governing such interactions are responsive to innate and established patterns of human behaviour and heterogeneous experiences and learning processes, then there is an irreducible element of randomness about the propensity of the economy to expand and contract.

There is a degree of uncertainty about the outcome of economic activities, about future profits and losses, and even about the mutable rules of behaviour and institutional structures. Economic uncertainty can, for instance, affect the behaviour of participants in fixed-income markets leading to anticipations of imminent recession, and bond pricing with invariably high yields similar to those demanded from debtors with high risk of default. Also, uncertainty about future tax regimes may be differently perceived. As noted by Adam Smith (1776, [2007], p. 565), "[l]et the tax be light or heavy, uncertainty is always a great grievance." It is, thus, argued that a significant degree of inequality across taxpayers under a regime of light taxation can be perceived as "less insupportable than any degree of uncertainty." Given the pervasiveness of uncertainty in all aspects of economic life, aversion towards risk cannot justify its transfer to other parties. There is, thus, no logical justification for a pre-determined stream of income to accrue with certainty to the lender, despite the uncertain nature of profits and losses. Positive interest rates, it is usually argued, are justified by the presence of uncertainty, but it is the very pervasiveness of uncertainty that should justify sharing risk rather than diverting it away.

Thus, economic agents may behave differently because of uncertainty about the outcome of economic activities and business cycle fluctuations. Heterogeneous expectations result in different views about future rates of economic growth and inflation, cost of capital and cost of labour, and other time-varying economic parameters. As noted by Frank Knight (1935, pp. 37–38) on the theory of investment, the relation between capital and time is "one of the most vexed questions of economic theory which must be cleared up if the structure as a whole is to be sound." Uncertainty about the future dynamics of economic systems is the rule not the exception. Yet, it is investment under certainty that seems to constitute the rule, and uncertainty seems to be dismissed as an unnecessary impediment to theoretical analysis. Indeed, the theory of the firm provides, as argued by Mark Blaug (1992, p. 151), a textbook definition of business enterprise as an "ideal type" that is "patently unrealistic: for example, instead of conceiving of entrepreneurs as maximizing an index of preferences that includes pecuniary and non-pecuniary returns, on analogy with the consumer in the theory of demand, the utility function of businessmen is reduced to directly observable monetary returns; moreover, the elements of time, uncertainty, and the costs of obtaining information are put aside as unnecessary complications." Economic decisions are taken, thus inevitably, under conditions of uncertainty and incomplete information.

It is important to examine the impact of incomplete information and the relation between uncertainty, risk and statistical inference. Drawing inferences about the unknown properties of the entire population from the characteristics of sample observations is associated with two types of error. Type I error is about rejecting a hypothesis that is in fact true, and type II error of mistakenly accepting one that is found to be false. Making inferences about the true population and judgement about the relative significance of type I and type II errors are bound to influence the process of decision-making under uncertainty. An economic relationship accepted at conventional levels of statistical significance does not make it an undisputable fact. It may be argued that economic and social relations are inherently probabilistic in nature. There is a failure, however, to acknowledge the necessary element of risk associated with economic decisions under uncertainty eschew harm and risk is part of human nature and instinct, but it is also a conscious one. Thus, individual attitudes toward risk may differ, but aversion toward risk does not justify its transfer in order to maximize one's own utility at the detriment of others. Indeed, risk transfer is an attempt to redefine the risk and return tradeoff and dissociate risk from uncertainty by resticting the probability of losses.

Risk and uncertainty are inseparable, indeed. In his treatise about risk, uncertainty and profit, Frank Knight (1921 [1964], p. 198), "it is our imperfect knowledge of the future, a consequence of change, not change as such, which is crucial for the outstanding of our problem." With respect to the problem of profit and competition, it is also argued that it is "*conceivable* that all changes might take place in accordance with known laws, and in fact very many changes do occur with sufficient regularity to be practically predictable in large measure." However, even upon allowing for changes to occur with sufficient accuracy and regularity such as interest rates, and in accordance with known laws and forward guidance as with unconventional monetary policies, there still remains an element of risk associated with debt defaults that cannot be completely eliminated. Thus, even a systematic adjustment of interest rates does not alter the essential nature of pre-determined rates of return, which remain set on *ex ante* basis, independently from the outcome of economic activities. Thus, variations in interest rates do not entirely address the implications of uncertainty and risk in economic activities.

It is also argued that with respect to risk, the distribution of possible outcomes can be known a priori based on mathematical calculation or statistical inference from past observation or experience. With respect to uncertainty, however, it may not be possible to estimate the distribution of outcomes and quantify probabilities because of the uniqueness of the conditions under consideration. The amount of uncertainty depends, among others, on the degree of homogeneity in beliefs and dogmatic assumptions, as well as individual levels of confidence and capacity to form correct judgement. The distinction between measurable and unmeasurable uncertainty is further complicated by a time-dependent learning process that may undermine rational judgement about changing conditions.

The world of change in which people live is indeed a world of uncertainty. As argued by Knight, Frank H. (1921 [1964], p. 199), it is possible to live only by "knowing *something* about the future; while the problems of life, or of conduct at least, arise from the fact that we know so little. This is as true of business as of other spheres of activity." (italics in original text). Life and possessions cannot be completely protected from all peril, as noted also by Haynes (p. 409), who argues that "[e]ven when it is certain that an unfavourable event will happen, a risk may exist, because the time of the occurrence is uncertain. Death is a certainty for all, but the time of death is among the greatest of uncertainties." It is undeniable that no human being has control over the beginning of life or its end, and that life is shrouded with uncertainty. There remains, indeed, an element of uncertainty in the timing of death, which is the most certain of events. This implies that as change in society is inevitable, it is impossible to gain accurate a priori knowledge about the outcome of economic activities.

THE PERVASIVENESS OF RISK-TRANSFER RELATIONS

It is difficult to reconcile the notion that uncertainty and imperfect knowledge are part of economic life with the disturbing thought that some economic agents can be completely insulated from economic losses. This insulation is hard to defend on moral and economic grounds, and it cannot be sanctified by legally binding agreement because, notwithstanding the freedom of contract, its effects are determined by the *Shari'ah* not *fiqh* arguments that give precedence to economic growth over economic justice. The insulation of lenders from potential losses is inconsistent with the direct exposure of other economic agents such as entrepreneurs and workers to similar risk. Adam Smith (1776 [2007], p. 69) acknowledged that the "wages of labour in different employments vary according to the probability or improbability of success in them." Thus, for the sake of consistency, the same line of argument should apply to other forms of productive engagement including financiers. It may be also argued that lenders who provide funding for risky investments should be entitled to payoffs in excess of the risk-free rate of return. But the very exposure to risky enterprise should justify state-contingent payoffs rather than fixed incomes reflecting a risk premium commensurate with the probability of default.

The question arises as to what may constitute the moral grounds on which fixed payoffs can be justified for lenders when the income streams accruing to other parties, including workers, are invariably exposed to the risks of entrepreneurial endeavours. It is not clear, indeed, why the wages of labour should vary with the probability of success whereas the payoffs of lenders are invariant to the probability of loss. The general view of interest as an inevitable reality is indicative of the way in which beliefs about interest accumulated into social tolerance for economic irrationality. It is the uncritical understanding of facts in ways that defy logic that leads to the acceptance of interest despite clear evidence of prohibition on moral, historical, and theological grounds. The practice of interest-based lending is so pervasive in the society that, for tax collection purposes, arbitrary minimum rates of interest can be legally imposed on interest-free loans. Even if lenders charge no interest or offer rates below market interest rates on any loan transaction, taxes may be levied regardless of the existence of family relationship between parties.

A mandatory limit on interest rates may be aimed at preventing tax evasion on loans or gifts among family members, but the underlying message is clear. It can be argued that such a tax treatment of interest-free loans is intrusive and punitive, as interest payments are thrusted upon parties who freely consent to enter into interest-free agreements. It rests on the view that debt is necessarily interest-bearing, and it leaves little to room for benevolent loans or *qardh hasan* between relatives and friends, among others. Debt may be interest-free between parties but in the sight of tax collectors, it is not. Thus, interest-based loans are the *de facto* rule rather than the exception. As the innate conscience about benevolence and moral sentiments is flattened, it becomes difficult for societies to realize that rules should be enacted to provide solutions to debt problems not to exacerbate them. As secular ideologies dispense with historical and theological arguments about the prohibition of interest, it becomes difficult for governments, which are presumed to beget power from people, to prevent the entrenchment of interest in every aspect of social and economic life.

Financial regulation, which should be aimed at promoting economic and social outcomes, seems to be geared toward protecting the interest of creditors than ensuring financial stability. There is a policy failure to address the destabilizing role of financial practices such as repurchase agreements and the transfer of credit risk off the balance sheet of banking institutions. At the aggregate level, credit risk is difficult to assess because of the inevitable correlation between default probabilities and the contagious effects of counterparty defaults. The social costs of litigation and law enforcement through courts are also huge. Risk-transfer arrangements are also entrenched in the society through other regulations including the tax deductability of interest payments. Financial measures are also taking to shift the burden of losses during banking crises, providing relief to financial institutions at the expense of the large public. Given the pervasiveness of uncertainty in the real economy, financial measures that insulate certain parties from suffering losses due to aggregate shocks and economic downturns, condemn others to suffer economic injustice, leading to destitution, and poverty.

Thus, a failure to understand the implications of uncertainty cannot lead to fundamental change in the way risk is managed to serve economic justice. If belief in the importance of economic justice in ensuring social stability is abandoned, and lies about econmic laws are accepted with warm applause, it is difficult to pursue the vision of an ideal economy. If ends are allowed to justify the means, it is difficult to restore credibility to governments and to palliative measures that faciliate the bailout of banking institutions during financial crises. The hard truth is that debt problems cannot be solved with more debt, and that uncertainty cannot be accommodated with risk-transfer and risk-shifting *solutions* that, given their inherent flaws, cannot be sustainable.

DEBT AND FINANCIAL INSTABILITY

The most important challenge in macroeconomic modelling is to provide, as noted by Joseph Stiglitz (2018, p. 70), convincing explanations about repeated economic downturns and proposals for adequate remedies. There is, however, a failure of macroeconomic models, including the Dynamic Stochastic General Equilibrium (DSGE) model over the past quarter-century, to meet expectations, and part of the reason is due to the "inadequate modelling of the financial sector meant they were ill-suited for predicting or responding to a financial crisis; and a reliance on representative agent models meant they were ill-suited for analysing either the role of distribution in fluctuations and crises or the consequences of fluctuations on inequality." There is a failure of DSGE models, in particular, to explain the sources of perturbance in the economy, and the mechanism through which shocks are less likely to be absorbed, than to get amplified and persist. In fact, the inability to predict crises is hardly surprising the reluctance of most models to meaningfully incorporate debt instruments despite the established evidence that financial crises are essentially debt crises.

Also, Paul Romer (2016), expressed similar disenchantment, as he argued that macroeconomics has experienced more than three decades of intellectual regress. The economics profession, Richard A. Werner (2016, p. 362) argues, "has singularly failed over most of the past century to make any progress in terms of knowledge of the monetary system, and instead moved ever further away from the truth as already recognised by the credit creation theory well over a century ago." As a result of repeated financial crises associated with the cyclical nature of credit, it is becoming extremely difficult to manage risks to the stability of the financial system, with the traditional instruments of monetary and fiscal policies. In this regard, the Bank for International Settlements (2015, p. 3) noted that "interest rates have been extraordinarily low for an exceptionally long time, in nominal and inflation-adjusted terms, against any benchmark. Such low rates are the most remarkable symptom of a broader malaise in the global economy: the economic expansion is unbalanced, debt burden and financial risks are still too high, productivity growth too low, and the room for manoeuvre in macroeconomic policy too limited. The unthinkable risks becoming routine and being perceived as the new normal."

Many years later, the BIS suggests also in its Annual Report (2022, p. 27) that nominal and inflation-adjusted interest rates remain at historically low levels partly because of "a weaker impact of monetary policy on aggregate demand following the prolonged period of unusually low interest rates." Thus, it is not clear whether the persistence of low interest rates is the outcome of persistently lower aggregate demand or the other way round. The question arises as to whether there are limits to the ability of central banks to stimulate demand since the transmission channels of monetary policy are weakened under low interest rates. There is growing evidence that aggressive monetary policy easing has become gradually ineffective. Borio and Hofmann (2017) argue that the transmission mechanism may be weakened by headwinds, including debt overhang and heightened uncertainty, which often accompany balance sheet recessions, and by inherent nonlinearities in the relationship between interest rates and spending. Also, Ahmad, Borio et al. (2021) provide evidence about the diminishing traction of monetary policy on aggregate demand after accounting for potential nonlinearities associated with business cycle fluctuations, debt levels, and decreasing equilibrium interest rates.

The lack of responsiveness of aggregate demand to monetary easing is indicative of a flattening of the Philipps curve, which describes the inverse relation between inflation and unemployment. It is also accompanied with a flattening of the IS curve, which relates investment to savings, output to interest rates, or goods markets to money markets in the Keynesian IS-LM macroeconomic model. Theoretically, reducing interest rates to lower borrowing costs is expected to stimulate real investment, leading to stronger output and income. Given the narrow room for policy manoeuvre, however, the flattening of the yield curve may not be effective either, since short-term nominal rates can be regarded as proxies for *ex ante* long-term real interest rates, as suggested by Fuhrer and Moore (1995) in their analysis of inflation persistence.

There are conceptual difficulties in understanding the current economic conditions and the impact of limited policy manoeuvre, which may be partly attributed to the complex implications of interest rates for the real economy. Persistently low interest rates may affect bank profitability in various ways, including diminishing term premium, which reflects the differential between short-term deposit and long-term lending rates. An environment of lower interest rates may not necessarily provide stronger incentives for capital expenditure by firms that do not regularly adjust hurdle rates in the evaluation of investment projects. Since hurdle rates are not systematically aligned with the levels of interest rates, underinvestment may persist even under low borrowing costs. The conditions of underinvestment are conducive, in turn, to a shortfall in demand, and economic stagnation.

Interest Rates and the Transmission of Monetary Policy

It may be argued that interest rates should be reduced in order to discourage savings and avoid the *paradox of thrift*, where excessive savings lead to reduced aggregate demand, but heightened uncertainty about future income may provide even stronger incentives for saving rather than borrowing. Similarly, contractionary fiscal policies meant to curb inflation may be conducive to the *paradox of austerity*, where deficits cannot be reduced due to falling demand and diminishing tax receipts. As central banks continue to hold large shares of government bonds through asset purchase programs, debt is destined to rise faster than economic output.

The theoretical difficulties in understanding the role of interest rates in regulating the real economy and sustainability of sovereign debt have stimulated the development of new economic philosophy that monetary policy does not matter when there are no legal or institutional constraints on borrowing and spending by governments that are monetarily sovereign. The Modern Monetary Theory (MMT) is often criticized for its simplistic approach to economic analysis. The fundamental argument behind the MMT paradigm is that new money creation can be used to pay for government debt, and unlimited spending does not matter either as long as inflationary pressures remain under control. While it is true that governments borrowing in their own currencies can neither be subject to scrutiny nor forced default, the counter-argument is usually made that demand on government debt would necessarily depend on the availability of underused resources. Also, mounting burdens of public debt may increase the prospects of higher taxation to fund future government spending, shifting thereby the burden on the private sector, and raising the likelihood of debt crises.

Thus, losing traction of the transmission mechanism is losing control of monetary policy. It seems that the bond between inflation and targeted growth in money supply is rather missing. The flattening of the yield curve, Philipps curve, and IS curve may be symptomatic of losing control and faith in effective monetary transmission mechanisms at low interest rates. If monetary policy is found to be ineffective at low interest rates, then the question arises as to whether it can be effective at higher rates. The argument that higher rates are necessary in switching from an inflation-targeting regime to inflation-fighting one may fall apart for the same reasons that render lower rates ineffective. As traction of monetary policy is waning, aggregate demand can hardly be expected to respond better to higher interest rates. Indeed, positive and negative changes in the level of interest rates may have asymmetric effects on aggregate demand. It is more plausible that aggregate demand would not be so much boosted by the lower savings resulting from lower interest rates as suppressed by the lower disposable income resulting from higher interest rates. Monetary policy is further complicated by expectations of higher inflation rates, which lend little support to the argument for raising interest rates in the presence of weak demand and anaemic growth.

Despite the compelling evidence about the theoretical difficulties emanating from the introduction of interest rates in economic thinking, there is a tendency for macroeconomic theorists, as argued by Paul Romer (2016), to "dismiss mere facts by feigning an obtuse ignorance about such simple assertions as 'tight monetary policy can cause a recession.'" There are indeed serious concerns that tight monetary policies can lead to recessions, but there are equally perturbing thoughts that loose policies can fuel speculative activities and asset bubbles followed by banking crises and economic recessions. The deliberate policies aimed at discouraging savings and encouraging borrowing may increase the incentives for speculative strategies in order to compensate for lower returns from bank deposits and bond markets. The greater exposure to riskier assets fuelled essentially by increased borrowing is conducive to higher equity valuation and it may be appealing to policymakers as well as it increases perceptions of greater wealth. Conventional wisdom suggests that the wealth effect ensures stronger consumer spending, but it is not clear whether higher asset valuation is sustainable when economic growth is essentially driven by debt, which increases the prospects of financial instability.

It is rather difficult to articulate convincing arguments for policy tightening or expansion given a dearth of investment irrespective of the level of interest rates. With high savings and historically low net investment as a share of total capital stock, the reality of secular stagnation poses serious policy challenges. For instance, the theory of stagnation proposed by Alvin Hansen (1939), is reflective of economic and philosophical conundrums about the ineffectiveness of orthodox and unconventional policies. He argued that unemployment should be used as an instrument to control inflation, and that monetary that monetary policy should pursue negative real interest rates in order to achieve full employment with equilibrium savings and investment. The notion that adjustments to policy rates can effectively determine inflation and fine-tune the goods and financial markets seems to be rather implausible given the inherent flaws of the transmission mechanism. Given the risk-transfer nature of interest rates and financial systems, low inflation constitutes an impediment against the lowering of real interest rates in order to increase demand. Also, Lawrence Summers (2014, p. 29) discusses the new secular stagnation hypothesis and notes that "it may be impossible for an economy to achieve full employment, satisfactory growth and financial stability simultaneously simply through the operation of conventional monetary policy."

Monetary Policy as a Source of Economic Uncertainty

The Taylor rule of central banking operations implies that adjustments of interest rates should be based on the significance of output gaps and deviations of actual inflation from target rates. For instance, policy tightening to control aggregate demand and ensure price stability is reflected by measures to increase interest rates if actual output surpasses potential levels and inflation rates exceed desired ones. As argued by Randall Wray (2016, p. 54), this is "just a slightly updated Phillips curve notion -if the unemployment rate gets too low, inflation results- but with far more concern shown for inflation than unemployment." The primary objective of inflation targeting is to promote economic stability by restricting increase in the general price level. The target inflation and growth rates of money supply are considered to be the appropriate quantities that ensure the operation of the economy near full employment levels. As the ability to control fluctuations in the general price level depends on inflationary tendencies and deviations from inflation targets, monetary policy rests on the accuracy of economic outlooks that capture the perceptions of households and firms about the long-term stability of the general price levels. The logic of setting a future path of inflation and adjusting interest rates on the basis of the observed deviations of actual price levels from target ones depends, however, on a better understanding about the determinants of inflation. It is difficult to argue for contractionary policies, for instance, when inflationary forces are essentially driven by external shocks to global fuel and food systems rather than increase in domestic demand.

If monetary policy is expected to achieve, concurrently, a multitude of objectives ranging from price stability to economic growth and full employment, it is necessary to consider the question of whether the adjustment of interest rates to transmit monetary policy and achieve its objectives is, in fact, the source of balance or distortion. From a theoretical perspective, it should be noted that, according to Keynes (1937, p. 221), *The General Theory* is "a theory of why output and employment are so liable to fluctuations." The effectiveness of monetary policy depends on the inner workings of interest rates, which should determine the optimal levels of saving and investment to attain equilibrium output at full employment. Despite near-zero interest rates, the reality of imbalanced and anaemic growth persists, however. It is clear also that quatitative easing with asset purchase programs aimed at providing further liquidity in the financial system are distortive of the price discovery process in financial markets. The unlimited balance sheet of central banks acting as *de facto* price makers and purchasers-of-last resort implies that asset prices are bound to increase regardless of the content of economic information. Money creation to purchase financial assets seems to take precedence over the informational efficiency of financial markets. As monetary policy becomes an additional source of uncertainty, the prospects of inflation, asset bubbles, and financial crises increase because it is axiomatic, as suggested by Kindleberger and Aliber (2005) that inflation is function of the growth of money and that asset bubbles depend on the expansion of credit.

Thus, monetary policies aimed at promoting price stability through the adjustment of interest rates can constitute a source of economic instability. Further evidence from Husted et al. (2020) suggests that increased uncertainty about monetary policy results in protracted declines in firm investment. Also, De Pooter et al. (2020) argue that the reaction of bond yields depends on market perceptions of uncertainty about the future path of policy rates. There is a degree of market complacency in building large positions in interest rates when policy uncertainty is low followed by abrupt reversals in response to monetary policy surprises. Thus, the very instrument of interest rate, with which monetary policy is purported to seek escape from economic uncertainty is itself found to be embroiled with controversy. The traditional sense of security and certainty in interest-based mechanisms is perhaps waning, and part of the reason has to do precisely with the uncertain nature of economic activities.

The theoretical and empirical arguments about secular stagnation are not merely suggestive of the Keynesian conundrum of low investment. They are also indicative of the fact that central banks are losing traction of the channels for policy transmission to the real economy in terms of aggregate expenditure and income. As noted earlier, the ability of central banks to boost demand and influence inflation expectations by inflating financial assets may be technically unlimited, but there are also concerns about credibility given the increased risks of asset bubbles and financial instability. Given the history of debt accumulation, financial crises, and balance-sheet recessions, it is rather difficult to concur with the argument that interest rates can be an effective instrument of monetary policy. The growing literature suggests that the occurrence of banking crises is not limited to countries with low levels of income, and that government debt is likely to increase not just as a result of bank bailouts and government spending but also in association with lower tax revenues.

Debt and the Making of Financial Crises

It is argued that though economic theory does not provide sufficient guidance about the exact timing of duration, financial crises, they may occur in advanced and developing economies. It is rather the reliance on leverage that makes financial markets markets and institutions vulnerable to crises of confidence. Reinhart and Rogoff (2009, p. xxxix) suggest that highly leveraged economies can be unwittingly sitting on the edge of financial precipice, and that part of the reason for *this-time-is-different syndrome* is the "failure to recognize the precariousness and fecklessness of confidence—especially in cases in which large short-term debts need to be rolled over continuously." Clear signals of impending crises may be, indeed, dismissed as irrelevant based on new theories about the implications of new economic dynamics, new rules of valuation, or new productivity-boosting technologies. But falling into the financial precipice is rather a certainty because asset bubbles, where prices are not driven by economic fundamentals but by debt and speculative trading, always implode.

Price increases driven by erratic shifts in market sentiment are consistent with individual rationality do not render asset bubbles rational. The notion of "rational bubbles" is proposed to describe market conditions under which price deviations from economic fundamentals are consistent with a behaviour of economic agents governed by "rational expectations." Since the theory of rational expectations implies only that changes in asset prices are driven by expectations conditional on all available information, rationality in this narrow meaning does not exclude the possibility of "rational" speculative bubbles. Arguably, the implosion of bubbles is inevitable and independent of their theoretical characterization as rational or otherwise. The inevitable implosion of speculative bubbles is a natural outcome of the inherent fragility of the financial structure. In this respect, John Maynard Keynes (1937, p. 210) argues that "the increased demand for money resulting from an increase in activity has a backwash which tends to raise the rate of interest; and this is, indeed, a significant element in my theory of why booms carry within them the seeds of their own destruction."

The financial instability hypothesis, proposed by Hyman Minsk (1977), provides an interpretation of Keynesian theory of the business cycle. The distinction is made between three classes of firms depending on their ability to meet debt obligations. Firms in hedge-finance positions are expected to generate stable income sufficient to cover all debt payments including interest and principal. Depending on the present value of future income relative to that of debt payments, the expected income of speculative units may not be sufficient to meet debt obligations, increasing thereby the need for new debt commitment or asset sales. The fragility of speculative units derives from a mismatch between long-term assets and short-term liabilities, and rising cost of refinancing with new debt, among others. Finally, Ponzi finance units are characterized by limited income and assets, where payments can only be met by increasing the amount of debt outstanding. Thus, the financial instability hypothesis implies that higher interest rates can transform hedge units into speculative units, and the latter into Ponzi units, which may be in turn forced into extinction or constrained to short-term debt rolled over continuously. A decline in the levels of investment and future income resulting from liquidity problems or lower aggregate demand would amplify the risk of debt defaults, bank runs, and financial crises.

The exact timing of financial crises may not be predictable, but vital signs emanating from money markets cannot be ignored. The Office of Financial Research (2022) argues that monetary market uncertainty is conducive to elevated treasury market volatility and reduced liquidity. More generally, it sends warning signals that "bond market stress measures are showing levels comparable to March 2020 and the early days of the 2007–09 financial crisis." Also, the market for repurchase agreements is regarded as the epicentre of the US financial crisis. Repurchase agreements allow banks, hedge funds, and investment funds to borrow overnight against collateral, and the rise of the repo rate above the federal-funds rate is often regarded as a sign of liquidity problems. The Federal Reserve may intervene with large-scale overnight funding, lowering thereby the repo rate, but concerns about shortage of liquidity may linger longer. Because the balance sheets of banks are characterized by long-term illiquid assets against short-term demand deposits, perceptions of liquidity shortage in repurchase markets increase the risk of old-fashioned bank runs. Non-bank institutions such as insurance companies are also exposed to bank-like maturity mismatch, which increases the risk to financial stability. There are also concerns about negative returns in the hedge fund industry, the largest decline since the onset of the US credit crisis, and about the ability of highly leveraged hedge funds to hedge against adverse price movements and rising inflation.

Prudential Regulation and the Procyclicality of the Financial System

It is clear that the conventional financial systems existing financial systems are inherently unstable, and that they do not match the pulse of the real economy. They constitute rather an unmistakable source of unwarranted fluctuations in aggregate demand and economic activity. As suggested by Minsky (1977), fine-tuning in the prevailing financial systems is rather impossible, but restraining the speculative activities of banks and businesses is warranted. Thus, attempts by central banks to promote price stability and economic growth by fine-tuning interest rates, which constitute the very source of financial instability, are also misguided. It is usually argued that the procyclicality of the financial system, which reflects the tendency for banks to increase lending during economic expansions and contract credit during economic downturns, exacerbates business cycle fluctuations. As noted by Rochet (2008), procyclicality is intrinsic to financial systems, as an alternation of credit expansions during growth phases and credit crunches during downturns produces endogenous financial cycles. Indeed, the accumulation of credit losses can trigger a crisis of confidence in the banking and financial sectors, lower investment, and a decline in economic activity. Prudential regulation can itself be a source of procyclicality as capital requirements imply that banks are bound to suffer credit losses during economic downturns rather than expansions. The question remains as to whether countercyclical measures and changes to accounting and regulatory rules can effectively reduce the risk of financial instability. Indeed, the financial instability hypothesis implies that it is debt-fuelled speculative activities that essentially cause, not merely exacerbate, fluctuations in the levels of output and employment.

Thus, it is not clear whether a regime of countercyclical capital buffers aimed at attenuating the propensity for credit contraction during downturns can eliminate the risk of financial instability. Additional capital requirements may, to some extent, constrain the supply of credit during economic expansions, but they do not necessarily diminish exposure to default risk. Indeed, higher capital-to-asset ratios during expansions may increase bank resilience to shocks during economic downturns, but they do not ensure lower exposure to default risk. There is empirical evidence, Ayyagari, Beck, and Martinez Peria (2017, 2018), that macroprudential policies result in slower growth of credit for smaller firms, and from Auer et al. (2022) suggest that higher growth in bank lending to smaller and riskier borrowers is associated with higher interest rates, which are reflective of larger default risk premia. It is also argued by Bhargava et al. (2023) that the riskiness of corporate credit deteriorates as the tightening of household-specific macroprudential measures increases. Thus, it can be argued that countercyclical capital buffers may be instrumental in smoothing the volume of credit over different phases of the business cycle, but the risks to financial stability from bad debt, liquidity problems, and financial contagion remain. Given the failure to address the causes of financial instability, it seems that financial regulation is not so much concerned about preventing the next banking crises than increasing the capacity of the banking system to withstand one.

It is difficult to expect the financial sector to smooth out economic fluctuations when it constitutes, in fact, the very source of economic instability. As macroprudential policies do not consider the economic rationale behind bank credit, and do not address the source of instability, there is no reason to believe that static or dynamic capital buffers would alter the nature of systemic risk. The bank business models are founded on the generation of revenues from the differentials between lending rates on long-term loan assets and borrowing rates on short-term demand-deposit liabilities. Under the current system of fractional reserve banking, banks are required to hold only a fraction of deposits as reserves for withdrawal purposes, allowing thereby for money creation to take place with each act of lending based on the remaining fraction. The reality, as noted by Michael Kumhof (2013), is that the power to create money is "an extraordinary privilege not enjoyed by any other type of business."

Historically, fractional reserve banking, which has also a legal basis in Roman law, is regarded to be inherently unstable. As noted by Collins and Walsh (2014, pp. 203–204), "there is little evidence of the type of large, destabilizing asset bubbles seen in modern economic history. Nevertheless, the Roman economy was not free from the potential instability of fractional reserve banking: both the attested credit crises of 49 BC and AD 33 prompted government to action to stabilise the credit markets, and most probably, the banking system." To lament a history of banking crises in ancient and modern economies without a desire to address the structural flaws in the financial architecture can only perpetuate the cycle of credit booms and busts, economic meltdowns, and job losses. The accumulated experience justifies action rather than a *status quo* over fractional reserve systems that are inherent unstable. It is important to realize that banks are not just financial intermediaries that channel preexisting funds from saving into investment, but also creators of money *ex nihilo*, and architects of wealth destruction. Thus, no amount of regulation, deregulation, and reregulation can be effective in preventing banking crises without promoting a full-reserve banking system operating under the principle of risk-sharing rather than interest-based debt financing.

Risk-Sharing and Economic Stability

It may be argued that the mechanics of monetary policies entwined with inherently unstable financial systems involve equal measures of complexity and paradox. From a philosophical perspective, the conundrum derives from the fact that economic activities are essentially associated with unknown outcomes with unknown probability distributions, and that it is impossible to circumvent the risks inherent to economic uncertainty by merely altering the level of interest rates. No amount of quantitative easing may be sufficient in rebalancing economic growth and employment with equilibrium levels of saving and investment when the economic environment is dominated pessimistic views about future yields and prospects of financial crises. Monetary policy based on the adjustment of policy rates and yield curves cannot be part of the problems and their solutions. The question, thus, arises as to whether the levels of output and employment should be determined by a rate of interest that provides a fixed premium as a reward for not hoarding money, or by a variable return of return on investment, which despite economic uncertainty and risk, constitutes an act of faith in the future.

The irrefutable evidence that interest-based debt is at the heart of banking crises and economic fluctuations strengthens the argument that the banking system's unique forces of destabilization in terms of credit expansion and money creation should be severed. The Chicago Plan, proposed by eminent scholars in association with the Great Depression, points out to the serious flaws of the prevailing financial systems. A full-reserve banking system would prevent banks from drawing on demand deposits to fund their lending activities, precluding thereby the boom-bust credit cycles, which are the source of economic fluctuations. It would also eliminate the risk of bank runs since no losses can be incurred by depositors in the event of debt default and deterioration of the bank's balance sheet. It was also argued that the reformed monetary system would allow the government to issue money at zero interest, and permit banks to draw from reserves at the central bank in order to fully cover liabilities, reducing thereby the net government and debt in the private sector.

As argued by Phillips (1992), the plan was defeated, however, as a matter of political expediency in favour of the institution of Federal deposit insurance and separation of commercial and investment banking. However, further evidence from Benes and Kumhof (2012) lends support to the economic rationale of the Chicago Plan, which can be theoretically achieved without diminishing the credit function of banks in extending funding to real investment. It is also argued that the interest rate on the treasury credit facility available to banks does not represent an opportunity cost of money but a borrowing cost to fund physical investment in the real economy. There is also evidence that a steady-state output is attainable given the reduction in distortive factors such as net interest rate spreads and unnecessary costs of bank supervision. Further analysis by Fiebiger (2014) suggests that money-financed fiscal stimulus would be also instrumental in promoting sustainable employment.

Interest Rates and Expected Rates of Return

The Chicago Plan has the merit of separating the monetary issuance and credit functions of banks, but it only lowers the level of debt without eliminating it. It is clear that interest rates are, unmistakably, the primary source of complexity and confusion. The distortive role of interest rates stems from a historical failure to deal with the inevitable implications of economic uncertainty in terms of exposure to risk. The debate about the concept of "natural" rate of interest, notably between David Davidson and Knut Wicksell, which centred on the existence of a rate that ensures full employment and price stability, provided some insights on the essence of interest rates. From the Keynesian perspective however, uncertainty contaminates, as noted by Robert Skidelsky (2020, p. 183) "the investment demand schedule as a whole, and not just enterprise. There is no 'normal' rate of return: there is simply an expected rate of return, governed by uncertainty." It is not clear, thus, whether interest rates, "natural" or otherwise, can be incorporated into models of economic equilibrium.

As argued by Tyler Cowen (1983, pp. 610–611), indeed, if interest rate is defined as an intertemporal price ratio for money, then the General Equilibrium (GE) model proposed by Arrow and Debreu model (1954) would fail to provide insights about the conditions of economic equilibrium under perfect competition. Indeed, it is by construction that the notion that "equilibrium" rate of interest should be explained with reference to the relative prices of other commodities. It is difficult, then, to impose predetermined rates of return as exogenous variables into a system of simultaneous equations when they should be determined rather endogenously. There is a need for a consistent theory of interest relating, internally, the prices of various commodities, but a coherent theory does not, or rather, exist. The inclusion of fixed rates of interest presents the problem of overdetermination with a system of more equations than unknowns unable to provide solutions that are internally consistent from an economic perspective. The essential argument is that a mathematical framework designed to identify equilibrium conditions for the optimal allocation of resources cannot be saddled with predetermined rates of interest as no economic role for money, except for accounting purposes.

Thus, the GE model of equilibrium under uncertainty assumes the existence of Arrow–Debreu securities or state-contingent claims, where a payoff defined in terms of one unit of a specific consumption good is obtained only if a particular state of the world occurs in the future, and zero otherwise. It precludes state-independent claims that deliver payoffs under every possible future state of nature because such securities are designed to circumvent the implications of economic uncertainty about future payoffs. It is not difficult to identify interest-debt claims as the only fixed-income arrangements that essentially transfer the risks inherent to economic activity from lenders to borrowers. The notion that rates of return should be predetermined *ex ante* in order to promote savings is inconsistent with the uncertainty that shrouds virtually all aspects of economic activity. However, with rates of interest, the financial economy is allowed to grow indefinitely independent from the reality of random payoffs that accrue from the real economy. Since the nature of economic activities is characterized by uncertainty, investment outcomes cannot be predetermined *ex ante*. If cashflows generated from real assets to service debt remain uncertain and unrelated to speculative or Ponzi financing, then it is impossible to enforce fixed claims on uncertain cashflows without breaking the relationship between the financial economy and the real economy. It is with the onset of credit crises stemming from debt defaults that the weak link between finance and the real economy is ultimately strained.

Iqtiṣād and the Islamic Financial System

In an ideal economy based on *Iqtiṣād* rules, monetary policy precludes the multiplication of money capital irrespective of the real and physical output. Essentially, the same policy instruments are available to Islamic and conventional monetary authorities, except that open market operations are driven by buying and selling of equity shares rather than bonds. In contrast to conventional monetary policy where interest rates are indirectly used to regulate money supply, the latter is directly adjusted through asset market activities. As in the standard apparatus of Arrow–Debreu general equilibrium, there is no room for state-independent financial claims. There is no recourse to fixed-income securities such as government bonds to induce portfolio adjustments, or direct lending to the banking sector with lower discount rates to increase liquidity in the financial system. Instead, it is possible for governments to adjust reserve requirements and use risk-sharing instruments rather than interest rates to create incentives to channel real savings toward productive investments.

The *Iqtiṣād*-based monetary policy depends on risk-sharing instruments rather than interest-rate mechanisms, which foster a decoupling of the financial system from the real economy. But the central challenge is about the design and issuance of risk-sharing instruments that can be used by the government to implement sustainable fiscal policies, and finance its operations and development expenditure beyond tax revenues. It is these risk-sharing instruments that would allow monetary policymakers also to manage liquidity and portfolio adjustment by the private sector to stabilize the real economy. It can be argued that it is possible to achieve these objectives through the issuance of sovereign *sukuk*. According to the Accounting and Auditing Organization for Islamic Financial Institutions (AAOIFI 2003), investment *sukuk* can be defined as "certificates of equal value representing undivided shares in ownership of tangible assets, usufruct and services." The negotiable financial certificates can be regarded as *pro rata* ownership claims on *Shari'ah*-compliant tangible assets and usufructs until maturity. Unlike conventional bonds, there is however no guarantee of redemption of *sukuk* capital prior to maturity, and theoretically, there is no assurance about fixed income.

Indeed, with reference to the issuance of investment sukuk, the *Shari'ah* Standard (17) issued by AAOIFI (2003, pp. 477–478) stipulates that "[t]he prospectus must not include any statement to the effect that the issuer of the certificate accepts the liability to compensate the owner of the certificate up to the nominal value of the certificate in situations other than torts and negligence nor that he guarantees a fixed percentage of profit." Thus, there is regulatory clarity about the nature of income expected from investment into asset-backed *sukuk*. Thus in theory, as there is no promise of a fixed rate of return, it is difficult to refer to *sukuk* as fixed-income securities. Depending on the nature of economic activity, the income streams generated by the underlying assets may be to, some extent, stable, but stability cannot legitimate promises of fixed income. The natural implication of this argument is that there is no theoretical basis for the notion of *sukuk* default because default is by definition a failure to honour a promise for payment of a fixed amount at a fixed point in time. The definition of the event of default on conventional bonds should not theoretically, apply to a failure by the *sukuk* issuer to pay a fixed amount at a fixed point in time because the issuance of the absence of guarantee of "fixed percentage of profit," according to the AAOIFI regulatory standards.

Thus, for the sake of resource mobilization in accordance with the risk-sharing principle of *Iqtiṣād* system, it is important to note that *Sharī'ah* compliance is not just about meeting the requirement of eligible underlying assets, but about the prohibition of interest charging as well. Given the economic definition of fixed-income security as one associated with state-independent payoffs, it is difficult to distinguish between conventional bonds and *sukuk* known as Islamic bonds. In fact, the labelling of *sukuk* as Islamic bonds similar to *conventional* bonds raises another regulatory conundrum. As *Sharī'ah* principles prohibit the trading of debt obligations except at face value, it is not clear how the debt-based *sukuk* would qualify for permissible trading on secondary markets, and constitute an effective instrument for monetary policy transmission. It may be also argued that, as a form of asset securitization, *sukuk* should not necessarily fall under the rubrique of debt. Whereas conventional bonds are issued without a designated underlying asset, it is the *pro rata* ownership of a *Sharī'ah* compliant underlying asset and its usufruct that distinguished *sukuk* apart from other securities including bonds and shares. This *sukuk* property may be regarded as a necessary, though, insufficient condition for *Sharī'ah* compliance because the securitization process should not culminate into a mechanism that guarantees fixed rates of return.

Insofar that demand is driven by promises of fixed-income streams based on asset ownership with reference to benchmark interest rates, it is difficult to eschew criticism that *sukuk* are nothing more than interest-based debt obligations. Theoretically, *sukuk* valuation should stem from the estimate appraisal of the underlying asset and its return-generating process, but they are rather subject to credit rating based on assessment of default probability. The credit rating of *sukuk* exposes the fact that they are perceived as debt instruments that can be subject to the likelihood of default. It should be noted that, despite promises of fixed payment, *sukuk ijārah* are permissible in Islamic finance on the grounds that they intrinsically differ from interest-*based* debt obligations. As demonstrated by Smith (1979) using option pricing theory, the value of *ijārah* does not depend on the financing decisions of the lessee, and does not affect its capital structure. As explained also by Maghrebi et al. (2016, pp. 214–215), *ijārah* depends, exclusively, on the value of the underlying asset net of usufructs until maturity whereas the value of debt is a function of promised fixed payments or the residual value of assets. It is noted, indeed, that "the valuation risk associated with the underlying asset is shared by both the lessor and the lessee. There is no risk transfer from the lessor to the lessee, as the potential fall in the asset value affects the former in terms of diminishing equity and the latter in terms of declining *ijarah* value. It is perhaps this risk-sharing element, which can be found in the ijarah but not in debt arrangements, that presents the economic rationale behind the permissibility of the former and prohibition of the latter." Thus, given the risk-sharing element and relative stability of future payoffs, *sukuk ijārah* should be regarded as a principal instrument of open market operations.

These conceptual distinctions are important because the design and issuance of *sukuk* in an *Iqtiṣād* system should not be driven by an unwarranted urge to mimic conventional instruments but by compliance with the tenets of risk-sharing in financial arrangements. The *pro rata* ownership of the underlying asset should be reflected by a commensurate exposure to risk. This is the case of pass-through securitization where the asset cashflows are channelled directly to investors. However, special-purpose-vehicles in structured finance are allowed to distribute cashflows to different tranches on prioritized basis. As actual earnings from *sukuk* may fall short of expected levels, it is the equity tranches that stand first to absorb potential losses. The sequential slicing of the loss function into additional mezzanine tranches to absorb residual losses implies that, unless all junior tranches are depleted, senior tranches are essentially protected against adverse cashflow fluctuations. The allocation of payoffs reflects an asymmetric distribution of risk, with a diminished exposure of senior tranches to payment shortfalls at the expense of subordinated tranches. Thus, the capital structure of structured finance products may provide opportunities for investors with different risk-return profiles, but the lower loss probability for senior tranches reflects the fact that cashflows are not distributed on *pro rata* basis. Hence, there is little evidence of risk-sharing when the loss function results in a fragmentation of payoffs that benefits senior tranches under unfavourable states of nature.

Structured finance can, thus, be instrumental in transferring risk across tranches and creating safe claims against risky assets. But it is difficult to argue for the use of financial securities based on credit enhancement mechanisms as instruments of monetary policy transmission. The complexity of structured finance lies in the implications of shock amplification to subordinated tranches and creation of debt-like obligations with respect to senior tranches. Ultimately, it is the degree of public trust in *Shari'ah*-compliant financial securities designed and issued on the basis of risk-sharing that would determine the demand and supply of financial instruments for the purposes of fiscal and monetary policies. It would be a misguided conviction for policymakers to promote financial systems based on risk-sharing while threatening their stability through the conduct of fiscal and monetary policies with instruments based on risk-transfer mechanisms.

Iqtiṣād, Equity Financing and State-Contingent Claims

The optimal instrument of risk-sharing remains the equity market because unlike fixed-income securities such as bonds, stocks represent state-contingent claims. The tightening of monetary policy can be conducted through the issuance of equity participation shares or asset-linked securities directly in the stock market to decrease money supply. The issuance of equity or national participation papers would offer, not only institutional investors but individual savers also, the opportunity to participate directly in the financing of government expenditures such as development projects. It is important, however, to issue low-denominated papers to induce individual investors, reduce transaction costs, and facilitate access to information in order to converge toward the optimal conditions of consumption and risk-sharing with complete markets. Investors would be entitled to a share of the expected revenues from the realization of development projects. It may be argued that for infrastructure projects that generate no direct revenues but are essential to economic activity, the government may be allowed to pay also dividends conditional on the rate of return in the real economy.

This argument is, to some extent, consistent with the notion of sovereign GDP-linked bonds, a financial innovation advocated by some economists including Robert Shiller (2003), who discusses the idea of trading a security that pays a quarterly "dividend" equal to a fraction of the GDP. Shiller (2018) further argues that the absence of such instruments is rather puzzling given the willingness of governments to tie debt with *fiat* money with no intrinsic value and no asset-backing as under the monetary system of gold or bimetallic standard. The binding of debt with the real economy can be instrumental in avoiding procyclical fiscal policies and provide the foundations for debt sustainability. But there are serious obstacles to the implementation of GDP-linked bonds, which stem from the behaviour of market participants and policymakers and their attitudes toward risk. Benford and Eguren-Martin (2018) contend that however large the benefits of macroeconomic and fiscal stability, there would be no market for such instruments if issuers are not willing to meet the expectations of investors. However, the main source of reluctance, as argued by Eduardo Borensztein, Maurice Obstfeld, and Jonathan Ostry (2018, p. 18), is not so much related to markets as to policymakers. Politicians, it is argued "tend to have relatively short horizons, and would not find debt instruments attractive that offer insurance benefits in the medium to long run but are costlier in the short run, as they include an insurance premium dirven by the domestic economy's correlation with the global business cycle." It may be further argued that the GDP-linked bonds have the potential to increase the capacity of the government to absorb shocks. As noted by Andy Haldane and Maurice Obstfeld (2018, p. 1), "[t]hey would provide the issuing government with debt relief when growth weakens and tax receipts decline." Given the limited room for policy manoeuvre under low interest rates and concerns of secular stagnation, the new instruments may provide innovative fiscal policy options that strengthen the linkage between the financial system and real economy.

The design and trading mechanics as well as pricing and regulatory issues related to GDP-linked debt are still a matter of intellectual debate. But the basic economic rationale is that the expected payoffs are defined as function of economic performance on *ex post* basis rather than naively predetermined as fixed income. GDP-linked bonds are state-contingent claims in the sense that payoffs are bound to vary during economic expansions and downturns. While recognizing, thereby, the implications of economic uncertainty about aggregate output, there remain, however, conceptual issues about the nature of debt or risk-sharing in GDP-linked bonds. Shiller (2018, p. 7) argues that "GDP-linked debt has to be issued into a world with existing outstanding nominal and inflation-indexed debt, with laws regulating the debt, such as national debt limits, and with public expectations and rules of thumb regarding the concept of debt, and even public hopes that the debt live up to religious principles, such as the Islamic Shari'ah compliant sukuk." In this respect, Arshadur Rahman (2018) suggests that governments interested in raising Shari'ah compliant

GDP-linked sukuk may opt for hybrid *ijārah* or *mudhārabah* partnership structures as *mushārakah* requires a symmetry of roles and responsibilities between parties that may not be appropriate for sovereign *sukuk*.

The central issue pertains to the nature and extent of debt and risk-sharing in the design of GDP-linked bonds. To the extent that there are binding promises of regular coupon payments and capital redemption at maturity, these securities are comparable to conventional bonds. It may be argued, however, that since the payout structure is not fixed a priori and the exact amount of coupon payments can only be determined after the calculation of GDP figures, it is difficult to strictly regard the GDP-linked bonds as fixed-income securities. There is indeed, to some extent, an element of risk-sharing since coupon payments are allowed to vary according to fluctuations in economic performance. As noted by Ostry and Kim (2018, p. 33), GDP-linked bonds "act as a perfect risk sharing device: giving the issuer a reduced obligation when its capacity to generate resources for debt service suffers, in exchange for a higher obligation when its capacity to pay is greater."

It is not clear, however, whether these securities represent, indeed, a "perfect" instrument for macroeconomic risk-sharing because fluctuations in coupon payments may not reflect the risk of negative growth. If the payoffs are calculated as a percentage of GDP *levels* rather than GDP *growth rates*, investors would be exposed to the risk of lower coupon payouts and diminishing returns rather than losses and negative returns resulting from negative growth. The calculation of coupon payments on the basis of GDP levels would insulate bond-holders from the risk of negative growth. Indeed, such GDP-linked debt obligations are reminiscent of the loss function applicable to holders of senior tranches in the multi-layered structured finance instruments, where shortages in cash-flows are absorbed first by equity tranches and subsequently by mezzanine tranches in order to reduce the risk of default to senior tranches. Hence, if GDP-linked bonds are designed so that the promised payouts are expressed in percentage of GDP levels rather than growth rates, then the loss of income from negative growth is bound to be absorbed in the real economy by the classes of entrepreneurs and workers only. This leaves the class of investors in GDP-linked bonds with lower probability of default on promised payments, a condition that resembles that of holders of senior tranches in structured finance.

Thus, the logic of fixed-income securities is glaringly contradicted by evidence of fluctuations in the real economy. This evidence renders adherence to the notion of linking the payoffs from government bonds to aggregate economic performance appealing indeed. But it appears from the above conceptual analysis that the element of risk sharing in GDP-linked bonds remains weak. Given the difficulties in understanding the nature of debt in GDP-linked bonds, important questions arise about the seniority ranking of GDP-linked bonds relative to other sovereign bonds, and about default probability despite the assumed indexation of debt with GDP. These issues underscore a tendency to treat GDP-linked bonds as pure debt obligations where coupon rates are fixed as a percentage of the bond principal represented by the GDP level, which varies over time. Indeed, in contrast to conventional sovereign bonds where a pre-fixed coupon rate applies to a principal that remains unchanged until maturity, GDP-linked bonds resemble rather inflation-index bonds where the principal is allowed to vary according to fluctuations in the consumer price index (CPI). Similar to a surge in the CPI which would force an increase in the principal amount, and in turn a rise in interest payments, an expansion in GDP would force an increase in the principal amount, and in turn a rise in GDP-linked bond payoffs.

The GDP-adjusted principal amounts can be determined in the same way that inflation-adjusted principal amounts are calculated as the product of the face value with an indexation coefficient that reflects the level of variations relative to the issuance date. Hence, it may be argued that the design of GDP-linked financial instruments with payoffs contingent on aggregate economic output does not constitute a clear departure from interest-based debt. The properties of perfect risk-sharing associated with equity financing in terms of sharing profits as well as losses may not be evident either in GDP-linked bonds. Hence, building confidence in GDP-linked bonds naturally raises the problem of interest, but it is clear that the idea holds, subject to further scrutiny, the prospects providing risk-sharing solutions to the problems of fiscal stability and monetary policy Insofar that financial innovation recognizes the importance of economic uncertainty and does not ignore its implications for risk-sharing finance, it deserves serious examination and perhaps fine-tuning to ensure economic justice.

Thus, uncertainty about future general price levels, economic growth, and employment should ideally lie at the heart of the economic thinking underlying not only monetary policies but corporate decisions as well.

This economic reality is implicitly recognized by Alan Greenspan (1998), who argues that "while the pursuit of price stability does not rule out misfortune, it lowers its probability." It may indeed, lower its likelihood, but it does not eliminate it. Yet, while firms and households make decisions about saving and investment under uncertainty, the mechanism of monetary policy transmission relies on interest rates that reinforce the misguided belief that fixed payoffs independent from future states of the economy are possible. There is indeed a deep logical inconsistency in the conduct of monetary policies, which are typically concerned with strategies leaning heavily on a perceived tradeoff between inflation and growth. Undue confidence is placed in policy rates and debt instruments that must, rather, bear the blame for the making of banking and financial crises, which constitute the primary source of financial instability and economic downturns.

It can, thus, be argued that only a shift toward equity financing can provide solutions to macroeconomic problems, including global imbalances. Indeed, Rogoff (2011) argues that "in a world of perfect financial markets, trade imbalances would not be a problem. They would simply be the outcome of efficient intertemporal trade and risk sharing." It is risk sharing, rather than risk transfer, that ensures that the payoffs to all contracts remain state-contingent, a necessary and sufficient condition that ensures financial stability and economic prosperity.

Risk-Sharing and Economic Prosperity

It is clear from the above examination that financial stability is *conditio sine qua non* for the pursuit of economic growth and full employment. The sources of financial instability do not seem to warrant serious thinking as there is a level of intellectual complacency in the uncritical dismissal of financial crises as unpredictable events or transitory disturbances. The question arises indeed, as to what major events would compel regulators to abandon fragile financial systems that are the primary source of economic instability and develop new architectures that are immune to financial crises. Contrary to conventional wisdom, financial instability is not inevitable. It is simply the natural product of credit risk accumulation in financial systems that rely on interest-bearing debt and fractional reserve on interest-bearing debt, and fractional reserve banking. A financial system based on the *Iqtiṣād* principle of risk-sharing would be resilient to shocks to aggregate demand and allow the conduct of effective fiscal and monetary policies with financial instruments designed to share rather than transfer risk.

Indeed, one of the central arguments of a paradigm shift toward *Iqtiṣād* for the organization of an ideal economy is that risk-sharing can be conducive to shared prosperity. The sharing of prosperity is not just a desirable proposition but a necessary condition for social and economic stability. It should be clear from the discussion throughout the book about the impossibility theorem of reconciling polar worldviews that economic life is not about self-interest, maximization of profit, and survival of the fittest. It is about adherence to normative rules of behaviour and institutional structure that ensure economic stability, and thus, shared prosperity. The inherent instability of debt-based financial systems is a descriptive proposition that has been proven to be true, it is incumbent on economists and policymakers to seriously consider the normative proposition that and ideal economy organized with the principle of risk-sharing should become a reality.

Given the historical evidence about the destabilizing effects of debt and balance sheet recessions, it is clear that equity financing should take precedence over debt financing. There are major difficulties in a paradigm shift toward equity because of institutional bias toward debt financing. Though the distortive effects of the latter can be easily identified, the regulatory remedies are often ignored. As noted by Brealey et al. (2013), it is possible to identify serious issues with capital-structure strategies based on debt-related conflicts of interest, which have adverse effects on the real economy. For instance, leveraged firms may prefer risky investment projects at the expense of bondholders, while firms in financial distress may distribute cash dividend or increase debt, a strategy that is consistent with Minsky theory of financial instability. Also, the incentive for issuing new equity to finance investment may be affected by higher levels of debt. Indeed, investment projects with positive net present values may be discarded solely on the basis that expected revenues may not be sufficient to cover the outstanding and future debt obligations. The suboptimal investment problem may be attenuated by the existence of sinking fund provisions, which reduce the risk of default, but as noted by Bodie and Taggart (1978), the underinvestment problem can be eliminated only when the firm exercises the option to redeem callable debt before maturity. As argued by Kish and Livingston (1992), call options on corporate bonds, which are useful in maximizing the market value of equity, are found to be, in turn, highly dependent on interest rates and debt maturities. The theoretical evidence implies that a solution to the underinvestment problem depends on a shift away from interest-bearing debt toward risk sharing.

Thus, future investment decisions cannot be entirely separated from past financing decisions. The risk structure of interest rates, game-theoretic behaviour, and complex designs of callable and convertible bonds further complicate the existing conflicts of interest between shareholders and bondholders over the capital structure and investment decisions. These conflicts of interest have the potential of curtailing the incentives to invest, which may lower firm valuation, and undermine economic activity. It is difficult, however, to eliminate the apparent bias toward debt. From the *Iqtiṣād*-oriented perspective, the elimination of the tax advantage of debt is a normative proposition that flows directly from the distortive effects of debt and stabilizing effects of equity and risk-sharing. The idea of eliminating the tax advantage of debt does not seem to be, as argued by Luigi Zingales (2015, p. 1356), "a very politically feasible proposal. But it is certainly the right proposal to eliminate many financing distortions. Ignoring it and marketing alternative proposals only contributes to making it more difficult to eliminate such distortion."

The idea of debt-equity swap to provide a viable solution to the U.S. financial crisis was also soundly rejected, perhaps not on the basis of economic rationale but because it contains an element of value judgement. Indeed, the right proposal to eliminate debt financing distortions is a value-based proposition to promote equity. It is difficult, indeed, to promote debt-equity swaps as such unconventional proposals are likely to be dismissed as irrelevant and not germane to the traditional debate about palliative solutions including bailouts and capital adequacy measures to which regulators typically resort at times of financial instability. As argued by Zingales (2008), debt-equity swaps or debt forgiveness arrangements should be mandated on financial institutions because these resolutions would not constitute a greater violation of private property rights than massive bailouts resulting in wealth redistribution from taxpayers to the financial system. The notion of swapping debt for equity resonates with the *Iqtiṣād*-based financial systems founded on the principle of sharing rather than transferring or shifting risk. Indeed, equity-driven financial systems preclude the formation of speculative bubbles leading to financial crises. As explained by Mirakhor (2014), the stability of Islamic financial systems derives, in part, from the condition of materiality in financing contracts, which ties financial assets to real assets and from the definition of returns as a function of cashflows generated by the underlying assets rather than interest rates. Also, the risk-sharing nature of Islamic bank assets, which differs from loan portfolios in the balance sheets of conventional banks, allows the financial sector in an *Iqtiṣād* system to absorb exogeneous shocks without incurring the risk of default.

Thus, from the *Iqtiṣād* perspective, the growth of the financial sector is not driven by growth in credit but by economic growth from real investment. As argued by Askari et al. (2010), the two-tier financial system that allows for organic growth in the financial sector and real economy is founded on full-reserve monetary system and investment banking based on equity financing. There may be incremental costs incurred under investment banking in terms of monitoring and information gathering, but these costs are intrinsic to risk-sharing agreements, and they can be reduced through information sharing, trust, and transparency. The alternative of debt-driven financial systems, it should be reminded, is associated with immensely higher costs for the society, stemming from asymmetric information, moral hazards, underinvestment, asset bubbles, financial crises, and massive bailouts. As argued by Skidelski (2020, p. 118), information is treated as a measurable cost but "what causes people to bond together is not the cost of obtaining information but the fear of being alone in an uncertain world."

Given the pervasive uncertainty, the important question, thus, arises as to whether it is possible to share economic prosperity without organizing the exchange economy in accordance with the principle of risk sharing. Part of the answer lies with the recognition of the logical inconsistencies of the capitalist ideologies dominating the economic thinking and willingness to seek a paradigm shift. The central contradiction of capitalism, as argued by Thomas Piketty (2014), lies in the fact that the rate of return on capital is persistently higher than the rate of growth of income or output. This inequality is an inequality of income and wealth distribution. It represents the principal destabilizing force that ensures the accumulation of wealth at higher rates than output and wages. It is clear that such an inequality cannot result from a distributive rule based on the *Iqtiṣād* principle of risk sharing that achieves equity and allocative efficiency. The fundamental logical contradiction is the outcome of risk-transfer arrangements where the financier or "entrepreneur inevitably tends to become a rentier, more and more dominant over those who own nothing but their labor. Once constituted, capital reproduces itself faster than output increases. The past devours the future."

Under the *Iqtiṣād* system, it is impossible for the past to devour the future as social and economic interactions are governed by exchange relations based on risk-sharing rather than rent seeking, which constitutes a violation of property rights. It is clear that capital can reproduce itself faster than output only if the relation between the financial sector and the real economy is severed. It is important to note also that the destabilizing forces emanate from debt rather than equity financing. It is interest-bearing debt that entitles debtholders to fixed-income streams independent from the sign of economic growth, reinforcing thereby the forces of divergence between the rate of return on capital and the growth of output and income. In contrast, the return on equity is reflective of the rate of return in the real economy. It is this organic relation that precludes capital from reproducing itself faster than output. There is no room for risk premium on assets with no direct exposure to undiversifiable risk, and no attachment with the real economy. Therein lies the central logical consistency of risk-sharing finance in the *Iqtiṣād* paradigm.

Conclusion

Thus, the normative argument that economic stability and economic prosperity can be achieved through risk sharing arrangements would lose its entire meaning if there is no desire to confront reality. The economic reality is that it is difficult to provide an intellectual justification for a synergetic projection of financial arrangements driven by risk transfer onto *Iqtiṣād*-based principles of economic organization. The impossibility theorem proposed in the previous chapter reflects the reality that given the radical differences in worldview and philosophical foundations between the Islamic and secular economic thinking, it is impossible to graft one polar case onto another. It is impossible to ignore pervasive uncertainty and imperfect knowledge, and graft the conflicting principles of risk transfer and risk sharing one onto another.

The crude reality is that there should be a constant ingredient of risk-sharing that ensures financial stability, which should, in turn, pave the way to the pursuit of sustainable economic growth and full employment. Debt is distortive of the relationship between the real economy and the financial system because financial claims for fixed payoffs independent of the outcome of real investment are inconsistent with the uncertain nature of economic activities. Speculative activities arise chiefly from the existence of state-independent claims that essentially ignore economic uncertainty. In the absence of risk-sharing, there is no viable solution to the central contradiction of capitalism and the unnecessarily complex relation between the financial sector and the real economy. No amount of financial regulation, bank supervision, monetary policy tightening and expansion, and financial inclusion can diminish the distortive effects of credit cycles and prospects of banking crises and financial instability without a genuine reform of the debt-based financial system. As noted in the previous chapters, *Iqtiṣād*, as a paradigm governed by immutable rules derived from *Qur'an* and *Sunnah*, not fallible human judgement, is a theonomy that provides practical guidance for the organization of economic life. It seeks justice in all economic interactions, without exception. As it recognizes the implications of uncertainty, the vicissitudes of seeking livelihood, and the risks associated with economic activity, it leaves no room for rent seeking in lieu of risk-sharing. It is impossible to accommodate risk-transfer agreements without distorting the system of incentives for investment and saving, which ensure economic growth and economic stability. The impossibility theorem, thus, implies that no coherent policies can be derived from a synthetic discipline that rests on grafting Islamic values onto conventional economics or secular ones onto Islamic economics through the processes of misguided secularization of Islamization of knowledge. There is certainly no merit in the grafting of economic ideas from conflicting worldviews that can only increase criticism and scepticism about a discipline that has so far failed to take off. And without a wholehearted shift to an internally consistent *iqtiṣād* paradigm that provides a vision for the organization of an ideal economy based on the principles of risk sharing with normative rules of behaviour and institutional structure, it is not clear, if it ever will.

References

Accounting and Auditing Organization for Islamic Financial Institutions, 2003. "*Shari'ah standard no. (17): Investment Sukuk*", pp. 464–488.
Arrow, Kenneth J., and Gerard Debreu. 1954. "Existence of an Equilibrium for a Competitive Economy." *Econometrica* 22: 265–290.
Rahman, Arshadur. 2018. "The Case for GDP-linked Sukuk," In *Sovereign GDP-Linked Bonds: Rationale and Design*, edited by Benford, James, Ostry Jonathan D, and Robert Shiller. VoxEU.org Book: CEPR Press, London, U.K.

Askari, Hossein, Zamir Iqbal, Noureddine Krichene and Abbas Mirakhor. 2010. "*The Stability of Islamic Finance: Creating a Resilient Financial Environment for a Secure Future*," Singapore: John Wiley & Sons (Asia) Pte Ltd.

Auer, Raphael, Alexandra Matyunina, and Steven Ongena. 2022. "The Countercyclical Capital Buffer and the Composition of Bank Lending." *Journal of Financial Intermediation* 52: 100965.

Ayyagari, Meghana, Thorsten Beck, and Maria Soledad Martinez Peria. 2017. *Credit Growth and Macroprudential Policies: Preliminary Evidence on the Firm Level*. BIS Papers No. 91.

Ayyagari, Meghana, Thorsten Beck, and Maria Soledad Martinez Peria. 2018. "*The Micro Impact of Macroprudential Policies: Firm-Level Evidence*," IMF Working Paper No. 2018/267.

Bank for International Settlements. 2015. "*85th Annual Report*," June 28, 2015, Basel, Switzerland.

Benes, Jaromir, and Michael Kumhof. 2012. "*The Chicago Plan Revisited*," IMF Working Paper WP/12/202.

Benford, James, Fernando Eguren-Martin. 2018. "Sovereign GDP-linked Bonds: Pros and Cons," In *Sovereign GDP-Linked Bonds: Rationale and Design*, edited by Benford, James, Jonathan D. Ostry, and Robert Shiller. VoxEU.org Book: CEPR Press, London, U.K.

Benford, James, Jonathan D. Ostry, and Robert Shiller. 2018. *Sovereign GDP-Linked Bonds: Rationale and Design*. VoxEU.org Book: CEPR Press, London, U.K.

Bhargava, Apoorv, Lucyna Górnicka and Peichu Xie. 2023. "*Leakages from Macroprudential Regulations: The Case of Household-Specific Tools and Corporate Credit*," European Central Bank Working Paper Series No. 2784.

Blaug, Mark. 1992. *The Methodology of Economics: Or How Economists Explain (2nd ed., Cambridge Surveys of Economic Literature)*. Cambridge: Cambridge University Press.

Blaug, Mark. 2003. The Formalist Revolution of the 1950s. *Journal of the History of Economic Thought* 25 (2): 145–156.

Bodie, Zvi, and Robert A. Taggart Jr. 1978. "Future Investment Opportunities and the Value of the Call Provision on a Bond." *The Journal of Finance* 33: 1187–1200.

Borensztein, Eduardo, Maurice Obstfeld, Jonathan D. Ostry. 2018. "Overcoming the Obstacles to Adoption of GDP-Linked Debt," In *Sovereign GDP-Linked Bonds: Rationale and Design*, edited by Benford, James, Jonathan D. Ostry, and Robert Shiller. VoxEU.org Book: CEPR Press, London, U.K.

Borio, Claudio and Boris Hofmann. 2017. "*Is Monetary Policy Less Effective When Interest Rates are Persistently Low?*" BIS Working Papers No. 628.

Boulding, Kenneth E. 1987. "The Epistemology of Complex Systems." *European Journal of Operational Research* 30: 110–116.

Brealey, Richard A., Stewart C. Myers, and Franklin Allen. 2013. *Principles of Corporate Finance*. 11th ed. MacGraw-Hill Education.
Collins, Andrew, and John Walsh. 2014. "Fractional Reserve Banking in the Roman Republic and Empire." *Ancient Society* 44: 179–212.
Cowen, Tyler. 1983. "The Rate of Return in General Equilibrium: A Critique." *Journal of Post Keynesian Economics* 5: 608–617.
De., Pooter, Giovanni Favara Michiel, Michele Modugno, Wu and Jason. 2021. "Monetary Policy Uncertainty and Monetary Policy Surprises." *Journal of International Money and Finance* 112: 102323.
Fiebiger, Brett. 2014. *The Chicago Plan Revisited: A Friendly Critique*. Elgaronline: Edward Elgar Publishing.
Fuhrer, Jeffrey, and George Moore. 1995. "Monetary Policy Trade-offs and the Correlation between Nominal Interest Rates and Real Output." *American Economic Review* 85: 219–239.
Greenspan, Alan. 1998. *The Federal Reserve's Semiannual Monetary Policy Report*," Testimony of the Chairman Alan Greenspan, February 24, 1998.
Hansen, Alvin H. 1939. "Economic Progress and Declining Population Growth." *American Economic Review* 29: 1–15.
Haynes, John. 1895. "Risk as an Economic Factor." *Quarterly Journal of Economics* 9: 409–499.
Husted, Lucas, John Rogers, and Bo Sun. 2020. "Monetary Policy Uncertainty," *Journal of Monetary Economics*, 115: 20–36.
Hyman P. Minsky. 1992. "*The Financial Instability Hypothesis*," The Jerome Levy Economics Institute of Bard College.
Keynes, John Maynard. 1937. "The General Theory of Employment." *Quarterly Journal of Economics* 51: 209–223.
Kindleberger, Charles P. 1989. *Manias, Panics and Crashes: A History of Financial Crises*. Basic Books.
Kindleberger, Charles P., and Robert Z. Aliber. 2005. *Manias, Panics and Crashes: A History of Financial Crises*, 5th ed. Palgrave Macmillan.
Kish, Richard J., and Miles Livingston. 1992. "Determinants of the Call Option on Corporate Bonds." *Journal of Banking & Finance* 16: 687–703.
Knight, Frank H. 1921 [1964]. *Risk, Uncertainty and Profit*. Augustus M. Kelley. New York.
Knight, Frank H. 1935. The Theory of Investment Once More: Mr. Boulding and the Austrians. *The Quarterly Journal of Economics* 50 (1): 36–67.
Kumhof Michael. 2013. "We Should Seriously Consider Revisiting "The Chicago Plan" of the 1930s which Separates the Monetary and Credit Functions of the Banking System," London School of Economics Blog.
Maghrebi, Iqbal, and Mirakhor,. 2016. *Intermediate Islamic Finance*. Singapore: John Wiley.

Maghrebi, Nabil, and Abbas Mirakhor. 2015. "Risk Sharing and Shared Prosperity in Islamic Finance." *Islamic Economic Studies* 23: 85–115.

Minsky, Hyman. 1977. "The Financial Instability Hypothesis: An Interpretation of Keynes and an Alternative to "Standard" Theory." *Nebraska Journal of Economics and Business* 16: 5–16.

Mirakhor, Abbas. 2014. "Regulatory Framework for Islamic Finance." *Islamic Banker* 11: 50–53.

Office of Financial Research. 2022. "Annual Report to Congress 2022"

Ostry, Jonathan D., Jun I. Kim. 2018. "On the Role of GDP-linked Debt in Expanding Fiscal Space", In *Sovereign GDP-Linked Bonds: Rationale and Design*, edited by Benford, James, Jonathan D. Ostry, and Robert Shiller. VoxEU.org Book: CEPR Press, London, U.K.

Phillips, J. Ronnie. 1992. *"The "Chicago Plan" and New Deal banking reform,"* The Jerome Levy Economics Institute of Bard College Working Paper No. 76.

Piketty, Thomas. 2014. *Capital in the Twenty-First Century*. Translated by Arthur Goldhammer. Cambridge, MA and London, UK: The Belknap Press of Harvard University Press.

Wray, Randall L. 2016. *Why Minsky Matters*. Princeton and Oxford: Princeton University Press.

Rashad Ahmad, Claudio Borio, Piti Disyatat and Boris Hoffmann. 2021. "*Losing Traction? The Real Effects of Monetary Policy when Interest Rates are Low,*" BIS Working Papers No. 983.

Reinhart, Carmen M., and Kenneth S. Rogoff. 2009. *This Time is Different: Eight Centuries of Financial Folly*. Princeton and Oxford: Princeton University Press.

Rochet, Jean-Charles. 2008. "Procyclicality of Financial Systems: Is there a Need to Modify Current Accounting and Regulatory Rules?" *Banque De France Financial Stability Review* 12: 95–99.

Rogoff, Kenneth. 2011, March 4. "What Imbalances after the Crisis?". In *Banque de France International Symposium on Regulation in the Face of Global Imbalances*.

Romer, Paul. 2016, January 5. "The Trouble with Macroeconomics". In *Speech at the Commons Memorial Lecture of the Omicron Delta Epsilon Society*.

Skidelski, Robert, 2020. *What's Wrong with Economics? A Primer for the Perplexed*, New Haven, London: Yale University Press.

Smith, Adam. 1776, [2007]. *"The Wealth of Nations"*, Harriman House Ltd, UK.

Smith, Clifford W. Jr. 1979. "Applications of Option Pricing Analysis." In *The Modern Theory of Corporate Finance, Handbook of Financial Economics*, edited by J. L. Bickster, 79–102, North-Holland Publishing Company.

Shiller, Robert J. 2018. "Introduction", In *Sovereign GDP-Linked Bonds: Rationale and Design*, edited by Benford, James, Jonathan D. Ostry, and Robert Shiller. VoxEU.org Book: CEPR Press, London, U.K.
Shiller, Robert J. 2003. *The New Financial Order: Risk in the 21st Century*. Princeton, New Jersey: Princeton University Press.
Stiglitz, Joseph E. 2018. "Where Modern Macroeconomics Went Wrong". *Oxford Review of Economic Policy* 34 (1–2): 70–106.
Summers, Lawrence. 2014. "Reflection on the 'New Secular Stagnation Hypothesis." In *Secular stagnation: Facts, causes and cures*, edited by Coen Teulings and Richard Baldwin, 27–38. London, UK: CEPR Press.
Werner, Richard A. 2016. "A Lost Century in Economics: Three Theories of Banking and the Conclusive Evidence," *International Review of Financial Analysis*, 361–379.
Zingales, Luigi. 2008, "Why Paulson is Wrong," *The Economists' Voice*, 5 (5).
Zingales, Luigi. 2015. "Presidential Address: Does Finance Benefit Society?" *The Journal of Finance* lxx (4): 1327–1363.

Index

A
Absolute freedom, 262
Absolute ownership, 262
Accountability, 157, 169, 172, 173, 229, 230
Agency costs, 152
Agency problems, 168, 174
Agnostic, 128
Agnostic humanism, 128
Altruism, 81, 101
Altruistic, 256
Arrow Debreu, 347, 348
Arrow Debreu Framework, 88, 89
Arrow Debreu Model, 84
Asset based distribution, 298, 314
Asset based financing, 169
Asset based redistribution, 288, 304–308, 312–314, 316, 318
Asset bubbles, 88, 104, 106
Asset linked securities, 352
Asset redistribution, 18
Asset securitization, 350
Asymmetric distribution, 351

Asymmetric information, 168, 292, 359
Austrian School, 82
Axiological, 226, 232

B
Banking crises, 167, 327, 334, 338, 341, 344–346, 361
Behavioural norms, 134
Behavioural rules, 119
Benevolence, 128, 160, 163
Business cycle, 331, 336, 342, 344
Business ethics, 172, 175

C
Capitalism, 138, 139, 152–154, 160
Capital scarce, 104
Capital structure, 351
Catholic, 129
Central banks, 17
Character traits, 161, 162, 164, 172
Christian, 215

Christianity, 189, 190
Christian values, 4
Collective behaviour, 9, 50
Colonialism, 192
Colonization, 183, 186, 192, 206, 216
Compassion, 4, 40, 128
Complexity, 129
Consumer behaviour, 101, 102, 104
Consumer choices, 102
Consumption, 348, 352
Contract enforcement, 132
Contractionary policies, 340
Corruption, 13
Credit booms, 345
Credit contraction, 344
Credit creation, 170, 336
Credit crises, 345, 348
Credit crunches, 344
Credit enhancement, 352

D
Debt crises, 328, 338
Debt financing, 345, 357, 358
Deceitfulness, 164, 173
Depression, 82
Desacralization, 37
Desacralize, 3, 18
Desacralizing, 23
Desecularization, 39
Despiritualized society, 183
Destabilizing effects, 357
Destitute, 21, 280
Diminishing returns, 354
Disequilibrium, 14
Dishonesty, 152
Disintegration, 186, 188
Distribution, 117, 118, 121
Distributive justice, 21, 242, 253, 260, 261
Dogmatic, 89

E
Ecological capital, 26
Ecological crisis, 20
Economic agent(s), 12, 25, 27–29, 64, 97, 101, 119, 123, 222, 223, 272
Economic behaviour, 85, 106, 119, 123, 131
Economic choices, 151, 153
Economic crises, 12, 13, 106, 152, 167
Economic decisions, 102, 103
Economic development, 61, 117, 132, 138, 169, 198, 201
Economic doctrine(s), 90, 198, 199, 203, 204
Economic equilibrium, 87, 95, 98
Economic exploitation, 166
Economic growth, 14, 26, 64, 94, 168, 170, 172
Economic ideology, 113
Economic injustice(s), 85, 121, 234, 286
Economic institutions, 122, 141
Economic justice, 116, 124, 157, 162, 216, 241, 246, 248, 251, 259–261, 274, 275
Economic man, 22, 26, 28
Economic models, 83, 94
Economic order, 91, 93, 94
Economic Policy(ies), 15, 16, 39, 82, 83, 85, 103, 106
Economic power, 183, 187, 188, 190
Economic prosperity, 117, 135, 138, 246, 255
Economic rationality, 100–105
Economic recessions, 263
Economic risks, 273
Economic stability, 132
Economic systems, 119, 122, 124, 132–135, 139

INDEX

Economic theory, 83, 84, 93, 95, 98–101, 104–106
Economic thought, 115–117, 123
Efficiency, 96
Efficient equilibrium, 85
Enlightenment, 216, 217, 229
Entrepreneurship, 87, 138, 142
Environmental degradation, 209
Environmental disasters, 26, 36, 58
Environmental equilibrium, 64
Epistemological, 5, 9, 36, 44, 92, 144, 190, 214, 220, 226, 230, 232
Epistemology, 39, 45, 51, 52
Equality, 15
Equilibrium, 217–219
Ergodic axiom, 96
Ethical beliefs, 105
Ethical dimension(s), 151, 152, 165, 174
Ethical norms, 200
Ethics, 2, 42, 48
Ethics theory, 159
Etymological, 3, 5
Etymology, 215, 224
Exploitation, 85, 263, 267

F

Fairness, 43
Fascism, 14
Felicity, 215, 225
Financial architecture, 345
Financial contagion, 344
Financial crises, 82, 89, 104, 105, 170, 263, 285, 287, 293, 299, 302, 303, 315, 319, 327, 335, 336, 341, 343, 346, 356, 358, 359
Financial distress, 357
Financial inclusion, 361
Financial instability, 167, 170, 335, 339, 341–344, 357, 358, 361

Financial institutions, 349
Financialization, 167, 171
Financial market(s), 87, 151, 309, 339–341
Financial regulation, 344, 361
Financial repression, 170, 171
Financial sector, 344, 345, 359–361
Financial stability, 339, 343, 344, 356, 360
Financial system(s), 59, 257, 273, 327, 328, 336, 343, 345, 346, 349, 352, 353, 356–361
Fiqh, 231–233
Fractional, 167, 169, 170
Fractional banking, 167, 169, 170, 345, 356
Fractional reserve, 169, 170
Fragility, 342
Free markets, 139
Fundamental inequality, 289, 290, 299, 304

G

Game theory, 88, 89
GDP growth, 354
GDP linked bond, 352–355
GDP linked debt, 353
GDP linked sukuk, 354
General equilibrium, 83, 84, 87–89, 93, 94, 98
Gharar, 165
Governance, 46, 59, 132
Government debt, 337, 338, 341, 346
Government spending, 82, 341

H

Hedonistic, 222
Heidegger, 4
Hellenic, 27
Human action, 189

Human behaviour, 25, 28, 29, 32, 45, 51, 103
Human capital, 155
Human choice, 213
Human conduct, 199
Human conscious, 222
Humanism, 128
Human well-being, 201

I
Ideologically, 61
Idiosyncratic risk, 301, 302
Immutability, 2, 55
Immutable, 212, 233
Impossibility theorem, 253, 357, 360
Incentive compatible contracts, 305
Income-based redistribution, 288, 289, 306
Income distribution, 166
Income inequality, 29, 30, 36, 87, 287, 288, 306, 310, 312, 316
Individual actions, 82, 85
Individual bias, 103
Individual choice, 275
Individual freedom, 13, 24, 43
Individualism, 216, 221
Individual liberty, 15
Individual rights, 263, 268
Inductive, 42, 59
Inequality(ies), 13, 17, 18, 44, 52, 86, 262, 274, 330, 359
Inequity, 228
Inflation, 14
Inflation adjusted, 336, 355
Inflation index, 353, 355
Inflation rates, 338, 339
Inflation targeting, 339
Injustice, 13, 47, 50, 85, 188, 199–201
Instability, 85, 94, 183, 339, 341–345, 357, 358, 361

Institutional, 8, 12, 51
Institutional behaviour, 119
Institutional development, 122
Institutionalized injustice, 250
Institutional scaffolding, 8, 13, 21
Integrity, 206
Intellectual disorder, 245
Interest-based contracts, 273
Interest prohibition, 269, 276
Internalizing virtues, 159, 160, 172
Invisible hand, 82
Irrational behaviour, 101
Irrationality, 334
Islamic civilization, 38, 155, 187, 268
Islamic ethics, vi
Islamic Institutions, 141
Islamic jurisprudence, 5, 6, 115, 133–135, 137, 140, 141, 143, 144
Islamic norms, 257
Islamic society, 46, 52–54, 57, 59
Islamic values, 2, 3, 22, 58
Islamization, xii, xiii, 6, 7, 9, 19, 23, 36–39, 66, 114, 118, 130, 133, 142, 185, 187, 198, 211, 223, 231–234, 253, 361

J
Judaism, 189, 190
Juridical ethics, 161
Just distribution, 118
Just market, 271

K
Keynesian, 12, 14, 15, 82, 83, 103, 336, 341, 342, 347
Key virtues, 162
Kuala Lumpur declaration, 306

L
Liberty, 200

INDEX

Logical impossibility, 35

M
Macroeconomic policy(ies), 318, 319, 336
Macro-market securities, 307, 308
Maldistribution, 19, 22, 87, 227, 228, 234
Malthusian theory, 86
Maqasid, 62, 63, 198
Market capitalism, 43, 153
Market economy, 87, 124, 263, 264
Market efficiency, 271
Market failure(s), 17, 85–87
Market pricing, 117
Material development, 188
Materialism, 184, 186, 193, 213, 216
Medinah society, 210
Meta-ethics, 155
Metamorphoses, 190
Metaphysical, 7, 9, 13, 21, 23, 31
Metaphysical beliefs, 120
Metaphysically, 232
Metaphysical order, 130
Metaphysics, 7
Modernists, 136, 193, 257
Modernity, 3, 4, 25, 38
Monetarism, 82
Monetarist School, 83
Monetary policy, 83, 336–341, 346, 348–350, 352, 355, 356, 361
Monopolies, 85
Moral character, 152, 159, 160, 172
Moral failure, 152
Moral hazard(s), 152, 170, 359
Morality, 128, 198, 202, 241
Moral law, 90
Moral order, 90
Moral philosophy, 23, 28, 159, 174
Morals, 151, 160
Moral sentiments, 100, 309, 334
Moral thoughts, 155
Moral values, 158, 173
Mortality, 121
Muslim civilization, 189, 195
Muslim societies, 6, 8, 37, 38, 41

N
Natural order, 90, 91
Neoclassical, 114, 121
Neoclassical economics, 79, 84, 89, 95, 98, 100, 105
Neoliberal economic(s), 1, 9, 10, 12–15, 17, 22, 32, 33, 35, 39, 44, 62, 63, 66
Normative system, 256

O
Ontological, 18, 19, 23, 34, 36, 47

P
Paradigm shift, 184, 198, 205, 206, 259
Pareto optimal, 219
Pareto optimality, 86, 100
Pass through, 351
Perfect competition, 84, 87
Personal freedom, 24
Phillips curve, 339
Philosophical foundation, 10, 33, 36, 52
Political economy, 10–12, 23, 78–81, 83, 90, 95, 97–99, 101, 106, 246, 247
Political freedom, 124
Political ideology, 13
Political instability, 183
Political philosophy, 116
Political virtues, 188
Positive character, 204
Positive economic, 132

Positivism, 219–221
Poverty, 13, 18–20, 22, 49, 154, 171, 250, 262–264, 274, 275, 335
Predatory capitalism, 9, 10, 23, 35, 37
Price stability, 339, 340, 343, 347, 356
Price takers, 87
Primordial, 30, 31
Primordial human, 2
Principal–Agent, 168, 170
Production distribution, 117
Property ownership, 44, 55, 59, 62, 141
Property rights, 158, 165, 166, 173
Prosperity, 7, 8, 41, 54, 56, 58, 64, 210, 225
Protestant, 2, 4, 60
Protestant Ethic, 4
Prudence, 154, 160, 164, 173
Public Basic Asset Fund, 313, 315, 318

R
Rational behaviour, 12, 28, 88, 101, 222
Rational individuals, 24
Rationalism, 193, 195
Rationalistic, 216
Rationality, 113, 120, 342
Rationality axiom, 30
Rationalization, 12
Real assets, 348, 358
Recession, 14
Redistribution, 85, 174, 221, 232
Redistribution policies, 13, 22
Redistributive justice, 165
Relative scarcity, 104
Renaissance, 185, 189, 198, 206
Renaissance humanism, 128
Rent seeking, 85, 106, 263, 328, 360

Resacralization, 19, 36, 37, 39
Resources scarcity, 104, 105
Righteous conducts, 156
Risk aversion, 154
Risk premium, 333, 360
Risk sharing, 47, 52, 59, 67
Risk-sharing asset redistribution, 289, 303
Risk-sharing universal basic assets, 308
Risk shifting, 166, 167, 327, 335
Risk transfer, 5, 165–167, 170, 171, 174, 273
Risk uncertainty, 267
Rule compliant, 225, 229, 239
Rules compliance, 41, 227, 230

S
Sacralized, 37, 38
Sacred, 187
Sacred tradition, 238
Scarcity, 11, 12, 18–23, 27, 32, 80, 102–104, 118, 121, 221, 222
Scholastics, 215, 216
Schumpeterian, 93, 144
Secularism, 189, 193
Secularization, xi, xii, 26, 36, 37, 114, 127–130, 132, 136, 140, 142, 144, 185, 194
Secular systems, 137, 142
Secular worldviews, 185, 197, 198
Securitization, 167, 350, 351
Self-interest, 4, 13, 23–28, 30, 32–34, 51, 56, 64, 81, 82, 101, 102, 104, 105, 120, 122, 144, 257
Shared prosperity, 289, 308, 311, 313–315, 357
Social capital, 56, 58, 68, 155, 184, 268, 272
Social choice, 85
Social cohesion, 56
Social contract, 135, 241, 253, 265

Social development, 200
Social economy, 28
Social good, 265
Social harmony, 57, 58
Social inclusion, 171, 174
Socialism, 14
Social justice, 165, 166, 174, 200, 201, 210, 242, 263
Social values, 189
Sociology, 48, 58, 190, 191
Spiritual, 157, 158
Spiritual discernment, 193, 197
Spirituality, 56, 187
Stabilizing effects, 358
Stagflation, 82
Stakeholders, 172–174
State contingent claims, 348, 352, 353
State contingent payoffs, 333
Stewardship, 249
Sukuk, 307, 308

T
Tawheed, 62
Teleologically, 232
Too big to fail, 327
Transmission mechanism, 336, 338
Trust, 56, 58
Trustfulness, 172, 173
Trustworthiness, 81, 162, 173
Truthfulness, 201, 243, 256, 267

U
Uncertainty, 106

Unequal distribution, 11
Unity, 189, 248, 252, 264
Universal Basic Income, 309, 318
Universal law, 103
Utilitarianism, 11, 80, 81, 217, 218, 241
Utilitarian philosophy, 99
Utility maximizing, 100–102
Utility-maximizing agents, 84

V
Value free economic, 243
Value judgements, 146, 248, 263
Value neutral, 276
Vicegerents, 255, 262
Virtue based ethics, 159, 161
Virtue ethics, 159
Virtues, 51
Virtuous behaviour, 200

W
Walrasian theory, 84, 98
Wastefulness, 201
Wealth distribution, 288, 289, 291, 294–296, 298, 308, 310, 311
Wealth inequality, 232, 285–291, 293–297, 299, 300, 302–304, 306–308, 311–313, 315, 317, 318
Wealth redistribution, 308, 309, 358
Wealth residual, 288, 289, 291, 295–297, 299, 302, 303, 310–312, 318

Printed in the United States
by Baker & Taylor Publisher Services